Minority Marketing: Issues and Prospects

Developments in Marketing Science: Proceedings of the Academy of Marketing Science

More information about this series at http://www.springer.com/series/13409

Robert L. King *Editor*

Minority Marketing: Issues and Prospects

Proceedings of the 1987 Minority
Marketing Congress

Presented by the Academy of Marketing Science,
The Citadel, and North Carolina A & T State University

Greensboro, North Carolina

November 12-14, 1987

Editor
Robert L. King
The Citadel
Charleston, NC, USA

Reprint from Original edition
Minority Marketing: Issues and Prospects, Special Conference Series, Vol III edited by Robert L. King
Copyright © Academy of Marketing Science 1987
All rights reserved.

Developments in Marketing Science: Proceedings of the Academy of Marketing Science
ISBN 978-3-319-17391-7   ISBN 978-3-319-17392-4   (eBook)
DOI 10.1007/978-3-319-17392-4

Library of Congress Control Number: 2015938794

Springer Cham Heidelberg New York Dordrecht London
© Academy of Marketing Science 2015

Printed on acid-free paper

Springer International Publishing AG Switzerland is part of Springer Science+Business Media (www.springer.com)

SPECIAL ACKNOWLEDGEMENTS

MINORITY MARKETING: ISSUES AND PROSPECTS represents the Academy of Marketing Science's first focused conference program effort in this field of significant concern and inquiry. The purpose of the conference was to assimilate and enhance knowledge of minority marketing practices, and to improve the general ability to market to minorities.

Initial indicators of the success of the conference include active participation of about 70 registrants from across the United States and Canada, and the presentation of more than 40 diverse research papers, most of which are included in these Proceedings. Further indication of the conference's success will come in the future, as new researchers are encouraged to enter this field of inquiry, and as the resulting body of knowledge is expanded.

The conference was the end product of much time and effort on the part of many individuals, only a few of whom are named here. The conference committee included the following people:

Program Chairperson:
    A. Coskun Samli (Virginia Tech)

Program Co-Chairpersons:
    Robert L. King (The Citadel)
    Japhet Nkonge (North Carolina A&T State University)

Track Chairpersons:
    Non-Profit Marketing and Minorities
        Sundar Fleming (South Carolina State University)
    Advertising and Other Types of Promotion
        Joseph Sirgy (Virginia Tech)
    Minority Consumer Behavior
        William Wilkinson (Governors State University), and
        Marcus Alexis (University of Illinois, Chicago Circle)
    Pricing and Marketing Analysis
        Mary K. Erickson (Southwest Texas State University), and
        Karen Walker (Southwest Texas State University)
    Inner City Enterprise Marketing and Entrepreneurship
        C. B. Claiborne (North Carolina A&T State University), and
        Jerry Hills (University of Illinois at Chicago)
    Product Planning and Management
        Sayeste Daser (Wake Forest University), and
        Edward Easely (Wake Forest University)
    Consumer Protection Information and Ethical Issues
        Robert Davis (North Carolina A&T State)

Research Methodologies
    Lee Meadow (Bentley College)
Special Sessions
    Joel Saegert (University of Texas at San Antonio)

ACADEMY OF MARKETING SCIENCE OFFICERS

President
    Roger Jenkins (University of Tennessee)
Executive Vice President/Director
    Harold W. Berkman (University of Miami)
Vice President for Programs
    John Mentzer (Virginia Tech)
Vice President for Publications
    Bill Lundstrom (Old Dominion University)
Vice President for Membership-USA
    Roy D. Adler (Pepperdine University)
Vice President for Membership-Canada
    Peter Banting (McMaster University)
Vice President for Membership-International
    Mai Antilla (Helsinki School of Economics)
Vice President for Academic Affairs
    Subhash Jain (University of Connecticut)
Vice President for Development
    Rebecca Yates (University of Dayton)
Vice President for Publicity and Public Relations
    Paul Thistlethwaite (Western Illinois University)
Vice President for Finance and Treasurer
    Robert L. King (The Citadel)
Secretary
    L. Lynn Judd (California State University-San Bernadino)

BOARD OF GOVERNORS

Chairman
    Jay D. Lindquist (Western Michigan University)
Other Members
    Constance Bates (Florida International University)
    V. V. Bellur (Niagara University)
    Michael Czinkota (Georgetown University)
    Kent L. Granzin (Virginia Tech)
    Jon Hawes (University of Akron)
    Stanley Hollander (Michigan State University)
    David Kurtz (Seattle University)
    Bert Rosenbloom (Drexel University)
    Stanley J. Shapiro (Simon Fraser University)
    Mary Ann Stutts (Southwest Texas State University)
    Julian Vincze (Rollins College)

SPECIAL APPRECIATION...
...TO The Citadel and to North Carolina A&T State University for their financial and logistical support of the conference.

Program
The First Conference on Minority Marketing

<u>November 11, 1987</u>
(Courtyard Room)

For early arrivers
Registration and Reception

5:30-7:30 PM

<u>November 12, 1987</u> - 9:15-10:00 AM
(Terrace and Patio Room)

Welcome and Introduction
A. Coskun Samli, Robert L. King and Japhet Nkonge

10:15-12:00 AM Plenary Session

Chair: A. Coskun Samli, Virginia Tech

"Macro Consumption Patterns of Black American Households"
William Lazer and Eric Shaw, Florida Atlantic University

"Problems Associated with Treating the Elderly As a Homogeneous Market"
H. Lee Meadow, Bentley College

"How to Enhance the Quality of Life of the Poor? The Marketing of Social Mobility Services"
M. Joseph Sirgy, Virginia Tech

12:15-1:45 PM Luncheon

<u>November 12, 1987</u> CONCURRENT SESSIONS - 2:00-3:45 PM
(Courtyard Room)

Title: Consumer Behavior I - Differences and Measurement Issues

Chair: Robert L. King, The Citadel

"Determining Black Expenditure Patterns Using Elasticity Coefficients: Developing a Profile"
Wayne C. Lindhart, Lincoln University of Missouri

"The Notion of Social Class and the Minority Buyer"
Hudson P. Rogers, University of Southwestern Lousiana
Reginald Peyton, Memphis State University
Robert L. Berl, Memphis State University

"Consumer Behavior Patterns of the Old Order Amish in South-Central Pennsylvania"
Henry T. Wilkins, Shippensburg University
Margaretha M. Hsu, Shippensburg University

Discussant: Robert L. King, The Citadel

November 12, 1987 CONCURRENT SESSIONS - 2:00-3:45 PM
  (Terrace and Patio Room)

Title: Minority Opportunities in Small Scale Retailing

Chair: Japhet Nkonge, North Carolina A & T State University

"Retailing Particularly Multi-Level Direct Selling, The Ease-of-Entry Opportunity"
    Ernest F. Cooke, Loyola College in Maryland
    Richard Baxter, Belmont College
    Mon-le Lee, Indiana University at South Bend

"The Roller Coaster Theory of Retailing and Implication for Minority Enterprises"
    Walter E. Greene, Pan American University

"The Role of Black Entrepreneurship in the Self-Actualization of Blacks in the Labor Force"
    William T. Ryan, Florida Atlantic University

Discussant: Japhet Nkonge, North Carolina A & T State University

3:45-4:00 PM - Coffee Break
━━

November 12, 1987 CONCURRENT SESSIONS - 4:00-5:30 PM
  (Courtyard Room)

Title: Special Issues Related to Minority Enterprises

Chair: C.B. Claiborne, Virginia Tech

"Black Entrepreneurs and Use of SBA Loans for Business Start-ups: A Field Study"
    Vicki L. Bolden, Southern University
    Winston Awadzi, Southern University

"Incubators for Minority Entrepreneurs"
    Richard Ellis, North Carolina A & T State University

"Attitudes and Experience of Minority Consumer Manufacturing Firms Toward Test Marketing"
    Bhagaban Panigrahi, Norfolk State University

Discussant: Bill Dowe, Director
             Tri-Ad Regional
             Small Business and Technology Development

November 12, 1987 CONCURRENT SESSIONS - 4:00-5:30 PM
  (Terrace and Patio Room)

Title: Consumer Behavior II - Motivation, Perception and Cognitive Styles

Chair: William C. Wilkinson, Governors State University

"Subcultural Differences in the Ability to Disembed Package Information"
    Stephen Calcich, Norfolk State University
    Karen Dale Hankel, Towson State University

"A Conceptual Framework for Examining Color Preference, Importance and Categorization in a Multiattribute Context Among Blacks"
    Margaret Mary Liebman, Trenton State College

"Subcultural Differences Among Direct Marketing Television Shoppers"
    E. Lincoln James, Michigan State University
    Allen Harris, Michigan State University

Discussant: Thomas I. Kindel, The Citadel
━━

<u>Friday, November 13, 1987</u> - CONCURRENT SESSIONS 9:00-10:30 AM
   (Courtyard Room)

Title: Consumer Behavior III - Sub-Cultural Differences

Chair: Thomas I. Kindel, The Citadel

"Perceptions of Health Care Services Among Black, Hispanic and White Consumers"
     Benjamin Sackmary, University of Hartford
     E. Marie Wilson, Connecticut Department of Health Services

"Tourism Marketing to Ethnic Travelers"
     Muzaffer Uysal, Clemson University
     Joseph T. O'Leary, Purdue University

"Black-White Differences in the Consumption of Cosmetics: Aggregate and Socio-Cultural Dimensions"
     Thaddeus H. Spratlen, University of Washington
     Pravat K. Choudhury, Howard University

Discussant: William C. Wilkinson, Governors State University

<u>Friday, November 13, 1987</u> CONCURRENT SESSIONS 9:00-10:30 AM
   (Terrace and Patio Room)

Title: Issues in Methodology

Chair: Joel Saegert, University of Texas at San Antonio

"An Exploratory Examination of Racial Bias in Measures of Consumer Socialization"
     Rose L. Johnson, Georgia State University

"Can Standard Research Methods Be Used in Studying Minority Segments?"
     Lee Slurzberg, Lee Slurzberg Research Inc.

"Sub-Segments of the Hispanic Market"
     Joel Saegert, University of Texas at San Antonio
     Robert J. Hoover, Corpus Christy State University
     Marye Hilger, University of Texas at Austin

Discussant: Rohit Deshpande, Darthmouth College

<u>Friday, November 13, 1987</u> Special Session - 11:00-12:15 AM
   (Courtyard Room)

Chair: Robert L. King, The Citadel

"The Changing Environment Surrounding the Personal Financial Investments of Minorities in the Market Place"
     Herrington J. Bryce, National Policy Institute

"Elderly Consumers and Life Satisfaction"
     Don Rahtz, William and Mary

"Minority Marketing to the North of the Border: The Case of French Canadians"
     Stanley Shapiro and Robert Tamilia, Simon Frazer University

Discussant: A. Coskun Samli, Virginia Tech

12:30-1:45 Lunch

Friday, November 13, 1987 CONCURRENT SESSIONS - 2:00-3:30 PM
   (Courtyard Room)

Title: Marketing By Minority Business

Chair: James Littlefield, Virginia Tech

"For the Small Minority Business: A Trade Show May Be Your Best Alternative"
      Grant M. Cunningham, Clemson University
      Brian Mihalik, Clemson University

"Advertising by Accountants: Implications for Minorities"
      William D. Cooper, North Carolina A & T State University
      Benton Miles, University of North Carolina at Greensboro
      Sarah A. Dunn, North Carolina A & T State University

"Black Consumers and Black Businesses: Income Spending and Sales Relationships"
      Thaddeus H. Spratlen, University of Washington

Discussant: James Littlefield, Virginia Tech

Friday, November 13, 1987 CONCURRENT SESSIONS - 2:00-3:30 PM
   (Terrace and Patio Room)

Title: Black Consumers and Advertising

Chair: M. Joseph Sirgy, Virginia Tech

"Questions on the Portrayal of Blacks in Magazine Advertising"
      Von D. Corbett, Miami University
      Lynette S. Unger, Miami University

"Developing an Advertising Strategy to Reach Blacks in the Market Place"
      Angela M. Airall, Graduate Management Admission Council

"Examining the Effectiveness of Celebrity Advertising to Blacks: Entertainers vs Athletes"
      Jerome D. Williams, Penn State University

Discussant: H. Lee Meadow, Bentley College
_____

Friday, November 13, 1987 CONCURRENT SESSIONS - 3:45-5:15 PM
   (Courtyard Room)

Title: Specific Issues in Minority Marketing

Chair: Anyansi Archibong, North Carolina A & T State University

"Portrayal of Blacks in Advertising: A Critical Review of the Literature"
      Thelma Snuggs, Purdue University
      William J. Qualls, University of Michigan

"Perceptions and Behaviors of Minority Consumers Toward Generic Consumer Products"
      Bhagaban Panigrahi, Norfolk State University
      Jon C. Stuart, Norfolk State University

"Marketing of Health Care Services for Minorities"
      Vanessa Hodges, University of Seattle
      Japhet Nkonge, North Carolina A & T State University

Discussant: William C. Wilkinson, Governors State University

Title: Profit and Non-Profit Marketing

Chair: Sundar Fleming, North Carolina Central University

"Non-Profit Marketing for Minorities"
    Herrington J. Bryce, National Policy Institute

"Marketing Effectiveness of the National Funeral Directors and Morticians Association"
    Alexander Okrah, North Carolina Central University

"Sales-Promotion Relationship in Urban Public Transportation and Impact on Minorities"
    Kofi Obeng, North Carolina A & T State University

Discussant: Sayeste Daser, Wake Forest University

Dinner: 7:00-9:00 PM "Minority Marketing: Where do we go From Here?"
    Linda L. Edmonds, Dupont Company

Saturday, November 14, 1987 - CONCURRENT SESSIONS 9:00-10:45 AM
    (Courtyard Room)

Title: Consumer Behavior IV

Chair: Japhet Nkonge, North Carolina A & T State University

"Race as an Influence on Health Care Information Sources and Provider Usage by the Elderly"
    Don Rahtz, College of William and Mary
    Rustan Kosenko, Ohio University

"Attribute Vs Activity Orientation As Related to Sub-Culture Purchase Behavior Differences"
    Linda L. Edmonds, DuPont Company
    A. Coskun Samli, Virginia Tech

"Functional Dysfunctional Consumer Behavior: A Normative Framework for Public Policy"
    M. Joseph Sirgy, Virginia Tech
    A. Coskun Samli, Virginia Tech

Discussant: H. Lee Meadow, Bentley College

Saturday, November 14, 1987 - CONCURRENT SESSIONS 9:00-10:45 AM
    (Terrace and Patio Room)

Title: Special Topics II

Chair: Edward Easely, Wake Forest University

"Chain Merchandising Policies for Ethnic Haircare Products in a Major Urban Market"
    Thaddeus H. Spratlen, University of Washington
    Ronald Robinson, Howard University

"Marketing of Historically Black Colleges"
    Sundar Fleming, North Carolina Central University

"Asian Americans: An Ignored Target Market"
    Mon-Le Lee, Indiana University at South Bend
    Ernest Cooke, Loyola College, Maryland

Discussant: A. Coskun Samli, Virginia Tech

Title: Special Session on Research in Progress

Chair: A. Coskun Samii, Virginia Tech

"An Analysis of Black Consumers"
Angela Airall, Graduate Management Admission Council

"Evaluation of Clothing Color Preferences"
Margaret Rucker, University of California, Davis
Young Fu Kim, University of California, Davis
Helene Ho, University of California, Davis

FOREWORD

These Proceedings bring together thirty-five papers presented at THE FIRST CONFER-
ENCE ON MINORITY MARKETING: ISSUES AND PROSPECTS, co-sponsored by the Academy of Marketing Science, The Citadel, and North Carolina A & T State University. The conference was
held in Greensboro, North Carolina, during the period of November 12 - 14, 1987.

Academicians, marketing practitioners, and government policy makers at all levels
were encouraged to submit empirical, conceptual, and theoretical papers for presentation
at the conference. Preference was given to papers focussing on strategic planning for
minority enterprises and field research findings in related areas, and to papers with a
managerial and futuristic orientation. The conference's overall objectives were to assimilate and enhance knowledge of minority marketing practices in the broadest sense, and
to improve the general ability to market to minorities.

This volume will serve as a permanent record of the conference, and of its success
in bringing together a substantial body of concerned professionals to share their research
findings, and in encouraging others to become involved and to carry on related research
efforts. The conference was a very "special" one, unique not only in its topical focus,
but also in its involvement of many persons not previously active in programs of the
Academy of Marketing Science, and in the intensity of discussion which characterized most
of the sessions. Hopefully, much of that provocative quality of the conference has been
captured and retained within the papers included in this volume.

As Editor of the Proceedings, I would like to thank each of the contributing authors,
not only for the quality of their papers, but also for their valiant effort in meeting my
deadlines, and in accommodating the demands of my style sheets when preparing their camera-
ready copy. All of us owe a debt of gratitude to Josh Samli and Jephet Nkonge for their
organizational leadership in creating the conference structure, and to all of the program
track chairs (identified on page iii) for "fleshing out" that structure. Finally, special
appreciation is expressed to The Citadel for its financial support of the Proceedings.

December 23, 1987   Robert L. King
                                                                    The Citadel

TABLE OF CONTENTS

PLENARY SESSION

"Minority Marketing: Then and Now" 1
        A. Coskun Samli, Virginia Polytechnic Institute and State University

"Macro Consumption Patterns of Black American Households" 3
        Eric H. Shaw, Florida Atlantic University
        William Lazer, Florida Atlantic University
        Allen E. Smith, Florida Atlantic University

"Problems Associated with Treating the Elderly as a Homogeneous Market" 8
        H. Lee Meadow, Bentley College

ISSUES IN METHODOLOGY

"An Exploratory Examination of Racial Bias in Measures of Consumer Socialization" 13
        Rose L. Johnson, Georgia State University
        Harash Sachdev, Georgia State University

"Determining Black Expenditure Patterns Using Elasticity Coefficients: Developing a Profile" 18
        Wayne C. Linhardt, Lincoln University of Missouri

"Can Standard Research Methods Be Used in Studying Minority (Hispanic) Segments?" 23
        Lee Slurzberg, Lee Slurzberg Research, Inc.

CONSUMER BEHAVIOR

"The Notion of Social Class and the Minority Buyer" 28
        Hudson P. Rogers, University of Southwestern Louisiana
        Reginald Peyton, Memphis State University
        Robert L. Berl, Memphis State University

"Attribute vs. Activity Orientation as Related to Sub-Culture Purchase Behavior Differences" 33
        Linda Edmonds, Dupont Company
        A. Coskun Samli, Virginia Polytechnic Institute and State University

"Subcultural Differences in the Ability to Disembed Package Information" 37
        Stephen Calcich, Norfolk State University
        Karen Dale Hankel, Towson State University

"Black-White Differences in the Consumption of Cosmetics: Aggregate and Socio-Cultural Dimensions" . . . 41
        Thaddeus H. Spratlen, University of Washington
        Pravat K. Choudhury, Howard University

"Tourism Marketing to Ethnic Travelers" 46
        Muzaffer Uysal, Clemson University
        Joseph T. O'Leary, Purdue University

"Subcultural Differences Among Direct Marketing Television Shoppers" 51
        E. Lincoln James, Michigan State University
        Allen C. Harris, Michigan State University

"A Conceptual Framework for Examining Color Preference, Importance and Categorization in a
Multiattribute Context Among Blacks" 57
        Mary Margaret Liebman, Trenton State College

"Evaluation of Clothing Color Preferences: A Comparison of Asian and White Consumers" 64
    Margaret Rucker, University of California at Davis
    Yong-Ju Kim, University of California at Davis
    Helene Ho, University of California at Davis

"A Study of Hispanic New Car Buyers" 65
    Joel Saegert, The University of Texas at San Antonio
    Robert J. Hoover, Corpus Christi State University
    Marye Tharp Hilger, The University of Texas at Austin

"Perception of Health Care Services Among Black, Hispanic and White Consumers" 69
    Benjamin Sackmary, University of Hartford
    E. Marie Wilson, Connecticut Department of Health Services

"Race as an Influence on Healthcare Information Sources and Provider Usage by the Elderly" 74
    Don R. Rahtz, College of William and Mary
    Rustan Kosenko, Ohio University

"Functional/Dysfunctional Consumer Behavior: A Normative Framework for Public Policy" 78
    M. Joseph Sirgy, Virginia Polytechnic Institute and State University
    A. Coskun Samli, Virginia Polytechnic Institute and State University

"Consumer Behavior Patterns of the Old Order Amish in South-Central Pennsylvania" 83
    Henry T. Wilkens, Shippensburg University
    Margaretha M. Hsu, Shippensburg University

"Asian Americans: Demographic of an Ignored Target Market" 87
    Monle Lee, Indiana University at South Bend
    Ernest F. Cooke, Loyola College in Maryland

"The English and Non French Market in Quebec: Issues and Prospects" 92
    Robert D. Tamilia, University of Quebec at Montreal
    Stanley J. Shapiro, Simon Fraser University

MINORITIES AND ADVERTISING AND PROMOTION

"Portrayal of Blacks in Advertising: A Critical Review of the Literature" 97
    Thelma L. Snuggs, Purdue University
    William J. Qualls, University of Michigan

"Perceptions and Behavior of Minority Consumers toward Generic Consumer Products" 103
    Bhagaban Panigrahi, Norfolk State University
    Jon C. Stuart, Norfolk State University

"Examining the Effectiveness of Celebrity Advertising to Minorities: Entertainers vs. Athletes" 107
    Jerome D. Williams, The Pennsylvania State University

MINORITY ENTERPRISES

"Retailing, Particularly Multi-Level Direct Selling, The Ease-of-Entry Opportunity" 112
    Ernest F. Cooke, Loyola College in Maryland
    Monle Lee, Indiana University at South Bend
    Richard Baxter, Belmont College

"The Roller Coaster Theory of Retailing and Implications for Minority Enterprises" 117
    Walter E. Greene, Pan American University

"The Role of Black Entrepreneurship in the Self Actualization of Blacks in the Labor Force" 121
    William T. Ryan, Florida Atlantic University

"Black Entrepreneurs and Use of SBA Loans for Business Start-Ups: A Field Study" 126
    Vicki L. Bolden, Southern University
    Winston Awadzi, Southern University

"Incubators for Minority Entrepreneurs" 130
    Richard Ellis, North Carolina Agricultural and Technical State University

"Marketing Effectiveness of the National Funeral Directors and Morticians Association (NFDMA)". 133
    Alexander M. Okrah, North Carolina Central University
    Tyronza R. Richmond, North Carolina Central University

"Black Consumers and Black Business: Income, Spending and Sales Relationships" 139
    Thaddeus H. Spratlen, University of Washington

"Advertising by Accountants: Implications for Minorities" 144
    Sarah Dunn, North Carolina Agricultural and Technical State University
    William Cooper, North Carolina Agricultural and Technical State University
    Mark Kiel, North Carolina Agricultural and Technical State University
    Benton Miles, University of North Carolina at Greensboro

"For the Small, Minority Business: A Trade Show May Be Your Best Marketing Alternative" 147
    M. Grant Cunningham, Clemson University
    Brian J. Mihalik, Clemson University

"Chain Store Merchandising Policies for Ethnic Hair Care Products in a Major Urban Market". 152
    Thaddeus H. Spratlen, University of Washington
    Ronald Robinson, Howard University

"The Marketing of the Historically Black College" 155
    Sundar W. Fleming, North Carolina Central University

INDEX OF AUTHORS. 161

MINORITY MARKETING: THEN AND NOW

A. Coskun Samli, Virginia Polytechnic Institute and State University

American marketing traditionally has been mass marketing where majorities in the market place are involved in the "exchange" or the "need-satisfaction" process. It seems neither the literature nor the political entities acknowledged the existence of certain minorities, particularly the underprivileged. Andreasen (1976) maintained that even though there have been earlier articles and books on blacks and the poor, Caplovitz (1963) was the bench mark study of a new era of awareness. In his book, The Poor Pay More, he posed the problems of minority markets. However, even then race and ethnicity were not acknowledged. The general thinking was as follows:

"Studies suggest that the market system works to the disadvantage of the poor simply because they are poor not because of their race or ethnicity" (Sturdivant 1968).

In fact, marketing discipline was inclined not to acknowledge even the first premise (Goodman 1968). Sturdivant (1968) and Sturdivant and Wilhelm (1968) set out to prove that both of these premises are correct. Indeed, their research supported a hypothesis that the market system may work to the disadvantage of the poor because of their race or ethnicity. In addition to "overt" discriminatory practices which were exposed by Sturdivant, Samli (1971) pointed out the presence of a de-facto discrimination. This was due to some poor being forced to buy from smaller high-priced stores because long wage barriers or lack of mobility or some other type of technicality. A third type of implicit discrimination was also brought into focus by Samli (1970). Here it was found that as prices for goods and services went up inflationary pressures became more prominent for the poor and other minorities. The root cause of this type discrimination is the "market baskets" of these groups. It appears that some of the products and services they use more readily than their upper income counterparts are more sensitive to upward price pressures (Samli, 1970).

Decline and Causes

As Andreasen (1976) maintained, during the late 60's and early 70's, literature relating to minority marketing flourished. Many articles explored many minority marketing related issues. However, by the mid 70's the whole activity came to a halt.

It became to be considered almost being prejudiced to undertake particularly racial type of minority marketing studies. Once again inefficiencies and unfairness of marketing practices were being ignored and mass marketing was re-emphasized. This decline was, at least partially, due to:

1. Not having enough scholars interested in this topic.
2. The topic not being a popular area of investigation.
3. Inadequate training to undertake this type of studies.
4. Changing academic research environment which is not conducive to this type of research.

The Future

Peters (1987) maintains that marketing has been mass markets and mass advertising. However, it must become "market creating, niche focus, innovation from being closer to markets, thriving on market fragmentation and ceaseless differentiation...." American marketing scholars and practitioners must understand that the mass markets of yesteryears are almost all gone. They are being replaced by numerous new (and old) minority markets. Thus, it may be maintained that the future mainstream American marketing will be minority marketing. Minority markets should not be considered to be only the poor or ethnic minorities, but the women, the elderly and other fragments or segments as well. Furthermore, in these segments there are noticeable and significant sub-sub-markets which need to be taken care of.

It is necessary to develop an agenda to study minority markets. Such an agenda must have a minimum of four steps:

1. Different minority markets must be identified.
2. These markets must be analyzed
3. Minority markets must be understood.
4. The needs of each and every market must be satisfied separately, particularly and as effectively as possible.

Enhanced abilities of American marketing practice to satisfy special needs of minority markets of all kinds, will most likely increase consumer satisfaction, enhance the quality of life and improve overall marketing efficiency. There is no doubt that during the forthcoming decade there will be many minority marketing studies providing direction to marketing practice. As American marketing theory and practice becomes more and more attuned to minority markets, the society as a whole will benefit.

References

Andreasen, Alan R. (1976), "The Ghetto Marketing Life Cycle: A Case of Underachievement," Journal of Marketing (February), pp. 20-28.

Caplovitz, David (1963), <u>The Poor Pay More</u>, New York: The Free Press.

Goodman, Charles S., "Do The Poor Pay More?", <u>Journal of Marketing</u>, pp. 18-24.

Peters, Tom (1987), <u>Thriving on Chaos</u>, New York: Alfred A. Knopf.

Sturdivant, Frederick D. (1968), "Better Deal for Ghetto Shoppers," <u>Harvard Business Review</u> (March-April), pp. 130-139.

Sturdivant, Frederick D. and Walter T. Wilhelm (1968), "Poverty Minorities and Consumer Exploitation," <u>Social Science Quarterly</u> (December), pp. 643-50.

Samli, A. Coskun and Larry French (1971), "De-Facto Price Discrimination in the Food Purchases of the Rural Poor," <u>Journal of Retailing</u> (Fall).

Samli, A. Coskun (1970), "Comparative Price Indexes for Negroes and Whites," <u>Mississippi Valley Journal of Business and Economics</u> (Winter), pp. 63-73.

MACRO CONSUMPTION PATTERNS OF BLACK AMERICAN HOUSEHOLDS

Eric H. Shaw, Florida Atlantic University
William Lazer, Florida Atlantic University
Allen E. Smith, Florida Atlantic University

Abstract

This paper compares the similarities and differences in macro consumption patterns between Black and non-black households. The analysis is based on data recently made available by the Bureau of Labor Statistics for 1984. The data indicate that Black households own less, earn less, and spend less than non-black households. However, despite the absolute differences, the data also reveal surprising similarities within categories of the relative income and purchasing patterns of Black and non-black households.

Introduction

Income and consumption are two fundamental factors in determining the standard of living for the members of a society. Most research in consumer behavior tends to focus on pre-purchase decision-making at the brand level of analysis. However, some scholars in marketing have recognized the necessity for more comprehensive analysis of macro purchasing behavior at the aggregate level of product and service categories (Arndt 1976).

According to Olander (1980, p. 59), in providing a solid foundation for consumer research more studies are necessary on "...priority patterns among goods, budgeting habits, the allocation of income among saving and some gross categories of spending (food, housing, travel, etc.)." The present study continues the process of filling this gap by taking a global approach to consumption patterns.

This research focuses on Black American households because they are widely recognized as a disadvantaged minority in the United States. Blacks thereby offer a clear contrast in income and purchasing patterns compared with non-black households.

Methodology

The comparisons in this study are based on Consumer Expenditure Survey data for 1984, recently made available by the U.S. Bureau of Labor Statistics. The data are collected by two independent methods, each using separate samples and questionnaires, which are used as a cross check on each other. One is the Diary Survey to develop weekly expenditure patterns, and the other is the Interview Survey to develop annual expenditure patterns.

The present study uses data from the quarterly Interview Survey. The survey is continuous and respondents report information to an interviewer, in person, once every three months on a rotating basis for five consecutive quarters. The sample follows a wave pattern, with a new 20 percent of the sample added as the oldest 20 percent complete their participation.

The Bureau uses a stratified area probability sample, known as "principle person" weighting, of the entire U.S. population. Of the 33,658 consumer dwelling units designated in the sample frame for the 1984 Interview Survey, 5,631 were vacant, nonexistant or otherwise ineligible. Of the remaining 28,027 dwelling units, interviews were obtained from 23,977. This resulted in a response rate for the sample of 85.6 percent.

The interview questionnaires are designed to obtain data on expenditures that respondents can be expected to recall for a period of three months or longer. These include relatively large expenditures, such as automobiles or television purchases, and spending that occurs on a regular basis, such as monthly rent, telephone bills or insurance premiums.

The consumer unit of analysis in the sample is a household, which is defined as a person living alone or sharing a dwelling unit, or two or more persons living together who pool their incomes to make joint purchasing decisions. A household is categorized as black when the head of the household is black and non-black when headed by whites or any other ethnics exclusive of blacks.

Demographics

Table 1 shows selected demographic characteristics comparing Black households with non-black households. Blacks represent a significant component of the national economy, comprising over 10 percent of all households in the United States. Black households tend to be larger in

TABLE 1
SELECTED HOUSEHOLD DEMOGRAPHICS 1984

	BLACK HOUSEHOLDS	NON-BLACK HOUSEHOLDS
Number of households (x1,000)	7,897	66,987
Number living in household unit	2.9	2.6
Number of earners	1.3	1.4
Number of children under 18	1.0	0.7
Number of persons 65 and over	0.2	0.3
Number of vehicles	1.2	1.9
Percent homeowner	42	63

Source: Compiled from BLS data; Consumer Expenditure Survey: Interview Survey, 1984, Table 8, pp 38-41.

size but have fewer earners compared with their non-black counterparts; and they have more children but less older persons living at home. They are only two-thirds as likely as other households to own their homes, and more likely to own only one car per household compared with two cars for non-blacks.

Household Income and Taxes

Table 2 presents data comparing Black and non-black households on components of 1984 income and taxes. Three views of the data are provided: (1) actual dollar amounts, (2) percentages of total income, and (3) income for Black households in dollars expressed as a percentage of non-black dollar income.

Black households pay half the personal taxes ($2,814) as do non-blacks ($5,629). The bulk of personal taxes for both groups is the Federal income tax. Despite the regressive nature of income taxes, the attempt at income redistribution appears relatively insignificant; since disposable incomes of Black households, that which remains after taxes are deducted, is only 64 percent of the after tax income of non-black households.

With their limited earnings from physical and financial capital and their greater reliance on public assistance, it is clear that Blacks have not as yet been well integrated into the main-stream economy.

TABLE 2
HOUSEHOLD INCOME AND TAXES 1984

	BLACK HOUSEHOLDS		NON-BLACK HOUSEHOLDS		BLACK $ / NON-BLACK $
	$	%	$	%	%
Income before taxes	16,046	100.0	25,566	100.0	62.8
Wages and salaries	12,654	78.9	20,057	78.5	63.1
Self-employment income	250	1.6	1,187	4.6	21.1
Social Security, other retirement income	1,761	11.0	2,449	9.6	71.9
Interest, dividends, rental income	120	0.7	1,113	4.4	10.8
Unemp & workers' comp, vet benefits	335	2.1	256	1.0	130.9
Pub assis, supp sec inc, food stamps	756	4.7	193	0.8	391.7
Reg contrib for support	111	0.7	220	0.9	50.5
Other income	60	0.4	92	0.4	65.2
Personal taxes	1,418	8.8	2,815	11.0	50.4
Federal income taxes	1,094	6.8	2,224	8.7	49.2
State & local income taxes	302	1.9	521	2.0	58.0
Other taxes	22	0.1	69	0.3	31.9
Income after taxes	14,628	91.2	22,751	89.0	64.3

Source: Compiled from BLS data; Consumer Expenditure Survey: Interview Survey, 1984, Table 8, pp 38-41.

The most significant differences are the imbalances in total household income, both before and after taxes, the total amount paid in taxes and the variances in the manner in which income is earned. Income before taxes for Black households is $16,046 compared to $25,566 for their non-black counterparts. Thus, Blacks receive only 63 percent of the total income of non-black households.

As expected, wages and salaries are the major component of income for both groups of households. Wages and salaries as a percentage of total income are about the same for Black (78.9 percent) and non-black households (78.5 percent). However, that is where the similarity ends. Almost every other category of income reflect considerable differences.

Black households earn only 63 percent of the wages and salaries earned by non-black households, $12,654 compared to $20,057. They receive 72 percent of the retirement income, but only 21 percent of the self-employment income, and just 11 percent of the interest, dividend and property income of non-blacks. On the other hand, Blacks receive 31 percent more unemployment, worker's compensation and veteran's benefits, and almost 300 percent more public assistance than non-blacks.

Household Purchasing Patterns

Table 3 compares total expenditures and purchasing patterns, in 1984 dollars, for Black and non-black households. Again, there are three views of the data: (1) actual dollar expenditures, (2) percentages of total expenditures, and (3) Black household purchases expressed as a percentage of non-black dollar spending.

With lower disposable incomes, purchases of products and services by Black households are only 63.5 percent that of their non-black counterparts. As a percentage of their total expenditures, Blacks spend 57 percent on food, clothing and housing--the necessities--compared to 51 percent for other households. Thus, Black households not only have lower disposable incomes, but they also have even less discretionary income available for spending than non-black households.

While a large variation was found in the sources of income between the two groups, there are far smaller variations in spending categories. Both Black and non-blacks spend more of their income on housing than any other category (33.3 and 30.2 percent, respectively). Similarly, in rank order are expenditures on transportation (19.0 and 20.2 percent), food (17.5 and 15.4 percent), personal insurance and pensions (8.1 and 9.4 percent), and

4

TABLE 3
HOUSEHOLD PURCHASING PATTERNS 1984

	BLACK HOUSEHOLDS		NON-BLACK HOUSEHOLDS		BLACK $ / NON-BLACK $
	$	%	$	%	%
Average Annual Expenditures	14,395	100.0	22,659	100.0	63.5
Food	2,520	17.5	3,493	15.4	72.1
Food at home	2,059	14.3	2,376	10.5	86.7
Food away from home	461	3.2	1,118	4.9	41.2
Housing	4,796	33.3	6,842	30.2	70.1
Shelter	2,581	17.9	3,884	17.1	66.5
Owned dwellings	1,083	7.5	2,318	10.2	46.7
Rented dwellings	1,359	9.4	1,149	5.1	118.3
Utilities, fuels & public service	1,614	11.2	1,686	7.4	95.7
Household operations	175	1.2	352	1.6	49.7
Telephone	483	3.4	449	2.0	107.6
Domestic services	148	1.0	284	1.3	52.1
Other household expenses	27	0.2	67	0.3	40.3
Housefurnishings & equipment	427	3.0	920	4.1	46.4
Furniture	142	1.0	291	1.3	48.8
Major appliances	97	0.7	150	0.7	64.7
Small appliances, misc housewares	39	0.3	67	0.3	58.2
Misc. household equip.	88	0.6	257	1.1	34.2
Apparel and services	896	6.2	1,227	5.4	73.0
Males (2 and over)	213	1.5	317	1.4	67.2
Females (2 and over)	336	2.3	502	2.2	66.9
Transportation	2,738	19.0	4,579	20.2	59.8
Cars & trucks, new (net outlay)	451	3.1	1,153	5.1	39.1
Cars & trucks, used (net outlay)	500	3.5	798	3.5	62.7
Vehicle finance charges	147	1.0	227	1.0	64.8
Gasoline & motor oil	799	5.6	1,077	4.8	74.2
Maintenance & repairs	321	2.2	468	2.1	68.6
Health care	474	3.3	950	4.2	49.9
Health insurance	145	1.0	297	1.3	48.8
Medical services	226	1.6	494	2.2	45.7
Prescription drugs, medical supplies	102	0.7	158	0.7	64.6
Personal care	184	1.3	207	0.9	88.9
Entertainment	506	3.5	1,103	4.9	45.9
Fees & admissions	116	0.8	375	1.7	30.9
TV, radios, sound equipment	241	1.7	336	1.5	71.7
Other equip and services	149	1.0	392	1.7	38.0
Reading	70	0.5	148	0.7	47.3
Education	190	1.3	326	1.4	58.3
Tobacco & smoking supplies	191	1.3	229	1.0	83.4
Alcoholic beverages	143	1.0	318	1.4	45.0
Miscellaneous	193	1.3	325	1.4	59.4
Cash contribution	334	2.3	788	3.5	42.4
Personal insurance & pensions	1,160	8.1	2,125	9.4	54.6
Life & other personal insurance	247	1.7	308	1.4	80.2
Retirement, pensions, SS	913	6.3	1,817	8.0	50.2

Source: Compiled from BLS data; Consumer Expenditure Survey: Interview Survey, 1984, Table 8, pp 38-41.

apparel (6.2 and 5.4 percent). Comparing the percentage of income spent across all product and service categories reveal more similarities than differences between the two groups.

Transportation expenditures, for example, are $2,738 and $4,579 for Black and non-black households, respectively. Although blacks spend 40.2 percent less than non-blacks for transportation, members of both households spend about 20 percent of their average annual expenditures on transportation; 19.0 percent by Black household compared to 20.2 percent for their non-black counterparts.

Education offers a similar example. Total educational expenditures are $190 for Black households and $326 for non-blacks . Although blacks spend 41.7 percent less than non-black households, the latter spends 1.4 percent of its total expenditures for education compared to the average Black household figure of 1.3 percent.

When spending is expressed as a percentage of total expenditures, there is a striking similarity between Black and non-black households for all but two other categories of expenditures. One is rented dwellings, where Blacks spend 18.3 percent more than non-blacks, $1,359 compared to $1,149. Black households apparently spend more on rentals because their ownership of homes is only 67 percent of non-blacks.

The second exception, where Blacks outspend non-blacks, is telephone expenditures. Black and non-black households spend $483 and $449, respectively. As a percentage of total expenditures, Blacks spend 3.1 percent and non-black households 2.0 percent. This disparity may reflect greater
Black usage of pay telephones and fewer subscriptions to lower cost telephone services, such as Sprint or MCI.

Some of the categories showing similarities between Black and non-black household spending in dollars are utilities, personal care, and tobacco. Black and non-black households annually spend $1,614 and $1,686 for utilities, a difference of only 4.3 percent. For personal care expenditures the figures are $184 and $207, respectively, with blacks spending 11.1 percent less. Spending for tobacco is $191 for Blacks compared to $229 for non-blacks, a difference of 16.6 percent. Another interesting similarity is that both Black and non-black households spend four times as much on tobacco, alcohol and entertainment than they do on reading and education.

In the area of differences, Blacks spend 27.9 percent less than non-black households for food. They spend only 13.3 percent less on food at home, but 58.8 percent less on food away from home. Black households spend 29.9 percent less on housing than do non-black households. Household operations are 50.3 less and furnishings and equipment 46.4 percent less. Blacks also spend 27 percent less for apparel and 40.2 percent less for transportation. They spend 50.1 percent less for health care; however, only 35.4 percent less for drugs and medical supplies. Finally, Black households spend 45.4 percent less for personal insurance and pensions than non-black households.

Discussion

In summary, among the findings between Blacks and non-blacks are three major differences: (1) in the demographic composition of the households, (2) in the sources and amount of income, and (3) total dollar expenditures. The most striking similarity found between the two groups is the percent of total annual expenditures allocated across individual product and service categories.

The data indicate that Black households own less, earn less, and spend less than non-black households. Lower expenditures, of course, result from lower incomes. This gap in income might be further reduced by encouraging Black entrepreneurs. Since entrepreneurship has historically provided opportunities for economic progress among minorities, research on Black entrepreneurs and programs to directly assist Blacks business owners are likely to prove beneficial.

Despite the disparity in incomes, and the fact that Black households still lag behind non-blacks, significant progress has been made. In 1940 Black households earned only 43 percent of the annual income of non-black households (Smith and Welch, 1981). The 1984 data show that Blacks have reached 63 percent of non-black income.

What might the future hold? The dominant economic factors most likely to affect future standards of living, particularly for Black American households, include continuing growth in the areas of services, high technology, and international competition.

The service sector accounts for the majority of employment opportunities in today's economy. Estimates are that 74.3% of U.S. jobs will be in the service sector by 1995 (Fortune 1987). It is likely that the greatest opportunities await workers with advanced skills, while the non-skilled are not expected to fare as well. According to Berger (1986, p. 81): "The economy's tilt toward services may worsen the already dire employment outlook for black adult males, whose 13% jobless rate is more than twice as high as for white adults."

Some Black workers may face difficulties in assimilating into the future service economy because the highest paying service jobs, such as business services, telecommunications, and computing, require advanced education, specialized training, or technical skills which many disadvantaged people lack. If the assimilation problem holds true, Personick's (1985, p.27) projection that overall employment rates will continue to drop," to 6.3 percent in 1990 and 6.0 percent in 1995," will offer little hope for disadvantaged Black households.

In the area of high technology, Laczniak and Lush (1987,p.7) indicate that rapid advances offer "the potential to sustain an ever improving quality of life." However, technological developments in robotics as well as office and factory automation are likely to have a severe impact on less educated and unskilled workers.

These technologies offer a two edged sword. They are expected to displace some unskilled and semi-skilled workers. However, for those who acquire additional education and training Personick (1985, p.37) notes: "Employment in these high tech industries account for 6.1 percent of all wage and salary jobs in 1972, 6.4 percent in 1984, and is projected to represent 7.0 percent by 1995."

In the world arena, the trend is toward ever increasing international competition. (Dymsza 1984, Porter 1986, among others). American workers must now compete for their wages in the global labor pool.

International competition forces manufacturers to reduce prices and cut costs. Lower prices make products more affordable for all household consumers. On the other side of the coin, efforts to cut costs reduce wages and employment opportunities for household workers. In a more dramatic cost-cutting strategy, some U.S. firms are increasing their direct foreign investment in overseas manufacturing, thereby eliminating domestic jobs. Unions have not been effective in reducing these trends.

The trends toward increasing growth in services, high technology and international competition offer little hope for some workers, although they do provide opportunities for others. Those workers willing and able to acquire the necessary skills through training and education are more likely to fulfill their expectations for an improved standard of living.

References

Arndt, Johan (1976), "Reflections on Research in Consumer Behavior," in B.B. Anderson, ed. Advances in Consumer Research, Vol 3, Cincinnatti: Association for Consumer Research, 213-221.

Berger, J. (1986), "The False Paradise of a Service Economy: If Basic Industry is Allowed to Wither, the Service Sector Can't Thrive," Business Week, (March 3), 78-81.

Bureau of Labor Statistics (1987), Consumer Expenditure Survey: Interview Survey, 1984, Table 8, pp 38-41.

Carnevale, A.P. (1984), Jobs for the Nation: Challenges for a Society Based on Work, American Society for training and Development, 600 Maryland Avenue, S.W., Washington, D.C. 20024, 1-45.

Dymsza, W.A. (1984), "Trends in Multinational Business and Global Environments : A Perspective," Journal of International Business Studies, 15 (Winter), 25-46.

Ebel, K. (1986), "The Impact of Industrial Robots on the World of Work," International Labor Review, 125 No. 1 (January-February), 39-51.

Fortune (1987), "The Economy of the 1990s: Special Report," 115 (February 2), 22-63.

Jelinek, Mariann and Joel D. Goldhar (1985), "Strategic Implications of the Factory of the Future," The McKinsey Quarterly, (Autumn), 20-33.

Johnson, K.P. and H.L. Friendenberg (1985), "Regional and State Projections of Income, Employment and Population to the Year 2000," Survey of Current Business, (May), 39-63.

Laczniak, G.R. and R.F. Lusch (1987), "Environment and Strategy in 1995: A Survey of High-Level Executives," Journal of Business and Industrial Marketing, 2 No. 1 (Winter), 5-23.

Personick, V.A. (1985), "A Second Look at Industry Output and Employment Trends Through 1995," Monthly Labor Review, 108 (November), 26-41.

Olander, Folke (1980), "Recent Developments in European Consumer Policy Research," in J.C. Olson, ed., Advances in Consumer Research, Vol 7, Ann Arbor: Association for Consumer Research, 56-65.

Porter, M.E. (1986), "Changing Patterns of International Competition," California Management Review, 28 (Winter), 9-40.

Quinn, J.B. and C.E. Gagnon (1986), "Will Services Follow Manufacturing into Decline?" Harvard Business Review, 64 (November-December), 95-103.

Smith, James P. and Finis R. Welch (1981), "Closing the Gap: Forty Years of Economic Progress for Blacks," Rand Corporation.

Schwartz P. and J. Saville (1986), "Multinational Business in the 1990s--a Scenario," Long Range Planning, 19 (December), 95-103.

PROBLEMS ASSOCIATED WITH TREATING THE ELDERLY AS A HOMOGENEOUS MARKET

H. Lee Meadow, Bentley College

INTRODUCTION

For some time marketing researchers have called upon their practitioner counterparts to take heed of a growing segment in the U.S. -- that segment known as the elderly. As early as 1960 demographers began to chart the growing population trend that those 55 years and older were increasing at a rate much faster than than other age segments of the population (Business Week 1960). By the mid 1970's it was concluded that the elderly population was growing at twice the rate of the population as a whole (Brotman 1977) and this was confirmed by the research of Linden (1986) who found that the 65 years and older age segment was growing at a 2.52 percent annual pace, while the rest of the population was growing at only a 1.16 percent rate. And even as late as 1985 it was argued that the elderly market was still a neglected target for consideration (Visvabharathy and Rink 1985). Though one could develop support for this argument, the prepon-derance of evidence appears to be quite the contrary.

Marketing practioners and academics have appeared to respond in recent years to the calls for attention. They have paid increasing attention as evidenced in attempts made to both study the elderly market more closely and in the development of marketing programs directed at what is estimated to be upwards of between a $200+ billion market segment (Media Decisions 1977) and an $800+ billion market segment (Linden 1986). Most recently Schewe (1984), Hoy and Fisk (1985), and Fox et al. (1985) provided cogent commentary and support for the contention that marketers are, indeed, paying increased attention. Rather than viewing the senior citizen market as a not very unique and identifiable segment (as Reinecke 1964 earlier suggested), Schewe (1984) and the Marketing News (1982) report that marketers are, in increasing numbers, beginning to respond by targeting effort uniquely for this group. Contrary to the argument that the elderly is a market segment still being ignored, recent history seems to support the notion that marketers are beginning to jump on the 'elderly bandwagon' and are attempting to address this groups' consumer needs.

One problem still exists, however, relative to targeting the elderly. That is, the mythical assumption that the elderly population as a whole can be stereotyped as one homogeneous mass. Too often those who attempt to deal with the senior citizen market assume that there is a homogeneity that runs across most of the socio-economic, demographic and behavioral variables used to characterize this segment (Merrill and Weeks 1983). This plays into the myth often heard in describing a variety of minority groups: "Seen one and you have seen them all!" If the practitioner in the attempt to respond to meeting the needs of this exciting new market opportunity fails to further segment the elderly market or uses a total market approach, the marketing strategy chosen will stand a high probability of achieving less than optimum results at best, and at worst, a high probability of absolute failure.

SEGMENTS FOUND IN THE ELDERLY MARKET

Given that the argument has been made that the elderly market can be categorized as a heterogeneous sub-culture, then the logical next step is to present evidence demonstrating that there are a variety of sub-segments which can be developed from an examination of the elderly population. The following discussion provides a abridged overview of the research efforts which have attempted to identify unique sub-segments among the elderly. The discussion is divided into efforts to segment on the basis of demographics, psychological variables, and behavior patterns.

Two attempts at demographic segmentation were presented by Tongren (1975) and Gelb (1978) in their examinations of consumption patterns and consumer characteristics of the elderly market. They found that income segments do, indeed, exist and that each of these groups have different needs which need to be fulfilled. In fact Gelb (1978) stated:

> To look at the 65-and-over group as low income shoppers can be misleading .... it means over-looking the possibility that a senior citizen with a $500-per-month income may be ready for a round-the-world trip. Assuming that income breaks down to $180 for Social Security, $320 from investments, the $320 may be a 5 percent return on about $77,000. (p. 45)

Using telephone longitudinal usage data from AT&T customers, Fox et al. (1984) studied the elderly along demographic dimensions. Their data consisting of demographics and psychographics, demonstrated that the elderly could be divided into two sub segments: those 65-74 years of age and those 75+ years of age, with each group possessing unique psychographic characteristics.

As for psychological attempts at segmentation, Towle and Martin (1976) conducted research using psychographic and buying study data, and concluded that the elderly can be divided into a variety of sub-segments. They identified six key sub-segments: (1) Saver/Planner--those who buy unknown brands and can be described as being frank, self-assured, and confident; (2) Brand Loyalist--those who don't buy for approval of friends and can be described as brave and not stubborn; (3) Information Seeker--those who are persuasible and can be described as kind and sincere; (4) Economy Shopper--those who are not brand loyal and can be described as not brave, not demanding, and possessing bland personalities; (5) Laggards--those who are not persuasible and can be described as liberal, unreserved and cold to others; and (6) Conspicuous Consumer--those who change brands and can be described as seekers of friends' approval, dominant, and stubborn.

In an other effort to psychologically develop discrete elderly sub-segments, Lumpkin (1985) developed a detailed analysis of the elderly using a shopping orientation segmentation strategy. Shopping orientation strategy is defined as those people who engage in the behavior of shopping for a variety of reasons including economic, leisure, and socializing. His focus was to develop a typology of shopping orientation exclusively for the elderly segment of the population. Based on the results obtained, Lumpkin concluded that at least three segments could be identified: (1) Active Apparel Shoppers--socially active opinion leaders who enjoy the shopping experience; (2) Economic Shopper--persons who seek maximum value by equating price and quality and who are not likely to engage in much comparative shopping; and (3) Uninvolved--shoppers described as apathetic consumers who minimalize the shopping experience and tend to be the least fashion conscious.

Using a classification scheme offered by Neugarten (1974), which classified the elderly on the psychological basis of how well they adjusted to old age, King et al. (1982) examined a sample of elderly and found that marketers could use the following scheme to segment this segment: (1) Reorganizers--those who attempt to 'stay young' and refuse to grow old by being active and substituting activities they might have lost due to the aging process for new ones; (2) Focused--those elderly who focus upon the attempt to achieve satisfaction with life by concentrating on one or two roles; and (3) Disengaged--those senior citizens with minimal social contact roles who have withdrawn from others, yet are content with their

general lives.

Merrill and Weeks (1983) similarly attempted to use a segmentation analysis on a sample of senior citizens. One of the patterns they employed for segmentation was the Beveridge (1980) model of retirement adjustment classifications. A second pattern chosen was the benefit segmentation device. The research attempted to determine if discrete segments could be identified combining both patterns. The results provided moderate support for stating that the elderly market is composed of discrete and identifiable benefit sub-segments along the retirement adjustment dimension.

Also using a segmentation model based on elderly adjustment patterns to retirement life, French and Fox (1985) attempted to divide the elderly market using an expert sample of social gerontologists to characterize each sub-segment. Their findings indicated that sub-segments can be produced from the employment of two factors: the "extent to which old age is viewed as another stage of life to be experienced and enjoyed... (and) the degree of insecurity and dependence associated with the adjustment pattern" (p. 65, parentheses added). They found the following sub-segments to exist among the elderly: (1) Reorganizers/Focused--constituting 40 percent of the market, they tend to be the most affluent and mainstream oriented and lead socially active lifestyles; (2) Angry/Self-Blaming/Apathetic--constituting 17 percent of the market, they tend to be cynical, suspicious, and resistent to efforts which attempt to change current behavior (e.g., marketing communication messages); (3) Holding-On--constituting 10 percent of the market, they focus on self-esteem, and who fear growing old and are reluctant to try anything new; and (4) Disengaged--constituting 9 percent of the market, they are confident, independent, but socially withdrawn.

Along a different vein, Festervand and Lumpkin (1985) conducted a study of how elderly consumers respond to the portrayals of elderly citizens by advertisers. Not only did they find advertisers using inappropriate stereotypical portrayals based upon commonly help myths of society, but they found their data could be used to find unique sub-segments within this growing market. Based on an attitude analysis of their responses, relative to how attracted or unattracted they were to current portrayals, three different groups were identified: those positively attracted to portrayals, those turned off by the portrayals, and those who did not feel one way or another toward portrayals.

As a by product of research conducted on the elderly market, it was noted that the elderly can be segmented behaviorally. The research was an attempt to investigate life satisfaction outcomes resulting from interactions with mass media (Rahtz et al. forthcoming). One of the outcomes from this investigation provided evidence that the elderly who were heavy users of television for information acquisition, had significantly different demographic and behavioral characteristics than those who were light users.

In sum, it should be apparent that the elderly segment is not monolithic and should not be treated as such. Regardless of how one approaches the segmentation effort, finding discrete and identifiable segments is quite likely when based upon sound theoretical and empirical bases.

PROBLEMS CREATED BY AGGREGATING THE ELDERLY

What faces the marketer attempting to reach the elderly in a naive fashion is the possible creation of a host of problems which could undermine the overall effectiveness of the marketing effort. What follows is a discussion of some of the problems that the naive marketer might encounter.

First and foremost, the marketer who aggregates assumes the elderly market possesses a consistent set of needs. This means all market members will be treated the same and the marketer will only reach those few who exhibit the need pattern assumed held by the entire group. The marketer will assume he/she knows why the consumer behaves/buys and that assumption will at best be, most imprecise. Certainly it is possible that by meeting the assumed needs of the whole market, the marketer will miss, what in actuality drives most of its participants.

Second, in responding to the assumed needs, the marketing strategy employed may not parallel the market demands. In essence, both the positioning strategy and the marketing mix developed, will fail to penetrate or stimulate enough response to warrant the effort. If people don't need what is offered, why should they be expected to respond in favorable manner?

Third, by treating all the elderly the same, management may tend to get quite complacent. Since developing decisions using managerial judgement from a production orientation perspective is the spawning ground for assuming homogeneity, the probability is high that the marketer will remain rather passive, or worse yet non-reactive to market

changes. Hence, the firm will stagnate if by some chance success has been achieved while employing the original aggregating assumption. This circumstance is most unlike the decision-maker whose drive is the marketing concept, which operationalizes by using research as the driving force; so that when the research shows market changes, the firm responds appropriately. Since there is no built in alarm mechanism (e.g., examining a continuous stream of market derived data), marketers assuming homogeneity may be more inattentive to market change conditions.

Fourth, one of the major keys to marketing success in a highly competitive environment is developing a distinctive competency (i.e., competitive advantage) that will effectively meet market demand. Locating and staying on top of a firm's competitive strengths and weaknesses is a key to the determination of distinctive competencies, a task made more difficult using a market aggregating assumption. Though the marketer may know competitive inroads are being made, it will be difficult to determine the causal reasoning behind competitive success. Competing marketers can take proactive market positions by carving out key elderly segments whose needs are not being met by the aggregating marketer. Since the aggregating marketer may not be able to track strength and weaknesses, anticipating competitive reaction or forecasting competitive inroads will be most difficult. Further, combating such competition by playing upon the strengths offered in determining distinctive competencies, will be all but impossible.

Fifth, not segmenting the elderly can lead to an inefficient allocation of marketing resources. Mass appeals not directed appropriately may reach uninterested or unresponsive audiences, making the dollars spent wasted.

For example if a marketer takes the stereotypcial approach to product development and designs a package with large print and containing small amounts of the item being sold, a significant portion of the elderly will be missed since "the elderly are not terribly concerned about package size and label print size" (Schewe 1984, p. 558). A clothing marketer who treats all elderly as not fashion conscious, will find a significant portion of the market 'turned-off' by the out-dated offerings (Martin 1976; Richards 1981). Assuming the elderly seek out the most reasonable bargains due to reduced income sources during retirement, will cause the marketer to miss a significant portion of the market seeking to obtain the very best (Forbes 1969) or those seeking status symbols in the purchases made with price acting as a status cue (Towle and Martin 1976). Advertisers portraying the old as infirmed, incapacitated, unhealthy, uninteresting, and unflattering may be reaching the 'old-old' (i.e., 75+) and be missing the 'young-old' (65-74), who outnumber the 'old-old' three to two and want to live life to its fullest (Harris and Feinburg 1977; Schewe 1984). Some of the earliest studies of the elderly consumer seem to confirm the image of the elderly as immobile and needing distribution outlets near their residences. By taking this myth 'to-heart' and only planning retail outlets close to senior communities, marketers may be missing those elderly willing travel to locations where special treatment and leisure satisfaction are built into the shopping experience (Gelb 1978; Samli 1967; Zbytniewski 1978).

Sixth, the marketer who aggregates has no idea how effectively market objectives are being achieved. Without targets being precisely defined operationally, what standards can be used to evaluate marketing performance? As Engel et al. (1972) point out, segmentation analysis will produce answers to such questions as:

> Should we add another brand?
> Should we drop or modify
> existing products, or should
> we attempt to reposition a
> faded and obsolete brand
> image?   (p. 3)

Finally, by not segmenting the elderly market, the marketing practitioner fails to achieve the long run goals of optimizing profitability by satisfying the target market. In essence the marketing integration that results from a segmentation strategy puts marketing effectiveness in jeopardy. Knowing that aggregation may be an inappropriate strategy choice, means that substantial portions of the elderly and their attendant needs will go unfulfilled; thus the goal of consumer satisfaction will not be achieved. When consumer satisfaction is then sub-optimized, it follows that profitability goals for the long run will also be less than ideally reached.

CONCLUSION

Over the past decade a number of academics and practioners have devoted much energy in developing a conceptual base for both the understanding of and catering to this dynamic segment as evidenced by the numerous articles which have appeared in both the professional/academic journals and business periodicals. Much progress has been made by practitioners and academics relative to understanding this dynamic market.

However, what has been ignored time and time again by both practioners and academics is the fact that the elderly segment is not a monolithic entity. Rather it is a group of persons whose commonality is based upon an arbitrary age classification as well as presumed cohort effects. As this paper has attempted to illustrate, there are a host of ways one could sub-divide this heterogeneous grouping into homogeneous clusters using a variety of dimensions. Given that such division is possible, the real key for marketing effort in the future is for those concerned with the senior citizen to begin to identify more precisely which subset is being addressed. Then, and only then will there be both an understanding and meeting of the needs possessed by this increasingly important age segment.

REFERENCES

Beveridge, W. E. (1980), "Retirement and Life Significance: A Study of the Adjustment to retirement of a Sample of Men at Management Level," Human Relations, 33 (1), 69-78.

Brotman, H. B. (1977), "Population Projection Part I: Tomorrow's Older Population (to 2000)," The Gerontologist, 17 (June), 203-209.

Business Week (1960), "How the Old Age Market Looks," February 13, 37-38.

Engel, J. F., H. F. Fiorillo, and M. A. Cayley (1972), "Introduction and Overview," in J. F. Engel et al., eds. Market Segmentation: Concepts and Applications. NY: Holt, Rinehart and Winston, Inc. 1-19.

Festervand, T. A. and J. R. Lumpkin (1985), "Response of Elderly Consumers to Their Portrayal by Advertisers," in J. H. Leigh and C. R. Martin, Jr., eds. Current Issues and Research in Advertising -- Volume 1: Original Research and Theoretical Contributions. Ann Arbor, MI: University of Michigan. 203-226.

French, W. A. and R. Fox (1985), "Segmenting the Senior Citizen Market," The Journal of Consumer Marketing, 2 (Winter), 61-74.

Forbes (1969), "The Forgotten Generation," January 15, 22-29.

Fox, M. C., A. M. Roscoe, Jr., and A. M. Feigenbaum (1984), "A Longitudinal Analysis of Consumer Behavior in the Elderly Population," in T. C. Kinnear, ed. Advances in Consumer Research: Volume 11. Provo, UT: Association for Consumer Research. 563-568.

Gelb, B. D. (1978), "Exploring the Grey Market Segment," MSU Business Topics, 26 (Spring), 41-46.

Harris, A. J. and J. F. Feinberg (1977), "Television and Aging: Is What You See What You Get," The Gerontologist, 17 (4), 464-468.

Hoy, M. G and R. P. Fisk (1985), "Older Consumers and Services: Implications for Marketers," in R. F. Lusch, et al., eds. AMA Educators' Conference Proceedings. Chicago: American Marketing Association. 50-55.

King, R. H., B. J. Dunlap, and G. S. Bagley (1982), "Segmenting the Elderly Market: Back to Demographics?" in D. R. Corrigan, et al., eds. 1982 Proceedings, Southwestern Marketing Association, 66-69.

Linden, F. (1986), "The $800 Billion Market," American Demograhics, 8 (February), 4

Lumpkin, J. R. (1985), "Shopping Orientation Segmentation of the Elderly Consumer," Journal of the Academy of Marketing Science, 13 (Spring), 271-289.

Marketing News (1982), "Research Suggests Nine Rules for Advertising to the Elderly," April 16, 1 & 9.

Martin, C. R., Jr. (1976), "A Transgenerational Comparison: The Elderly Fashion Consumer," in B. B. Anderson, ed. Advances in Consumer Research: Volume 3. Ann Arbor, MI: Association for Consumer Research. 453-456.

Media Decisions (1973), "Don't Write Off the Senior Citizen Market," 8 (July), 64-67 & 112-116.

Merrill, J. R. and W. A. Weeks (1983), "Predicting and Identifying Benefit Segments in the Elderly Market," in P. E. Murphy et al., eds. AMA Educators' Conference Proceedings. Chicago: American Marketing Association. 399-403.

Neugarten, B. L. (1974), "Age Groups in American Society and the Rise of the Young-Old," Annals of the American Academy of Political and Social Science, Political Consequences of Aging, 415 (September), 187-198.

Rahtz, D. R., M. J. Sirgy, and H. L. Meadow (forthcoming), "Elderly Life Satisfaction and Television Viewership: An Exploratory Study," in M. J. Houston, ed. Advances in Consumer Research: Volume 13.

Reinecke, J. (1964), "The 'Older' Market -- Fact or Fiction?" Journal of Marketing, 28 (January), 60-64.

Richards, M. L. (1981), "The Clothing Preferences and Problems of Elderly Female Consumers," The Gerontologist, 21 (3), 363-367.

Samli, A. C. (1967), "The Elusive Senior Citizen Market," Business and Economic Dimensions, 3 (November), 7-16.

Schewe, C. D. (1984), "Buying and Consuming Behavior of the Elderly: Findings from Behavioral Research," in T. C. Kinnear, ed. Advances in Consumer Research: Volume 11. Provo, UT: Association for Consumer Research. 558-562.

Tongren, H. N. (1975), "Consumer Credit and the Over-65 Age Group," Journal of Consumer Credit Management, 5 (Spring), 117-123.

Towle, J. G. and C. R. Martin (1976), "The Elderly Consumer: One Segment of Many?" in B. B. Anderson, ed. Advances in Consumer Research: Volume 3. Ann Arbor, MI: Association for Consumer Research. 463-468.

Visvabharathy, G. and D. R. Rink (1985), "The Elderly: Still the 'Invisible and Forgotten' Market Segment," Journal of the Academy of Marketing Science, 13 (Fall), 81-100.

Zbytniewski, J-A (1979), "The Older Shopper: Over 65 and Overlooked," Progressive Grocer, 58 (November), 109-111.

AN EXPORATORY EXAMINATION OF RACIAL BIAS IN MEASURES OF CONSUMER SOCIALIZATION

Rose L. Johnson, Georgia State University
Harash Sachdev, Georgia State University

Abstract

The problem of racial bias in measurement has achieved great attention with respect to I.Q. and other achievement tests, and, more recently, in social scientific measurement as well. The advancement of knowledge through research requires that valid measures be used. However, differential validity, i.e. differences in validity across groups, is rarely assessed by marketers. This paper provides a discussion of the problem of racial bias in marketing-related measures and demonstrates a method of testing for bias.

Introduction

The problem of racial bias in measurement instruments has come to the forefront in several fields. Standardized tests have been used historically in educational settings to place students and to identify them for special programs. Since the 1960's the validity of such tests for use in assessing students' ability has been challenged by several groups (Talbutt 1983). In some cases the validity of the tests was found to differ for white versus black children to the extent that their use was seen as discriminatory (see e.g. Bersoff 1982).

Other tests, such as those used in professional licensing examinations have also been called into question. Studying administrations of the Colorado bar examination, McClelland (1985) found that portions of the test were differently intercorrelated across whites, blacks, and Chicanos. Had no bias been present, the relationships among test elements should have been the same across groups. An item is generally considered biased if equally able members of different groups show unequal levels of success or are classified differently based on that item. Thus, a test for differential validity, i.e. differences in validity across groups, must involve a comparison of results for the two groups under consideration. However, standardized tests such as those described above are generally validated on all white or predominantly white samples (Bersoff 1982).

While achievement-type tests have been accorded the most attention with respect to the racial bias issue, bias in measurement is not restricted to this area. In their examination of 1190 social group comparisons in the psychology literature, Bartlett, Bobko, Hannan, and Mosier (1977) found differential predictive validity across groups for 282 (23%) of the measures (Bobko and Bartlett 1978). Allen and Chaffee (1977) note: "Racial bias may be less obvious but it is not necessarily less pernicious, with less precise types of social measurement [than with intelligence testing] and with the theories of social behavior that are based on them" (p 9.) An example of racial bias identified in social-scientific research is the family communications patterns model. The model is based on two dimensions: the family's socio-orientation, in which deference is given to elders, and concept orientation, in which the child is encouraged to express his/her own ideas. This typology has been used to explain a number of mass communication and interpersonal behaviors and processes. However, Allen and Chaffee (1977) reported that the typology is valid for white families but not for blacks.

Several studies have examined the effects of race on consumer behavior directly (eg. Christiansen 1979, Moschis and Moore 1985), and indirectly, through its effects on socialization processes (eg. Moschis, Moore, and Smith 1984). Since the existence of racial bias in measurement instruments is rarely assessed, these studies may be affected by the same problem as the achievement tests and the family communication typology.

The purpose of this paper is to provide a discussion of the problem of racial bias in marketing-related measures. A method of testing for racial bias will be described and an empirical investigation of the presence and extent of racial bias in measures of parent-child interaction concerning consumption will be performed.

The family communication patterns typology, studied by Allen and Chaffee, has been adapted for use in studying consumer socialization by others. This study seeks to extend Allen and Chaffee's (1977) findings of racial bias within the measure into the consumer behavior sphere. The applicability to blacks of other commonly used measures of consumer socialization, including the frequency of interaction and of positive and negative reinforcement, will also be investigated.

Validity Assessment

Reliability and validity are necessary conditions for sound consumer research. Validity refers to the degree to which instruments truly measure the constructs which they are intended to measure. Reliability, a necessary but not sufficient condition for validity, indicates the degree to which measures are free from error and thus yield consistent results.

For a test to be valid, scores should predict subsequent performance. The higher the correlation between a test and the performance criterion of interest, the more valid is the test for that particular use (Carmines and Zeller 1979). Problems in assessing validity may arise because the validity of the performance criterion is unknown, or there may be no appropriate criterion available (McClelland 1985). In such cases, an alternative is to examine tests with respect to their reliability, or internal consistency.

Marketing researchers rarely assess the reliability of their measures. Of the more than 400 consumer behavior studies surveyed by Peter (1979), less than 5% assessed the reliability of the measures employed. Even when reliability is assessed, however, racial bias in measures may go undetected (Bobko and Bartlett 1978). Bias is evidenced by differential predictive ability of a measure across groups of equal ability. Thus to demonstrate or assess the fairness of a test, a comparison of the predictive ability across relevant groups must be made.

The assessment of differential predictive ability is hindered by the same problems as is the assessment of single group validity. In fact, the lack of a valid criterion measure may prove even more problematic in this situation since the (unknowing) use of a biased performance criterion can make a fair measure appear biased (McClelland 1985). Internal consistency measures, however, can still prove useful.

Tests of internal consistency cannot signal that an entire scale is systematically biased; however, they can be used to identify biased items or differences in the extent of bias across items. McClelland (1985) studied differences in scores for components of the Colorado state bar examination. For a fair test, differences in ability across groups should be reflected to the same extent by all test components. Bias was thus suspected when group differences on one component were greater than differences on other components.

If all elements of a measure are non-biased, the intercorrelations among items will be the same across comparison groups. Conversely, differences in reliability across groups will signal bias. An analysis of item-to-total correlations for individual items thus can be used to identify biased items.

The Socialization Perspective

A great deal of consumption-related knowledge and behavior is believed to be learned, especially that obtained in the pre-adult years (Olshavsky and Granbois 1979 in Moschis and Moore 1985). Further, it is widely held that childhood experiences are of paramount importance in shaping patterns of cognition and behavior in later life (Ward 1974). Thus understanding socialization processes is an important part of the analysis of consumer development and behavior.

"Socialization" typically refers to the learning of social roles and the behavior associated with those roles. "Consumer socialization" refers to the processes by which people, especially young people, acquire skills, knowledge, and attitudes relevant to their functioning as consumers in the marketplace (Ward 1974). The social learning model of socialization seeks to explain socialization as a function of the interaction of a learner with his/her environment. Learning is seen as taking place during, and as a result of, the individual's interaction with socialization agents in various social settings.

A conceptual model of social learning developed in previous research (see e.g. Churchill and Moschis 1979) involves three types of variables. Antecedent variables include social structural and developmental variables such as social class, race and age. These variables indicate the location of the individual in his or her social environment. Socialization processes refer to the agent-learner relationships through which learning occurs. Interaction may be with parents, peers, the school, the media or others. Outcomes in the model include the development of consumer knowledge, attitudes and norms.

Research Questions

Socialization agent/learner interactions, or learning processes, can be divided into three categories (McLeod and O'Keefe 1972). Modeling involves imitation of the agent by the learner, either through a conscious attempt to emulate the socialization agent or because the agent's behavior is the most salient alternative open to the learner. Reinforcement may be positive and/or negative, and involves learning to duplicate past behaviors that have been rewarded and avoid those behaviors for which the learner has been punished. Social interaction may involve a combination of modeling and reinforcement. Within this process, the social norms involved in the learner's interactions with relevant others shape his behavior.

This research will provide an empirical investigation of the presence and extent of racial bias in commonly used measures of consumer socialization in the parent-child relationship. Specifically, it will examine the following question:
Does the internal consistency of 1) modeling, 2) reinforcement, and 3) social interaction measures differ when applied to black versus white populations?

Method

The sample for this study consists of 65 black and 145 white middle and high school students. To allow approximately equal sized racial groups, subjects represent all black respondents and a random subsample of white respondents taken from a larger study.

Respondents were selected from six counties in suburban, semi-rural, and rural Georgia. While the sampling was not random, the help of school officials was enlisted in an effort to select schools most representative of their respective counties. Questionnaires were self-administered and anonymous, and were completed during regular class sessions.

Variables include multi-item scales measuring the extent of parent-child modeling, reinforcement, and social interaction. Scale items are the same as or similar to those used in other consumer socialization studies (cf. Moschis, Moore, and Smith 1984). A listing of scale items is given in the Appendix.

Modeling is measured as learner observation of parental behavior. Nine consumer-related activities are evaluated. Individual items are dichotomous responses that the child often sees his parents doing the activity.

Reinforcement is measured on two five-point scales. The positive reinforcement scale involves six items measuring parental affection and rewarding behavior. The negative reinforcement scale measures parental punishment through physical, verbal and restrictive behaviors.

Social interaction is measured as family interaction with respect to consumer matters. The five-point scale includes six items measuring behaviors such as shopping with parents and talking with parents about consumer matters.

The family communication patterns model was included as an additional measure of social interaction. The socio-orientation scale includes six items measuring the extent to which deference to elders is demanded with respect to consumer matters. The concept-orientation scale includes six items measuring the extent to which the child is encouraged to express his own ideas.

Results

The first analysis involved a comparison of scale reliabilities for blacks versus whites for each of the six socialization measures. Cronbach's alpha coefficients were transformed to z-scores via Fisher's z transformation (for details, see Morrison 1976). Cross-racial comparisons were then made via a z-test. Results of this analysis are contained in Table 1. None of the differences in z-scores was significant.

Because it was recognized that bias in individual items may be hidden by the cumulative analysis, further analysis involved a comparison of item-to-total correlations for the individual scale items. If no bias in scale items were present, one would expect the item-to-total correlations for a particular item to be the same across racial groups.

The results for scale items for the six socialization measures analyzed are given in Figures 1-6. The figures show that four of the items differed significantly across racial groups; one within family interaction, one within behavioral observation, and two within the concept orientation scale. However, due to the large number of tests performed, these differences may be due to chance.

Unfortunately, failure to reject a null hypothesis does not provide conclusive evidence that no differences exist. An analysis of internal consistency may not reveal systematic bias that affects all items. Further, the analysis of item-to-total correlations gives no guidelines as to how much bias is acceptable. Thus researchers must use their own judgement in assuring test fairness. In this case, the small sample size and resulting large standard deviation may also have served to hinder the identification of differences. The method demonstrated, however, is valuable for its ability to provide a guide for the researcher.

Conclusion

It is widely recognized that blacks and whites exhibit differing consumer behavior; however, there is less consensus as to the reasons for racial differences (Moschis and Moore 1985). Since a great deal of consumer behavior is believed to be learned, several researchers have attempted to explain differences using socialization theory.

While cultural differences in socialization patterns can result in different behavior, the differing life experiences of black versus white subcultures may also result in differences in

TABLE 1
Comparisons of Scale Reliabilities

	Blacks	Whites	$\lvert Z_B - Z_W \rvert$
Family interaction	.713	.619	
	.894	.723	.141
Socio orientation	.759	.697	
	.993	.861	.132
Concept orientation	.486	.545	
	.531	.611	.080
Positive reinforcement	.591	.634	
	.679	.749	.070
Negative reinforcement	.549	.571	
	.617	.649	.032
Behavioral observation	.552	.499	
	.621	.548	.073

Table entries = alpha coefficient
Z - score

the way questions are construed. In addition, questions may be misunderstood by respondents who speak "Black English" or other non-standard dialects.

An understanding of the reasons for and process of consumption by blacks is vital for an adequate servicing of this market. In order to insure a true understanding of consumer behavior of any group, researchers must insure the reliability and validity of measures for their intended purpose. Many researchers in the past have validated measures on all white or predominately white samples (Allen and Chaffee 1977, Bersoff 1982). This paper sought to demonstrate that such a procedure is inadequate to ensure validity of measures for use with black consumers. Rather, researchers must begin separately assessing validity for blacks and whites, and care must be taken when "standardized" measures are adopted for use on black samples.

FIGURE 1
Comparisons of Item-to-Total Correlations

Family Interaction

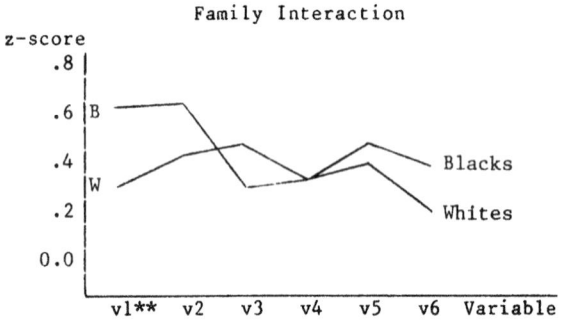

FIGURE 2
Comparisons of Item-to-Total Correlations

Socio Orientation

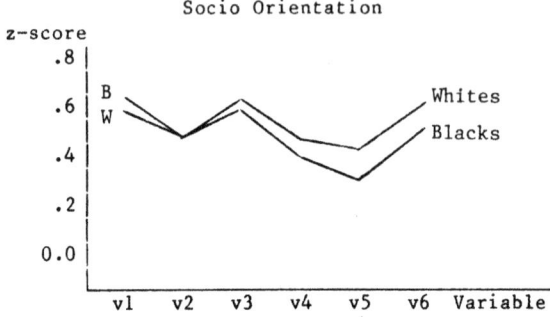

FIGURE 3
Comparisons of Item-to-Total Correlations
Concept Orientation

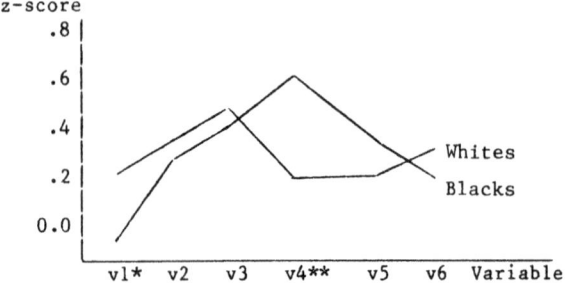

FIGURE 4
Comparisons of Item-to-Total Correlations

Positive Reinforcement

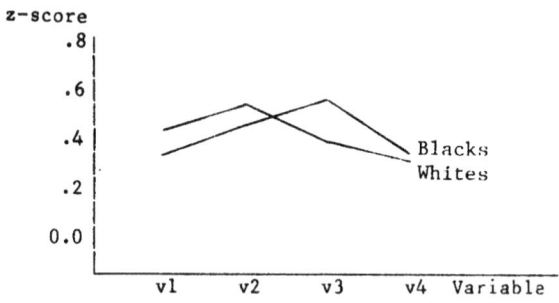

FIGURE 5
Comparisons of Item-to-Total Correlations

Negative Reinforcement

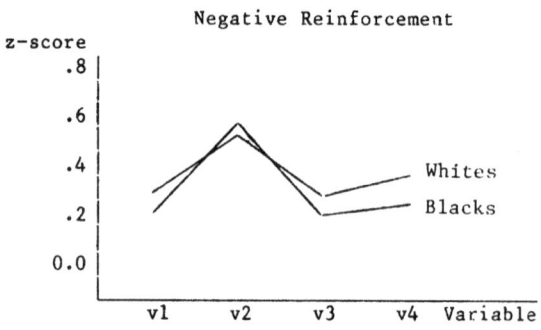

FIGURE 6
Comparisons of Item-to-Total Correlations

Behavioral Observation

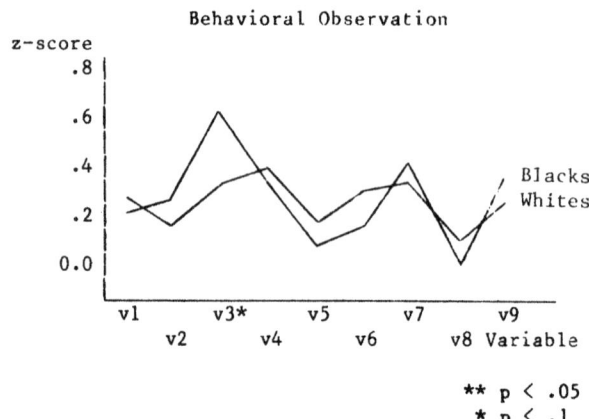

** p < .05
* p < .1

References

Allen, Richard L. and Steven H. Chaffe (1977), "Racial Differences in Family Communication Patterns," Journalism Quarterly, 55 (Spring), 8-13, 57.

Bobko, Philip and C. J. Bartlett (1978), "Subgroup Validities: Differential Definitions and Differential Prediction," Journal of Applied Psychology, 63:1, 12-14.

Bersoff, Donald N. (1982), "Larry P. and PASE: Judicial Report Cards on the Validity of Individual Intelligence Tests," Child and Youth Services 5:1-2, 101-120.

Carmines, Edward G. and Richard A. Zeller (1979), Reliability and Validity Assessment, Beverly Hills, CA: SAGE.

Christiansen, J.B. (1979), "Television Role Models and Adolescent Occupational Goals," Human Communication Research, 5 (Summer), 335-337.

McClelland, Gary H. (1985), "Assessing Bias in Professional Licensing Examinations by Checking Internal Consistency," Law and Human Behavior, 9:3, 305-318.

McLeod, Jack M. and Garrett O'Keefe Jr. (1972), "The Socialization Perspective and Communication Behavior," in Current Perspectives in Mass Communication Research, edited by G. Kline and P. Tichenor, Beverly Hills, CA: SAGE, 121-168.

Morrison, Donald F. (1976), Multivariate Statistical Methods, New York: McGraw-Hill Book Company.

Moschis, George P. and Roy L. Moore (1985), "Racial and Socio-Economic Influences on the Development of Consumer Behavior," in Advances in Consumer Research, vol. 12, edited by E. Hirschman and M. Holbrook, Provo, UT: Association for Consumer Research, 525-531.

Moschis, George P., Roy L. Moore, and Ruth B. Smith (1984), "The Impact of Family Communication on Adolescent Consumer Socialization," in Advances in Consumer Research, vol. 11, edited by Thomas C. Kinnear, Ann Arbor, MI: Association for Consumer Research, 314-319.

Peter, J. Paul (1979), "Reliability: A Review of Psychometric Basics and Recent Marketing Practices," Journal of Marketing Research, 16 (February), 6-17.

Talbutt, Lou Culler (1983), "The Counselor and Testing: Some Legal Concerns," The School Counselor, 30 (March), 245-250

Ward, Scott (1974), "Consumer Socialization," Journal of Consumer Research, 1 (September), 1-14.

Appendix
Socialization Measuses

FAMILY INTERACTION
Your parents:
- v1   My parents and I talk about things we see or hear advertised.
- v2   I try to get my parents to buy things I see advertised.
- v3   I get my parents to buy things that are advertised.
- v4   I ask my parents for advice about buying things.
- v5   I go shopping with my parents.
- v6   My parents and I don't agree on what things I should or shouldn't buy.

SOCIO-ORIENTATION
Your parents:
- v1   Tell you what things you should or shouldn't buy.
- v2   Want to know what you do with your money.
- v3   Complain when they don't like something you bought for yourself.
- v4   Say that they know what is best for you and you shouldn't question them.
- v5   Say you shouldn't ask questions about things that teen-agers like you don't normally buy.
- v6   Say you may not buy certain things.

CONCEPT-ORIENTATION
Your parents:
- v1   Ask you to help them buy things for the family.
- v2   Ask you what you think about things they buy for themselves.
- v3   Ask your advice about buying things.
- v4   Say you should decide what things you should or shouldn't buy.
- v5   Say that buying things you like is important even if others do not like them.
- v6   Say that you should decide yourself how to spend your money.

POSITIVE REINFORCEMENT
Your parents:
- v1   Give you money to buy the things you want.
- v2   Let you pick out some things for the family.
- v3   Buy you presents.
- v4   Let you know you are a smart buyer.

NEGATIVE REINFORCEMENT
Your parents:
- v1   Act as if they don't care about things you buy.
- v2   Make you feel guilty about some things you buy.
- v3   Punish you by taking away your allowance.
- v4   Punish you by saying they won't buy you things they promised you.

BEHAVIORAL OBSERVATION
- v1   They try not to waste energy.
- v2   They show what things one should have in order to get ahead in the world.
- v3   They keep track of the money they spend and save.
- v4   They shop around before buying something that costs a lot of money.
- v5   They let you know what others think of you if you buy certain products.
- v6   They return for refund things they are not happy with.
- v7   They plan before buying things.
- v8   They show what things to buy to make good impressions on others.
- v9   They read packages or labels of some products.

DETERMINING BLACK EXPENDITURE PATTERNS USING ELASTICITY COEFFICIENTS: DEVELOPING A PROFILE

Wayne C. Linhardt, Lincoln University of Missouri

Abstract

The purpose of this paper is to draw an expenditure profile of black consumers and to develop a model to measure the purchasing patterns of blacks. Data from the Bureau of Labor Statistics is analyzed using an income elasticity model based on Engel curves to establish elasticity coefficients for expenditure patterns by blacks.

Introduction

The consumer behavior patterns of black Americans have long been misunderstood and neglected by major marketing firms. Black consumers have usually been considered as a part of the general market for consumer goods without any major distinction in their purchasing habits. Marketers for most major firms believed that they could reach the black market through their undifferentiated advertising in media that black consumers viewed. This is not true. The extent of the misconception of the black consumer can be seen from an unfortunate remark that was made at a Small Business Institute Directors meeting held in 1985. An SBI director remarked that, "Every black person with a recipe for barbecue sauce thinks he should go into business". The lack of understanding of the black consumer and the subsequent neglect of this market has led to the development of a group of convenient and most often erroneous myths that filled the vacuum left by the lack of supporting research.

The purpose of this paper is to determine the purchasing behavior patterns of the black consumer and develop a model to measure these patterns.

Maggard (1971) states that some authorities contend that the so-called black market is inseparable from the total market, and that no need therefore exists for a special approach in the promotion of goods and services. Others insist that the social, economic, and political isolation of blacks has practically forced them into a distinctive market of their own. It would appear that while a black may not desire to be so distinct, he does recognize that he is. It is now generally agreed that a distinct black market does exist, and that it is a market which is based somewhat upon geographical concentration, but even more so upon sociological background, cultural history, and elements of a color cast system in modern society, as well as upon various psychological needs, desires, and frustrations which tend to emerge as a result of employment and income limitations.

McNatt (1984) using U. S. Department of Commerce data shows that the black population for the United States was 27.7 million in 1982, with projections of 28.2 million in 1983 and 28.6 million in 1984. This represents 11.9, 12.0, and 12.1 percent of the population respectively. Actual black income was $126.1 billion, $160.5 billion, and $179.9 billion for the respective years. This was a 7.1 percent increase in 1982, 7.3 percent in 1983 and 7.5 percent in 1984. This shows that while black population increased only 0.1 percent in both 1983 and 1984, black income increased 2.7 percent for the respective years.

Even though blacks make up 12 percent of the population, they are conspicuous consumers, particularly in certain product groups. A Management Review (1986) article shows that blacks purchase 222 percent more malt liquor, 141 percent more frozen yogurt, and 139 percent more hair coloring products than the national average. Maggard points out that statistical verification shows that blacks also consume 28 percent of all soft drinks, 23 percent of all shoes, and up to 50 percent of imported Scotch. Swisshelm (1986), using a use index for consumption patterns shows that consumption for black individuals was 70 percent higher than average for bottled barbecue sauce, 53 percent for butter, 67 percent for pancake syrup, 74 percent greater in heavy usage of non-frozen orange juice, and a whopping 795 percent higher for rice consumption.

O'Hara (1987) using 1984 BLS data shows that blacks account for 33 percent for all expenditures of rental televisions, 25 percent of inter-city mass transportation, 17 percent of expenditures on encyclopedias and other reference material, and accounted for only 1.6 percent for all new truck and van sales.

Methodology

Millican (1967) used the 1960-61 Consumer Expenditure Survey (CEX) published by the U. S. Department of Labor, Bureau of Labor Statistics to verify Engel's Laws for the economy.

Income elasticity was calculated by the author for the fifteen major expenditure categories listed in the CEX for households with a black head. The 1972-73, 1980-81, 1982-83, and the 1984 CEX was used as the source data.

The use of Engel curves, as modified by Wright (1875) has long been recognized in economic thought as a method of measuring the income-expenditure relationship (Duesenberry 1949, Ackley 1961, Brennan 1964, Ferguson & Gould 1975, Mansfield 1979, Henderson & Quandt 1980, Maurice & Phillips 1986).

The general model developed for measuring the elasticity coefficient is:

$$EC = \frac{\Delta CE/CE}{\Delta I/I} = \frac{\Delta CE}{\Delta I} \cdot \frac{I}{CE} \geqq 0 \qquad (1)$$

However, for manipulation of the data, a more practical statement of the formula was used.

$$EC = \frac{CE_1 - CE_0 / \; CE_1 + CE_0}{I_1 - I_0 \; / \; I_1 + I_0} \qquad (2)$$

Where:

EC is the elasticity coefficient.
CE_1 is the consumer expenditure after an income change.
CE_0 is the consumer expenditure before an income change.
I_1 is the income level after change.
I_0 is the income level before change.

All coefficients were calculated using mean values from matching category data in the CEX.

The hypothesis can be stated that if:

$EC \geqq 1.0$, then the expenditure category shows a significant responsiveness to income change.

$EC < 1.0$, then the expenditure category is not responsive to income change.

Elasticity coefficients may be either positive or negative to reflect the absolute change in the expenditure patterns.

The BLS in reporting the data for the CEX shows a standard error of 0.00002 for all consumers.

No evidence of a coefficient of correlation being calculated for black expenditure patterns has surfaced. However, Fareed and Riggs (1982) and Hammermesh (1984) has cross-indexed the 1972-73 BLS Consumer Expenditure Surveys for the elderly and found an R^2 factor of 0.90.

Results

Table 1 shows the elasticity coefficients calculated for the years 1972-73, 1980-81, 1982-83, and 1983-84. Table 2 shows the expenditures as a percentage of income made by black consumers for the same years.

All coefficients were calculated using mean values. The categories used in the study are matching categories as presented in the CEX for the corresponding years.

Discussion and Interpretation

As a general observation, the elasticity coefficients for 1983-84 are highly distorted due to an extremely small increase in reported income. The absolute increase in income was only $96 with a 1984 average income before taxes of $16,040 as compared to $15,950 in 1983. The data for 1983-84 is included in this study. The implication of this phenomenon is that black consumers relied on other forms of financial funding such as savings, credit or liquidation of assets to support the increase in expenditures.

Following the hypothesis stated in the first part of the paper, elasticity coefficients of 1.0+ would show that black consumers would have a greater propensity to spend additional money on that category of item with an increase in income. Conversely, categories with a coefficient of less than 1.0 would show a reluctance to increase expenditures for items within the categories.

Each of the categories will be analyzed in the following sections:

Food at Home

The profile for expenditure patterns for black consumers for Food at Home shows a declining pattern. Coefficients of 1.71, 0.45, -3.48, and -0.90 support this observation. The percentage of income observations for this category also shows a declining pattern with a consistent decline from 16.4 percent in 1972-73 to a mean percentage of 13.1 percent during the 1980's.

Food Away From Home

Food Away From Home shows increasing expenditure patterns for black consumers in both elasticity coefficients and percentage of income. Black consumers are eating out more, with the percentage of income increasing approximately 2.0 percent from 1972 through 1983. Elasticity coefficients of 0.44, 0.21, 0.33, 1.34, and 10.06 point to increasing expenditures.

Alcoholic Beverages

The mean elasticity coefficient for consumption of alcoholic beverages by blacks is -1.84. The mean percentage of income for the category is 0.9 percent. The implications are that blacks are clearly consuming less alcohol as income increases. The coefficients are in the majority of cases in a negative trend indicating even less absolute dollars being spent than previously.

Tobacco Products

The mean expenditure for tobacco products as a percentage of income is only 1.2 percent of income. However, the expenditure pattern as shown by the elasticity coefficients are very volatile from year to year with 0.34, -1.55, 1.25, 5.18, and 8.96 for the respective years. This apparent paradox might be explained by the fact that for black consumers the absolute amount of tobacco consumption is fixed and is not influenced by changes in income and is not sensitive to promotional claims after a clear smoking pattern is established.

Housing

Housing is the single largest expenditure category for black consumers. It comprised a mean of 29.7 percent of total income for the respective years. The income elasticity coefficients were 1.00, 1.13, 0.92, 1.94, and 15.30; showing a rise in responsiveness to income change.

TABLE 1
Expenditure Elasticity Coefficients For Black Consumers

	1972-73	1980-81	1981-82	1982-83	1983-84
Food at Home	1.71	0.45	-3.48	-0.90	14.26
Food Away From Home	0.44	0.21	0.33	1.34	10.00
Alcoholic Beverages	-0.66	0.34	-4.96	-5.19	333.33
Tobacco Products	0.34	-1.55	1.25	5.18	8.96
Housing	1.00	1.13	0.92	1.94	15.30
Clothing/Apparel	0.46	1.23	0.86	-3.76	24.57
Transportation	0.79	0.29	2.29	-6.66	32.54
Health Care	0.56	2.73	-0.16	-1.15	-5.87
Personal Care	-0.59	1.02	1.52	-3.43	20.17
Recreation (Entertainment)	1.02	0.50	0.40	-4.49	52.63
Reading Materials	0.10	-1.89	1.32	***	14.93
Education	1.49	0.53	12.75	-3.71	5.13
Miscellaneous	1.41	-1.46	8.89	-7.04	9.78
Personal Insurance & Pensions	0.95	0.76	10.05	4.27	20.76
Gifts & Contributions	-0.05	0.75	0.31	1.33	-7.32

TABLE 2
Expenditure Patterns By Blacks As Percentage Of Income

	1972	1980	1981	1982	1983	1984
Food at Home	17.4	17.5	17.1	14.6	14.7	12.8
Food Away From Home	4.0	3.4	3.2	3.2	3.4	2.9
Alcoholic Beverages	1.5	1.5	1.5	1.2	1.1	0.9
Tobacco Products	1.8	1.5	0.6	1.2	1.4	1.2
Housing	31.2	20.1	31.3	31.4	34.0	29.9
Clothing/Apparel	8.5	6.1	6.4	6.5	6.0	5.6
Transportation	19.4	20.0	19.2	20.3	17.5	17.1
Health Care	4.7	3.3	4.0	3.8	3.8	3.0
Personal Care	2.0	1.1	0.5	1.1	1.3	1.1
Recreation (Entertainment)	5.0	3.2	3.2	3.1	2.9	3.2
Reading Materials	0.6	0.6	0.2	0.5	0.5	0.4
Education	1.3	0.6	0.5	1.7	1.5	1.2
Miscellaneous	0.8	1.3	1.1	1.7	1.4	1.2
Personal Insurance & Pensions	8.9	7.6	3.8	7.5	8.0	7.2
Gifts & Contributions	6.3	1.7	0.8	2.4	2.7	2.1

Both the percentage of income and the rise in the elasticity coefficients prove that the Housing category is elastic for black consumers. Blacks are apparently very willing to make changes in their housing facilities with a small income increase incentive.

Clothing/Apparel

Apparently the clothing picture has changed for black consumers from the decade of the 70's. This is manifested by the over 30 percent decrease in expenditures as a percent of income, from 8.5 percent in 1972 to 5.6 percent in 1984. The elasticity coefficients show an ambivalent market with a highly volatile profile. The black consumer is unsure whether or not to conform to conventional dress standards or continue to make large expenditures for distinctive fashions.

Transportation

Transportation remains constant with a mean percentage of income of 18.9 percent. This is the second highest expenditure category, after housing, among black consumers. The elasticity coefficients for the 1982-83 and 1983-84 records show a dramatic shift of 2.29 and -6.66 respectively.

This may represent a major shift in black transportation usage from public transportation systems to private vehicles. Analysis of the subcategories of transportation shows percentage increases of 10.4, 32.2, -30.4, and 52.6 percent for the years 1980 through 1984 for private transportation compared to increases of 5.9, 8.1, -0.4, and 9.9 percent respectively for public transportation.

Health Care

Elasticity coefficients for three of the five years calculated for this study were negative and all occurred in the last three years. This would indicate a negative trend in the propensity to spend income on health care. The percentage of income spent on health care remained relatively constant with a mean of 3.7 percent. Analyzing the subcategories of Health Care, we find that over the four year span of the 1980's Health Insurance had a mean elasticity of 0.61, Medical Service declined with a mean coefficient of -3.61 and Prescription Drugs had a mean coefficient of 2.45. Apparently black consumers are funding Health Care services from sources other than out-of-pocket expenditures. The use of Federal and State sources such as Medicare, Medicaid, and ADC payments appear to be assuming an increasing role in this area for the black consumer.

Personal Care

Personal Care expenditures for blacks dropped approximately a full percentage point during the last decade from 2.0 percent in 1972-73 to a mean of 1.02 percent in the 1980's. Elasticity coefficients are ambivalent with -0.59 in 1972-73, 1.02 in 1980-81, 1.52 in 1981-82, -3.43 in 1982-83, and a staggering 20.17 in 1983-84. Brand loyalty is a strong psychological variable among black consumers in this area. Blacks tend to use the same products regardless of income (Martin 1985).

Recreation (Entertainment)

Black expenditures for Recreation have significantly declined during the last decade with an elasticity coefficient of 1.02 and a 5.0 percent of income expenditures being recorded in 1972-73. With the exception of 1983-84, expenditures in this category have considerably declined, with elasticity coefficients of 0.50, 0.40, and -4.49 recorded in 1980-81, 1981-82, and 1982-83 respectively. This is confirmed by a decline in expenditures as a percentage of income. Mean percentage for the 1980's is 3.4 percent.

Reading Materials

Purchase of reading material does not play a major role in black consumption patterns. Percentage of income expenditures range from 0.6 percent over the years included in the study. With the exception of 1983-84, elasticity coefficients for the 1980's were -1.89 and 1.32 for 1980-81 and 1981-82. 1982-83 recorded absolutely no change in expenditures. The 1972-73 coefficient was 0.10.

Education

While education does not make up a large percentage of expenditures within black income, it is very sensitive as an elasticity coefficient. With the exception of 1980-81 (0.53) all coefficients are above/below elasticity by significant margins. The elasticity coefficients for this category show the largest change of any category. In comparing the change within the last decade, we find a coefficient of 1.49 for 1972-73 with a mean coefficient of 3.69 for the 1980's. Individual coefficients range from a high of 12.75 in 1981-82 to a low of -3.71 in 1982-83. To black consumers, education appears to be viewed as a viable means of improving their position; however, they are inconsistent in their expenditure pattern.

Miscellaneous

Miscellaneous item expenditures expressed a strong elasticity coefficient in each year of the study. There was a significant increase in the amounts spent by blacks in the 1980's as compared to 1972-73. The mean coefficient for the 1980's was 2.54 with the 1972-73 coefficient at 1.41. The category remained relatively stable as a percentage of income with 0.8 percent in 1972-73 and a mean of 1.3 percent from 1980 to 1984.

Personal Insurance & Pensions

The purchase of personal insurance (life) and the development of retirement systems for black consumers has remained relatively stable as a percentage of income within the last decade. The category made up 8.9 percent of expenditures during 1972-73 and averaged 6.8 percent from 1980 to 1984. However, elasticity coefficients rose rapidly during the last three years. 1981-82 shows a coefficient of 10.05; 1982-83, 4.27; and 1983-84, 20.76. An examination of the subcategories shows that purchase of life insurance significantly increased with coefficients of 0.86 in 1972-73 and a mean of 5.55 for the 1980's. Pension and retirement funds showed a dramatic change with 0.86 and a mean of 6.12 respectively for the years of the study

Gifts and Contributions

Black consumers have significantly changed their habits of making contributions since 1972. Contributions/Gifts constituted better than 6 percent (6.3%) of income in 1972-73 and has fallen to an average of 1.4 percent for the 1980's. The most significant factor is the negative elasticity coefficient of -7.32 in 1983-84. This represents a major shift in attitude toward contributions.

Conclusion

1. Evaluating the prior research done on black consumers, it appears that the researchers attempted to determine the extent of purchases made by black consumers in specific individual product categories. Little attempt was made to develop a consistent longitudinal profile of expenditure patterns by blacks as to the importance of the purchases when compared to income. This study is an attempt to create a model that will measure the relative importance of each expenditure category to the black consumer.

2. The effect of the abnormal 1984 expenditure patterns by black consumers needs further research. The patterns may represent a one-time phenomenon or a major departure from previous patterns.

3. The results of the study show the following implications for marketers selling products to black consumers:

a) The Food category, in general, is not responsive to income change. Growth within this category (Food, Food Away From Home, Alcoholic Beverages, Tobacco Products) appears to be limited to demographic growth. Changes in black population, shifts from urban to suburban residence, etc. appear to have more impact on the market growth of this category than do increases in income.

b) Housing remains consistently elastic within this study and is very sensitive to income change. Blacks will spend disproportionately more on housing as income increases. As black consumers become more affluent, marketers in this category will benefit from the increase in wealth.

c) Clothing/Apparel does not show a definite trend among black consumers over the years contained in the study. Both elastic and inelastic coefficients occur that are positive and negative.

d) Transportation seems to be declining in importance as a category of black consumption The expenditures on transportation do not take on disproportionate influence.

e) Black Personal Care items (Health Care, Personal Care, Recreation, Reading Materials, Education, Miscellaneous) have mixed results. Health Care is clearly declining as more blacks participate in health insurance plans and Medicare-Medicaid programs. The other categories do not show a definite trend.

f) Personal Insurance & Pension expenditures show the greatest increase of any category in importance to black consumers. Blacks are purchasing life insurance, annuities, and pension plans in disproportionate numbers. This is of special importance to marketers in this area.

g) The category of Gifts & Contributions has significantly declined. Black organizations that depend on charitable contributions may find it hard to secure funds.

References

Ackley, Gardner (1961), Macroeconomic Theory, New York: The Macmillan Company.

Askin, Steve (1983), "The Hidden Power of Pension Funds," Black Enterprise, 13 (January), pp. 35-37.

Brennan, Michael J. (1965), Theory of Economic Statics, Englewood Cliffs, N. J.: Prentice-Hall, Inc.

Dingle, Derek T. (1986), "Seeking An Agenda for Economic Growth," Black Enterprise, 16 (June), pp. 201-208.

Duesenberry, J. S. (1949), Income, Saving and the Theory of Consumer Behavior, Boston: Harvard University Press.

Fareed, F. E. and G. D. Riggs (1982), "Old-Young Differences in Consumer Expenditure Patterns," The Journal of Consumer Affairs, 16 (Summer), 152-160.

Ferguson, C. E. and J. P. Gould (1975) Microeconomic Theory, Homewood, IL: Richard D. Irwin, Inc.

Fitch, Ed. (1986), "Agencies Playing For Equality From Advertisers," Advertising Age, 57 (August 25) pp. 15-30, 31.

Graves, Earl G. (1985), "Recognizing Our Value As Consumers," Black Enterprise, 16 (December), p. 9.

Hammermesh, Daniel S. (1986), "Consumption During Retirement: The Missing Link in the Life Cycle," Review of Economics and Statistics, 66 (February), pp. 1-7.

Henderson, James M. and Richard F. Quandt (1980) Microeconomic Theory: A Mathematical Approach, New York: McGraw-Hill Book Company.

Joseph, Franklyn W. (1986), "Despite Growth In Market, Strong Resistance Continues," Advertising Age, 57 (August 25), pp. 5-1, 5-2.

Lewis, Sir Arthur (1983), "Black Americans And The Changing World Economy," Black Enterprise, 13 (March), pp. 36, 39.

Maggard, John P. (1971), "Negro Market-Fact or Fiction," California Management Review, 14 (Fall), pp. 71-80.

Management Review, (1986), "Debunking Ethnic Marketing Myths," 75 (April), pp. 5-6.

Mansfield, Edwin (1979), Microeconomics, New York: W. W. Norton.

Marketing & Media Decisions, (1984), "A Segmentation Approach To The Market," 19 (May), pp. 134-136.

Martin, Joel P. (1984), "Segmenting the Black Market," Marketing Communication, 10 (July), 17-19, p. 69.

Maurice, S. Charles and Owen R. Phillips (1986), Economic Analysis: Theory and Application, Homewood, IL: Irwin.

McNatt, Robert (1984), "Black America In a State of Crisis," Black Enterprise, 14 (January), pp. 28-32, 34, 36-39.

Millican, Richard D. (1967) "A Re-examination of Engel's Laws Using BLS Data (1960-61)," Journal of Marketing, 31 (October), 18-21.

O'Hare, William (1987), "Black and Whites: One Market or Two?," American Demographics, 9 (March) pp. 44-48.

Paskowski, Marianne (1986), "Shades of Grey," Marketing & Media Decisions, 21 (March), pp. 30-32, 34, 38, 40.

Swisshelm, George (1986), "Black Income Expected to Surpass $204 Billion in '86," Television/Radio Age, 33 (February 17), pp. A3-A4, A6-A8.

U. S. Department of Labor, Bureau of Labor Statistics (1974) Consumer Expenditure Survey Series: Interview Survey, 1972 and 1973, Report 455-3.

_____ (1985), Consumer Attitude Survey: Interview Survey, 1980-81, Bulletin 2225.

_____ (1986a), Consumer Attitude Survey: Interview Survey, 1982-83, Bulletin 2246.

_____ (1986b), Consumer Attitude Survey: Interview Survey, 1984, Bulletin 2267.

Wright, Carroll D. (1875), Sixth Annual Report of the Bureau of Statistics and Labor, Boston: State Printers.

CAN STANDARD RESEARCH METHODS BE USED IN STUDYING MINORITY (HISPANIC) SEGMENTS?

Lee Slurzberg, Lee Slurzberg Research, Inc., Fort Lee, New Jersey

Introduction

Can standard research methods be used in studying minority (Hispanic) segments? We will be talking about marketing research which is merely a different application of survey research-technology than social research.

1. The components of the research methods:

> Problem definition
> Universe
> Drawing the sample
> Interview method
> Questionnaire

2. Is the problem always/ever the same in the Hispanic market as in the Anglo market?

We know it isn't necessarily so, but the hispanic consumer research assignment usually comes to us in the same form. We've been told there's no problem with the product because it "has been selling very well" in Puerto Rico (Cuba or wherever), therefore, there is no problem with the product, but why aren't hispanics in the United States buying it. That seems to preclude any recommendation for a product test in the United States. We've been told the problem is lack of shelf facings for the brand in bodegas, but the client had no idea of what distribution he had in bodegas—and of course, no product manager had made a field trip to bodegas. A word about the term—bodega—which can mean the hold of a ship or a "mom and pop" store catering to hispanics. On the West Coast, the term tiendita is the more common term. In fairness, its tricky to do. Then, the client may ask us why hispanics say they can't find the product in stores where they shop. These are oversimplified examples to make the point.

3. Defining the universe

Again, this is easier said than done. Most clients say something like..... we want to know if spanish people are eating/using our paper napkins. watches, batteries,brandy, wine or whatever.

There are, of course, a variety of ways to define spanish people. Of course, the definitions are related to the ends to which the findings are to be applied as we as the survey methodologies to be employed.

Spanish descent Perhaps the easiest definition for the novice to comprehend. Its the definition that the Census Bureau uses. Here's how the Census asked the question in 1980.

TABLE 1

CENSUS BUREAU QUESTIONNAIRE

----

7. Is this person of Spanish/Hispanic origin or descent? (Fill one circle.)
    No (not Spanish/Hispanic)
    Yes, Mexican, Mexican-Amer., Chicano
    Yes, Puerto Rican
    Yes, Cuban
    Yes, other Spanish/Hispanic

Instructions: 7. A person is of Spanish/Hispanic origin or descent if the person identifies his or her ancestry with one of the listed groups, that is Mexican, Puerto Rican, etc. Origin or descent (ancestry) may be viewed as the nationality group, the lineage, or country in which the person or the per-son's parents or ancestors were born.

Spanish descent and spanish speaking This is the definition used in the LSR National Hispanic Omnibus and which we recommend in most of the MARKET studies conducted by the firm. Basically, we start the interview in spanish by asking if the potential respondent is of spanish descent.

Spanish surname The Census Bureau compiled a list of 12,497 spanish surnames which is "based on the premise that a particular surname is Spanish if it has a geographic distribution similar to that of the Hispanic population." The derivation of the list is really more sophisticated than that description. That list is generally accepted in the industry. Here's part of what one page of the list looks like.

TABLE 2

1980 CENSUS LIST OF SPANISH NAMES IN ORDER OF FREQUENCY

Rank	Name	Rank	Name
1	Garcia	11	Torres
2	Martinez	12	Rivera
3	Rodrigues	13	Flores
4	Lopez	14	Gomez
5	Hernandez	15	Diaz
6	Gonzalez	16	Ortiz
7	Perez	17	Gutierrez
8	Sanchez	18	Ramos
9	Gonzales	19	Frenandez
10	Ramirez	20	Morales
			etc.

Note: Ranking based on 1977 Tax Returns

One can buy that list from the Census or buy samples with names and telephone numbers that match that list from sampling firms. One of these firms claims "early reports indicate about a 78% incidence rate for reaching actual hispanic households." There is no reason to doubt that hit rate. The development of the list is, of course, complicated with names such as Roman, Martin, Silva and Santos. The list contains only the name Santos.

To put the list in perspective, it doesn't contain the names of the principals at several leading spanish advertising agencies in New York. Alicia Conill, Carlos Rossi... Nor, does it contain the name of Ernest Bromley of Sosa & Associates...nor the name of Bibiana Grau of Grau & Garcia. Nor does it contain any names beginning with the letter K, but some of our spanish studies yield respondents whose names begin with the letter K.

Obviously, the list can only be applied to telephone sampling. More about that later.

<u>Viewers of Spanish TV</u>   This definition makes sense when one is concerned with making local market decisions respecting the medium. However, the definition creates problems in moving from market to market where the availability and appeal of spanish TV (media/programming) varies. That varies from about 60% to 75%).

<u>Acculturated or not</u>   This is a more elusive definition and may have more applicability in social issue studies than in marketing studies. Clients often change this definition to "length of time in the U.S. or on the mainland for Puerto Ricans". We have not used this definition, but if asked to, we would do it on a self-definition basis.

<u>Speaking spanish at home</u>   This definition too often depends on whether the spouse of the spanish person is also spanish speaking as we as on the inclination of the parents to attempt to "americanize" their children.

Most studies show about 90% of hispanics speaking spanish at home. Other studies indicate from 12% to 20% of hispanics can not speak spanish.

<u>Consider oneself spanish</u>   This definition has limited application in most marketing research studies, but could be useful in social science polling--political polling. I know a man of spanish descent whose grandparents came from Spain who considers himself spanish, but neither reads nor speaks spanish. Clearly, he is not part of the "spanish market" that can be reached with spanish media. Should we include persons like that in a definition of the spanish market? how about in the definition of the spanish population?

<u>Agree to be interviewed in spanish</u>   This is a more recent definition. In effect, we are saying to the respondent, you must speak spanish and prove it to me by speaking spanish in this interview. I have no data on how this affects information, I do have experience which indicates that younger people more often want to be interviewed in english than older people. Further, the subsample interviewed in spanish often have different brand usage patterns than those who were interviewed in english.

<u>Read spanish</u>   This one makes sense when we are conducting a print ad test. The definition deals with the issue of illiterates--at least in spanish. In 34 years of conducting ad tests for general market advertising agencies, I have never seen a print or TV ad test that screened for ability to read the language used in the stimulus to be tested.

4. Drawing The Sample

This subject is intertwined with the subject of the Interview <u>Method</u> which follows, but we teach them separately in market research courses and seminars, so let's talk about them separately.

National vs. regional vs. local. The issue here should be simple. What kind of decisions is the user of the data (research agency, advertising agency or client company) going to make with the data. We a know that the composition of the Hispanic market in New York is different than in Miami and so forth. Clients frequently remind me that Puerto Ricans are different than Cubans. However, is the user of the data able or willing to apply different decisions to different ancestry groups. For example, half of the hispanic population in the New York Area is <u>not</u> Puerto Rican. Can a marketer make different marketing decisions (packaging, advertising strategy, print ads, TV commercials) for Puerto Ricans and Colombians?

If the user of the data is only going to make one series of commercials for 4 or 5 hispanic markets, (a very common situation, I assure you) does it matter that Cubans have a different reaction to a specific stimulus tested (say a TV commercial) than do Mexicans? Most advertisers budget minimum amounts for production of spanish language commercials because the amount to be spent on commercial time is small compared with the Non-hispanic market. There are exceptions, of course. A brewer asked us to test different beer ads in Miami than in Los Angeles. The same is true for fast food marketers and soft drink marketers who are among the top spenders in spanish TV advertising.

5. Interview Method

Too often this is determined by budget considerations, but the need to use visual aids--storyboards, packages, product samples, concept statements--or the need to provide sensory stimuli will determine personal vs. telephone--but not mall vs. door-to-door.

Designing the questionnaire instrument

The use of visual aids is highly recommended to minimize cultural and language difficulties. Flash cards should contain alternate spanish expressions, e.g., bodegas in New York and tienditas in Los Angeles. We generally solicit these variations before fielding a study.

Avoid the tendency to replicate the old familiar anglo form--particularly be wary of things like life style lists. They may not have been "validated" in the Anglo market so how do you know they will apply in the (local) hispanic market?

Some comments about the advantages and disadvantages of each method.

Telephone. The extent of non-wired and non-listed are reasonably well documented--although the various sources do not agree. For purposes of this issue, I'm prepared to use data published by sources other than our company.

Here's some data from a Peter Roslow article in 1980--but the data haven't changed substantially. The following percentages of hispanics are listed in the telephone book:

New York (1976)   24%
Los Angeles (1976)   42%
San Antonio (1979)   52%
Miami (1975)   68%

Here's what a Channel 47 (Research Resources) study in New York reported in 1984. "36% of hispanic homes had no telephones and an additional 36% had an unlisted number. That means that 28% were listed in the current directory)-which is consistent with Peter Roslow's statistic above, and our own pattern of data over the last 12 years.

The limitations of spanish surnames as a statistically projectable data base have already been expounded.

There is a difference of opinion among my peers as to whether the telephone interviewer (even assuming that person is clearly spanish by her voice--a judgment interviewers may make) can establish the same rapport as an indigenous personal interviewer. Can a spanish speaking voice from Cincinnati establish rapport with a Puerto Rican lady in the Bronx as we as the Puerto Rican interviewer who comes to her door?

In the general market, we know the limitations of a New Yorker type interviewer from Long Island interviewing a respondent on the telephone in Dallas. Any professional field director listening in on hundreds of WATS interviews each week knows what I mean about rapport.

Clearly there is a limitation of the use of Flash Cards which serve to cover the need for multiple spanish definitions to meet regional/ancestry needs.

Let there be no misunderstanding on the next point. There are clearly differences in brand usage, advertising recall and other attitudes between samples of hispanics with and without telephones. Not always and not in every product category in every market, but that's the point. We never know in advance. Some writers have said "it doesn't make any difference". Well, I can't disagree with them. If it doesn't make any difference that non-telephone households use different brands of household cleanser than telephone households, then go right ahead and use telephone samples. (We conduct telephone studies among hispanics.)

Let me walk you through a hypothetical pattern of hispanics and telephones (See Figure 1). The data are based on several years of looking at field results from the four leading markets where spanish interviewing is done. However, its not inconsistent with data from our own national probability samples of hispanics.

FIGURE 1

HYPOTHETICAL RESPONSE RATES FOR HISPANIC TELEPHONE INTERVIEWING

(L.A., N.Y., MIAMI, SAN ANTONIO)

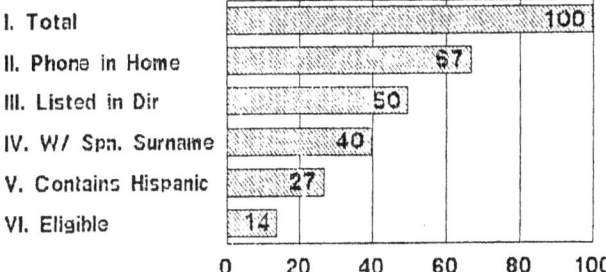

I. Let's assume our population consists of 100 hispanics.

II. My best estimate is that about 67% of them have a telephone in their home. That excludes those with a telephone available--someplace where they can be called. Our interviewers often record an amigo's phone to permit verification of the interview, but we're not counting them.

III. Now, let's assume that 75% of those with telephones in the home are listed in the current directory--and that percentage is less in New York City)--then 50% of a hispanics are listed in the current directory. Remember, the average directory is 9 months old--3 months from closing date to publication plus half a year for an annual directory. The non-listings are associated with mobility, desire to be unlisted and the time it takes to have your listing published in the current directory. About two out of five (42%) of the telephone households in Los Angeles are unlisted. In Miami, its 32%. These statistics are TOTAL MARKET, not just hispanics. However, the statistics are indicative of hispanic non-listings.

IV. When we draw samples from telephone directories, all the researchers I know use the Census list of 12,497 spanish surnames. In one wave of our omnibus, someone went through 1,000 names and compared them with the Census list. Almost 20% were not on the Census list. I also know that about 13% of hispanic women marry non-hispanic men (from 1984 birth information).

So if I assume 20% of hispanics with telephones listed in their name do not have a spanish surname, then we now have 40% of the hispanic population listed in the telephone directory with a spanish surname.

V. Some spanish surnamed households do not contain any spanish persons. Survey Sampling reported "about a 78% incidence rate for reaching actual hispanic households" as mentioned earlier. So the eligible pool goes to 27%. If anyone has reached more 78% using spanish surnamed samples, please let me know about your results.

VI. A very buttoned up telephone interviewer can complete about half the names she is given, that would reduce the yield to 14%.

This last statistic is the most tenuous, but I only ask you to consider the logic and insert your own estimates. For example, if one were to say 81% of hispanics have a telephone—which may be true in Miami or San Antonio among the four cities—the last estimate comes out 17% instead of 14%.

How can we put that statistic (14% or 17%) in perspective? If we start out with a list of households and telephone numbers, IN THE GENERAL MARKET we can complete about 55% to 65% with up to three callbacks on different days. The incompletes include not at home, language problems, (don't speak english), and refusals.

Given all of that, why bother using telephones at all.

Telephone interviewing clearly has cost advantages.

There are also advantages of replicability even if not projectability. Often, we want to measure changes over time. For example, what is the change in the level of advertising awareness after an advertising campaign. In that examples, we are less concerned with the absolute level than with the increments of change. That is, even assuming the ruler is"crooked", we are going to use the same ruler each time and use the differences from wave to wave in a tracking study, so the absolute levels for the parameters are not crucial.

I have been told the quality of interviewing is better and is more closely supervised. My opinion is the latter is true and the jury is out on the former. Do central location facilities attract better interviewers than are available to those services that provide in-home interviewers.

Do telephone interviews yield the same level of open end responses as personal in-home interviews? In my experience, the answer is negative.

Telephone samples more easily yield matched samples so often the more important need.

Personal, door-to-door

This approach permits better sampling because it includes non-wired and non-listed house-holds.

It includes persons without spanish surnames. These are generally of two types. Females who use a non-spanish husband's surname. The other type are persons of spanish descent whose ancestors came from a european country "a century" ago, have a european non-Hispanic surname, but migrated to a country like Brazil or Argentina and consider themselves to be Hispanic. Sampling surnames of respondents in the LSR National Hispanic Omnibus produces these kinds of names—including some that begin with the letter K.

Personal interviewing permits the use of FLASH CARDS.

We have been able to show cards with samples of denim and corduroy to clearly communicate the type of jeans being asked about. The Flash cards also permit multiple translations referred to earlier.

TABLE 3

TRANSLATIONS ACROSS CITIES

City	Translation
	Casual Slacks
Los Angeles	Pantalones Casuales
San Antonio	" "
New York	" " or
	Pantalones Sports
Miami	" de Mezclilla Casuales
Chicago	"Just Slacks"/Wash Pants
	Denim Jeans
Los Angeles	Pantalones Blue Jeans
San Antonio	" " "
New York	Denim Jeans or
	Mahones de Algodon
Miami	Pantalones Mezclilla
Chicago	Denims
	Corduroy Jeans
Los Angeles	Pantalones de Corduroy
San Antonio	" " "
New York	Corduroy Jeans or
	Mahones de Corduroy
Miami	Pantalones de Pana
Chicago	Cords

However, personal interviewing requires tremendous field controls. Drawing and executing samples requires "the patience of a saint" and the "luck of the Irish" according to our field director who has been involved in minority marketing research for over two decades.

Verification of field work—a term I prefer to validation—is difficult at best. Part of the problem is related to one of the benefits of personal interview sampling—picking up non-telephone households. We attempt to minimize that problem with post card verifications (clearly not absolute) and by asking for a work phone or "amigo's phone".

One of the other approaches used is to compare demographics from adjacent block samples used in successive waves of probability sample market studies.

Central Location Studies

These studies have many, but not all of the advantages of door-to-door interviewing. We can

show Flash cards, we can interview people
without telephones, we can include hispanics
without spanish surnames and establish good rapport. However, the sampling is clearly not as
good.

However, in those cases where we are conducting
controlled experiments:

Which of two ads is better for...?

Which of 3 nectars seems to taste sweeter?

Do spanish women serve (FOOD PRODUCT) in different ways than non-spanish women?

These situations and many others that we face in
consumer marketing research justify the use of
central location studies--sometimes called mall
intercepts. The great bulk of general market
consumer research is conducted in malls.

6. The Questionnaire

Since we are often asked to conduct a study in
the spanish market to compare that market with
the general market, the tendency is to ask for
an anglo market questionnaire--"that we know has
worked"--to be translated and replicated.

I have not witnessed any questionnaire
technique--sorting 10 points into three or four
brands, using semantic differential scales,
rating product attributes, etc.--which could not
be replicated in the spanish market. The differences show up in the composition of product
attributes, the listing of life styles,
psychographics, occasions for eating (between
meals, bedtime snacks) etc.

THE NOTION OF SOCIAL CLASS AND THE MINORITY BUYER

Hudson P. Rogers, University of Southwestern Louisiana
Reginald Peyton, Memphis State University
Robert L. Berl, Memphis State University

Abstract

Hill (1987) suggested that income classifications as defined by the U.S. Bureau of Census, be used as the single indicator for determining Black social class. However, a major weakness of this approach is that income, by itself, does not provide an adequate means of developing marketing strategy aimed at reaching the Black market. Therefore, marketers interested in reaching the Black market must seek more "involved" measures for defining social class. There seems to be no justifiable reason why Blacks should not be classified into social classes employing the same measures used in classifying Whites. This holds true even if it is argued that there are wide differences or distinctions (values, behavior patterns, mores, possessions, income, education, etc.) within the various classes as a result of racial/ethnic backgrounds.

Introduction

The marketing literature is replete with studies addressing the relative importance of social class on consumer behavior (Coleman 1983, Assael 1987). A central tenet of consumer behavior behavior studies is that marketing strategy must be guided by the needs and wants of a given target market. In determining market strategy, marketers often look to aspects of social class in order to define the marketing strategy suited to the target market (Assaels 1987, Engel, Blackwell and Miniard 1986).

However, these studies have been, for the most part, based on the notion of social class as it pertains to white Americans. Some circles have argued that there is a great degree of diversity between Blacks and Whites (Stamps 1986). Blacks differ from Whites in terms of: affluence, age, education, purchasing patterns, brand choice, possessions, and location of housing (Assael 1984 p 311, Larson 1968). Some researchers have noted that Blacks display different media behavior than Whites and show markedly different attitudes towards the use of credit (Choudhury, Connelly, and Kahlow 1976, Glasser and Metzger 1975, and Hiltz 1970).

To the extent that Blacks and Whites have different values, lifestyles, interests and behavior, researchers may find it pertinent to talk in

terms of separate, if not different class categorization for different ethnic groupings. If Blacks and Whites behave quite differently, what effect, if any, would this have on the study of social class? What are the implications for marketers? Are classes similar across racial/ethnic lines? What criteria should marketers use for determining class classification among different ethnic groups?

These questions are of critical importance to marketers interested in targeting minority markets. In a recent article, Hill (1987) notes that "it is essential to provide a clear working definition" of social class for Blacks. This reasoning is based upon the assumption that Blacks and Whites do not share the same social classes. The assumption is that Black social classes are somehow different from White social classes. However, should different class standards be used for Blacks and for Whites? Or should researchers rely upon one set of standards thereby identifying persons as being in certain social classes without respect to race or ethnicity?

The Notion of Social Class

The notion of social class is predicated upon the idea that social classes are hierarchical, dynamic, and serve as a frame of reference for class norms, attitudes and behavior (Assael 1987, p353). Social classes may be defined as relatively permanent and homogeneous social divisions within which persons and families with similar values, life-styles, interests and behavior can be grouped. As such, persons in the same social class are seen as equal to one another in social prestige and superior or inferior in prestige to other groups that make up the social classes above or below them (Engel, Blackwell and Miniard 1986, p 328, Runyon and Stewart 1987, p 80).

Towards a Unidimensional Measure of Social Class

The notion of social class is a difficult concept to measure. There is much confusion about the way it is measured and its uses. Berkman and Gilson (1976) hold that income is by no means a good measure of social class. Persons with similar incomes may probably spend their money differently and are perceived as belonging to different social strata.

DuBois (1973), on the other hand, used family income as the determining factor in deciding social class. According to this perspective, Blacks and Whites could both belong to the same social class as long as their income met the predetermined cut-off point for the particular class. However, Myers, Stanton and Haug (1971) held that while income may be a good indicator of class behavior,

The authors wish to acknowledge the support from the Avron B. and Robert F. Fogelman Academic Excellence Fund.

it could not be applied for all products.

More recently, Hill (1987) contended that income is "a more appropriate criterion for defining class among Blacks within the society-at-large." He goes further to look to the Tax Reform Act of 1986 to provide the monetary benchmarks for defining social classes.

Barth and Watson (1967) held that occupational class was the single most important measure of social class. Accordingly, all white-collar workers and skilled craftsmen were classified as "middle-class." However, this perspective almost always favored classifying Whites as middle-class and Blacks as lower class.

Hisrich and Peters (1974) resolve the issue somewhat by indicating that additional variables are needed. Martineau (1958) notes that persons fall into classes based on status characteristics. Further, psychological differences exist between the classes. Values, communication mixes and saving and spending patterns have also been shown to differ between the classes. However, within a class people tended to behave in like manner.

A Multidimensional Measure of Social Class

Coleman (1983) argues that the identification with class is influenced most heavily by educational credentials and occupation. It is also affected by social skills, status aspirations, community participation, family history, cultural level, habits, and social acceptance by a given social class. Thus, social class is a combination of many personal and social factors rather than just a single factor such as income or education.

In measuring social class, Warner (1940) suggests that a multidimensional measure is desirable. Warner's Index of Social Characteristics indicate that an individual's social class is a factor of four demographic characteristics: occupation, income, housing, and dwelling area. Similarly, the U.S. Bureau of the Census has developed a socio-economic status (SES) score based upon income, education, and occupation.

Kahl (1957) notes that there are seven basic determinants of social class: family, occupation, personal performance, possessions, value orientation, class consciousness, and class interaction. Accordingly, the essence of social class is the way the person is treated by others and the way the person treats others. While money and occupation are important determinants of social class, these two alone do not adequately establish social position. The notion of social class must include ranking people in superior and inferior social position by any and all factors.

Problems Encountered in Measuring Social Class

A major shortcoming of the unidimensional measure of social class is that they fail to employ the notion of prestige as a central tenet in the determination of social class. From the marketer's perspective, the study of social class is important only in as far as it can be used to segment the market and hence guide marketing strategy.

The employment of unidimensional measures to define social class greatly reduces the degree to which the concept of social class could be put to use. Marketers are more interested in the behavioral, attitudinal, and value orientation of particular classes. The use of income as the major determinant of social class does not enable the marketer to put social class to much use.

Warner, Meeker, and Eells (1960) note that social class is a relatively permanent and homogeneous division in a society into which individuals and families sharing similar values, lifestyles, interest, and behavior can be categorized. The notion of social class exists as a position without reference to a specific person.

The basic question stemming out of these studies is whether or not attempts to classify Blacks and Whites into social classes ought to employ markedly different measures. A major concern is whether the notion of social class also exists without reference to the race or ethnic origin of the person. Simply, should the same standards be applied to Blacks and Whites in the determination of social class?

That Blacks and Whites have markedly different demographic, behavioral, attitudinal and shopping traits is a major reason for the idea that the different races should not be pooled when it comes to deriving social classes. From a marketing perspective, it may be desirable that social classes be separately derived for each racial group. Accordingly, researchers can identify Black and White upper, middle, and lower classes.

Towards a Model For Defining Social Class Along Racial Lines

Any attempt to develop a model aimed at defining social class along racial lines must be such that it facilitates the decomposition of the society into racial groups. At the same time, the model should facilitate looking at social classes without respect to race. Where large differences are found to exist along racial or class lines, the model should be such that it facilitates the development of marketing strategy for each racial and class category. The model must also facilitate the development of standardized marketing strategy across class and racial lines where similarities are found to exist.

One approach that may prove viable is to divide the society along racial lines, then employ a standardized but multi-dimensional measure for deriving social class for each racial group (Figure 1). Accordingly, each racial grouping would have its own upper, middle, and lower class structure, comparable to class structures of other racial groupings.

While such an approach may prove helpful, the task is still to determine the measures to be employed. There seems to be no logical reason why the same measure should not be employed across the races. Thus, in developing a standardized measure of social class researchers must be careful to include objective (education, occupation and income) as well as subjective considerations (social position).

SOCIETY

Racial/Ethnic Divisions in Society

	Blacks	Whites	Hispanics	Other
Upper Class	-	-	-	-
	-	-	-	-
	-	-	-	-
Middle Class	-	-	-	-
	-	-	-	-
	-	-	-	-
Lower Class	-	-	-	-
	-	-	-	-
	-	-	-	-

Figure 1

A major reason for this approach stems from the fact that the notion of class is more a result of prestige, behavioral expectations, values, and lifestyles than a result of occupation or income alone, although these two factors contribute significantly to the determination of social class.

This approach would provide the marketer with a means of looking at classes within racial groupings, and at the same time facilitate comparison of similarities and differences across racial lines. It is only by utilizing a standardized set of measures that the researcher can compare classes across racial lines.

Social Class, Marketing and Minorities

While it can be argued that Black social classes are markedly different from White social classes these differences do not necessarily justify using different standards to arrive at class categorization. From the marketing perspective, social class should be derived by a set of measures without respect to race.

Social class can best be determined by using some combination of objective measures (occupation, education, and possessions) and subjective measures (one's perception of one's place in the class system, others perception of your place in the hierarchy). By combining these two measures the researcher can arrive at a classification that is not subject to as much variation as that suggested by Hill (1987), Frazier (1969), or DuBois (1973).

Race gives rise to variances within classes. These variances cannot be adequately addressed simply by pooling the races for the purposes of class studies. By separating the races, the researcher is able to improve the segmentation and marketing targeting process.

Traditionally, social class was viewed as important to marketing because of its relationship to lifestyles. Different classes have different buying behavior patterns and this affects the promotional strategy of the firm. Social class influences shopping outlet used; therefore can

be directly applied to market segmentation. In this way, research into social class reveals insights into consumer behavior in terms of product usage patterns which create problem recognition. Social class also provides the criteria for product evaluation and decision-making.

Social classes often mask wide variations in behavior and status within each social class. Different persons in the same social class may have markedly different statuses. To overcome the problems of different statuses within the same social class, Coleman suggests identifying consumers in each social class who are above and below the class average (Coleman 1983). Thus, he referred to those above the average class income as overprivileged and those below the average as underprivileged. This procedure has the potential of leading to similar classifications for the highly paid bluecollar worker and the wealthy lawyer (Assael 1987, p 358).

Peters (1970) finds that product usage varies between the over and the underprivileged regardless of social class. Thus, well-off blue collar workers are likely to exhibit buying behavior much more like that of the more affluent white-collar and professional worker rather than like that of the less well-off blue-collar worker (Peters 1970, Klipper and Monoky 1974). This indicates that income, as a unidimensional measure, is not a sufficient criteria for defining social class.

Social class helps in the understanding of consumer values and behavior. It can also be used for market segmentation and prediction in consumer behavior. However, Schaninger (1981) notes that social class is superior to income for areas of consumer behavior that do not involve high dollar expenditure, but do reflect underlying life-styles, and values. Income is usually superior for major appliances which are not status symbols within the class. The combination of social class and income is superior for product classes that are highly visible and which serve as symbols of social status within class (Peter and Olson 1987).

Assael (1987) notes that the use of a social class index may provide the marketer with no greater advantage than using demographic variables such as income, education, occupation. Some researchers have argued that income provides as good an indicator of buyer behavior as social class, and is much less cumbersome to employ (Myers, Stanton, and Haug 1971, Myers and Mount 1973, Wind 1969). Others have argued that social class gives a better indicator of the regularity with which a product would be purchased (Hisrich and Peters 1974, and Schaninger 1981). However, it is important to note that none of these researchers suggested that income was the equivalent of social class.

Conclusion

The notion of social class has become an important aspect in the development of market segmentation and strategy. However, as yet there has been no attempt to determine whether Blacks and Whites should be pooled prior to a determination of social class. Much of the literature suggests that demographic and behavioral, and lifestyle differences exist among the many racial groups. This would suggest that the races should be separated prior to being categorized into social classes. however, there seems to be no logical reason why different measures should be employed for different racial groupings. By using standardized measures for class determination, marketers may better determine the similarities and differences which exist among the different groups. This would be helpful for planning effective marketing strategy.

If income alone were used to define Black social class, researchers would be guilty of masking the fact that lifestyle, values, and prestige are central concepts in class determination. Further, income by itself does not provide a sufficient indicator of the behavioral and prestige aspects of class.

While occupation may provide a better indicator of the behavioral aspect of social class, it is not a sufficient means of deriving social class. Income provides the means whereby a person can afford to maintain a given lifestyle. However, there are many examples of persons employed in white-collar jobs who do not receive sufficient income to maintain the lifestyle suggested by their occupation.

Thus, we contend that multidimensional measures of social class are preferable to unidimensional measures regardless of whether the society is divided along racial lines. Further, while it may be desirable to divide the society along racial lines prior to a determination of social classes, the same measures ought to be employed without respect to race.

References

Assael, Henry (1987) Consumer Behavior, Boston: Kent Publishing Company.

Barth, Ernest A., and Watson, Walter B. (1967) "Social Stratification and the Family in Mass Society," Social Forces (March).

Berkman, H.W., and Gilson, C.C. (1976), "Social Class and Consumer Behavior: A Review for the 1970's," Journal of the Academy of Marketing Science, (Summer).

Choudhury, P.K., Connellym P.F., and Kahlow (1976), "The Effect of Income on Black Media Behavior," American Marketing Association Conference Proceedings, Chicago: American Marketing Association, pp. 422-425.

Coleman, Richard P. (1983), "The Continuing Significance of Social Class to Marketing," Journal of Consumer Research, pp. 265-280.

DuBois, W.E.B., (1973), The Philadelphia Negro, (Millwood, New York: Kraus-Thompson Organization Limited).

Engel, James F., Blackwell, Roger D., Miniard, Paul W. (1986) Consumer Behavior, Chicago: The Dryden Press, pp. 328-342.

Frazier, Edward Franklin (1969), Black Bourgeosie, (New York: The Free Press).

Glasser, G.J., and Metzger, G.D. (1975), "Radio Usage by Blacks," Journal of Advertising Research, (October): pp. 39-48.

Hill, Robert B. (1987), "The Black Middle Class," Ebony, pp. 30-32.

Hiltz, S. Roxanne (1970), "Black and White in the Consumer Financial System," American Jouranl of Sociology, (May): pp. 987-998.

Hisrich, Robert D., and Peters, Michael P. (1974) "Selecting the Superior Segmentation Correlate," Journal of Marketing (July): pp. 60-63.

Klipper, R. Eugene and Monoky, John F. (1974), "A Potential Segmentation Variable for Marketers: Relative Occupational Class Income," Journal of the Academy of Marketing Science (Spring): pp. 351-354.

Kahl, Joseph A. (1982), The American Class Structure: A New Synthesis (Homewood: The Dryden Press).

Larson, Carl M. (1968), "Racial Brand Usage and Media Exposure Differentials," in Keith Cox and Ben Enis (eds.), A New Measure of Responsibility for Marketing, Chicago: American Marketing Association.

Martineau, Pierre (1958), "Social Classes and Spending Behavior," Journal of Marketing (October) pp. 121-129.

Myers, James H., and Mount, John F. (1973), "More on Social Class vs. Income as Correlates of Buying Behavior," Journal of Marketing (April): pp. 71-73.

_____, Stanton, Roger R., and Haug, Arne (1971) "Correlates of Buying Behavior: Social Class vs Income," Journal of Marketing (October):pp. 8-15.

Peter, J. Paul, and Olson, Jerry C. (1987) Consumer Behavior, Homewood: Illinois, pp. 430-435.

Peters, William H. (1970), "Relative Occupational Class Income: A Significant Variable in Marketing of Automobiles," Journal of Marketing (April) pp. 75-79.

Rotzoll, Kim B. (1967), "The Effect of Social Stratification on Market Behavior," Journal of Advertising (March): pp. 22-27.

Runyon, Kenneth E., and Stewart, David W. (1987), Consumer Behavior and the Practice of Marketing, Columbus, Ohio: Merrill Publishing Company, pp. 80-97.

Schaninger, Charles M. (1981), "Social Class versus Income Revisited: An Empirical Investigation," Journal of Marketing Research (May): pp. 192-208.

Stamps, Mariam B. (1986), "The Impact of Race, Social Class, and Demographics on Psychographic Variables," in Robert L. King (ed.) <u>Marketing in an Environment of Change</u>, Charleston, South Carolina: Southern Marketing Association, pp. 48-52.

Warner, W. Lloyd and Meeker, Marchia, and Eells, Kenneth (1960), <u>Social Class in America: A Manual of Procedure for the Measurement of Social Status</u> (New York: Harper and Row).

Wind, Yoram (1969), "Incongruency of Socioeconomic Variables and Buying Behavior," in Philip R. McDonald, Ed., <u>American Marketing Association Fall Conference Proceedings</u>, Chicago: American Marketing Association, pp. 362-367.

ATTRIBUTE VS ACTIVITY ORIENTATION AS RELATED TO SUB-CULTURE PURCHASE BEHAVIOR DIFFERENCES

Linda Edmonds, Dupont Company
A. Coskun Samli, Virginia Polytechnic Institute and State University

Abstract

In this study an attempt was made to contrast clothing purchase behavior of a group of employed black females and a group of employed white females. It was hypothesized that the blacks are more likely to be attribute oriented and whites activity oriented. The hypothesis was accepted. This implies that there some sub-cultural differences in clothing purchases. If understood and further verified, these differences can be used to satisfy consumer needs more readily.

Introduction

Most societies, but particularly the American society, are composed of many cohesive groups named sub-cultures. These sub-cultures are a subset of a larger culture with some different values, norms and symbols that are not common to all members of the larger culture (Gudykunst and Kim 1984). The presence of sub-cultures implies the applicability of some or all of the efforts that are made to dichotomize or classify cultures. This paper is based on the premise that Hall's (1976) high-context versus low-context culture dichotomy is applicable to American sub-cultures as well. It is further posited that American Blacks display behavior patterns and values which are closer to high-context culture whereas American whites are more likely to be classified as being close to low-context culture. According to Hall (1976), high context societies are less formal, people in these societies rely more on interpersonal communication rather than written communication. There are fewer attorneys, fewer contractual agreements than those that may be identified as low context societies. Agreements are made more on the basis of individual handshakes than official negotiations. Thus, high context societies appear to be less formal, people in these societies are more inclined to put emphasis on unwritten communication; personal interaction and other contextual factors such as appearance, aesthetic appeal, and verbal guidance from certain individuals play a key role in consumer behavior.

If this dichotomy is accepted, i.e. blacks display a behavior pattern closer to high context culture whereas whites behavior can be classified as low-contextual, then the Monroe and Guiltinan (1975) model can be utilized to distinguish black and white purchase behaviors.

Monroe and Guiltinan (1975) make a strong case about the existence of a dichotomy in retail purchase behavior or retail store selection. They introduced and explore the concepts "attribute orientation" and "activity orientation".

Attribute orientation implies paying attention to specific store attributes and merchandise attributes. Among other factors, attribute orientation can be pin-pointed to the attention paid to store layouts, windows, sales people's personality, interaction with store personnel, special sales, some aspects of advertising and other impulse buying factors. Activity orientation, on the other hand revolves around the individual. The individual consumer is more inclined to be self-reliant, information seeking and making decisions as the process of shopping progresses. In addition to trying to be free to make individual comparative analysis of merchandise, they use the sales people or store advertising to receive information which would aid their decision making process.

The relationship between cultural background and purchase behavior is based on Wallace's (1964) theory of culture and personality. This theory is presented, in a simplified form, in Figure 1. The figure illustrates that personality is the force behind behavior which is conditioned by culture. Thus, it is maintained in this paper that hi-context versus low-context dichotomy influences the personality which then is inclined to use attribute or activity orientation.

Monroe and Guiltinan (1975) posited that an all white sample of females follow basically activity orientation in their shopping behavior rather than attribute orientation. Samli et. al., (1980) however, dealing exclusively with a sample of black females found, on the whole, that the respondents were having a tendency towards attribute orientation. The present article explores this issue more closely. It attempts to answer the question: If similar samples of black and white females were to be utilized, will there be significant differences in their purchase behavior which may be related to attribute or activity orientation.

FIGURE 1
WALLACE'S THEORY

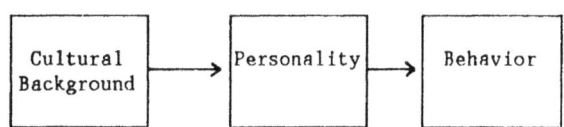

Methodology

Most store selection and purchase behavior studies particularly pertaining to clothing dealt with female samples (see e.g. Sirgy and Samli, 1985; Samli and Sirgy, 1981; Samli et. al., 1980; Samli et. al., 1978). Most of the studies dealing with black purchase behavior have been exclusively based on black female samples (see e.g. Samli et. al., 1980; Samli et.al., 1978; Smith, 1974; Portis, 1966). The present study is based on black and white female respondents. This paper is based on a portion of a larger data base dealing with the clothing purchase behavior of black and white working women.

The Sample

The information for this study was obtained from 239 black working women and 239 white working women. This data base was only partially utilized as the basis for analysis in this paper. The subjects were all members of professional women's organizations. In order to get access to both black and white respondents a purposive sample was taken. An attempt was made to collect data from both blacks and whites in similar professional groups. All respondents were employed and appeared to be middle-class in terms of their socio-economic background. A deliberate attempt was made to keep the two samples in equal sizes. In terms of age, education, occupation and income, the two groups were almost identical. Thus, the possible impact of socio-economic and demographic factors on the study outcome was neutralized. It was therefore assumed that if there are certain differences between these two groups they are bound to be due to racial or sub-cultural factors since there are no other clear-cut differences between the two. It must be reiterated that racial differences, if any, are not related to the color of skin as much as the existence of certain sub-cultural differences.

The Hypothesis

The hypothesis for this study was:
H1: Working black women are more attribute oriented whereas working white women are activity oriented.

The four sub-hypotheses were:
H1a: Blacks are more impulsive in their apparel purchases
H1b: Blacks prefer boutiques
H1c: Blacks have stronger inclination to pay to store features
H1d: Whites are more careful about the product features

Variables

In the context of research pursued in this study, it was assumed that certain impulsive approaches are more readily related to attribute orientation. Additionally, the type of store specific features of the store, and certain product features were utilized as indications of being activity or attribute orientation (see Exhibit 2).

In order to approximate impulsive purchase behavior two specific approaches were utilized. First, direct approach and second, indirect approach. The direct approach was implemented by using a scale with the wording of "I buy on impulse." Indirectly two bits of information were obtained: First, the response to one attitudinal

statement of "I stop to look at clothes even when I am not planning to buy anything," and second, the response to the attitudinal statement of "If I see a garment I like in a store window, I just may go in and buy it."

EXHIBIT 2
HYPOTHESIS TESTING

	High Context	Low Context
Impulsive behavior	+	-
Interaction	+	-
Store features	+	-
Product features	-	+

The store, where the purchase was made, is also an indicator of activity or attribute orientation. If the store is a department store the individual is left alone to explore and make decisions. Furthermore, there is much greater choice and therefore a greater basis for individual exploration and information gathering. A boutique, on the other hand, provides more opportunity for interpersonal interaction and possibility of being impressed by the appearance the merchandise and by atmospherics (Kotler 1973-74). In this case, department store versus boutique choice by the respondents was utilized as the indicator for attribute versus activity orientation.

More specifically than the type of store itself, store features may invoke attribute or activity orientation. Unfortunately there are not too many bits of information relating to this factor. Store features are articulated in terms of the type of advertising that the store has been undertaking and in terms of sales clerks' attitudes. These two and numerous other store features are likely to create attribute or activity orientation. Finally, exploring product features may indicate activity or activity orientation. Only one bit of information was utilized in this area, the fiber content. The response to the attitudinal statement of "I read fiber content labels on clothes before buying them", was used as a factor which may trigger an attribute or activity orientation.

Findings and Discussion

Table 1 presents survey results relating to this particular issue. In all three indicators of impulse, black respondents appeared to be significantly ahead of white respondents. Thus, they appeared to be more impulsive which is one aspect of being attribute oriented. As they see the product or the display, black respondents appeared to be more impressed and therefore, more influenced. This information is supportive of hypothesis 1a.

TABLE 1
COMPARATIVE ANALYSIS OF CLOTHING PURCHASES *

Impulse Factors:	Black Women (N=239) % Answered	White Women (N=239) % Answered
I stop to look at clothes even when I am not planning to buy anything	71.0	60.0
If I see a garment I like in a store window I just may go in and buy it	25.9	16.0
I buy on impulse	48.5	38.0
Store Where Comparisons Can Be Made:		
I buy mostly at department stores	51.0	61.6
I buy mostly at boutiques	31.9	17.0
Store Features:		
The attitude of sales people	46.6	59.6
Television advertisements	33.8	17.6
Exploring the Product Features:		
Fiber content	55.7	71.5

* The responses in this table reflect only those respondents who stated "most often" or "always".

Black respondents preferred boutiques where store attributes are more prominent and interaction with individual storekeeper and other people is more readily possible. Department stores, one may maintain, are more suitable for activity oriented behavior. White respondents preferred department stores. Thus, hypothesis 1b can be accepted.

The attitude of sales people was more important for white respondents than blacks. It is not clear if this because the sales clerks imparted with important information which enabled the activity oriented respondents to carry out their activities more effectively, or they are simply more impressed by the sales people's attitudes. Additionally, black respondents preferred TV ads which, again, goes against the hypothesis. Of course, it is not clear if blacks are impressed with the attributes of the store or the products presented in the ads. Or they used the information presented in ads to make comparisons and facilitate activity orientation. Thus, H1c was rejected.

Finally, white respondents indicated that they pay much more attention to fiber contents of the clothing they buy than their black counterparts. The evidence supported H1d.

Although all of the sub-hypotheses were not accepted, since three out of four were supported by the study data, the general hypothesis was accepted. The fact that the sub-hypotheses were not more decisively accepted implies that instead of a cultural dichotomy, our society may be on its way towards a stronger assimilation of sub-cultures.

Conclusions and Recommendations

Even though not very decisively, accepting the basic hypothesis of this study implies a number of practical implications for retailers. Retailers who own boutiques in metropolitan areas, where there are many working black women, may try to develop a strategy of creating an atmosphere that would facilitate attribute orientation. Showing off certain unique merchandise in special displays, putting particular emphasis on store windows, developing specific store atmospherics (Kotler 1973-74), and interacting with customers are some aspects of this strategy.

Similarly, department stores may develop a strategy to facilitate activity orientation. Providing a chance to certain consumers to be particularly active in terms of exploring, gathering information, comparing and making decisions for themselves, are the key tenets of this strategy. The attitude of salespeople appears to be critical in both cases. Thus, independent of study objectives a critical finding is that in the purchase of clothing, sales people must be trained very carefully so that they could display the proper attitude.

At a more theoretical level, there appears to be some differences between the sub-cultures. Unfortunately, this study is not conducted in a longitudinal manner so that the differences between the sub-cultures can be assessed in time. Future studies may consider this point.

It must be emphasized that in order to obtain two similar samples it was necessary to use purposive samples instead of a random sample. Hence, a number of statistical analyses could not be performed in this study. The post hoc nature of the study provided many limitations.

Future studies must use more and better variables indicating both the contextual characteristics of the culture as well as identifying attribute versus activity orientation. This preliminary study, by providing some important information, has clearly justified future exploration of this very important area of consumer behavior. Successful studies in this area are likely to enhance consumer satisfaction in our society for blacks and whites alike.

References

Gudykunst, William B. and Young Yun Kim (1984), Communicating With Strangers, Reading Massachusetts: Addison-Wesley.

Kotler, Philip (1973-74), "Atmospherics As a Marketing Tool," Journal of Retailing (Winter), pp. 50-58.

Monroe, Kent B. and Joseph B. Guiltinan (1975), "A Path Analytic Exploration of Retail Patronage Influences," The Journal of Consumer Research (June).

Portis, Bernard (1966), "Negroes and Fashion Interest," Journal of Business (April), pp. 314-323.

Samli, A. Coskun, Enid Tozier and D. Yvette Harps (1980), "Social Class Differentials in the Store Selection Process of Single Black Professional Women," Journal of the Academy of Marketing Science (Spring), pp. 138-151.

Samli, A. Coskun, Enid Tozier and D. Yvette Harps (1978), "Social Class Differences in the Apparel Purchase Behavior of Single, Professional Black Women," Journal of the Academy of Marketing Science (Winter).

Samli, A. Coskun, M. Joseph Sirgy (1981), "A Multidimensional Approach to Analyzing Store Loyalty: A Predictive Model," K. Bernhard, et.al. (eds.), The Changing Marketing Environment, Chicago: AMA, pp. 113-116.

Sirgy, M. Joseph and A. Coskun Samli (1985), "A Path Analytic Model of Store Loyalty Involving Self Concept, Store Image, Geographic Loyalty and Socio-economic Status," Journal of the Academy of Marketing Science (Summer), pp. 265-291.

Smith, Bernice (1974), "Fashion Preferences and Fashion Buying Practices of Professional Black Women," Unpublished Masters Thesis, Louisiana State University.

Hall, Edward T. (1976), Beyond Culture, New York: Anchor Press Doubleday.

Wallace, A.F.C. (1964), Culture and Personality, New York: Random House.

SUBCULTURAL DIFFERENCES IN THE ABILITY TO DISEMBED PACKAGE INFORMATION

Stephen Calcich, Norfolk State University
Karen Dale Hankel, Towson State University

Abstract

Individual variations in the ability of consumers to disembed package information may be the result of a number of factors such as learning, education, social class, and subculture. This study examines subcultural difference in the ability to disembed and therefore use package information.

Introduction

Individuals vary in their desire and ability to acquire and process information. The source of that variation may be due to a number of factors, including subcultural differences. Acquisition of product information is limited by the individual's desire and need for information to be used in the decision making process. However, even if the individual desires product information, his/her ability to acquire the desired information is further limited by the consumer's ability to perceive, disembed, and use that information. This ability may be influenced by characteristics such as culture. This study looks at subcultural differences in the ability of consumers to perceive and disembed the kind of information that is presented on product labels.

In the evaluation of the subcultural difference in the ability to disembed information in particular, a three-task experiment was used. In addition to supplying general information, the subjects had to complete both a general disembedding task and a package information disembedding task. To evaluate the differences, subjects were recruited from Black, Hispanic, and White subcultures.

Background

Accurate presentation of product information has concerned public policy makers since at least 1938, when the passage of the Federal Food, Drug and Cosmetic Act established the Food and Drug Administration. Since then, the FDA has been concerned with both the safety of food products and the labeling of those products. As a result of government regulations, the amount of information that must be presented on food product packages has increased dramatically, requiring greater consumer perceptual skills to be disembed and acquire the information.

Packaging information provides a depth of information not normally found in advertising, whether print, television, or radio. Food product packages, even for no-name brands, present information such as price, ingredients, nutritional values, and package size usually in a complex array of stimuli. Although public policy makers have attempted to simplify the acquisition of vital product information through policies such as unit pricing and ingredient lists, these same policies have increased the complexity of the product package and the information processing task. The consumer who recognizes the need for information before making a purchase decision must seek, acquire, and process that information before a choice can be made.

Intervening between the product package as a source of information and the consumer as acquirer, and integrater of information is the consumer's perceptual process. A simplified version of this relationship is illustrated in Figure 1. Information processing research to date has concentrated on the second half of the model: cognitive decision making rules. This emphasis has resulted in a call for research focused on more primary and fundamental processes such as perception (Chestnut and Jacoby, 1977). The research presented here concentrates on the first half of the model in general and perception in particular, while focusing on perceptual differences between Blacks, Hispanics, and Whites.

FIGURE 1
Simplified Model of Consumer Information Processing

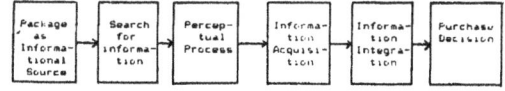

The most commonly used information acquisition investigation procedure in consumer research is the information display board (i.e., Bettman and Zins, 1979; McNeil and Wilkie, 1979; Lehmann and Moore, 1980). Other methods of simplifying product information presentation are to group either all attributes of a specific brand (Biehal and Chakarvarti, 1982) or all brands having a specific attribute on a card or in a booklet (Lussier and Olshavshy, 1979). These simplified information display formats have been useful in the objective measurement of consumers' information search and utilization patterns. However, the specific information format has been found to influence the processing of information even when in simplified form (Van Raaij, 1977; Bettman and Kakkar, 1977). Furthermore, actual product package information is not presented in a simplified format. Instead, the information is complex, and the actual presentation of the information varies with each brand.

The use of actual food packages as information sources should have a substantial effect on knowledge of consumer information acquisition and processing as well as being useful to public policy makers in determining quantity and quality of information required on food packages. Using actual product packages, Chestnut found that, although individuals took varying periods of time to search for and acquire information, the speed of locating package information did not have any significant effect on information acquisition (Chestnut, 1975). However, increasing the number of choices the consumer had to make decreased both the amount information acquired and the time taken to make a decision. Patton (1981), using simulated product package labels, found that increased quantities of information can have a detrimental affect on consumers. Furthermore, individuals may vary in their need or desire for information.

This study seeks to shed additional light on the causes of the individual differences in information search and acquisition when food packages are used as sources of product information. In particular, the study concentrates on variations in individual perceptual skills as they are related to cultural differences and the acquisition of food product label information.

In general, the packages of frequently purchased food items are extremely complex stimuli arrays. Table 1 gives some indication of the variety and types of information commonly present on food packages. For some products, all of this information appears on a single package. However, at least some of this information appears on all product packages. A package is, of course, three dimensional with the following variables interacting to increase the complexity of the perceptual task involved in extracting a specified piece of information from the package:

1. Shape
2. Size
3. Print type and size
4. Colors
5. Organization and emphasis

For example, a national brand of corn flakes has more than 45 different sizes and styles of print.

TABLE 1
Food Package Information Taxonomy

CLASSIFICATION	INFORMATION
OBJECTIVE	Price
	Weight
	Ingredients
	U.S. RDA
	Servings per package
	Serving size
	Nutrition
	Packaged, or sell-by-date
	Usage
	Storage
	Opening
	Filling
	Product
	Guarantee
	Recipes with illustrations
SYMBOLIC	Brand
	Product illustrations
	Trademarks and/or logos
	Product claims and descriptions
	Product associates (e.g. Bruce Jenner, Jolly Green Giant)
PROMOTIONAL	Special Offers
	Coupons
	Premiums
	Premium illustrations
	Proof of Purchase

Disembedding specific pieces of information from a complex stimulus object such as a food package requires a certain perceptual skill. This perceptual skill is hypothesized as being one of a "disembedding" nature and is measured by a psychological assessment procedure - the Embedded Figures Test (EFT) (Witkin, 1950). A subject's task on each of several trials is to locate a previously seen simple figure within a larger complex figure which has been so organized as to obscure or embed the sought-after simple figure. The construct applied to a person's perceptual style is "field-dependence versus field-independence." In a field-dependent mode of perceiving, perception is strongly dominated by the overall organization of the surrounding field, and parts of the field are experienced as "fused." In a field-independent mode of perceiving, parts of the field are experienced as discrete from organized ground (Witkin, Oltman, Raskin, and Karp, 1971).

Due to government regulation, manufacturers and retailers of food products must provide certain information for the consumer. For example, the manufacturer must provide information about the number of servings per container, the amount of protein, and percentage of U.S. RDA iron. The retailer must provide price information. As previously stated, consumers vary in their ability to perceive, disembed, and therefore, use that information. Some of that variation may be the result of cultural differences.

Research using the EFT in foreign cultures has shown that, in those which discourage antonomous functioning, a much greater degree of field dependence is exhibited (Berry, 1966; Dawson, 1967). To the extent that the Black and Hispanic subcultures in the U.S. also discourage antonomous functioning there may be differences in the perceptual skills among the three groups in this study.

Research Questions and Propositions

If the task of acquiring information from a food package is a perceptual one of a disembedding nature, then individual differences in acquisition times will be explained by differences in perceptual skills as measured by the EFT. In part, the individual differences in perceptual skills may be a result of subcultural differences.

Proposition 1: There will be differences between individual EFT scores based on subculture.

The second proposition is concerned directly with the consumer's ability to disembed the product information from the label. If there are subcultural differences in the ability to disembed information, it follows that there will be subcultural differences in the ability of the consumer to disembed package information.

Proposition 2: There will be differences between the individual's ability to acquire product information based on subculture.

Methodology

The study was conducted in a shopping center in a major southern city in three phases. Each subject had to complete three tasks. These were, in order of administration: 1) Embedded Figures Test (EFT), 2) Packing Information, and 3) Questionnaire.

The Embedded Figures Test was designed to test the ability of the subjects to discern a set of simple figures within a complex figure. Over 12 trials, plus a practice trial, a simple figure or shape was shown to a subject for 10 seconds. They then were shown a complex figure and asked to pick out the simple figure from it. The time taken to accurately trace the embedded figure was recorded. If the subject was unable to find the figure within three minutes, the score was recorded as 180 seconds and the next figure was attempted. The score for all twelve figures were used in determining the EFT score.

Package Test scores were determined based on the ability of the subjects to find specific information on a variety of product packages. The product categories were selected to meet four criteria: that the products would represent typical purchases by the subjects; that most grocery stores would carry at least five competing brands; that the typical product package would include a variety of information types; and that all the packages would include the selected information types. The product categories meeting these criteria and included in the experiment were: breakfast cereals, instant potatoes, instant rice, and macaroni and cheese. Of the five brands in each category, four were national brands and one was a store brand, which was consistent with the assortment to be found in most supermarkets.

The product information types or attributes selected were: price, number of servings per package, grams of portein per serving, and percentage of the U.S. recommended daily allowance (RDA) of iron. According to government regulation this information must be provided by the retailer or manufacturer. All information included on packages is presumably thought to be of potential use to consumers, either by the manufacturers or regulatory authorities or both.

Subjects were presented with two cards for each product category in the following order: (1) breakfast cereals, (2) instant potatoes, (3) instant rice, and (4) macaroni and cheese. The first card contained the piece of product information to be located on the five packages in that product category. The other card contained a list of the five brand names, and subjects were instructed to find the piece of information on each of the brands, in the order presented. Therefore, the elements of the task are brand identification, information search, and identification. Subjects were timed to determine how long it took them to find each piece of information on all five packages, yielding four scores for each subject. These four scores were then combined to provide an overall package test score.

The questionnaire was used to collect purchase information about the product categories used in the study and background information about the subjects. Data was collected to determine if the individuals were package readers as well as to determine the usage of product information for the categories used in the study.

Subjects

Forty female shoppers were each offered a small financial inducement ($2.50) to participate in the study. Female consumers are those who federal authorities would most like to be able to use the information present on food packages. Middle class white females tend to make the most use of this information, so a more specific target of regulators within the general female population are lower income consumers, including minority groups. For this reason, female shoppers were considered the most appropriate subject group, and the site of the study was located in a predominantly working class and ethnically mixed area of a major southern city.

Results

The data was analyzed to determine if there were differences between the subculture groups for the EFT scores and the package test scores. There were 14 White subjects, 15 Black subjects, and 11 Hispanic subjects. The educational levels of the three groups are shown in Table 2, and the mean age for each group was: Black 35.2, White 40.8, and Hispanic 24.7. Mean scores for each subsample were determined for both the EFT and the package test for the evaluation of the propositions.

TABLE 2
Educational Levels

Educational Level	Group		
	Black	White	Hispanic
Some High School	2	5	6
Completed High School	7	5	5
Some College	1	4	0
Completed College	5	0	0
Total	15	14	11

The first proposition suggested that there would be differences in the EFT scores depending on membership in the different subculture groups represented in the study. The means for the EFT scores are reported in Table 2. A similar pattern is evident for both the EFT and Package Test with the Black group having the highest times, the White group the lowest, and the Hispanic group somewhere in between. For the first proposition, t-tests (independent samples, two-tailed tests) were used to determine whether there were differences between the groups. The only statistically significant difference was the paired comparison between the Black and White subjects (t= 2.70, p= .013). The Black-Hispanic and White-Hispanic comparisons were not statistically different (t= 1.44, p= .164 and t= .96, p= .346 respectively). Thus, there was only partial support for the proposition.

TABLE 3
Group Means and Standard Deviations

Group	n	EFT Mean	S.D.	Package Test Mean	S.D.
Black	15	119.1	53.9	76.7	33.6
White	16	86.0	26.5	52.8	23.9
Hispanic	11	101.0	61.1	67.7	28.0

The second proposition suggested that there would be differences between package scores based on subcultural group membership. The means for the Package Test are reported in Table 2. Once again t-tests were used to determine if there were differences between the groups, and as with the EFT, only the comparison between the Black and White subjects showed a statistically significant difference (t= 2.41, p= .024). The Black-Hispanic and the White-Hispanic comparisons were not statistically different (t= 1.25, p= .225 and t= 1.04, p= .308 respectively). Again, there was only partial support for the proposition.

Discussions and Conclusions

The results of this study suggest that there are some differences in female consumers' perpetual skills. In addition, those differences may be in part related to subculture differences. Although the differences between the Black and Hispanic group and the White and Hispanic group were not statistically significant. However, this would seem to be due to the small sample sizes rather than lack of actual differences between means. Certainly lack of sample size is a weakness of the study. Statistically significant differences were found between the Black subjects and the White subjects for both EFT and package test scores. This would support the contention that there are subculture differences related to the ability to disembed information in general and package information in particular.

If one assumes that one of the FDA's objectives is to provide the individual with information that is useful in the decision making process, the individuals who want and need the information should be able to easily access and understand the information. Furthermore, if there are subculture differences in the ability of consumers to disembed the information present on product packages, these differences should be taken into account in formatting the information presented. If subjects find it difficult to disembed package information, new methods of information presentation should be considered so that subjects can better use that information. In particular, consideration needs to be given to revising and improving information presentation formats in view of the processing abilities of the consumers who currently find it difficult to process package information.

References

Berry, J.S. (1966), "Temne and Eskimo Perceptual Skills," International Journal of Psychology, 1, pp. 207-229.

Bettman, James R. and Pradeep Kakkar (1977), "Effects of Information Presentation Format on Consumer Information Acquisition," Journal of Consumer Research, 3, pp. 133-240.

_____ and Michael A. Zins (1979), "Information Format and Choice Task Effects in Decision Making," Journal of Consumer Research, 1, pp. 141-153.

Biehal, Gabriel and Dipankar Chakarvarti (1982), "Information Presentation Format and Learning Goals as Determinants of Consumers' Memory-Retrieval and Choice Processes," Journal of Consumer Research, 8, pp. 431-441.

Chestnut, Robert W. (1975), "Expenditure of Time in the Acquisition of Package Information," unpublished masters thesis, Purdue University.

_____ and Jacob Jacoby (1977), "Consumer Information Processing: Emerging Theory and Findings," in Consumer and Industrial Buying Behavior, eds. Arch G. Woodside and Jagdish N. Sheth, North Holland, NY, pp. 119-134.

Dawson, J.L. (1967), "Cultural and Physiological Influences Upon Spacial-Perceptual Processes in West Africa," Part 1 and Part 2, International Journal of Psychology, 2, pp. 115-128, 171-185.

Lehmann, Donald T. and William L. Moore (1980), "Validity of Information Display Boards: An Assessment Using Longitudinal Data," Journal of Marketing Research, 17, pp. 450-459.

Lussier, Dennis A. and Richard W. Olshavsky (1979), "Task Complexity and Contingent Processing in Brand Choice," Journal of Consumer Research, 6, pp. 154-165.

McNeil, Dennis L. and William L. Wilkie (1979), "Public Policy and Consumer Information: Impact of the New Energy Labels," Journal of Consumer Research, 1, pp. 1-11.

Patton, W.E. (1981), "Quantity of Information and Information Display Type as Predicators of Consumer Choice of Product Brands," Journal of Consumer Affairs, 15, pp. 92-105.

Van Raaij, W. Fred (1977), "Consumer Information Processing for Different Information Structures and Formats," in Advances in Consumer Research, Vol. 4, ed. William O. Perreault, pp. 176-184.

Witkin, Herman A. (1950), "Individual Differences in Ease of Perception of Embedded Figures," Journal of Personality, 19, pp. 1-15.

_____, Oltman, Philip, K., Raskin, Evelyn, and Karp, Stephen A. (1971), A Manual for the Embedded Figures Test, Consulting Psychologists Press, Inc., Palo Alto, CA.

BLACK-WHITE DIFFERENCES IN THE CONSUMPTION OF COSMETICS:[1]
AGGREGATE AND SOCIO-CULTURAL DIMENSIONS

Thaddeus H. Spratlen, University of Washington
Pravat K. Choudhury, Howard University

Abstract

Black-White differences in the consumption of
cosmetics are substantial, persistent and per-
vasive. Aggregate secondary data on consumption
patterns are used to describe such differences.
They are explained in terms of the socio-cultural
influences on cosmetics usage, such as styles of
personal grooming and prevailing beauty standards
in the society. Implications of the analysis for
minority marketing are presented. Key questions
and issues are suggested for future consumer behavior research on Black consumption of cosmetics.

Introduction

Consumer uses of cosmetics reflect many personal,
social and cultural dimensions of consumption behavior. Choices in personal grooming are expressed with varied hair styles, coloring and
skin preparations. Social status and approval
can be linked to the uses of fragrances and cosmetics accessories. Cultural norms are reflected
in various hair treatments, hair styles and nail
care as well as eye and facial makeup.

However, there are distinct patterns of cosmetics
consumption which can be delineated along racial/
ethnic lines. Suntan lotions and other tanning
treatments for Whites and hair straighteners or
bleaching cream for Blacks are illustrative. Yet
some patterns are not so physically obvious in
their variations. For example, Blacks buy five
times the level of color cosmetics in comparison
with the general market (Weil 1985). In the aggregate, Black spending is estimated to be between one-fifth and one-quarter of industry sales
or about $3.0 billion (Brown 1986). As a point
of general comparison, Blacks comprise about 12%
of the U.S. population and receive about 7% of
the nation's personal income. Thus, Black spending for personal care goods and services is disproportionately high. Further, estimates of
Black spending in specific product categories
such as hair care place Black consumption as high
as 36%-38% of the products sold. Clearly, Blacks
comprise one of the largest usage groups for cosmetics. The present and future potential of this
market is substantial.

In minority marketing terms, the importance of
ethnic hair care products, in particular, should
be noted. Black-owned companies now hold about

---

[1] Research for this paper was completed while the
first-named author was on sabbatical leave as
Visiting Research Professor in the School of Business Administration, Howard University. Special
thanks are due Dean Milton Wilson for the support
received during the 1986-87 academic year.

50% of the market (Newsweek 1986). There is
probably no other manufacturing industry in
which the stakes of successful minority marketing are as high as they are for Black-owned companies in cosmetics. They are a formidable,
yet vulnerable, competing group in that industry.
Historically, they have had a competitive advantage that is now diminishing. Since the mid-
1970's their overall market share has been lost
to the giants of the industry--Revlon, Clairol,
Avon, etc. Apparently Black consumer loyalty
has also declined dramatically. Such issues
suggest that the industry has considerable economic importance with respect to Black enterprise
and its role in the economy as a whole.

The main purpose of this paper is to provide an
analytical perspective on Black cosmetics consumption based on the literature and related
secondary information. It is presented in comparative terms with the consumption of Whites
whenever that is feasible or relevant. But the
primary focus is on interpreting the socio-cultural influences on Black consumption of cosmetics.

The paper is organized into five major sections.
Following this introduction, a section of the
paper is devoted to describing Black consumption
of cosmetics. Aggregate expenditure data are
summarized and major socio-cultural influences
on the consumption of cosmetics are identified
and discussed. Next, implications for minority
marketing are presented. Suggestions for further research are then summarized. Several conclusions are stated in the final section.

Black Consumption of Cosmetics

Total sales in the industries that include cosmetics are estimated to be in the range of $12.6-
$16.8 billion for 1985 (HAPPI 1986b, Product Mar-
keting 1985a). As already noted, Blacks spend
quite disproportionately on the product category.
We estimate that per capita expenditures by
Blacks in 1985 amounted to $104 or between 1.5-
2.0 times the level spent by Whites (e.g., $47
and $68, using the range of aggregate spending
noted above). The estimates are based on a population of 28.8 million Blacks and 202.3 million
Whites in 1985 (Statistical Abstract of the
United States 1986, p. 31). See Table 1 below
for other comparisons.

Put in store patronage terms, with 5% Black patronage, a store could generate 15% or more of
its health and beauty aids (HBA) sales from Black
consumers (Hersch 1986). Even in the case of a
single national manufacturer-marketer, the proportions can be dramatic. It is reported that

41

Blacks represent 9% of Avon's customers but purchase 14% of their cosmetics (Hersch 1986). It is of interest to make such a connection with Avon which is one of the world's largest marketers of cosmetics. As recognized by Gibson(1978, pp. 116-120), Avon has demonstrated corporate leadership in its economic and community relations programs with respect to Blacks. Further, overall growth rates in spending on cosmetics by Blacks have been placed as high as 15%-20% annually (Marketing News 1985). Such rates are consistently about 10% and are expected to remain at levels higher than for Whites.

Another illustration of the importance of cosmetics spending among Blacks is the emphasis on cosmetics advertising in the print media. In comparing full-page ads in Ebony (October 1986) 27 of 93 (29%) were for cosmetics as compared with six (6.5%) for cigarettes, six for women's apparel and four for automobiles (Spratlen 1986).

Historical Patterns of Black Consumer Spending

It is now well established that Black consumers spend disproportionately large sums for cosmetics in comparison with Whites (Wells 1987). This pattern has existed over a considerable period of time. In one of the earlier reported studies Blacks spent as much for cosmetics as they did for furniture (Johnson 1952, p. 108). An estimated 3% of Black disposable personal income was spent on cosmetics in 1946 (Johnson 1952, p. 108). Unfortunately, similar data were not provided for Whites. The comparative numbers for 1983 as a percent of total spending were as follows (U.S. Department of Labor 1986):

	Personal Care[2]	Furniture
Blacks	1.2%	1.2%
Whites	0.9%	1.4%

Historical comparisons are presented in Table 1. Note that the percent of expenditures devoted to personal care has declined for Blacks as well as Whites, as incomes have risen over time. Yet Blacks still allocate considerably more of their spending to the product category than Whites. In this connection, the comparison of per capita spending should be recalled. Consideration should also be given to the fact that Blacks have relatively and substantially less available for spending in the aggregate than Whites.

Consider median incomes for both groups. In 1984 median household income for Blacks amounted to $13,471. For Whites it was $23,647 (Statistical Abstract of the United States 1986, p. 445). Thus, the income gap was 43% for Blacks. However, sufficient data are not available to interpret the effects of income differences between Blacks and Whites on cosmetics consumption. This limits to some extent the generalizations that can be made based on the aggregate comparisons presented here.

Nevertheless, it should be noted that the data

---

[2]Spending on subgroups of products within this category is not available. The pattern is consistent with other relationships reported in the literature.

---

in Table 1 are quite consistent with the pattern associated with higher per capita spending in the product category by Blacks. Blacks allocate as much as one-quarter to one-third more to personal care spending than Whites. Although the proportion for 1972-73 is identical for both broups, it is clear by far for all other comparisons that relative spending for cosmetics by Blacks is substantially higher than it is for Whites. The question that should now be considered is why.

TABLE 1

Black-White Consumption of
Personal Care Goods and Services
Selected Survey Years,
1960-61 - 1982-83

Percent of Average Annual
Consumption Expenditures

Year	Group	Personal[a] Care Expenditures	Black/[b] White Index
1960-61	Black[c]	3.6%	128.6
	White	2.8%	
1966	Black	2.2	N.A.
	White	N.A.	
1972-73	Black	1.3	100.0
	White	1.3	
1982-83	Black	1.2	133.3
	White	0.9	

[a]Percent of total expenditures for personal consumption for each group.

[b]Black proportion/White proportion times 100.

[c]Expenditure data on Nonwhites of whom Blacks represent 90% or more. Original sources suggest that data can be considered comparable and adequately representative of Black spending patterns.

Cosmetics Consumption:
The Socio-Cultural Influences

At this time explanations of the socio-cultural influences on Black consumption of cosmetics must be based mostly on conjecture. Comments on the subject rely mainly on the opinions of practitioners and beauty consultants or industry professionals in trade and specialty magazines.

Some important categories and ideas that help to explain patterns of cosmetics consumption are categorized and summarized in EXHIBIT 1. Most of the categories are generally applicable to all groups of consumers of cosmetics. They also tend to overlap and reinforce each other. Because of these characteristics as well as their summary and tentative form, only a few comments about them are made at this time.

EXHIBIT 1

Types of Socio-Cultural Influences on Cosmetics Consumption

Type of Socio-Cultural Influence	Description	Product Examples
Personal Taste and Style in Appearance	Use of cosmetics in connection with complexion and skin condition or characteristics	Facial makeup, skin creme
Beauty Standards in the Culture and Society	Use of cosmetics to conform to prevailing norms such as "straight hair," light skin and youthful appearances	Hair coloring, straighteners, bleaching creme
Attractiveness and Sex Appeal	Use of cosmetics to soften the skin, remove blemishes, and enhance appeal to others	Lotions, powders to reduce oily skin condition
Ego Enhancement Self Esteem	Use of cosmetics to gain confidence, improve one's self-concept	Hair styles, makeup
Social Status and Acceptance	Use of cosmetics to impress others with one's expression of style and good taste	Preference for brand names, quality products and images

In the most immediate and functional sense cosmetics serve as an expression of personal grooming preferences. Because of the apparent importance attached to individuality and styling among Blacks (as reflected in disproportionate spending for hats, shoes and other selected items of apparel), spending for cosmetics complements the orientation towards such expressiveness.

Prevailing beauty standards in the culture and society contribute to the observed pattern of spending in a variety of ways. The standards reflect mostly European images and features.Thus, in striving for the European-look of straight and preferably long, silky-looking hair, Blacks must spend relaatively more for hair care than Whites. A similar comparison might be made regarding oily-appearing skin. Natural oils may be more visible against a darker complexion (Wells 1987). Cosmetics are then used to compensate for this characteristic. In this connection it might be instructive to recall the four-fold difference in Black spending levels for color cosmetics.

The remaining categories will eventually be singled out as separate examples. In the case of attractiveness and sex appeal, the motivations may not be separable at all from responses to the promises and hype of cosmetics promotion. But there may be aspects of natural ethnic differences which must be off-set by images that can be expressed through the use of cosmetics. Skin and hair coloring are probably the most obvious and sensitive aspects of Black presentations of self relative to cosmetics. Similar speculation could also be offered with aspects of self-esteem and social acceptance based on cosmetics usage. But in this early phase of the research, we suggest that these tentative comments can serve as initial guides and issues for future analysis.

Implications for Minority Marketing

The information and relationships presented in the paper have many potential uses in the marketing of cosmetics to Black consumers. Their economic, ethnic and other marketing implications for minority marketing are discussed briefly.

In economic terms, Black spending for cosmetics represents high growth rates and levels of sales for cosmetics marketers. Black business firms in the industry should be in a position to preserve at least a significant presence. They should be able to stay in closer touch with the Black consumer and protect their collectively strong position through adaptive and ethnically-sensitive marketing. If such a goal is pursued effectively, they should be able to maintain some of their historic, situational and political advantages relative to their much larger and more dominant national competitors -- Revlon, Avon, and other corporate giants in the industry.

In ethnic terms, it should be noted that Blacks as a group are extremely diverse. For example, it has been suggested that with respect to cosmetics consumption there are 33 different shades of Black skin preparations in covering the entire range of skin tones and complexions (Product Marketing 1985b). Such diversity and ethnicity should be recognized and responded to in sensitive and understanding ways. At the very least this important group of consumers must not be taken for granted by any marketers. In view of certain policies which have been followed in the past, it could be inferred that marketing mistakes have been made. Examples would include lack of market and product research and development on the part of Black firms and undifferentiated marketing on the part of the major national firms. Some have been ambivalent about the importance of this consumer segment.

Serving this large, high-growth market segment should be enhanced considerably through various types of market segmentation. Demographic, usage, benefits sought and psychographic methods are all needed in order to be more effective in reaching and meeting Black consumer needs. For example, among Black women as the primary target market, one study suggested that they exhibit at least five different life style characteristics (Marketing News 1981, p. 6). One category has been labeled as the "fashion-conscious" in which new hair styles and dressing for fashion are prominent attitudes and interests. Themes for marketing cosmetics could very likely be adapted to some of the other categories of life style as well.

Key Research Questions and Issues

An important research objective is to have empirically-based explanations of Black-White differences in the consumption of cosmetics. The following questions and issues illustrate what we need to know:

1. What are the real Black consumer motivations in cosmetics usage? Do they differ from the motivations of White consumers in measurable ways?

2. How do expenditures in the product category vary according to Black consumer demographic and psychographic characteristics?

3. How can the socio-cultural influences be measured and applied in developing marketing strategies aimed at meeting the cosmetics needs of Black consumers?

4. What are the main political, economic and ethnic issues associated with minority marketing and the cosmetics industry?

Answers to these questions (and others that might be phrased) would help to provide insights and strategies that contribute to more effective minority marketing.

Conclusions

Substantial economic and ethnic differences exist between Blacks and Whites in their patterns of cosmetics consumption. At present our knowledge is mainly aggregate, descriptive and speculative. Yet the patterns and relationships appear to be strong and consistent over time.

Basic theoretical as well as policy-oriented research is needed in order to increase our understanding of this important aspect of consumption behavior. The subject deserves far more financial and intellectual resources than it has received to date. We view this as a beginning effort at exploring, interpreting and eventually explaining Black consumption of cosmetics. Because of the unusually large stake and presence of Black-owned firms in the hair care segment of the industry, they should be challenged to identify and develop strategies which better serve the interests of Black consumers and the Black community generally. Their future depends on how soon and how well such a response is made to satisfy Black consumer demands for cosmetics.

References

Brown, Tony (1986) "Blacks Should Buy Commitment, Not Blackness," The Washington Afro-American (December 2), p. 6.

Gibson, D. Parke (1978) $70 Billion in the Black-America's Black Consumers. New York: Macmillan Publishing Company.

Hersch, Linda (1986) "Black Entreprenerus Enter Skin Care Market," Product Marketing, (October) 15, pp. 14, 16.

Johnson, Joseph T. (1952) The Potential Negro Market. New York: Pageant Press.

Spratlen, Thaddeus H. (1986) "Affluent Blacks as Travellers and Tourists: Group Characteristics and Targeted Advertising Themes," W. Benoy Joseph, et al, eds. Tourism Services Marketing Conference Proceedings, Cleveland, OH: Academy of Marketing Science and Cleveland State University, pp. 238-248.

Weil, Arthur W. (1985) "'Special' Needs Spur Growth of Ethnic Market," Product Marketing (September) 14, p. 11.

Wells, Linda (1987) "Enhancing Black Skin," The New York Times Magazine (January 18), p. 53.

Household and Personal Products Industry (HAPPI) (1986a) "Clairol Dominates Hair Color, Survey Shows," (December) 23, p. 12.

_____ (HAPPI) (1986b) "Sales of Toiletries, Cosmetics to Grow by 7.3% a Year to $25.5 Billion in '96," (November) 23, p. 10.

Marketing News (1981) "New Survey Reveals Five Life-Style Segments of Age 18-49 Black Women," (April 21), p. 6.

_____ (1985) "Minority-Marketing Growth Boosts Black Trade Journal," (March 29),p. 15.

Newsweek (1986) "Targeting Black Dollars: White Owned Companies Muscle Minority Firms Out of the Hair Care Market," (October 13), p. 54-55.

Product Marketing (1985a) "Beauty Aids Business Stands Firm at $15.8 Billion in '84," (July) 14, pp. 6, 13, 14, 16.

_____ (1985b) "State of the Industry Report," (December), p. 16, 20, 21.

Statistical Abstract of the United States 1986. U.S. Department of Commerce, Bureau of the Census Washington, D.C.: U.S. Government Printing Office

The Wall Street Journal (1986) "Business Bulletin," (December 18), p. 1.

U.S. Department of Commerce (1978)[3]Changing Minority Markets. (April), p. 4. Washington, DC: U.S. Government Printing Office.

_____. (1975) Minority Markets. (October), p. 5. Washington, DC: U.S. Government Printing Office.

U.S. Department of Labor (1986) Consumer Expenditure Survey: Interview Survey, 1982-83. Washington, DC: U.S. Government Printing Office, p. 37.

---

[3]Data presented in Table 1 were from the last three references. These are the principal sources of information on aggregate Black consumption patterns.

TOURISM MARKETING TO ETHNIC TRAVELERS[1]

Muzaffer Uysal, Clemson University
Joseph T. O'Leary, Purdue University

Abstract

Little research has been conducted on blacks as travelers and tourists, and what has been done is either anecdotal or is tied to black magazine readers who travel. This paper investigates whether differences exist in the travel motivations, activities, and travel group type of blacks and whites from a national sample of travelers in the U.S. population. Information from this study is intended to provide a basis for comparing the majority and minority traveling populations. There are sufficient differences between the two groups both in terms of the factors that push people to travel and in the activities that may pull the tourist to an area, to warrant different kinds of marketing action.

Background

Blacks in the United States comprise 12 percent of the total population, with some large urban centers having larger concentrations. Spratlen (1986) notes that little research has been conducted on blacks as travelers and tourists, and what has been done is either anecdotal or is tied to black magazine readers who travel. Analysis of the development or presence of black businesses (O'Hare 1987) indicate that a substantial percentage (64 percent) of all black businesses are located in 48 metropolitan areas. Questions that will be explored in this paper are whether these metropolitan black businesses might play a role in providing services and opportunities for tourists and whether these might be focused to differentiate between the black and white traveler.

Although there has been limited work in the area of tourism for black travelers, there is research in leisure and outdoor recreation that examines differences between the black and white participants. Differences which exist in participation in outdoor recreation among ethnic groups have been viewed from two perspectives, marginality and ethnicity (Washburne 1978, O'Leary and Benjamin 1981). The marginality perspective suggests that "blacks do not participate in the same recreation activities as the white dominant culture because of poverty and the various consequences of socioeconomic discrimination" (O'Leary and Benjamin 1981:10). The marginality explanation posits that blacks would develop similar leisure patterns as whites if similar resources and opportunities were available.

The ethnicity perspective proposes that black leisure patterns are "the result of distinct subcultural values and norms different from general American culture" (O'Leary and Benjamin 1981:11. Differences in participation would arise from cultural differences rather than opportunity or class differences.

Stamps and Stamps (1985) provided an extensive review of the literature related to studies done on social class, race and leisure since 1956. Their review suggested there is tremendous variation in the populations investigated as well as in the findings. Populations studied ranged from Canadian and American national samples to investigations of patrons of neighborhood taverns and lounges. Some studies of ethnic group behavior controlled for socioeconomic and residence factors, while others did not. The studies which did provide controls used a variety of methods, including simple comparison of rates of leisure participation among different race, income and other categories (Mueller and Gurin 1962); multiple classification analysis (Enosh 1975); multivariate analysis using chi-square (Wagner and Donohue 1976, Washburne 1978); and matched samples (Cheek et. al. 1976, Washburne 1978, Washburne and Wall 1979). Some of the earlier research had identified class differences (Burdge 1969, Clarke 1956, Noe 1974), race differences (Meeker et. al. 1973, Washburne 1978), and some assumed similarities (Blackwell 1975, Kronus 1971, O'Leary and Benjamin 1981) in leisure participation patterns. Stamps and Stamps concluded that "social class and race as variables explaining leisure participation were not conclusive as predictors" (Stamps and Stamps 1985:54). Further study is needed to clarify the relationship between race, class and recreation participation. This lack of clarity is further underlined by the work of Goodrich (1985) and Spratlen (1986) noting the paucity of research on the black traveler taking a trip as a leisure or recreation experience. These views are consistent with recreation literature described above suggesting the need to further develop understanding of the similarities or differences of the black and white travelers.

The purpose of this study was to determine whether differences exist in the travel motivations, activities, and travel group type of blacks and whites from a national sample of travelers in the U.S. population. Information from this analysis provides a basis for comparing the majority and minority traveling populations and a perspective of how minority business might approach marketing services to minority (or majority) tourists.

---

[1] The authors would like to acknowledge the research cooperation and assistance of Environment Canada-Parks and Southeast Regional Office of the National Park Service.

Methods

Data used to investigate black and white travelers were obtained from the 1985 Travel Study conducted with a national survey by National Analysts of Philadelphia for Tourism Canada. The overall purpose of the survey was to gather information about the perceptions and preferences of pleasure travelers from the United States.

A multi-stage area probability design was used to select participants in the study. A sequential probability plan, by quota, sampled area segments, housing units, and eligibles consumers within households. Three levels of urbanization (central cities, suburban, and non-metropolitan) were represented. Americans who were at least 16 years of age and had made at least one pleasure trip in the 36 months preceeding the study qualified for sample selection. A total of 9,033 in-home personal interviews averaging 50 minutes in length, were conducted during September and October, 1985. Of the respondents, 8,117 (91.4 percent) were white and 516 (5.8 percent) were black. Seven types of trips were initially examined: close-to-home leisure trips, touring trip, city trip, an outdoors trip, resort trip, cruise, a trip to a theme park, exhibition or special event. City trips were then chosen for additional analysis. The focus is on domestic city trip travel by the two groups and motivations for goals and activities associated with that choice. Chi-square analysis was used to examine the relationship between motivations (goals and activities) and race. Student t-tests for differences between means were used to compare the goals and activities scores between the two groups. Then factor analysis was used to examine the patterns that are associated with the motivations for each of the groups.

Results

Trip Types

In comparing the trips taken by black and white travelers, both differences and similarities emerge. Both groups identify a visit to friends and relatives as the most common type of trip they take. For whites the next important trip type taken is visiting some place close to home. However, blacks identify a city trip as their second choice and a close to home trip as the third choice. While black travelers do participate in other types of trips, on a percentage basis they do so at a reduced rate from their white counterparts. Because of the importance of city trips to black travelers, the subsequent analysis will focus on factors that are associated with this travel.

Who Do You Travel With?

Descriptive analysis of the data revealed that when blacks and whites travel with others for city trips, the patterns tend to be different. Whites are more inclined to travel with their spouse or partner. Black travelers appear to

travel with their family, friends, or some combination of these two groups. There are sufficient differences between the two patterns identified here to suggest that the motivations of the two groups could be affected by these different travel partners.

Motivations on City Trips

Table 1 indicates that for virtually all of the goal motivations associated with taking a city trip, there are differences between black and white travelers. Blacks appear to feel more intensely about those things that motivate one to take a city trip. For example, feeling safe for a black is highly important; having lots to do, being entertained, and finding thrills are also quite important. However, a major driving force behind a trip may have to do with visiting friends and relatives, with 88 percent of the black respondents identifying that as being very or somewhat important. Blacks are also more sensitive to reduced fares when they think about factors that influence travel.

TABLE 1
City Trip Motivations for
White and Black Travelers

Motivations	Very Important	Somewhat Important	Not Very Important	Not At All Important	Sig. Level
Visiting historical places	21/29[1]	38/36	19/22	22/14	.05
Being w/ someone special	66/66	21/21	5/9	8/4	NS
Being w/ family	62/64	17/21	7/9	15/6	.02
Going places people haven't seen	21/34	26/27	26/25	27/14	.00
Talking about trip after I return home	28/47	37/39	23/8	13/5	.00
Getting away from pressures	56/63	27/23	11/9	7/5	NS
Experience diff. cultures	29/38	33/32	20/19	18/11	.05
Traveling to places where feel safe	42/67	29/22	16/5	13/5	.00
Being physically active	34/48	37/25	17/17	13/10	.00
Being entertained	59/69	31/25	7/5	4/1	.05
Having lots to do	57/71	29/20	9/7	5/2	.01
Visit friends and relatives	44/70	22/18	14/6	20/6	.00
Visit place where family came from	21/44	23/23	19/16	37/17	.00
Rest and relax	51/65	32/24	10/9	7/2	.00
Take advantage of reduced fares	34/55	28/21	16/13	22/11	.00
Fulfilling a dream of visiting a place I've always wanted to visit	33/48	24/21	18/13	25/18	.00
Meeting someone of opposite sex	9/23	13/13	16/23	62/42	.00
Finding thrills	24/40	29/38	22/9	25/13	.00
Meeting people of same interest	27/43	36/34	17/13	19/10	.00
Being pampered	17/35	29/33	25/17	29/15	.00

[1] White %/Black %, and statistical test used was x²=chi square.

Table 2 shows a ranking of the mean importance scores of motivation goals for the black and white groups. There are a few differences in ranking the items, but generally the first ten items are similar, only changing position. However, as noted above, the black group appears to assign more importance to the items for a city trip. In addition, statistical differences exist between the mean scores for all the items except "spending time with someone special" and "getting away from pressure."

The factor analysis identifies several themes that appear to push each of these different travelers toward the city (Table 3). The analysis indicates that there are two more

TABLE 2
Importance Mean Score and Rank of Motivations for City Trip

Motivations[1]	Black Travelers Rank	$\bar{x}$	White Travelers Rank	$\bar{x}$
10) Having fun, being entertained	1.	1.3355	1.	1.5402
11) Having lots to do and see	2.	1.3484	3.	1.6041
12) Visiting friends and relatives	3.	1.4323	9.	2.0804
8) Traveling to places where I feel safe	4.	1.4387	7.	1.9767
14) Resting and relaxing	5.	1.4452	5.	1.7105
2) Spend time w/ someone special	6.	1.4710	1.	1.5307
6) Getting away from pressures	7.	1.5226	4.	1.6444
3) Being together as a family	8.	1.5355	6.	1.7122
5) Talking about trip after I return home	9.	1.6774	10.	2.1772
15) Taking advantage of reduced fares	10.	1.7290	13.	2.2481
4) Being physically active	11.	1.8452	8.	2.0640
14) Meeting people of similar interests	12.	1.8645	12.	2.3472
18) Finding thrills and excitement	13.	1.8903	16.	2.4209
16) Fulfilling a dream; visiting a place I've always wanted to visit	14.	1.9419	14.	2.3129
7) Experiencing different cultures	15.	1.9677	11.	2.2230
13) Visiting places my family came from	16.	1.9935	19.	2.6497
20) Being pampered	17.	2.0581	18.	2.5982
4) Going places many people haven't seen	18.	2.1097	17.	2.5575
1) Visiting places important in history	19.	2.1548	15.	2.3747
17) Meeting opposite sex	20.	2.7613	20.	3.2773

[1] T-tests indicated that statistical differences exist between the mean scores for all the items at the 5 percent or better probability level except item numbers 2 and 6.

factors that emerge for blacks than for whites. These two groups are interested in having social experiences, escape, fun and thrills, and going on an expedition to see or do something different. Perhaps the biggest difference in looking at the black "expedition" factor, is that the item of being together as a family appears here. However, for black travelers there also seems to be at least two additional factors described as "controlled fun" (with a safety item) and "party."

TABLE 3
Factor Analysis of Travel Motivations for City Trips

Black Travelers

Factor 1 Fun & Thrills	Factor 2 Expedition	Factor 3 Social
meet someone of opposite sex	places important in history	spending time w/ someone special
thrills and excitement	being together as a family	being together as a family
meeting people w/ like interests	going to places unseen by others	visit friends and relatives
being pampered	fulfilling a dream	visiting places my family came from

Factor 4 Controlled Fun	Factor 5 Escape	Factor 6 Party
experiencing different cultures	talking about trip	having fun
traveling where I feel safe	getting away from pressures	having lots to do
being physically active	rest and relax	
having lots to do		
take advantage of reduced fares		

White Travelers

Factor 1 Expedition	Factor 2 Social	Factor 3 Fun & Thrills	Factor 4 Escape
places important in history	spend time w/ someone special	physically active	getting away from pressures
going to unseen places	being together as a family	having fun	having fun
experiencing different cultures	visit friends and relatives	meet opposite sex	have lots to do
fulfilling a dream	visit where family came	thrills and excitement	rest and relax
	take advantage of reduced fares	meet people of similar interests	
	being pampered		

Activities and the City Trip

Table 4 demonstrates that the relationship between importance and group type is significant for all but three activities - sunbathing, shopping for arts and crafts, and playing golf. Table 5 reinforces these results with the importance rank for the activities for the two groups. For the first seven positions there are similar activities identified, with only slight

TABLE 4
City Trip Activities for White and Black Travelers

Activities	Very Important	Somewhat Important	Not Very Important	Not At All Important	Sig. Level
Visiting big cities	30/43[1]	37/33	15/16	17/8	.00
Being by the ocean	18/19	27/32	20/20	34/29	NS
Sunbathing	10/9	19/16	27/22	43/53	NS
Having predictable weather	29/39	35/38	18/9	19/14	.00
Dining at a variety of restaurants	32/46	42/30	17/16	9/9	.00
Dining in elegant and sophisticated restaurants	15/36	24/32	33/21	27/21	.00
Staying in 1st-class hotels	19/36	31/32	27/18	23/34	.04
Paying budget accommodations	23/41	37/34	22/15	18/11	.00
Shopping	26/51	39/30	23/11	13/8	.00
Going to night clubs and discos	11/32	20/27	24/15	43/26	.00
Gambling	11/10	10/18	19/17	65/53	.00
Going to live concerts or live theater	18/34	31/31	19/13	31/22	.00
Attending ethnic events	12/19	31/36	27/22	30/23	.01
Visiting museums, galleries	20/24	38/26	22/32	20/19	.00
Take rides at amusement parks	8/19	20/27	24/22	49/32	.00
Shop for arts & crafts	14/18	35/36	26/21	25/25	NS
Indoor activities, cards	7/18	20/34	30/20	43/28	.00
Attend sport events	13/28	25/27	22/19	40/17	.00
Playing golf	5/8	9/11	17/15	69/66	NS
Playing tennis	3/6	10/17	18/17	69/61	.00
Going to car or motorcycle races	5/14	10/10	18/22	67/54	.00
Going to race track	7/14	13/21	19/19	61/45	.00
Walking, strolling about	29/34	48/42	11/11	11/13	NS
Sampling local cuisine	31/34	42/42	14/13	13/11	NS
Taking guided tours	13/25	27/27	24/27	36/22	.00
Going to zoo or wildlife exhibits	17/22	33/29	19/27	30/23	.03
Viewing science exhibits	15/21	28/22	26/26	31/31	NS
Going to bars or pubs	9/15	19/31	20/16	51/39	.01

[1] White %/Black %, and statistical test used was a χ^2—chi square

TABLE 5
Importance Mean Score and Rank for City Trips

Motivations[1]	Black Travelers Rank	$\bar{x}$	White Travelers Rank	$\bar{x}$
9) Shopping	1.	1.7390	4.	2.1927
5) Dining at a variety of restaurants	2.	1.8323	1.	1.9888
1) Visiting big cities	3.	1.8452	7.	2.3526
8) Having budget accommodation	4.	1.8968	6.	2.3181
4) Having predictable weather	5.	1.9419	5.	2.2264
23) Walking, strolling about	6.	1.9613	2.	2.0233	NS
24) Sample local cuisine	7.	1.9806	3.	2.0459	NS
12) Going to live concerts or live theatre	8.	2.1613	11.	2.5964
10) Going to nightclubs or discos	9.	2.2903	19.	2.9542
6) Dining in elegant sophisticated places	10.	2.3326	15.	2.6645
7) Staying in first class hotels	11.	2.3419	9.	2.5039	NS
18) Attending sports events	12.	2.3613	18.	2.8600
25) Taking guided tours	13.	2.3871	17.	2.7752
14) Visiting museums and galleries	14.	2.4129	8.	2.3863	NS
13) Attending ethnic festivals or events	14.	2.4129	16.	2.6932
26) Going to zoo or wildlife exhibits	15.	2.4387	10.	2.5806	NS
16) Shopping for arts and crafts	16.	2.4581	12.	2.5972	NS
17) Indoor activities, playing cards	17.	2.5355	20.	3.0363
2) Being by the ocean	18.	2.5613	13.	2.6596	NS
15) Taking rides at amusement parks	19.	2.5742	21.	3.0691
27) Viewing science exhibits	20.	2.6194	14.	2.6776	NS
28) Going out to pubs or bars	21.	2.6839	22.	3.0769
22) Going to race track	22.	2.8645	23.	3.2818
11) Gambling	23.	3.0258	24.	3.3768
21) Going to car or motorcycle races	24.	3.0839	25.	3.4019
3) Sunbathing	25.	3.1290	19.	2.9542	NS
20) Playing tennis	26.	3.2129	27.	3.4780
19) Playing golf	27.	3.2968	26.	3.4468	NS

[1] T-tests indicated that statistical differences exist between 18 of the 27 activities for the two groups; and NS implies that the difference between the two mean scores is not significant at the 3 percent or better probability level.

48

differences in position. From this point on there is more variation in the item ranks. There are statistical differences between 18 of the 27 activities for the two groups. In general, black travelers identify the large majority of the activities as being more important to them on the city trip than their white counterparts.

Table 6 represents the results of the factor analysis done with the activities that visitors identified as important in taking a city trip. In general, the factors look somewhat similar. There is one additional factor for black travelers (Factor 4) that appears to be a subset of the white travelers' Factor 2, suggesting some additional focused interest in that array of activities. However, while this similarity is apparent, the result must be interpreted in the context of the above discussion showing that the two groups differ in the importance they assign to the activities.

TABLE 6
Factor Analysis of Important
City Trip Activities

Black Travelers

Factor 1	Factor 2	Factor 3	Factor 4
gambling	visit big cities	having budget accommodation	
taking rides at amusement parks	dining at variety of restaurants	walking or strolling about	shopping
indoor activities	dining at elegant restaurants	taking guided tours	attend ethnic events
attending sports events	staying in lst-class hotels	going to zoo or wildlife exhibit	visit museums and galleries
playing golf		view science exhibits	shop for arts and crafts of area
playing tennis			
go to car and motorcycle races			
going to race track			

Factor 5	Factor 6	Factor 7
go to nightclubs or discos	being by the ocean	shopping
go to concerts or theater (live)	having predictable weather	shopping for arts and crafts
go to bars and pubs	having budget accommodations	indoor activities
		walking or strolling about
		sampling local cuisine

White Travelers

Factor 1	Factor 2	Factor 3
gambling	attend ethnic events	visit big cities
indoor activities	visit museums and galleries	dine in variety of restaurants
attend sports events	take rides at amusement parks	dine in elegant restaurants
play golf	shop for arts and crafts	stay in lst-class hotels
play tennis	take guided tours	take rides
go to car and motorcycle races	go to zoo or wildlife exhibits	
go to race track	view science exhibits	

Factor 4	Factor 5	Factor 6
being by the ocean	go to nightclubs or discos	walking, strolling
sunbathing	go to concerts or theater (live)	sampling local cuisine
having predictable weather	go to bars and pubs	
budget accommodations		

CONCLUSIONS AND IMPLICATIONS

In much of the literature that has looked at comparing the recreation and leisure patterns of black and white participants, the general conclusion has been that there are many similarities between the two groups. Even in the limited research that has been done on the black American tourist (Goodrich 1985) this same type of conclusion is reached. However, the data examined in this survey would tend to suggest that for businesses that are interested in developing opportunities in the tourist service market, there are sufficient differences between the two groups both in terms of the factors that push people to travel and in the activities that

may pull the tourist to an area, to warrant different kinds of action.

Findings of this study suggest that black and white travelers are likely to be responsive to different vacation travel experiences during a city trip with shifting priorities of the same vacation related attributes and features, and consequently, to different promotional messages. For example, findings associated with city trip motivations suggest that black travelers are more sensitive to reduced fares and premium-priced vacation packages than white travelers. Featuring these attributes in promotional campaigns targeted at black travelers becomes important from a marketing point of view.

The broad marketing implication of this study for tourism related public/private businesses (e.g., chambers of commerce, departments of state tourism, travel agencies, and tour operators) is that they should always take into account possible differentiating characteristics of the traveling public and determine the level of importance attached to the same set of motivations and activities for travel in their marketing efforts. With more detailed and more clearly identified vacation behavior of different ethnic groups and thus tourism market segments, promotional efforts may be effectively directed at the specific purpose traveler.

Differences between black and white travelers in the importance they assign to the activities and motivations that push one to take a city trip reaffirm the need to develop different marketing strategies and messages for each of the two groups. From a service marketing perspective, recognition of this existence of subgroups of travelers will afford tourism related businesses clear understanding to what types of marketing strategies and policies are needed to ensure that diverse tastes, preferences and/or motivations of carefully selected targeted markets are accommodated.

References

Blackwell, J. (1975), The Black Community: Diversity and Unity, New York: Dodd, Mead.

Burdge, R.J. (1969), "Levels of Occupational Prestige and Leisure Activity," Journal of Leisure Research, 1, pp. 262-274.

Cheek, N.H., Jr., D. Field and R.J. Burdge (1976), Leisure and Recreation Places Ann Arbor: Ann Arbor Science Publishers.

Clarke, A. (1956), "The Use of Leisure and its Relation to Levels of Occupational Prestige." American Sociological Review, 21, pp. 301-307.

Cosenza, R.M. and D.L. Davis (1981), "Family Vacation Decision Making over the Family Life Cycle: A Decision and Influence Structure Analysis," Journal of Travel Research, 20(2), pp. 17-23.

Crask, M.R. (1981) "Segmenting the Vacationer

Market: Identifying the Vacation Preferences, Demographics, and Magazine Readership of Each Group, Journal of Travel Research, 20(2), pp. 29-34.

Dybka, J.M. (1986), "Focus on North American Tourism: Attracting U.S. Tourists to Canada," Tourism Management, (September), pp. 202-204.

Dybka, J.M. "A Look at the American Traveler: The U.S. Pleasure Travel Market Study,: Journal of Travel Research, 25(3), pp. 1-4.

Enosh, N., R.A. Christiansen, S.D. Staniforth, and R.B. Cooper (1975), Effects of Selected Socio-Economic Characteristics on Recreation Patterns in Low Income Urban Areas: Part I, Recreation Resources Center, University of Wisconsin-Extension, Dept. of Agricultural Economics, Madison, WI.

Gitelson, R.J. and J.L. Crompton (1983), "The Planning Horizons and Sources of Information Used by Pleasure Vacationers," Journal of Travel Research, 21(3), pp. 2-7.

Goodrich, J.N. (1985), "Black American Tourists: Some Research Findings," Journal of Travel Research, 24(2), pp. 27-28.

Hollingshead, A.B. and F.C. Redlich (1958), Social Class and Mental Illness, New York: John Wiley & Sons.

Kronus, S. (1971), The Black Middle Class, Columbus, Ohio: Charles E. Merrill Publishing Co.

Lounsbury, J.W. and L.L. Hoopes (1985), "An Investigation of Factors Associated with Vacation Satisfaction," Journal of Leisure Research, 17, pp. 1-13.

McClaskie, S.L., T.L. Napier and J.E. Christiansen, (1986), "Factors Influencing Outdoor Recreation Participation: A State Study, Journal of Leisure Research, 18, pp. 190-205.

Meeker, J.W., W.K. Woods and W. Lucas (1973), "Red, White and Black in the National Parks," North American Review, (Fall), pp. 3-7.

Miller, D.C. (1977), Handbook of Research Design and Social Measurement, (3rd ed.), New York: Longman.

Mueller, Eva and Gerald Gurin (1962), Participation in Outdoor Recreation: Factors Affecting Demand Among American Adults. Report to the Outdoor Recreation Resources Review Commission, ORRRC Study Report 20 (Washington, D.C.: Superintendent of Documents).

Murphy, J.F. (1974), Concepts of Leisure: Philosophical Implications, Englewood Cliffs, N.J.: Prentice-Hall, Inc.

Noe, F.P. (1974), "Leisure Life Styles and Social Class: A Trend Analysis," Sociology and Social Research, 58, pp. 286-294.

Nolan, S.D., Jr. (1976), "Tourists' Use and Evaluation of Travel Information Sources: Summary and Conclusions," Journal of Travel Research, 14, pp. 6-8.

O'Hare, William (1987), "Best Metros for Black Businesses," American Demographics, 9(7), pp. 38-41.

O'Leary, J.T. and P. Benjamin (1981), Ethnic Variations in Leisure: Studies, Theories and Directions for Future Research, Final Report, Cooperative Research Project, U.S. Forest Service, North Central Forest Experiment Station, Chicago and Purdue University.

O'Leary, J.T., F.A. McGuire and F.D. Dottavio (1985), Outdoor Recreation Activities and Limitations: 1960 vs. 1983, Report No. 15. Technical Report Series, Nationwide Recreation Survey Working Paper, Clemson Cooperative Park Study Unit, U.S. Department of the Interior, National Park Service.

O'Leary, J.T., M. Uysal, F.D. Dottavio and H.K. Cordell (1986), Travel Patterns of the American Public: Participation in Selected Outdoor Recreation Activities. W.B. Joseph, L. Moutinbo and I.R. Vernon, In Tourism Services Marketing: Advances in Theory and Practice, Proceedings of the Special Conference on Tourism Services Marketing, Cleveland, Ohio, (September), 2, pp. 30-40.

Rosenfeld, J.P. (1986), "Demographics on Vacation," American Demographics, (January).

Spratlen, T.H. (1986), "Affluent Blacks as Travelers and Tourists: Group Characteristics and Targeted Advertising Themes." In W.B. Joseph, L. Moutinbo, and I.R. Vernon, Tourism Services Marketing: Advances in Theory and Practice, Proceedings of the Special Conference on Tourism Services Marketing, Cleveland, Ohio, (September), pp. 238-248.

Stamps, S.M. and M.B. Stamps (1985), Race, Class and Leisure Activities of Urban Residents, Journal of Leisure Research, 17, pp. 40-56.

Tinsely, H.E.A. and D.J. Tinsley (1986), "A Theory of the Attributes, Benefits, and Causes of Leisure Experience," Leisure Sciences, 8(1), pp. 1-45.

Wagner, F.W. and T.R. Donohue (1976), "The Impact of Inflation and Recession on Urban Leisure in New Orleans," Journal of Leisure Research, 8, pp. 300-306.

Washburne, R.F. (1978), "Black Under-Participation in Wildland Recreation: Alternative Explanations," Leisure Sciences, 1, pp. 175-189.

Washburne, R.F. and P. Wall (1979), Cities, Wild Areas, and Black Leisure: In Search of Explanations for Black/White Differences in Outdoor Recreation, Unpublished Paper, Intermountain Forest and Range Experiment Station, U.S. Forest Service, Missoula, Montana.

SUBCULTURAL DIFFERENCES AMONG DIRECT MARKETING TELEVISION SHOPPERS

E. Lincoln James, Michigan State University
Allen C. Harris, Michigan State University

This study was made possible by a grant to one of the authors from the Direct Marketing Policy Research Center, University of Cincinnatti.

Abstract

A national mail survey was used to gather information from direct marketing television shoppers about their attitudes, motivations, social environment, and attributions about their shopping behaviors. Subcultural differences between Black, White and Hispanic shoppers were analyzed by means of multiple discriminant analysis. The data revealed more differences between Black and White shoppers than between Blacks and Hispanics or Hispanics and Whites.

Introduction

Past studies of ethnic subcultures have demonstrated a variety of critical relationships between subcultural membership and consumer behavior. For example, studies of Blacks and Hispanics have indicated that minorities tend to differ from non minorities in the following ways: (1)Blacks and Hispanics tend to be more conservative in shopping behavior (Saegert, Hoover, and Hilger, 1985; Gillett and Scott, 1975; Hoyer and Deshpande, 1982; Segal and Sosa, 1983); (2) Hispanics tend to be more brand loyal (Yankovitch, Skelley, and White (1981); (3) Blacks and Hispanics tend to display greater preference for familiar businesses and products (Bellenger and Valencia 1982; Cervantes, 1980; Kizibash and German, 1975-76; Sturdivant, 1969); and (4) Blacks and Hispanics tend to hold greater negative attitudes toward business (Deshpande, Hoyer, and Dontu, 1986; Cervantes, 1980).

Researchers have paid attention to minority consumers because they comprise a large segment of the American consuming public, and appear to be different from non minorities in a variety of important ways, which when identified, can facilitate the marketing and advertising strategies of retailers. Most subculture studies, however, while they provide important insights into consumer behavior, tend to be more relevant to traditional rather than non traditional retailers. Few investigations have provided information about subcultural influences relevant to the non traditional retailer--the direct marketer. Indeed, a survey of the literature reveals a surprising dearth of empirical research focusing on the relationship between subcultural influences and in-home shopping behavior. In one of these few studies, Feldman and Star (1968) found that Whites were twice as likely as non-Whites to engage in in-home shopping by telephone at lower levels of income. This did not hold true, however, at higher income levels. In another investigation Gillett (1970) found that when classified by race, Blacks were less likely to be involved in in-home shopping than Whites. However, when controlling for income, there was no significant difference in racial spending among respondents. More recently, James and Cunningham (1978) found that Blacks were the least likely minority group to engage in direct response television shopping.

This lacuna in subcultural/consumer behavior type research is inexplicable given the phenomenal explosion over the past decade in the number of purchases made by in-home shoppers. According to the most recently compiled industry reports on the direct marketing industry, direct response advertising expenditures rose from $25,022,800 in 1981 to $30,065,200 in 1983 with estimated spending on goods and services sold by direct marketing in 1983 at $150.3 billion (DMA, 1985). Spending in 1987 is projected to top the $250 billion mark.

Study Objectives

The present investigation is an attempt to fill this void about subcultures and in-home shopping by identifying some key differences among in-home shoppers. Understanding the relationship between in-home shopping and subcultural group membership can contribute to advertising and marketing practice by providing descriptive knowledge which can help direct marketing practitioners to be more adaptable to the needs and wants of current and potential consumers. Further, identification of descriptive and subcultural differences can lead to generalizable theoretical insights about the basic process of consumer shopping behavior.

Specifically, the study is concerned with direct marketing television (DMTV) shoppers. Whereas DMTV was once considered a speciality to be used only by record clubs, book publishers and sundry kitchen gadget merchants, the strategy is currently being embraced by more than half the number of Fortune 500 corporations (Nash, 1982). Typically, a direct marketing television commercial makes a sales pitch for a product or service then invites a consumer to order or write for information by mail or telephone. The method of payment is either by check, money order or credit card. Products ranging from jumper cables and fitness kits to sophisticated video home computers have been offered for direct sale to the consumer via the medium of television. The "One-and-only-Veg-A-Matic dicer-slicer-splicer" of the 1960s, the "Fantastic Armourcote non-stick cookware" of the 1970s, and "The Amazing Lee Press-on Nails" of the 1980s have all entered the consumer's home directly by means of the television medium. While no current data are available, a conservative estimate based on past trends suggest that in 1987 consumers will spend more than $700 million on direct marketing television (DMTV) goods and services.

This study sought answers to three major questions: First, "What are the subcultural attributes of Black, Hispanic, and White direct marketing television shoppers?" Second, "Are there any significant differences between Black, Hispanic, and White direct marketing television shoppers?" Third, "If there are significant differences, are they identifiable and explainable?"

Independent Variables and Hypotheses

Based on a review of the general marketing literature on subcultures, shopping behavior, patronage, and in-home shopping behavior, five types of variables were identified as possible predictors of subcultural group membership. These variables were: attitudes, motivations, social environment, attributions made about DMTV shopping behaviors, and DMTV shopping intensity.

Attitudes

First, attitude has been a major focus of consumer behavior research since it is generally held that attitudes influence the shopping, buying, and consumption behaviors of individuals. While a number of shopping attitudes have been investigated by past researchers, this study confines itself to the examination of a few which have appeared in in-home shopping research and seem to have some bearing on subcultural shopping behavior. These are attitude toward risk, attitude toward credit, and attitude toward impulsive behavior.

In-home shopping literature indicates that an individual's attitude toward risk, attitude toward credit, and attitude toward impulsiveness are critical determinants of in-home shopping behavior (Cox and Rich, 1964; Gillett, 1970; Cunningham and Cunningham, 1974). Studies of subcultural influences on consumer behavior have shown that minorities tend to be more brand loyal, and more conservative, and by imputation less likely to have positive attitudes toward risk. Also, findings about conservatism and negative attitudes toward business among minorities imply that they are less likely to hold positive attitudes toward credit and impulsiveness.

Given the inherent risks in DMTV shopping such as non delivery of merchandise, or delivery of shoddy merchandise, the predominant credit card form of payment, and the conservatism of minority shoppers, this study hypothesized that:

(1) Blacks, Hispanics, and Whites will differ when classified respectively by their <u>attitude toward risk</u>, <u>attitude toward credit</u>, and <u>attitude toward impulsive behavior</u>.

Motivations

As early as 1923, Copeland proposed a typology of convenience-shopping-speciality goods, but it was Martineau (1952) some decades later, who, drawing upon the early work of motivational psychologist, Kurt Lewin (1930) verbalized the presence of social-psychological motives for shopping. Researchers such as Cattel (1957), Maslow (1970), Murray (1978), and McGuire (1974) have attempted to identify and categorize human motives. However, it was Tauber (1972) who inferred a number of specific shopping motivations based on satisfactions that individuals derived from a particular action. His hypothesized shopping motivations were supported in a recent study by Westbrook and Black (1985).

Five motivations were examined in this study: (1) power and authority motivation -- associated with satisfactions derived from acquiring momentary dominance over the activities of others in the marketplace, (2) affiliation motivation -- associated with the satisfactions derived from socially interacting, communicating, and identifying with others in the marketplace, (3) choice optimization motivation -- associated with satisfactions derived from intensively searching for and finding the right product at the right price, (4) self stimulation motivation -- associated with satisfactions derived from encounters with new and interesting stimuli in the shopping environment, and (5) convenience motivation -- associated with satisfactions derived from saving shopping time. A more complete discussion of these variables can be found in Westbrook and Black (1985).

The first four motivations were hypothesized by Tauber (1972) and supported by the Westbrook and Black (1985) study. The last motivation variable, convenience motivation, was included in the study because DMTV practitioners as well as researchers have shown that this is a basic characteristic of DMTV shoppers (Cox and Rich, 1964; Cunningham and Cunningham, 1973; Gillett, 1970; James, 1983).

The second hypothesis made in this study was that (2) Blacks, Hispanics, and Whites will differ when classified respectively by their <u>power and authority motivation</u>, <u>affiliation motivation</u>, <u>choice optimization motivation</u>, and <u>convenience motivation</u>.

Social Environment

Socio-environmental influences in this study are dealt with in terms of <u>social categories</u> and <u>social relations</u>. Social categories refer to traditional socio-demographic variables. The four social category variables examined here are sex, age, income, and education.

DMTV is a non traditional form of shopping, which

is associated with adequate income, a certain degree of cosmopolitanism, average education, and possession of the means of credit (Cunningham and Cunningham, 1973; Cox and Rich, 1964). Census data show that minorities score less on the attributes of income and education than non minorities, with minority females at the lower end of the educational and income scale. Based on the national trend, therefore, one can expect income, sex, and educational differences among Black, Hispanic, and White DMTV shoppers. Some findings suggest that through a process of accultration younger minorities tend to possess similar profiles to non minorities while older group members tend to differ (Deshpande, Hoyer, and Donthu, 1986; Franklin, Hair, and Anderson, 1972).

The third hypothesis made in this study was that (3) Blacks, Hispanics and Whites will differ when classified respectively by their sex, age, education, and income.

Social relations refer to reference group influence. Social influence has been posited as having a significant impact on subcultural group behavior. Social influence is seen to operate as a function of contextual group situations as demonstrated in the findings of role theory. Findings have shown that the spheres of influence exerted by reference groups on an individual is informational, comparative, and normative. Social relations, in effect, provide a point of comparison which helps the individual define his/her own beliefs, values, attitudes, and opinions.

In the realm of social relations, sociologists have consistently demonstrated that the extent of an individual's social ties or lack of ties, is shaped by the society in which he lives and impacts on his behavior. These scholars have further argued that a major dysfunction of urbanized society is the high incidence of lack of social ties or lack of group identification among individuals. This lack of ties is defined as social isolation. Seeman (1959) and Srole (1965), among others, have noted that social isolation is reflected in feelings of anonymity, low social participation, low membership in social groups, and few visits from friends. Stone (1954) was able to identify a socially isolated type of urban shopper in his study of consumer behavior and urban identification. Deshpande et. al. (1986) indirectly investigated this variable by identifying low and high identity Hispanics based on their degree of acculturation. More recently, James (1986) identified this variable as a key discriminator between DMTV shopper and non shopper groups.

The fourth hypothesis made by this study was that (4) Blacks, Hispanics and Whites will differ when classified respectively by their social isolation

Attributions About DMTV Shopping Behavior

In addition to these variables, this study investigated seven attributions made by consumers about their DMTV shopping behaviors. The seven attributions were identified as important by five focus group studies conducted with convenience samples over a six month period. These attributions were: (1) perceived price advantage, (2) convenience, (3) ability to use credit, (4) acceptable product quality, (5) dislike of in-store shopping, (6) opportunity to secure unique products, and (7) impulsiveness.

The fifth hypothesis made by this study was that (5) Blacks, Hispanics and Whites will differ when classified respectively by their attributions about. (1) perceived price advantage, (2) convenience, (3) ability to use credit, (4) acceptable product quality, (5) dislike of in-store shopping (6) opportunity to secure unique products, and (7) impulsiveness.

Methodology

Subjects for this study were drawn from a national sample. The names of 2250 known DMTV shoppers plus the names of 2250 other residents were randomly selected from an amalgamated direct mail broker's list. The sample of known DMTV shoppers was randomly drawn from a database of 175,000 individuals who had purchased a DMTV product at least once during the month prior to the survey. The other half of the sample was drawn from a national database consisting of over thirty million individuals generated by a match and purge of utility listings, voter registration listings, college listings, and automobile registration listings. All potential subjects were at least 18 years old. The entire sample was drawn from a total of 1551 zipcode areas. Since the incidence of DMTV shopping was unknown it was felt that this sampling approach would provide enough representative responses from DMTV shoppers and non shoppers.

A four page instrument was used to gather information in a national mail survey. The questionnaire was pretested on a random sample of 200 residents in a midsized Southwestern city and adjustments were made to insure clarity of the items. Both a premailer and a follow up card were used in this survey.

Results

There was a 20.53% response to the survey with 905 of the 924 returns being usable. Almost 68% or 613 were DMTV shoppers. Demographic distribution of the sample is shown in Table 1. There was a greater proportion of female than male DMTV shoppers across subcultural groupings. While there was a somewhat proportional distribution of subjects across age groups there were smaller proportions of Blacks in the lowest and highest income segments across subculture groups. An unexpectedly large proportion of Hispanics (24.3%) and Blacks (13.3%) seemed to fall into the highest income and education categories respectively.

Differences between Blacks, Hispanics and Whites

Table 1: Demographic Distribution of the Sample

VARIABLE	ETHNIC SUBCULTURE		
	Black (N=75)	Hispanic (N=55)	White (N=642)
SEX			
Male	67.6%	54.1%	65.3%
Female	32.4	45.9	34.7
AGE GROUP			
18 - 24	23.7	27.0	18.9
25 - 34	36.8	25.1	36.4
35 - 44	21.1	13.5	30.2
45 - 54	13.2	18.9	9.3
54 +	5.2	5.4	5.2
INCOME			
$9,999	7.9	16.2	11.9
$10,000 - $19,999	23.7	21.6	19.6
$20,000 - $29,999	42.1	16.2	22.8
$30,000 - $39,999	13.2	18.9	16.0
$40,000 - $49,999	7.9	2.7	11.1
$50,000 +	5.2	24.3	18.5
HIGHEST LEVEL OF EDUCATION COMPLETED			
grade school	2.6	13.5	7.5
high school	57.9	43.2	50.5
college	25.2	37.9	33.6
graduate school	1.1	5.4	8.4

Table 2: DISCRIMINANT ANALYSIS OF DIFFERENCES BETWEEN BLACK, HISPANIC, AND WHITE DIRECT MARKETING SHOPPERS

Variable	Coefficient		Means			Differences in Means
	$F1$ [1]	$F2$ [2]	Blacks (N=38)	Hispanics (N=17)	Whites (N=495)	
DMTV Shopping Frequency	-.05	-.28	2.82	2.41	2.52	
DMTV Spending	-.08	.23	3.0	3.26	2.98	
Price as a Reason	-.34	.10	1.61	1.48	1.46	
Convenience as a Reason	.08	-.24	1.61	1.52	1.68	
Ability to Use Credit as a Reason *	.27	-.41	1.77	1.70	1.89	C
Acceptable Product Quality as a Reason	-.28	.16	1.81	1.74	1.67	
Dislike of In-Store Shopping as a Reason *	.50	-.04	1.74	1.88	1.93	AB
Unique Product Opportunity as a Reason *	-.32	.36	1.45	1.44	1.28	A
Impulsiveness as a Reason *	.26	-.06	1.74	1.81	1.89	A
Attitude Toward Risk	-.01	.03	11.9	11.81	11.2	
Attitude Toward Credit	-.09	.06	6.93	6.74	6.40	
Attitude Toward Impulsive Behavior	.22	.15	10.93	12.0	11.4	
Social Isolation *	.29	.48	25.64	29.81	21.24	B
Power and Authority Motivation	.11	.11	4.58	4.81	4.79	
Need for Affiliation Motivation *	.05	-.14	8.54	8.11	9.04	
Choice Optimization Motivation	-.29	-.31	4.84	3.48	3.95	AB
Environmental Stimulation Motivation	-.03	-.14	6.06	6.27	6.04	
Convenience Motivation	.11	.21	10.51	11.09	11.04	
Sex (male)	.20	.24	.29	.48	.35	
Education Level	-.07	-.10	2.95	2.96	2.65	
Age Group	.27	-.07	2.19	2.00	2.03	
Income Level	.21	.39	3.16	3.50	3.57	

1 $X^2=79.71$, df=44, p<.001
2 $X^2=47.39$, df=21, p<.05
A Difference between Blacks and Whites, p<.05
B Difference between Blacks and Hispanics, p<.05
C Difference between Whites and Hispanics, p<.05

NOTE: Percent of sample correctly classified is 70.1%. Within-group correctly classified: Blacks 80%, Hispanics 60%, Whites 73%

were assessed by multiple discriminant analysis. Table 2 shows the coefficients, means and differences between means for the three groups. Six variables were significant discriminators of subcultural group membership. There was no support for the first hypothesis that Blacks, Hispanics and Whites would differ when classified by attitude toward risk, attitude toward credit, and attitude toward impulsive behavior. There was only partial support for the second hypothesis. The only significant motivational discriminator of subcultural group membership was "choice optimization." None of the social category variables was significant and the third hypothesis was rejected. The data supported the fourth hypothesis that Blacks, Whites and Hispanics would differ when classified by their social isolation. Three of the seven attributions about DMTV shopping were significant and provided partial support for the final hypothesis. The three groups differed on attributions about ability to use credit, dislike of in-store shopping, the opportunity to acquire unique products, and impulsiveness.

A more detailed examination of each significant variable was made by conducting posteriori difference of means test (Duncan's Multiple Range Test). The analysis reveals that
(1) Hispanics ($\bar{X}$=1.70) and Whites ($\bar{X}$=1.89) differ on the attribution that their DMTV shopping is based on their ability to use credit.
(2) Blacks ($\bar{X}$=1.74) when compared to Hispanics ($\bar{X}$=1.88), and Whites ($\bar{X}$=1.93) differentially attribute their DMTV shopping to a dislike of in-store shopping.

(3) Blacks ($\bar{X}$=1.45) and Whites ($\bar{X}$=1.28) differ on the attribution of their DMTV shopping behavior to the opportunity acquire unique products.
(4) Blacks ($\bar{X}$=1.74) when compared to Whites ($\bar{X}$=1.89) differ in their attribution of impulsiveness as a reason for DMTV shopping.
(5) Blacks ($\bar{X}$=25.64) and Hispanic ($\bar{X}$=29.81) DMTV shoppers differ in terms of their social isolation.
(6) Blacks ($\bar{X}$=4.84) are different from Hispanics ($\bar{X}$=3.48) and Whites ($\bar{X}$=3.95) in terms of their choice optimization motivation.

Discussion

In summary, the results show that there are more differences between Black and White DMTV shoppers than between Hispanic and White shoppers. The results indicate that Blacks when compared to both Hispanics and Whites are less likely to attribute their DMTV shopping to a dislike of in-store shopping and more likely than Hispanics but less likely than Whites to be guided in their marketplace behaviors by the motivation to optimize choices. When compared to Hispanics, Blacks also appear to be less socially isolated. On the other hand, when compared to Whites, Black DMTV shoppers appear to be more likely to attribute their shopping behavior to the opportunity to acquire unique products and services and less likely to cite impulsiveness as a reason. Hispanics, though, when compared to Whites appear to be less likely to attribute their DMTV shopping to the ability to use credit.

The generalizeability of these results is limited in a number of ways. First, the investigation was concerned with DMTV shoppers and the results cannot be projected to cover either other types of response television shoppers or consumers who subscribe to different direct marketing modes. Second, although a national sampling frame was used, and respondents were drawn from 1551 zip-code areas, there was no distinction made between urban and rural dwellers. The implication is that there was no way of knowing how far the incidence of DMTV shopping, and the differences are common to urban and rural dwellers. Third, in the interest of parsimony and time and money limitations, only a limited set of variables were analyzed, although it was recognized that there could be other identifiable variables, such as the degree of ethnic identification, which exert an influence on DMTV shopping behavior. A fourth limitation was the lack of a comparative basis for these results since there are few prior published works on in-home subcultural characteristics. However, despite these limitations the results of this investigation can facilitate a general understanding of the determinant subcultural characteristics of DMTV shoppers.

References

Bellenger, Danny N. and Hunberto Valencia (1982), "Understanding the Hispanic Market," Business Horizons, (May-June), 47-50.

Cattel, R.B. (1957) Personality and Motivation: Structure and Measurement, New York: World Book.

Cervantes, Fernando Javier (1980) "The Forgotten Consumers: The Mexican Americans," in Richard Bagozzi and Alice Tybout (eds.) Educators' Conference Proceedings, Chicago, Ill.: American Marketing Association, pp. 180-183.

Cox, Donald F. and Stuart V. Rich (1964) "Perceived Risk in Consumer Decision Making-The Case of Telephone Shopping," Journal of Marketing Research, Vol. 1 (November), 32-39.

Cunningham, Isabella C.M., and William H. Cunningham (1973) "The Urban In-Home Shopper: Socioeconomic and Attitudinal Characteristics," Journal of Retailing, Vol. 49 (Fall), 42-50.

Copeland, Melvin T. (1923) "Relation of Consumer's Buying Habits to Marketing Methods," Harvard Business Review, (April), 282-289.

Deshpande, Rohit, Wayne D. Hoyer and Naveen Donthu (1986) "The Intensity of Ethnic Affiliation: A Study of the Sociology of Hispanic Consumption," Journal of Consumer Research, Vol. 13 (September): 214-220.

Direct Marketing Association (1985) Direct Marketing Fact Book: Statistical Update, New York, NY.: Direct Marketing Association.

Feldman, Laurence P., and Alvin D. Star (1969) "Racial Factors in Shopping Behavior," in Keith Cox and Ben Enis (eds.) A New Measure of Responsibility for Marketing, Chicago, ILL.: American Marketing Association, pp. 216-226.

Gillett, Peter (1970) "A Profile of Urban In-Home Shoppers," Journal of Marketing, Vol. 34 (July), 40-45.

Gillett, Peter L., and Richard A. Scott (1975) "Shopping Opinions of Mexican-American Consumers: A Comparative Analysis," in Richard C. Curhan (ed.) Combined Proceedings of the American Marketing Association, pp. 135-141.

Hair, J.F., Jr., and Rolph E. Anderson (1972) "Culture, Acculturation and Consumer Behavior: An Empirical Study," in Boris W. Becker and Helmut Becker (eds.) Combined Proceedings of the American Marketing Association, No. 34, pp. 423-428.

Hoyer, Wayne, and Rohit Deshpande (1982) "Cross Cultural Influences on Buyer Behavior: The Impact of Hispanic Ethnicity," in Educators Conference Proceedings, B.J. Walker et. al. (eds.) Chicago, Ill.: American Marketing Association, pp. 89-92.

James, E. Lincoln (1983) "What Makes Direct Marketing television Work-As Perceived By Practitioners," Unpublished Masters Theses, University of Florida.

James, E. Lincoln (1986) "Motivations, Attitudinal, and Socioenvironmental Characteristics of Direct Marketing Television Shoppers," Unpublished Doctoral Theses, The University of Texas at Austin.

James, E. Lincoln and Isabella Cunningham (1986) "A Profile of Direct response Television Shoppers Working Paper, Dept. of Advertising, The University of Texas at Austin.

Kizilbash, A.H. and E.T. Garman (1975-76) "Grocery Retailing in Spanish Neighborhoods," Journal of Retailing, Vol. 51 (Winter), 15-21.

Lewin, Kurt (1938) The Conceptual Representation and Measurement of Psychographical Forces. Chapel Hill, N.C.: University of North Carolina Press.

Martineau, Pierre (1952) Motivation and Advertising, New York: McGraw-Hill.

Maslow, Abraham H. (1970) Motivation and Personality, 2nd ed. New York: Harper and Row.

McGuire, William (1974) "Psychological Motives and Communication Gratification, in J.F. Blumier and E. Katz (eds.) The Uses of Mass Communications: Current perspectives on Gratification Research, Beverley Hills, Ca.: Sage Publications, pp. 106-167.

Murray, Henry A. (1968) "Components of an Evolv-
ing Personological System," in D.L. Sills (ed.)
International Encyclopedia of the Social Sciences
New York: Macmilan.

Nash, Edward L. (1982) Direct Marketing Strategy,
Planning, and Execution. New York: Macmilan.

Saegert, Joel, Robert J. Hoover and Marye Tharp
Hilger (1985) "Characteristics of Mexican-Ameri-
can Consumers," Journal of Consumer Research,
Vol. 12 (June), 104-109.

Seeman, Melvin (1959) "On the Meaning of Alienation," American Sociological Review, Vol. 24
(December), 783-791.

Segal, Madhav N. and Lionel Sosa (1983) "Marketing to the Hispanic Community," California Management Review, Vol. 26 No.1 (Fall), 120-134.

Srole, Leo (1956) "Social Integration and Certain
Corrolories: An Exploratory Study," American
Sociological Review, Vol. 21 (December), 700-716.

Stone, Gregory P. (1954) "City and Urban Identification: Observations on the Social Psychology
of City Life," American Journal of Sociology,
Vol. 60 (July), 36-45.

Sturdivant, Fredrick D. (1969) "Business and the
Mexican-American Community," California Management Review, Vol. 11 (Spring): 73-80.

Tauber, Edward M. (1972) "Why Do People Shop?"
Journal of Marketing, Vol. 36 (October): 46-59.

Westbrook, Robert A., and William C. Black (1985)
"A Motivation Based Shopper Typology," Journal
of Retailing, Vol. 61 (Spring): 78-103.

Yankovitch, Skelley, and White, Inc. (1981)
"Spanish USA: A Study of the Hispanic Market,"
Yankovitch, Skelley and White, New York, N.Y.

A CONCEPTUAL FRAMEWORK FOR EXAMINING COLOR PREFERENCE, IMPORTANCE AND CATEGORIZATION IN A MULTIATTRIBUTE CONTEXT AMONG BLACKS

Mary Margaret Liebman, Trenton State College

Abstract

This paper develops a conceptual framework that investigates the salience of color in the presence of price, brand name and quality, using two distinct products, and examines the subsequent differences in purchase behaviors and color preferences between black males and females. A conjoint analysis revealed significant differences in the perceived relative importance among the four attributes, differences were evident for general and product specific color preferences and relationships among past/ intended purchase behaviors were established. Implications for future research on an "antecedent color choice model" are introduced.

Introduction

Existing research on color preferences in a marketing context is scattered and the knowledge of color's effects on choice processes is virtually non-existent. The literature suggests that although private researchers have been able to forecast color trends, position certain colors as important and influence manufacturers' product color decisions, theoretical considerations and implications of color preferences in a choice setting have been largely overlooked. Multidisciplinary research suggests that males tend to rank the color yellow higher than females (Stimpson and Stimpson 1979), but yellow is generally less preferred than red or blue, yet more preferred than black (Adams and Osgood, 1973; Birren 1963, pp. 175-176, 189-18; Cheskin 1948; Choungourian 1968). Also, results are inconclusive for differences between male and female preference rankings of red and blue (Birren 1961 p. 75; Cheskin 1948; Choungourian 1968), and differences across sexes for color preferences in general (Granger 1952; Sloane 1968; Sharpe 1974). With the exception of Gotz and Gotz (1974a, 1974b) who found a positive perception of black, in at least twenty studies, black has been shown to be the least preferred or negative color across sexes and ethnic groups. Although research tends to support the notion that red and blue are more preferred than yellow and that black is the least preferred color, considerable research supports the premise that evaluative responses to color are object-category referenced (Osgood et al, 1957; Rosch et al 1976; Slatter and Whitfield 1977; Whitfield 1979, 1984; Whitfield and Slatter 1978, 1979). Whitfield (1979) posits that "colors vary in the extent to which they are appropriate or correspond with the learned specifications of different object categories". The color of one product will often affect the color of other products selected (e.g., women's fashion accessories, paint, household appliances carpeting, furniture, etc.)(Chemical Week 1980). Color also affects individuals' responses to store layouts and merchandise displays (Bellizzi et al, 1983), direct mail catalogues (Hill 1981), automobiles (Doehlert 1968; Lonial and Van Auken 1982), and magazine layouts (Schindler 1986). If color is presumed to be object-categorized, than how influential is color in a decision choice setting when an individual must assess other variables? Are there differences across product categories and genders?

Although researchers generally agree that the importance of price in determining choice behavior is typically either overrated or under-rated (Haines 1966, pp. 665-685), multiattribute studies that consider price, brand and quality simultaneously show that the importance of price varies with both quality and brand as well as with product type (Monroe 1984). However, existing economic and marketing models (Alpert 1971) do not fully explain the price, brand and quality relationships with respect to choice behavior. Studies to date have not preferred a conceptual framework to assess the impact of color in the presence of price, brand name and quality using different product categories for either the population as a whole or, more specifically, for black consumers. Also, very little is known about blacks' general color preferences or preferences that may be product specific because previous color studies have focused on the emotive aspects of color connotations and racial perceptions across different ethnic groups and sexes. In order to develop a preliminary conceptual framework for color in the presence of price, brand name and quality, it is tentatively posited that if an individual possessed the information necessary to evaluate the price, quality and brand name attributes of a product, exclusive of other variables, then the "ideal" choice of levels for these attributes could be defined as a low price, high quality and a well known brand name. Individuals may possess this "ideal" picture of attributes in their intention to purchase a specific product. However, in a realistic choice setting, where economic exchange is necessitated, intervening variables (e.g. style, size, location of store, discretionary time and product availability) will motivate the individual to trade-off the "ideal" variables in the presence of the intervening ones. The resulting decision will probably not reflect the original "ideal", but an individual will still attempt to satisfy his/her individual needs and desires by choosing a combination of variables that is closest to their perception of the "ideal".

Experimental Design

A conjoint analysis approach was employed to research the issues under consideration. Conjoint analysis is a multivariate technique concerned primarily with measuring consumer preferences. By developing a fractional factorial design for a main effects model, it is possible to generate a set of multiple factor evaluation (MFE) cards, or stimulus profiles, which display all studied attributes, each at a particular level (Green 1974; Green et al, 1978), and to examine the specific trade-offs that subjects make when they evaluate these multiattribute profiles (Green and Rao 1971). This is accomplished by first defining the number of levels of each attribute. In this study, the following attribute levels were employed: price=3, (low,medium,high); brand name=2, (lesser known, well known); quality=3 (good,better,best); color=4 (red,yellow,blue, black). Second, the total number of possible attribute combinations is determined, which in this case was 3x2x3x4=72. However, 72 stimulus profiles for each product would surely generate information overload, thereby confusing and frustrating the subjects (Bettman 1979; Green and Srinivasin 1978; Hulbert 1975; Jacoby 1984; Malhotra 1982). To edit the number of stimulus profiles to a more manageable number while preserving a set of orthogonal combinations, the attributes and their corresponding levels were subjected to the Conjoint Designer (1986) program that effectively reduced the number of stimulus profiles to 16 orthogonal arrays (i.e. a fractional factorial design) for each product and then subsequently randomized the profile order for administration. The subjects' responses to each stimulus profile were recorded on single nine-point behavioral expectation scales, ranging from least likely to buy (1) to most likely to buy (9). A dummy coded orthogonal matrix of the levels for each of the 16 stimulus profile cards was developed and subjects' responses were appended to this matrix. This response matrix was then subjected to multiple linear regression and the resultant betas (part-worths or utility scores) examined to ascertain overall preferences or utilities for each particular attribute at the assigned levels (Green and Carmone 1970; Green and Srinivasin 1978). Rather than using specific dollar figures for the price levels and/or the names of existent or fictitious brands, generic terms such as "high" for price and "well known" for brand name, were employed thereby allowing subjects to conceptualize what each particular attribute level meant to them, not prompted by pseudo price ranges, imaginary or real brand names and implied quality criteria. The colors used were the three primary ones of red, yellow and blue with black as the fourth. These are familiar to the subjects, easy to conceptualize and assess, and, since concern with the qualities of color (i.e. hue, saturation and (Munsel, 1973) intensity, are not at issue in this study, standardized color plates (Munsel, 1973) were not required. Providing only the names of colors to subjects rather than showing them particular renditions of each color allows the subjects to conceptualize the color attribute

in the same manner as the price, brand name and quality attributes. Red, blue and yellow have been used in numerous previous studies of color preferences across sexes. Black, defined as the total absence of color, was chosen because it has consistently been selected as the least preferred color when subjects were asked to rank their preferences. It was felt that the results of previous research would at least serve as a benchmark for the current study as a first attempt in assessing the salience of color in a multiattribute context.

Although the use of students in academic research is controversial, color preceptions are characterized by perceptual color theory (Burnham et al, 1963), which maintains that color preferences are well established by college age. Therefore, using a student sample poses no major threat to the external validity of the color preference results. The hypothesis to be examined in the study are as follows:

Hypothesis 1: It is expected that the most preferred or "ideal" attribute level choices will be low price, best quality and a well known brand name with color attribute levels different across products with no differences between sexes.

Although the "ideal" price, brand, quality combinations may be in evidence, the color attribute levels are expected to render the prdoucts more or less attractive, depending on the individuals' perception of the appropriateness of the color levels to the products in question with no differences across sexes in preferred color levels.

Hypothesis 2: The color attribute in general will not be perceived as more important than price, but color is expected to exact more influence on the perceived relative importance of brand and quality with differences across both product categories and between sexes.

Given the limited financial resources of college students, it is expected that in general, price will be considered dominant in relative importance over color, brand and quality, but previous research does not support any assumptions concerning the relative importances among color, brand and quality. However, it is suspected that differences in the perceived relative importance of the attributes will differ between sexes and across product categories.

Hypothesis 3: No differences are expected between sexes for general color preferences, but it is conjectured that individuals' color choices will exhibit differences across sexes for color choices and purchase behavior relationships.

Previous research has not revealed significant differences in color preferences between males and females. However, if color is presumed to be object categorized, then individual's color preferences could conceivably affect purchase behaviors with color differences being gender embedded.

Methodology

Subjects

Sixty four undergraduate subjects (32 black males, 32 black females), from two eastern universities voluntarily participated in the study as part of classroom exercises.

Pretest

A pre-test was administered to 12 non-sample member undergraduate volunteers who were participating in a cross-cultural seminar in international business. Pretest subjects first indicated whether or not they had purchased each of the 15 products within the last year or intended to purchase them in the near future. The items were diverse, ranging from clothing (personal item) to an apple (non-personal item), where neither brand loyalty nor gender differences in purchase behavior were expected. A ballpoint pen and a sweater were purchased (intended) by all pretest subjects and therefore were chosen for the study. Second, the students were asked to designate five product attributes that they consider important when purchasing a product. No rank order was indicated nor were any attributes presented to aid recall. The students were free to make their own judgments regarding perceived importance. The results indicated that price, quality, color and brand name were the most important attributes across each group.

Questionnaire

The experimental subjects reviewed the MFE profile on the first page of the questionnaire, where all of the attributes and their levels were displayed. Subjects next read that they would be shown 16 randomized permutations of these attributes for each of the two products: a plain, long sleeved sweater and a ballpoint pen. The subjects were then instructed to view a sample profile and to evaluate it by circling the number on the attendant nine point scale (1=least likely to buy to 9=most likely to buy) that best described their appraisal of that particular item and then to proceed with the randomized profiles for the sweater and pen. The next section of the questionnaire asked subjects to rank order the importance for them of the attributes price, brand, quality and color separately for the pen and the sweater and then to rank order in terms of general preference the colors used in the stimulus profiles. Subjects were then asked to name their favorite color in general as well as for a sweater and a ballpoint pen. Plus, their past purchase behavior concerning sweaters and pens was requested. These past purchase questions were identical in content and presentation for both products except for those concerning the price variable, where the price range for the sweater was [1] $1.00-$9.99 to [6] $ > $60.00 while that for a ballpoint pen was [1] $.01-$.99 to [6] > $5.00. In each case 'don't' and 'did

did not buy' responses were also available. Subjects were also asked the quantity (1 to 8) of the sweaters and ballpoint pens that they had purchased within the last year, the brand name of the most recent purchase (lesser known, well known), the quality (good,better,best), and its color. General socio-demographic questions were asked at the end of the questionnaire.

Results

For the pen Fig. 1(b), the major differences between subjects was that male utility scores were highest for a better (.39) quality rather than a best (.02) quality pen while the opposite was true for the females, who exhibited scores of better quality (.12) and best quality (.18). Cross-over effects (i.e. differences in the preference utility scores for different levels of the same attribute) were also evident for the color attribute levels. For males, the most to least preferred colors for the pen were blue (1.1), black (1.07), red (00) and yellow (-.45) and for the females they were blue (.66), black (.37), red (00) and yellow (-.23). The attribute levels for the sweater (i.e. low price, high quality and well known brand name), although different in magnitude, were similar across groups. The utilities for the color preferences of a sweater showed differences with males preferring blue (1.25), black (.95), red (00) and yellow (-.45), while females showed preferences for red (00), black (-.29), yellow (-.54) and blue (-.70). An analysis of the regression coefficients indicates differences across groups for the sweater ($F=24.31$, $p < .05$) and pen ($F=20.20$, $p < .05$). The R^2 results for the sweater (R^2_s) and pen (R^2_p) were ($R^2_s=.3432$) ($R^2_p=.3876$) across groups, for males ($R^2_s=.4101$) ($R^2_p=.3604$), and for females ($R^2_s=.3942$) ($R^2_p=.4682$).

FIGURE 1

Figure 1(a)
Sweater

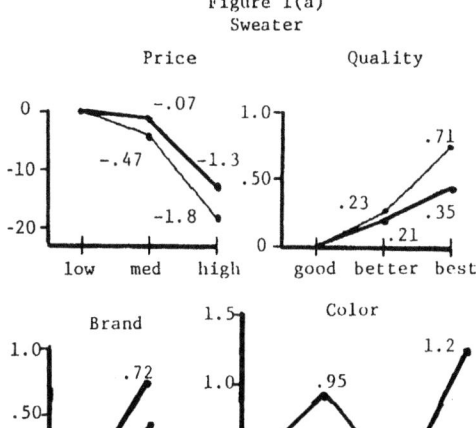

Males =
Females =

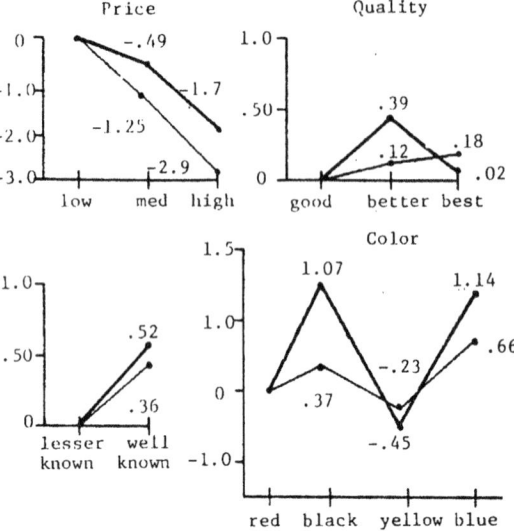

Figure 1(b)
Ballpoint Pen

TABLE 1

RELATIVE PERCEIVED IMPORTANCE OF PRICE, BRAND,
QUALITY AND COLOR ATTRIBUTES EXPRESSED AS
PERCENTAGES OF THE TOTAL UTILITY SCORES*

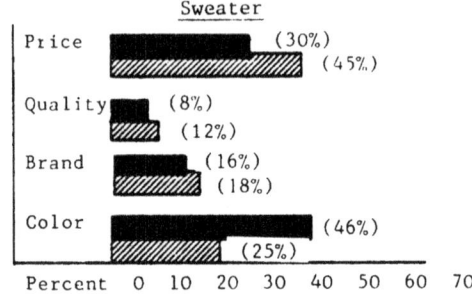

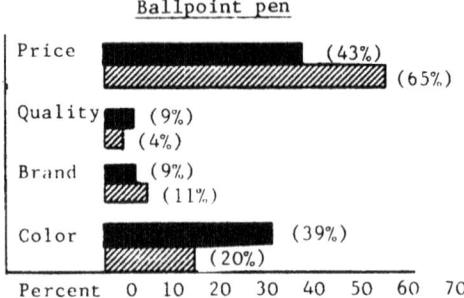

*Note: The perceived relative importance of
each attribute is calculated by taking the
difference between the highest and lowest betas
for each attribute, summing the differences and
then taking the individual range differences as
a percentage of the total differences in the
betas.

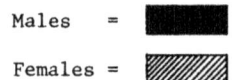

Males   =

Females =

The following results reflect the respondents'
most preferred choices of price, quality, brand
and color (i.e., they would be most likely to
buy the product given this configuration). The
results are derived from the utility scores
depicted in Figure 1(a)(b). For the sweater
[Fig. 1(a)], males most preferred combinations
were low price (00), best quality (.35), well
known brand (.72), and the color blue (1.2),
while femles' preferred a low price (00), best
quality (.71), well known brand (.47) and the
color red (00). The pen [Fig. 1(b)], preferences for males were a low price (00), better
quality (.39), well known brand (.36) and the
color blue (1.14), with females indicating
preferences of low price (00), best quality
(.18), well known brand (.52) and the color blue
(.66). In order to predict how the average
individual's overall utility score would deviate
from the "ideal" combination for a specific
product, merely substitute another utility score
for a different level of an attribute. For
example, the males' highest utility configuration
for a pen is (1.89). If the utilities for the
color blue (1.14) and low price (00) were substituted with the color black (1.07), and low
price (00), the difference in overall utility
would be negligible (.07). However, if yellow
(-.45) was substituted, the overall utility
would be considerably less vis-a-vis the ideal
configuration of the attribute levels. This
does not imply that the lesser valued configurations for the two products will never be purchased, since individuals in a choice setting
will make trade-offs in their decision processes
(e.g., the time required to search for a more
ideal alternative may be deemed too costly).
The color attribute levels had considerable
influence in the configurations. Namely,
subjects' choices showed considerable differences
in color preferences across sexes for the sweater
(personal item) but not for the pen (impersonal
item), implying that the color level preference
is product specific.

Table 1 shows the results of the perceived relative importance of each attribute across sexes.
Black males ordered the sweater attributes, from
most to least important, as color, price, brand
and then quality. For the pen, their corresponding importance ratings were price, then color,
with brand name and quality of equal importance.
For black females, however, the sweater ordering
was price, color, brand and quality and for the
pen it was price, color, brand and then quality.
With the exception of the sweater results for
males, the price criterion overcame the other
attributes for blacks in general, with color
perceived as more important than quality or
brand and the brand attribute consistently more
important than quality for both product categories.

Color Choices and Purchase Behavior Results

Tests of differences were performed on the ranking importance of price, quality, and color for
the sweater and pen as well as the personal

preferences of the colors used in the study (i.e. red, blue, black, yellow) that were not associated with a specific product category. No differences were found for the sweater attributes, but the price attribute for the pen was significant ($z=1.88$, $p < .05$) which lends some support to the results shown in (Table 1) regarding perceived relative importance of the pen price. Differences were also evident across sexes for the colors red ($z=2.89$, $p < .05$), blue ($z=1.63$, $p < .10$), yellow ($z=2.03$, $p < .05$) and black ($z=2.89$, $p < .05$) thereby offering more credibility to the differences in the color utility levels. Interestingly, when respondents were asked to name their favorite color in general, using ten self-generated colors, (red, blue, black, yellow, green, orange, brown, grey, purple, white), no significant differences were evident, but when the categories were reduced to four colors (i.e. red, blue, black, yellow), the differences appear. Also, differences are shown across sexes in the relationships between past/intended purchase behaviors for a sweater and pen with differences in color preferences (using the ten self-generated colors) between males and females shown for their favorite color of pen ($z=1.65$, p .10) as well as the color of the last pen ($z=1.79$, $p < .05$) and sweater purchased ($z=2.03$, $p < .05$). To ascertain the existence of any relationships among the individuals' past purchase behavior variables (i.e. price, quality, quantity, brand and color), their favorite color in general, and favorite colors for a sweater and pen, Pearson correlations were performed on the variables. The results show that both males ($r=.47$, $p < .01$) and females ($r=.37$, $p <.05$) exhibited a direct relationship between their favorite color in general and their favorite color of sweater with males showing an inverse relationship ($r=.54$, $p < .05$) between the brand of sweater and the quantity of sweaters purchased. All subjects exhibited a direct moderate relationship between their favorite color and the color of the last sweater purchased ($r=.42$, $p < .01$). The results for the pen show direct relationships between their favorite color of pen and the color of the last pen purchased [males ($r=.50$, $p < .01$) females ($r=.49$, $p < .01$)], the favorite color of pen and the quantity of pens purchased [males ($r=.47$, $p < .01$)], females ($r=.40$, $p < .05$), and lastly, an inverse relationship for females ($r=.43$, $p < .05$) between the quality and quantity of pens purchased.

Discussion

The results indicate that color is a salient attribute when viewed in a multiattribute context with price, brand name and quality with the color attribute capable of rendering different products more or less attractive in an "ideal" setting with differences across sexes. Although it may be argued that the "ideal" choice preferences of the first three attributes are not reflective of a realistic choice situation, logic dictates that if a particular color for a product was perceived as unacceptable in this instance, then the importance of color would be more pronounced in a realistic decision setting where the "ideal" combinations may be few and far between.

Differences in the perceived relative importance of the four attributes were evident across sexes, for both products. Price was perceived as more important than color, with brand and quality utility scores nearly equal but perceived as considerably less important than color. In general, these results imply that the differences across sexes are gender embedded and product specific. The results for a favorite color, using the ten self-generated colors, lend support to previous studies which showed no significant differences across sexes for color (Birren 1978; Eysenck 1941; Garth 1931; Granger 1952; Sharpe 1964; Sloane 1968). This study also evidences support for the general preferences of males and females for red and blue as defined by (Garth and Eysenck) in Birren (1978). However, significant differences were found when ten colors were associated with product specific color preferences and past purchase behaviors adn when the number of color categories for general color preferences was reduced from ten to four (red, blue, black, yellow). Differences between males and females were also evident when the four colors were product specific.

Since the resultant differences in color preferences were markedly product oriented and gender embedded, the results also lend support for the theory that evaluative responses to color are object-category referenced and that these color preferences will vary from one object to another depending upon the individual's perception of the object and corresponding color preference for it (Osgood et al, 1957; Rosch et al, 1976; Slatter and Whitfield 1977; Whitfield 1984; Whitfield and Slatter 1978, 1979). The utility preferences across groups for the color black is an excellent example of an object-category evaluation. Heretofore, with the exception of Gotz and Gotz (1974b), black has consistently been shown to be the least preferred color among various cultural groups and across sexes. However, in this study, black possessed the second highest utility score for both a sweater and pen across both groups. Males significantly preferred black over yellow and red with a minimal utility difference between black and the most preferred color of blue for both products. Females showed a preference for black over blue and yellow with a minimal utility difference between black and red for the sweater but the pen results were identical to the color preference order exhibited by males. Preferences for the color yellow have been addressed in the past, results typically showing that yellow is less preferred than blue or red but more preferred than black (Staples 1932, Stimpson and Stimpson 1979). However, the results of this study indicate that yellow was the least preferred color in both product categories for males. For females, yellow was more preferred than blue, but less preferred than red or black for the sweater and the least preferred color for a pen. Clearly color preferences that are product specific yield different preferences as compared to color assessments that are not object categorized with gender embedded differences. That these differences have not surfaced in previous studies suggest that although an individual may possess a "favorite color" in an affective sense (i.e. one that is emotive and understood only by the individual), this color may or may not be object categorized. An individual, although preferring a particular color, may not perceive this color as "appropriate" for objects outside a specific group. Consequently, the individual may develop a "contingency" set of color preferences that are more representative of the "appropriateness" of different objects.

It is postulated that color may actually be an antecedent choice variable, with specific color preferences already having been "decided upon" by the individual before the other choice variables in the situation are evaluated. Although the correlations were weak in certain instances, it seems clear that an individual's overall favorite color may or may not be his or her favorite color for a particular object (e.g. sweater or pen). However, one's favorite color for a specific object is reflected in the color chosen the last time that object was purchased. Although color preferences associated with a personal item such as clothing may differ across sexes, an individual's favorite color will probably be more influential than other choice variables in a choice set.

The intent of this study was to develop a rudimentary framework that would provide some direction and structure for future research on color in a multiattribute setting. Although external validity is weak, particularly regarding the price, brand, name, quality and color relationships that were limited to two products, it is felt that a contribution to a conceptual framework has been achieved in that the color preference results were able to demonstrate the gender embedded differences, some inferences were made regarding the object categorization process and the question of color as an "antecedent choice" variable has evolved.

Although residual analysis indicates that a linear model is appropriate, the low R^2 values suggest that a main effects model does not capture the interactions suspectedly present among the attributes and considerable variation needs to be examined. It is also suggested that multidimensional scaling techniques be employed in a future study since these techniques are able to depict specific product preferences as well as segmentation clusters in a more efficient manner. Future conjoint measurement research should examine the impact of specific monetary values assigned to price, use actual or contrived brand names, and test a broader spectrum of colors, across a broader range of products in order to refine the relationships that have been discussed here. It is posited that the results of this study have more implications for multiattribute models of price, brand, quality and color. More importantly, this study raises several questions regarding the categorization and formulation of color preferences and their subsequent effects on choice behavior. This study has attempted to examine the salience of color in a multiattribute

model with moderate success, in that associations are evident. However, the strength of the relationships suggests that further research is required in order to define what may be termed an "antecedent color-choice model". How important are individual's predetermined color preferences and what influence do they have on the importance of the price, quality, brand and color attributes for a specific product? Are there differences across other ethnic groups and are these differences culturally and/or gender embedded?

The results of this study have provided a framework that establishes association and influence among the attributes examined as well as some support for existing interdisciplinary hypotheses on color preferences and color-object categorizations. By augmenting the knowledge of the price, quality, brand and color relationships, another measure has been contributed that helps shed light on choice differences between black males and females, thereby differentiating and refining the market preference structures of each group.

References

Adams, F.M. and Osgood, C.E. (1973), "A cross cultural study of the effective meaning of color." Journal of Cross Cultural Psychology 4, 135-156.

Alpert, M.I. (1971), "Identification of determinant attributes a comparison of methods." Journal of Marketing Research 8 (May) 184-191.

Bellizzi, J.A., Crowley, A.E. and Hasty, R.W. (1983), "The effects of color in store design." Journal of Retailing 59 (Spring) 21-45.

Bettman, J. (1979), "Memory factors is consumer choice: a review." Journal of Marketing 43 (Spring) 37-53.

Birren, F. (1961), Color psychology and color therapy. New York: University Books.

_____(1963), Color. New York: University Books.

_____(1978), Color and human response. New YOrk: Van Nostrand Reinhold.

Burnham, R.W., Hanes, R.M. and Bartleson, J.C. (1963), Color: a guide to basic facts and concepts. New York: John Wiley.

Cheskin, L. (1948), Colors. New York: Liveright.

Chougourian, A. (1968), "Color preferences: a cross sectional study." Perceptual and Motor Skills 26, 1203-1206.

Color it right and it will sell. (1980), Chemical Week (September) 33-36.

Conjoint Designer. (1986), New York: Bretton Clark, Inc.

Doehlert, D.H. (1968), "Similarity and preferences mapping: a color example." in Proceedings of the Fall Conference, Chicago: American Marketing Association.

Eysenck, H.J. (1941), "A critical and experimental study of color preferences." American Journal of Psychology 54, 385-394.

Gotz, K.O. and Gotz, K. (1974), "Color preferences of art students." Perceptual and Motor Skills 38, 63-70.

Green, P.E. (1974), "On the design of choice experiments involving multifactor alternatives." Journal of Consumer Research 1 (September) 61-68.

_____Carroll, D.J. and Carmone, F.J. Jr. (1978), "Some new types of fractional factorial designs for marketing experiments." in Research in Marketing 1, J.N. Sheth, ed. Greenwich: JAI Press.

_____and Rao, V. (1971), "Conjoint measurement and qualifying judgmental data." Journal of Marketing Research, 8 (August) 355-363.

_____and Srinivasin, V. (1978), "Conjoint analysis in consumer research: issues and outlook." Journal of Consumer Research 5 (September) 103-123.

Haines, G. (1966), "A study of why people purchase new products." in R.M. Hass, ed. Science, Technology and Marketing. Chicago: American Marketing Association, 665-685.

Hulbert, J. (1975), "Information processing capacity and attitude measurement." Journal of Marketing Research, 12 (February) 104-106.

Jacoby, J. (1984), "Perspectives on information overload." Journal of Consumer Research, 1 (March) 432-43.

Lonial, S.C. and Van Auken, S. (1982), "Perception and preference congruency: a color replication study." Decision Sciences, 13 (January) 60-70.

Malhotra, N. (1982), "Information overload and consumer decision making." Journal of Consumer Research, 9 (March) 419-430.

Monroe, K.B. (1984), "Theoretical and methodological developments in pricing." in Thomas C Kinnear (ed). Advances in Consumer Research XI Provo Utah: Association for Consumer Research 636-37.

Munsell, A.H. (1973), Munsell book of color. Baltimore: Kollmorgen Corp.

Osgood, E.C., Suci, G. and Tannenbaum, P. (1957), The measurement of meaning. Urbana, Ill.: University of Illinois Press.

Rosch, E. and Mervis, C.B., Gray, W.D., Johnson, P.M. and Boyes-Bream, P. (1976), "Basic objects in natural categories." Cognitive Psychology 7, 573-605.

Schindler, P. (1986), "Color and contrast in magazine advertising." Psychology and Marketing, 3 (Summer) 69-78.

Sharpe, D.T. (1974), The psychology of color and design. Chicago: Nelson-Hall.

Slatter, P.E. and Whitfield, T.W.A. (1977), "Room function and appropriateness and color." Perceptual and Motor Skills, 45, 1068-1070.

Sloan, P. (1968), Color: basic principles and new directions. New York: Reinhold.

Staples, R. (1932), "The responses of infants to color." Experimental Psychology, 15, 119-141.

Stimpson, D.V. and Stimpson, M. (1979), "Relation of personality characteristics and color preferences." Perceptual and Motor Skills, 49, 60-62.

Whitfield, T.W.A. (1984), "Individual differences in evaluation of architectural colour: categorization effects." Perceptual and Motor Skills, 59, 183-186.

EVALUATION OF CLOTHING COLOR PREFERENCES: A COMPARISON OF ASIAN AND WHITE CONSUMERS

Margaret Rucker, Yong-Ju Kim and Helene Ho, University of California at Davis

Data on United States apparel consumption indicate it is a major market, accounting for over 50 billion dollars per year in consumer expenditures, according to the American Apparel Manufacturers Association. Industry experience as well as empirical research indicate that color is one of the more important factors affecting salability of garments at retail.

Previous research suggests that cultural heritage and ethnic identification are related to clothing color preferences. However, this research is limited and largely focused on black consumers. Research on other minorities, such as Hispanics and Asians would be useful in determining how to best meet the needs of these expanding markets.

The present study was designed to determine whether ethnic identity was related to clothing color preference for one type of apparel, female sleepwear. To assess the effect of context on these preferences, color ratings were requested for both general use and a special situation. Purchase for a wedding trousseau was selected as the special situation since trade data indicate that this market is experiencing a revival. If preferences for wedding wear were found to differ from preferences for general wear, this fact would have obvious implications for meeting the needs of this developing market. Furthermore, consumer research has largely ignored ritualized activities and events in spite of evidence that these are frequent and important components of human experience. Based on Rook's analysis of the relationship between ritual vitality and prescription of artifactual consumption, it was hypothesized that cultural norms associated with weddings would decrease differences in preference that might ordinarily be found between people in different ethnic groups.

Subjects for this study were 71 female university students who volunteered to participate in a study of color preferences. Of these, 50 indicated White as their ethnic identity and 21 checked Asian. Analysis of the subjects by major indicated that there was a good cross-section of the general university population.

Selection of colors was based on the Cromarama® color wheel cross-referenced with the Pantone® professional color system. Eight hues, a gray and a brown were chosen along with the corresponding lightest tint, medium tint, and medium shade. Squares of each color were affixed to a questionnaire and rated by each subject once as to preference for inclusion in a trousseau and again as to preference for lingerie for general use. Ratings were made on a seven-point scale ranging from like very much to dislike very much.

Stepwise discriminant analysis was used to determine whether color preferences differed by ethnic identity. Separate analyses were run for the light tints, medium tints, hues and shades. Rank order correlations were computed to determine whether, within each ethnic group, the order of preference was different for weddings compared to general use.

The stepwise discriminant analyses of ratings for a wedding trousseau indicated that the two ethnic groups could be differentiated on the basis of preference for tints but not hues or shades. Among the lightest tints, preferences for pale pink provided for a significant differentiation between Whites and Asians with Asians indicating a higher preference. Univariate analyses indicated that Asians also showed a higher average preference for pale orange and pale purple, but these latter values did not add significant information to the multivariate analysis. With respect to medium tints, preference for orange differentiated between the two groups, with Asians having higher average ratings. The univariate analyses indicated that the value between red and purple (rose) was also rated higher by Asians. These findings suggest that some segmentation of the trousseau market by ethnic identity may be useful, although similarities in preference are much more in evidence than differences. The similarities with respect to this special situation suggest that the normative values associated with a cultural ritual may be related to small variations in preferences for the regalia associated with that ritual.

More significant differences were found with respect to preferences for general use. Asians gave significantly higher ratings to the two tints and hue for brown. For the lightest tints, their higher average preference for pink added significant information to the multivariate prediction equation. With respect to shades, Asians gave significantly higher average ratings to yellow. The univariate analyses indicated that ratings of the tints of orange, rose, purple, green and a medium gray also were significantly higher for Asians compared to Whites. These data suggest that for the general use market, it may be more important to segment on the basis of ethnic identity, especially with respect to the tints.

A comparison of trousseau ratings with general use ratings within ethnic groups suggested that both Asians and Whites were consistent in the order in which they preferred different colors. For Asians, the Spearman Rank-Order Correlation Coefficient was .95 (p < .001) and for Whites, it was .93 (p < .001). These data suggest that once the market has been segmented by ethnic identity, having separate stock plans for general versus wedding wear, at least in terms of color, may not be worth the effort.

(References available upon request.)

A STUDY OF HISPANIC NEW CAR BUYERS[1]

Joel Saegert, The University of Texas at San Antonio,
Robert J. Hoover, Corpus Christi State University,
and
Marye Tharp Hilger, The University of Texas at Austin

Introduction

Although a number of studies designed to determine distinctive characteristics of Hispanic shoppers have recently been reported (e.g., Deshpande, Hoyer & Donthu, 1986; Saegert, Hoover & Hilger, 1985; Wilkes & Valencia, 1986), they have chiefly focused on consumption of non-durable products. It is certainly true that Hispanics must also be said to constitute an appreciable market for durable-goods products, and it would seem important to attempt to discover what characteristics distinguish Hispanics from non-Hispanics in durable goods purchasing. This study surveyed Hispanics who had recently purchased a new automobile, and asked questions concerning search behavior, expectations, make of car purchased, and satisfaction with the purchase. Earlier work has raised the issue of whether differences between Hispanics and non-Hispanics are attributable to socioeconomic factors rather than cultural differences. In this case, since Hispanics who can afford to purchase a new car have at least some purchasing power, such a study could point to true cultural characteristics of Hispanic buyers.

We formulated several research hypotheses about Hispanic consumer behavior based on an earlier review of literature about Hispanic consumer behavior (Saegert and Hoover, 1985). For example, several studies have identified "familiarity" as a variable which characterizes Hispanic purchase patterns (e.g., Sturdivant 1969; Saegert, et al., 1985). That is, Hispanics are said to be drawn to products and stores which are familiar to them, rather than to those which are unknown. Such an idea would lead to the prediction, for example, that Hispanics might prefer to buy cars which are domestically produced, rather than those which are imported. Another hypothesis which comes from the notion that Hispanics are generally more "conservative" in shopping is that Hispanic consumers will have more extensive search behaviors than non-Hispanics; that is, they may seek advice of a greater number of other individuals, such as family members, or other information sources prior to purchasing. Similarly, they may shop for their purchase at a greater number of dealers than non-Hispanics.

Finally, it is possible that Hispanics may have different experiences with the actual purchase process. For example, they may be more likely to perceive that sales representatives are aggressive in the sales dyad than non-Hispanics. The study attempted to address such questions through a questionnaire sent to recent new car purchasers, both Hispanic and non-Hispanic.

[1] The authors express thanks to Corpus Christi State Univ. for project support.

Method

A questionnaire was mailed to recent purchasers of new automobiles in the Corpus Christi, Texas vicinity; this city is located in an area of South Texas which is greater than 50% Hispanic, and which is approximately 150 miles away from the nearest large city. It was thus considered a good example of a community which has a high incidence of purchase by Hispanics who are limited to the local community for purchase opportunities.

The sample was drawn from the county records of new car purchases and included 1,000 Hispanic surname and 500 non-Hispanic surname individuals. The over-sampling of Hispanics was considered necessary in light of earlier work (Saegert and Benitez, 1984) which indicated a low survey response rate from Hispanic consumers. A total of 169 (16.9%) responses were received from the Hispanic surname sample while 171 (34.2%) of the non-Hispanics (Anglos) responded. Nearly all of the respondents indicated that they had indeed purchased a new car within the past month.

Comparisons were made on the basis of self-classification of ethnic background, rather than surname. However, there was a close correspondence between these two designators. Respondents who classified themselves as Black, Oriental or Other were excluded from the analyses. In addition, the demographic variable of education level was used as a surrogate for socioeconomic status and was included in factorial analyses of the dependent variables of the study.

Results

An obvious first difference between the two sets of respondents was their demographic characteristics. Table 1 shows that the Hispanics in

TABLE 1

DEMOGRAPHICS OF THE SAMPLE

	Anglo	Hispanic	p
AGE			
Under 30	23.4	52.7	
31-50	44.4	37.3	
51 or over	32.2	10.1	.001
MARITAL STATUS			
Single	14.0	25.6	
Married	70.2	63.1	
Divor./Wid.	15.8	11.3	.05
EDUCATION			
No College	21.1	37.3	
Some College	32.2	31.4	
Col. Grad	46.8	31.4	.001

the sample were relatively younger, more likely to be single than married, and of lower education level than the Anglo respondents. In spite of this, however, the fact that nearly two-thirds of the Hispanic respondents have at least some college education, does seem to indicate that the Hispanic sample is of at least middle socioeconomic status.

Other data suggest (Table 2), however, that the Hispanics in the sample are relatively inexperienced in car-buying, compared to the Anglos; for example, on a question concerning the perceived importance of a "trade-in" in the purchase, nearly half of the Hispanics (44.6%) indicated that they had not traded in another car, compared to only about a third (32.8%) for the Anglos (comparisons by Pearson Chi Square). In addition, the Hispanics seems to have picked their new car from a smaller "evoked set," consisting most characteristically (54.4%) of only one other alternative, compared to two or more alternatives for the Anglo buyers.

TABLE 2

TRADE-IN AND ALTERNATIVE CONSIDERED
(Percents)

	Anglo	Hispanic	p
How important was trade-in?			
Not impt.	11.7	01.8	
Somewhat impt.	24.0	19.1	
Very impt.	31.6	34.5	
No trade	32.8	44.6	.001
How Many Alternatives?			
None	30.4	21.3	
One	31.6	54.4	
Two	22.8	16.0	
Three or More	15.2	08.3	.001

Such inexperience may have lead to a lower sense of self-confidence in the buying situation. This idea is supported by the data in Table 3

TABLE 3

CONFIDENCE IN CAR-BUYING
Scale means (std. dev. in parentheses)

	Anglo	Hispanic	p
How difficult to make up mind?	2.1 (1.1)	2.5 (1.2)	.003
How confident about which car?	1.8 (1.9)	2.1 (1.0)	.004
Expectations (low to high)	4.3 (0.8)	4.0 (0.9)	.05
How likely same decision?	4.4 (2.8)	3.6 (3.0)	.001

which show that Hispanics had a significantly more difficult time making up their minds about their purchase (p=.003), and that they were significantly less confident about their selection after it had been made (p=.004, comparisons by Analysis of Variance). Moreover, they indicated that they had lower expectations about the car in the first place (p=.05), and that they were less likely to make the same decision, even though they had only recently made their purchase selection (p<.001).

If Hispanics are less confident about buying a new car, and if they reflect a cultural conservatism in purchasing, they might be expected to engage in more extensive search behavior than Anglos, prior to making their purchase. Table 4 shows that this was not the case: Hispanics did

TABLE 4

SEARCH VARIABLES
Scale means (std. deviations)

	Anglo	Hispanic	p
How many dealers?	3.2 (1.7)	3.0 (1.6)	ns
How much time shopping?	3.2 (2.0)	3.4 (2.0)	ns
How many info. sources?	1.8 (1.1)	1.8 (1.2)	ns
How many other people?	2.6 (1.5)	2.8 (1.5)	ns

---

not differ from Anglos in the number of dealers visited, amount of time spent shopping, number of information sources sought, or number of other people consulted before purchase. In addition, Table 5 shows that there was no difference between the two groups in degree of satisfaction with the purchase made.

TABLE 5

SATISFACTION WITH PURCHASE
Means (std. deviations)

	Anglo	Hispanic	p
How satisfied with purchase?	9.2 (1.0)	9.0 (1.5)	ns
How good a deal did you get?	4.1 (0.8)	4.0 (1.1)	ns

Another prediction which follows from the hypothesis that Hispanics are more conservative than non-Hispanics in car-buying is that Hispanics may be drawn to domestically produced products; Table 6 shows that there was no greater likelihood that Hispanics would buy domestic cars than Anglos. Thus, Hispanics seems to have been very similar to the Anglo respondents in their purchase behavior for automobiles.

TABLE 6

MAKE OF CAR PURCHASED
(Percents)

	Anglo	Hispanic	p
General Motors	42.0	41.8	
Ford	18.9	12.3	
Chrysler	4.7	7.0	
American Motors	2.4	0.6	
Japanese	23.1	21.6	
European	3.5	4.7	
No Response	5.3	12.3	ns

In all of the above analyses, education level was included as a factorial variable; however, in only on case out of 10 comparisons was a significant, was a significant interaction between ethnic group and education indicated. This interaction was such that for Anglo respondents, "expectations of purchase satisfaction" increased as education level increased, while expectations remained relatively constant across education levels for the Hispanic respondents. In other words, the interaction did not suggest variation in expectations as a function of socioeconomic level for Hispanics, even though it did for Anglos.

Finally, an indication of a propensity by Hispanics to be drawn to familiar aspects of a purchase situation was noticed in a comparison of the ethnicity of the salesperson from whom respondents bought their new cars. The top of Table 7 shows that Hispanics bought their cars from a Hispanic salesperson 55% of the time, even though nearly two-thirds of the salespersons represented in the survey were Anglos. Thus, there appears to be a propensity for Hispanics to buy their cars from other Hispanics. The reason for this phenomenon is not known, because it is impossible to ascertain from the questionnaire, whether the car buyers chose their salespersons themselves or whether the salesperson is assigned to customers by the

TABLE 7

ETHNICITY OF SALESPERSON
(Percents)

| | Salesperson Ethnicity | | | |
	Anglo	Hispanic	Total	p
Customer Ethnicity				
Corpus Christi Sample				
Anglo	81.6	44.8	63.7	
Hispanic	18.4	55.2	36.3	.001
San Antonio Sample				
Anglo	70.0	45.8	49.3	
Hispanic	30.0	54.2	50.7	.001

automobile retailer. Follow-up interviews with representatives of several retail showrooms suggest that customers are assigned to salesmen (95% of the salespersons were men) on an "arrival" basis, rather than according to a plan to match salesmen with customers on ethnicity.

Of course, it can be pointed out that a similar tendency, to buy a car from a salesman of the same ethnic group as the customer, was observed among the Anglo sample; that is, the phenomenon is certainly not idiosyncratic to Hispanics. Nevertheless, the overall effect can be seen to have profound implications for sales strategy for auto retailers, namely, that customers tend to "gravitate" to members of their own ethnic group in car sales situations.

To further investigate the propensity for Hispanics customers to have bought their cars from Hispanic salespersons was not specific to the particular area sampled or the survey method used, a follow-up study was conducted in another city with high Hispanic representation, San Antonio, Texas. In this case, the data were collected via telephone from persons listed in county records as having purchased a car in the past two weeks. An equal number of Hispanic and non-Hispanic surname buyers were interviewed. The results replicated the phenomenon from the first study exactly.

Discussion

While the results of this survey are far from conclusive, some conclusions can be made about Hispanic new car buyers which may have strategic implications. The most telling result was that the Hispanic customers in the study were different demographically from the Anglos: they tended to be younger, single, and of somewhat lower education level. Consistent with this, the data suggested that Hispanic car buyers may have been buying their first new car more often than their Anglo counterparts, given their lower propensity to trade in an older car for their purchase, and their lower confidence in their choice. However, expectations about Hispanic search behavior were not supported, nor did the Hispanics express lower satisfaction with their purchases. Moreover, Hispanics were no more likely to purchase domestic car makes than Anglos. In fact, it could be argued that the car buying process, as engaged in by the Hispanics, was essentially similar to that of the Anglo customers. Such a result could be taken as argument that there is little basis for special marketing effort toward Hispanics as a target market for automobiles, other than as young, single, lower socioeconomic consumers.

Perhaps the most interesting datum of the study was the discovery that Hispanic (and Anglo) customers in the study tended to have bought their cars from salespersons of their own ethnic group. While the reason for such an effect remains unexplained, its consistent demonstration suggests that it may be useful to include a matching strategy in sales efforts of auto retailers. Of course, the critical effect would be to show that customers who have an a salesman of the same ethnic background are in fact more likely to make a purchase, but this remains to be demonstrated. It would not be inconsistent with the theory that similarity in the customer-salesperson dyad leads to greater likelihood of purchase.

References

Deshpande, Rohit, Hoyer, Wayne D., and Donthu, N. (1986) "The Intensity of Ethnic Affiliation," Journal of Consumer Research, 13 (September) 214-220.

Saegert, Joel and Benitez, Patti (1983) "Response Rates to Mail Questionnaires in an Ethnic Minority Population," Proceedings of the Division of Consumer Psychology of the American Psychological Association, 132-135.

Saegert, Joel and Hoover, Robert J. (1985) "A Catalog of Hypotheses about Hispanic Consumers," Proceedings of the Division of Consumer Psychology of the American Psychological Association, 56-61.

Saegert, Joel, Hoover, Robert J., and Hilger, Marye Tharp (1985) "Characteristics of Mexican American Consumers," Journal of Consumer Research 12 (June) 104-109.

Sturdivant, Frederick D. (1969) "Business and the Mexican-American Community," California Management Review 11 (Spring) 73-80.

Wilkes, Robert E. and Valencia, Humberto (1986) "Shopping Orientations of Mexican-Americans," Proceedings of the American Marketing Association, 26-31.

PERCEPTION OF HEALTH CARE SERVICES AMONG BLACK, HISPANIC AND WHITE CONSUMERS

Benjamin Sackmary, University of Hartford
E. Marie Wilson, Connecticut Department of Health Services

Abstract

This paper compares black, Hispanic and white consumer attitudes toward three types of health care services: prehospital emergency medical services, women's health care services and obstetrical services. Research results from two consumer surveys indicate significant differences across the three consumer groups in importance of convenience factors such as location and office hours. There are also variations in interest in women's health care services and hospital obstetrical services. Results suggest that health care services for minorities require marketing programs built on perceptions and specific needs of these markets segments.

INTRODUCTION

Neglect of Minorities in Marketing

The field of health care services marketing has grown rapidly during the past decade. However, much of the research has focussed on broad issues relating to adoption of marketing, marketing strategies for health care organizations and development of specialized marketing techniques appropriate to the health field. There has been little discussion or research on marketing health care to minority market segments. Similarly, there has been little discussion of differences among minority and majority consumers in perception of health care services.

Such neglect of minorities is unfortunate for the field of marketing. This is especially true for health care areas where minorities may be at greater risk than whites. In addition, lack of knowledge about consumer behavior and attitudes toward health services among minorities can impede program development and may impact the success of health promotion and health care programs.

Objectives

This paper presents a comparison of black, white and Hispanic consumer attitudes toward three types of health care services: obstetrical services, women's health care and prehospital emergency medical services (EMS). The intent is to identify areas of similarity and difference among the three consumer groups and to apply these results in recommendations for development of health care programs for minority populations.

Obstetrical service, women's health care and EMS represent very different types of health care services. Selection of obstetrical service and women's health care entails a high-involvement decision process with considerable opportunity for consumer information search and evaluation. The consumer of emergency medical services is usually in serious distress or is helping a person in distress. While EMS usage is clearly a high-involvement situation (i.e., life threatening), the time for decision making is extremely brief (or should be!). Comparison of attitudes toward the different services should offer some insight into factors of importance in decision making by the three consumer groups.

Minorities As Consumers

A review of the research literature shows that there have been studies of a number of aspects of minority consumer behavior and marketing to minorities. Brief bibliographies of marketing articles and publications on black and Hispanic consumer behavior can be found in Assael (1987, p. 330-350) and Engel et al (1985, p. 410-423). During the past few years, there have been relatively few journal articles on minority consumer behavior but there have been a number of publications in proceedings. In general, there is limited continuity in the literature, few theoretical or conceptual linkages across studies and no clear focus on a research agenda.

The broad range of topics in the recent literature about black consumer behavior include: advertising imagery (Johnson 1982); interest in fashion (Tat 1982); psychographics (Stamps 1986); use of direct marketing (Friedman et al 1987); buyer behavior (Sexton 1972); food shopping patterns (Solomon and Bush 1980); marketing performing arts (Robbins and Robbins 1982); and radio usage (Glasser and Metzger 1975).

Studies of the Hispanic consumer are equally diverse and cover the following topics: segmentation strategies (Loudon and Simpson 1982); use of radio (O'Guinn and Meyer 1983/4); misuse of language and cross-cultural marketing blunders (Valencia 1983/4); market characteristics (Cervantes 1980); buyer behavior (Hoyer and Deshpande 1982); shopping behavior (Valencia and Bellenger 1982); and media usage and communication strategy (Guernica 1982).

Throughout the literature on minority consumer behavior, there are few references to health-oriented behavior among minorities or use of health care services. In this regard, the research results presented in this study can be considered an exploratory inquiry with implications for health care marketing to black and Hispanic consumers.

Emergency Medical Services

EMS is a statewide medical system for providing medical care to seriously injured and critically ill persons in need of rapid and specialized treatment. It is a high-involvement service dealing with life-threatening circumstances.

Research on consumer decision processes in serious medical situations shows that there is often delay and resistance to the use of EMS. That is, when faced with serious medical symptoms, many consumers attempt "denial" of symptoms and delay entry into the system (Sackmary 1986).

The decision to call an ambulance when confronted with a medical emergency is influenced directly by consumer perception of components of the EMS system. The more favorable the evaluation of aspects of EMS, the more likely a consumer is to take appropriate action in life-threatening medical situations. In this paper, a comparison of black, white and Hispanic consumer perception of EMS will serve as an indicator of the need for a differential marketing approach to minorities about EMS and usage of the system.

Obstetrical Services and Women's Health Care

Obstetric services are a high-involvement type of service. Selection of a physician and a hospital for childbirth may entail extended search behavior and a lengthy decision process. In addition, there are now many options for childbirth including length of stay, preparatory education classes, type of birthing facility and use of medication (Kotler and Clarke 1987).

As with EMS, there are few studies of consumer attitudes toward obstetrical services or women's health care services. In fact, the introduction of marketing into the area of obstetrical services is still very recent. Much of the literature takes an applied approach with a focus on strategies for integrating marketing into obstetrical services and women's health care programs (MacStravic 1986; Dearing et al 1987; Lee 1980; Hardy and Ekbladh 1979).

There does appear to be a general pattern of consumer satisfaction with obstetrical services. Danko and Boucher (1985) examined consumer attitudes and found little difference in patient evaluation of obstetrical services at three competitive hospitals. After childbirth, the primary determinants of service satisfaction, as measured by intention of future usage of the hospital, are quality of nursing care and concern for the patient (Anderson 1982). A literature search was unsuccessful in locating research or analysis on ethnic and/or racial differences in perception of or response to obstetrical and women's health services.

The research results discussed in this paper derive from two random samples, marketing research telephone surveys. Both survey research efforts had a broader intention than documenting minority consumer behavior. The results presented in this paper are based on a secondary analysis of the databases for these surveys.

EMS Survey

The EMS survey was conducted during November of 1985 for a state department of health. The EMS survey consists of 604 completed telephone interviews. A custom computer program was used for random selection of telephone exchanges and phone numbers. Only residences are included in the sample. A comparison of the sample with characteristics of the state population showed no significant variations in demographic characteristics between the sample and population. Survey results are considered representative of state residents.

The minority sample is roughly proportionate to representation in the state population. The EMS sample includes 40 blacks, 20 Hispanics and 525 whites. The number of minority respondents is not large and care should be taken in drawing conclusions based on this sample size.

Obstetrical/Women's Health Survey

The data are a combination two types of samples: a systematic sample from a listing of women who had live births during a recent twelve month period at a large urban hospital and a random digit dialing survey of women within the Hartford metropolitan area. The women on the hospital list were also contacted by telephone. The interviews covered a number of health-related topics including obstetrical services and interest in women's health services. A comparison of the two sample sources shows no significant differences in terms of attitude toward health care matters. The sample of 541 respondents includes 52 blacks, 33 Hispanics and 449 whites.

Results

Emergency Medical Services

Table 1 indicates consumer response to a series of questions about hypothetical medical emergencies involving serious illnesses such as a facial burn or heart attack. Responses were categorized in terms of their appropriateness for the symptoms. Overall, whites are the most likely to make a correct choice in contacting EMS (57%), followed by blacks (51%) and then Hispanics (40%). The most significant feature of this table is that, regardless of the severity of the symptoms, a substantial percentage of consumers will not contact EMS at all. Nonuse of EMS is not related to proximity to a hospital. This resistance to the use of medical services, usually involving a denial of the significance of symptoms, is a common phenomenon in the health care field.

Table 2 deals with the related issue of cost of ambulance service. The Hispanic consumers are the most likely to perceive the service as extremely or very expensive (60%) followed closely by the black consumers (58%). Whites are more moderate in their assessment of the cost of ambulance service with only 40% rating the service as at least very costly. The cost question is important as willingness to use EMS in an emergency is related to the perception of service cost. Based on Tables 1 and 2, minorities are at higher risk in medical emergencies than whites.

Table 1
Response to Medical Symptoms*

	Did not call EMS for any medical symptoms	Incorrect use of EMS	Correct use of EMS	Total
Black	43	6	51	100%
Hispanic	53	7	40	100%
White	38	5	57	100%

*Chi Square significant at the .01 level.

Table 2
Perceived Cost of Using an Ambulance*

	Extremely costly	Very costly	Some-what costly	Not very costly	Not at all costly	Total
Black	22	36	25	17	0	100%
Hispanic	33	27	7	7	26	100%
White	15	25	37	8	15	100%

*Chi Square significant at the .01 level.

Respondents were also asked to evaluate specific aspects of the EMS program in their own community. A series of seven questions using a five point rating scale with values from excellent to poor was applied to assess consumer perception of EMS components. The results are presented in Table 3. These mean ratings of service features are important indicators. A positive evaluation can directly influence appropriate use of EMS.

There are no statistical differences among the three groups and there are few consistent variations in ratings. It is concluded that there is no systematic relation between ethnic/racial background and perception of EMS.

Table 3
Evaluation of Ambulance Service in Community

	Mean response*				
	Black	Hispanic	White	F-value	Signi-ficance
Ambulance response time in your town	2.32	2.29	2.24	1.265	.8812
Ambulance crew training	2.18	2.00	2.08	.221	.8014
Ambulance equipment	2.07	2.13	2.11	.028	.9727
Concern of ambulance crews for victims	2.17	1.94	2.00	.478	.6203
Treatment of victims by ambulance crews	2.19	1.94	2.04	.506	.6031
Overall quality of ambulance service in your town	2.28	2.47	2.15	1.132	.3232
Ability of ambulance in your town to get a victim to the hospital quickly	2.32	2.39	2.09	1.638	.1955

*Mean on a five point scale where "1" = excellent and "5" = poor.

Additional data analysis of attitudes of recent users of ambulance service confirm this lack of relationship. No significant difference was found between black, white and Hispanic recent ambulance users in their ratings of either ambulance crews or hospital emergency departments.

Obstetrics and Women's Health

Table 4 presents mean importance ratings of factors in the selection of a doctor or hospital for childbirth. Blacks, whites and Hispanics are in agreement about the importance of reputation in selecting a doctor. The major difference is that black and Hispanic women place a much higher level of importance on convenience of the doctor's location, convenient office hours and ease of getting an appointment.

This concern with location may relate to problems of mobility, difficulty in obtaining childcare services, cost of travel, problems with leaving work to see a doctor or a desire to have a local physician. In any case, locational convenience is a more important factor for minority women than for whites.

With regard to selecting a hospital for childbirth, the largest variation in importance ratings is for location. Blacks and Hispanics rate hospital location as significantly more important than white females. All three groups are in agreement about the importance of reputation in selection of a hospital.

The groups differ on the importance of staff quality and variety of services offered by the hospital. Whites and blacks are more concerned with staff quality than Hispanics and blacks appear to favor a multi-service hospital more than the other groups.

The respondents were asked how likely they are

to use specific women's health care services within the next 12 months. There are significant differences among the three groups for only three of the eight proposed services. Among women under age 40, whites have the lowest interest in family planning (12%) and Hispanics have the most interest (52%). Hispanics are also the most likely to make future use of obstetrical services (56%). The Hispanic group shows the most concerned with breast cancer screening (50%).

Blacks have the most interest in the medical information telephone line (40%), weight management (40%), fitness and stress management (43%) and sex counselling (15%). Whites are least likely to be interested in the proposed services for women.

Table 4

Importance of Factors in Selection of a Physician

and a Hospital for Childbirth

	Black	Hispanic	White	F-value	Signi-ficance
Importance of factors in selecting a physician					
Doctor's reputation	1.82	1.71	1.88	.632	.5319
Convenient location	2.28	2.14	2.66	5.493	.0044
Convenient office hours	1.85	2.11	2.62	13.622	.0000
Easy to get an appointment	1.78	1.93	2.30	7.451	.0007
Importance of factors in choosing a hospital for childbirth					
Location of hospital	1.92	2.04	2.45	6.819	.0012
Reputation of hospital	1.72	1.96	1.76	1.008	.3656
Variety of services	1.80	2.26	2.22	3.615	.0277
Quality of medical staff	1.49	1.81	1.47	3.149	.0439

Header over Black/Hispanic/White: Mean response*

*Mean response on a five point scale where "1" = extremely important and "5" = not at all important.

Discussion And Implications

There are both similarities and differences among white, black and Hispanic consumers in their perception of high-involvement health care services. The results of the two studies presented in this paper should dissuade health program planners and health services marketers from making easy generalities about the needs and interests of minority consumers. It appears that ethnicity operates in a subtle and selective manner in influencing attitudes toward and usage of services.

For example, whites, blacks and Hispanics may be equally concerned with certain factors such as reputation and quality of health service suppliers but they can differ greatly on the importance of location and convenience of service delivery. Black, Hispanic and white females share some interests in common for

health services for women but there are significant differences in concern with family planning, sex counselling and fitness programs. In contrast, the three groups are similar in their rating of local EMS service.

The most direct marketing management implications of these studies relate to distributional strategies for health care services. There seems to be a definite difference in concern about access to health services among blacks and Hispanics. In addition, differences in response to medical emergencies indicate a need for greater emphasis on correct use of emergency medical services among blacks and especially among Hispanics. Such information may have life saving significance to minority populations.

The development of health care programs for minorities should be based on a systematic effort at information collection through marketing research. Such information may have a preventive importance for minority consumers. It may also be of value for whites. With regard to breast cancer screening, results show that the Hispanic women were the most interested in the service. However, breast cancer "occurs most frequently among white women, with an incidence of 85 per 100,000 population, compared with 75 per 100,000 in black women and 48 per 100,000 in Hispanic women (Page 1985, p. 22)." In this instance, greater emphasis on white females may be needed in marketing programs.

In conclusion, effective health care marketing initiatives aimed at minority consumers are not likely to be totally different than programs for whites but they will have to be fine tuned for these specific market segments. It is strongly recommended that health care marketers avoid any stereotypes and search for real differences among white, black and Hispanic populations.

Table 5

Interest in Health Services for Women

	Black	Hispanic	White
Breast cancer screening	35	50	37
Medical information telephone line	40	36	36
Weight management program	40	25	23
Fitness/stress management*	43	14	29
Sex counselling*	15	11	3
Asked only of women under age 40			
Premenstrual syndrome clinic/support group	18	24	12
Obstetrical care	36	56	46
Family planning*	36	52	12

Header over Black/Hispanic/White: Percent who might use the service in the next 12 months

*Chi Square significant at the .05 level.

REFERENCES

Anderson, Douglas C. (1982), "The Satisfied Consumer: Service Return Behavior in the Hospital Obstetrics Market," Journal of Health Care Marketing, 2(Fall), 25-33.

Assael, Henry (1987), Consumer Behavior and Marketing Action, 3rd edition, Boston: Kent Publishing Company.

Cervantes, Fernando Javier (1980), "The Forgotten Consumers: The Mexican Americans," 1980 Educators' Conference Proceedings, Richard P. Bagozzi et al, eds., Chicago: American Marketing Association, 180-183.

Danko, William D. and David L. Boucher (1985), "Perspectives From Users of Obstetric Services: Implications for Providers," Health Marketing and Consumer Behavior, NY: The Haworth Press, 41-48.

Dearing, Ruthie H. et al (1987), Marketing Women's Health Care, Rockville, MD: Aspen Publications.

Engel, James F., Roger D. Blackwell and Paul W. Miniard (1986), Consumer Behavior, 5th edition,Chicago: The Dryden Press.

Friedman, Marshall M., Yacob Haile-Mariam and Charles S. Broadfeld (1987), "A Comparison of the Attitudes Toward and Use of Direct Marketing Channels by Blacks and Whites," in Jon M. Hawes, ed., Developments in Marketing Science, Vol. 10, Academy of Marketing Science, 96-100.

Glasser, Gerold J. and Gale D. Metzger (1975) "Radio Usage By Blacks," Journal of Advertising Research, 15(October), 39-45.

Guernica, Antonio (1982), Reaching the Hispanic Market Effectively, New York: McGraw-Hill.

Hardy, C. T. and Lamar Ekbladh (1979), "The Birth of a Service," Health Care Marketing: Issues and Trends, Philip D. Cooper, ed., Germantown, MD: Aspen Publications, 193-198.

Hoyer, Wayne D. and Rohit Deshpande (1982), "Cross-Cultural Influences on Buyer Behavior: The Impact of Hispanic Ethnicity," 1982 Educators' Conference Proceedings, Bruce J. Walker et al, eds., Chicago: American Marketing Association, 89-92.

Johnson, Elizabeth (1982), "Black Market Segmentation Based on Black as Well as White Symbols," in Vinay Kothari, ed., Developments in Marketing Science, Vol 5, Academy of Marketing Science, 82-86.

Kotler, Philip and Roberta N. Clarke (1987), Marketing for Health Care Organizations, Englewood Cliffs, NJ: Prentice-Hall.

Lee, John M. (1980), "Marketing Ensures Success of Maternity Care Program," Hospitals, (December), 91-94.

Loudon, David L. and Claude Simpson (1982), "The Hispanic Consumer Segment," in Vinay Kothari, ed., Developments in Marketing Science, Vol 5, Academy of Marketing Science, 104-108.

MacStravic, Robin S. (1986), "Relationship Marketing in Maternity Care," Journal of Hospital Marketing, 1(Fall/Winter), 115-123.

O'Guinn, Thomas C. and Timothy P. Meyer (1983/84), "Segmenting the Hispanic Market: The Use of Spanish Language Radio," Journal of Advertising Research, 23(December/January), 9-16.

Page, Harriet S. (1985), Cancer Rates and Risks, 3rd edition, Washington, D.C.: U. S. Department of Health and Human Services.

Robbins, John E. and Stephanie S. Robbins (1982), "Marketing the New Orleans Symphony to Blacks: A Strategic Analysis," A Spectrum of Contemporary Marketing Ideas, John H. Summey et al, eds., Charleston, S.C.: Southern Marketing Association, 234-237.

Sackmary, Benjamin (1986), "Service Selection in Serious Medical Situations: Implications for Marketing EMS," Creativity in Services Marketing, M. Venkatesan et al, eds., Chicago: American Marketing Association, 58-62.

Sexton, Donald E. (1972), "Black Buyer Behavior," Journal of Marketing, 36(October), 36-39.

Solomon, Paul J. and Ronald F. Bush (1980), "Profiling the Food Shopping Patterns of Rural Low Income Blacks: A Cluster Analysis Apprach," 1980 Educators' Conference Proceedings, Richard P. Bagozzi et al, eds., Chicago: American Marketing Association, 488-491.

Stamps, Miriam B. (1986), "The Impact of Race, Social Class, and Demographics on Psychographic Variables," Marketing in an Environment of Change, Robert L. King, ed., Charleston, S.C.: Southern Marketing Association, 48-52.

Tat, Peter K. (1982), "An Examination of Income Differentials on Black Buyer Behavior of Fashions," in Vinay Kothari, ed., Developments in Marketing Science, Vol 5, Academy of Marketing Science, 139-142.

Valencia, Humberto (1983/84), "Point of View: Avoiding Hispanic Market Blunders," Journal of Advertising Research, 23(December-January), 19-22.

_____ and Danny N. Bellenger (1982), "Ethnic and Income Influences on Hispanic Shopping Behavior," A Spectrum of Contemporary Marketing Ideas, John H. Summey et al, eds., Charleston, S.C.: Southern Marketing Association, 190-194.

RACE AS AN INFLUENCE ON HEALTHCARE INFORMATION SOURCES AND PROVIDER USAGE BY THE ELDERLY

Don R. Rahtz, School of Business
College of William and Mary, Williamsburg, Virginia 23185

Rustan Kosenko, Ohio University, Athens, Ohio 45701

ABSTRACT

Using data generated from a sample of 752 elderly this research examines the influence of race (a dichotomy of white and black) on use of information sources and actual provider usage in the healthcare market. Results from oneway ANOVA's indicate that there are significant differences between blacks and whites on a number of variables. Blacks find information from television more helpful than do whites, have a much higher degree of direct mail healthcare information usage than do whites, believe the yellow pages offer useful information to a higher degree than do whites, and find newspapers a greater source of healthcare information than do whites. They also report a higher degree of personal information search and have a higher usage of healthcare facilities.

INTRODUCTION

Continued growth in the elderly market has drawn increasing attention from marketers (e.g., Sherman 1987; Swayne and Greco 1987). One of those marketing areas of interest has been the healthcare field. In the healthcare field many new programs are being developed aimed at the elderly market (Lazer 1985). Blacks within the overall elderly market and the elderly healthcare market, however, have received very little attention, if any, as compared to their white counterparts, outside of overall public policy research. One possible reason for this lack of interest on the part of marketers is an historical misconceived perception that the elderly are a homogeneous group, a perspective which is now beginning to fall by the wayside (Rahtz and Moore, 1987).

As interest in the elderly market continues to grow, marketers could be expected to seek better access to the elderly market through more segmentation based strategies. When one considers the continued growth of minority ethnic segments in the United States, it seems only appropriate for marketers to explore the possible role that race may play in elderly market segmentation. The purpose of this paper is to explore the influence of race on one such product/service area which has been shown to be highly relevant to the elderly population: healthcare. The race variable for this study is operationalized as a simple dichotomy of white and black.

THE STUDY

Sampling

Data for this study were collected through the use of a mail survey questionnaire. The sample of 5,000 was drawn through a systematic random sampling of a mailing list. The mailing list of approximately 20,000 contained the names of households in the region (a Mid-Atlantic, three county, urban and rural area) with a member sixty years of age or older. Total response rate was 16 percent (n = 791). Thirty-nine of the returned questionnaire were unusable yielding a 15 percent usable response rate (n = 752). It is recognized that the low response rate may create strong non-response bias in the results. However, following suggestions by Feber (1981) methods were employed to assess the impact of that bias. Comparisons were made between the sample and the true demographic profile of the sample area on the age and income demographics. As table 1 shows, the sample and sample area are very comparable.

TABLE 1

DEMORGRAPHIC PROFILE COMPARISON: PERCENTAGE OF POPULATION COHORTS FOR THE SAMPLE AREA AND RESPONDENTS 65+

Population	Demographic Characteristics					
	Sex		Income ($)			
	Male	Female	<15,000	15-24,999	25-34,999	35-Up
Sample Area 65+	40.3	59.7	44.0	26.9	12.9	16.2
Study Sample	40.1	59.9	36.9	26.5	17.7	18.8

Source: National Planning Data Corp: 1980 U.S. Census

Operationalizations of the Variables

The six demographic variables were measured through nominal, ordinal, and continuous scaling methods. Respondents checked categories for their responses on all demographics except for age. For the age variable they simply filled in their age in the blank provided. Table 2 provides a summary of the results of the demographics.

The information source and health rating variables were operationalized through the use of six-point likert type scales The subjective health rating scale includes a four point scale taken from Maddox and Douglass (1978). This scale was combined with two six-point items for the overall subjective health rating scale used for this study. Table 3 provides a summary of constructs and items used in the operationalizations as well as their descriptive statistics. Table 4 summarizes the item and descriptive statistics for the healthcare provider usage scale. For the latter scale, respondents were asked to check the appropriate space for visits over the past year. This scale was assumed to have interval properties for analysis.

ANALYSIS AND RESULTS

To test the influence of race on health ratings,

TABLE 2
SAMPLE DEMOGRAPHIC CHARACTERISTICS

| | % in Category | | | | % in Category | |
	White	Black			White	Black
AGE				EDUCATION*		
55-60	3.6	3.2		Grammar School	5.5	20.2
61-64	13.6	23.8		High School	38.0	41.9
65-68	24.5	28.6		College (Attended)	37.1	25.0
69-72	21.8	13.5		Grad (Attended)	15.2	10.0
73-76	16.9	14.3		Trade	4.1	2.4
77-80	11.3	6.3				
81-85	5.4	6.0		YEARLY GROSS INCOME*		
over 85	2.8	4.0		0 - 999	.3	0.9
				1,000 - 4,999	5.4	20.5
SEX				5,000 - 9,999	9.4	25.5
				10,000 - 14,999	10.8	22.6
Male	41.5	36.1		15,000 - 19,999	12.5	16.6
Female	58.5	64.0		20,000 - 24,999	10.8	4.9
				25,000 - 29,999	8.7	2.0
				30,000 - 34,999	8.7	2.9
				35,000 - 39,999	5.4	.9
MARITAL STATUS				40,000 - and Up	13.4	2.9
Married	56.7	44.0				
Widowed	4.5	7.2				
Divorced	4.6	5.6				
Single	34.2	43.2				
EMPLOYMENT STATUS						
Full-Time	6.4	9.5				
Part-Time	6.8	11.1				
Unemployed	86.8	79.4				

* Note: Chi-Square significant at p<.0001

TABLE 3
SUMMARY OF INFORMATION
USE AND HEALTH RATING ITEMS

Construct		Item	X	SD
Subjective Health		I would rate my health at the present time as...	2.18	0.73
	(+)	I enjoy the physical pleasures life.	4.83	1.87
	(+)	I am in good physical condition.	4.41	1.38
Personal Information	(+)	I often seek out the advice of friends and/or family about my healthcare decisions.	3.29	1.62
	(+)	I attend health education programs	2.85	1.62
	(+)	I rely more on friends and family for advice than I do on newspapers, TV, radio, or magazines.	3.46	1.70
	(+)	Friends are a useful source of information about healthcare.	3.77	1.26
	(+)	Family are a useful source of information about healthcare.	4.28	1.26
Television Information	(+)	I pay close attention to TV commercials about healthcare.	3.47	1.61
	(+)	Television is a useful source of information about healthcare.	3.45	1.38
Mail Information	(+)	I gain valuable information from things sent to me in the mail about healthcare programs.	3.59	1.58
	(+)	I try to read all healthcare information that is sent to me through the mail.	3.96	1.59
	(+)	Mail is a useful source of information about healthcare.	3.21	1.48
Newspaper Information	(+)	Newspapers are a useful source of information about healthcare.	3.81	1.35
Yellow Pages Information	(+)	The telephone yellow pages are a useful source of information about healthcare.	3.45	1.62

TABLE 4
SUMMARY OF HEALTHCARE
FACILITY USE RESPONSES

| | % in category | | |
	White	Black	Total
Once a week or more	1.5	2.6	1.7
Twice a month	3.2	7.7	3.9
Once a month	6.9	6.8	6.9
Once every 2 month	7.0	14.5	8.3
Once every 3 to 5 months	40.1	36.8	39.6
Once every 6 months	7.7	8.5	7.9
Once a year	30.5	21.4	29.8
More than a year	3.0	1.7	2.8

information sources and healthcare provider usage, a series of oneway ANOVA's were performed. Simple Chi-square analysis was conducted between whites and blacks on the demographic variables to assess any major demographic differences between the two groups. Table 5 provides a summary of the ANOVA results for the health rating, information sources and usage variables

TABLE 5
ANOVA RESULTS OF REACE INFLUENCE ON
INFORMATION SOURCE
HEALTH RATING AND FACILITY USE

Variable	N	X	SD	SE	F Ratio	P Value
Personal Information						
White	544	17.27	4.55	.195	7.36	.0070
Black	103	18.58	4.15	.409		
Total	647	17.47	4.52	.777		
Television Information						
White	574	7.20	2.01	.084	12.92	.0003
Black	116	7.95	2.14	.199		
Total	690	7.33	2.05	.078		
Mail Information						
White	571	10.36	3.52	.147	35.96	.0000
Black	116	12.54	3.73	.346		
Total	687	10.73	3.64	.139		
Newspaper Information						
White	589	3.69	1.31	.054	24.17	.0000
Black	120	4.34	1.36	.124		
Total	709	3.80	1.34	.050		
Yellow Pages Information						
White	590	3.34	1.58	.065	11.09	.0009
Black	121	3.87	1.75	.159		
Total	711	3.43	1.62	.061		
Health Rating						
White	578	12.12	2.64	.109	2.08	.1501
Black	113	11.73	2.79	.236		
Total	691	12.06	2.67	.107		
Facilty Use						
White	585	6.40	1.51	.063	13.24	.0003
Black	119	5.84	1.62	.148		
Total	704	6.30	1.54	.058		

Demographics

As table 2 shows, there are no significant differences (p<.05) between whites and blacks on four of the six demographics. There are significant differences, however, on the age and income variables. These items are traditionally different demographics between the black white segments (O'Hare 1987).

Health Ratings

There are no differences between the two groups on subjective health ratings. As can be seen in table 3 and table 5 both groups have a fairly mid-range rating of their own health. The one-way ANOVA results shows very little difference between the two groups. The F-value of .075 suggests that race plays almost no role in the elderlys' perception of their own health.

Healthcare Facility Use

Although there is no significant influence of race on perceived health among the elderly, there is a significant influence on the amount of usage of healthcare facilities. Blacks are heavier users of healthcare facilities than are whites. As table 4 shows the mean score for whites is 6.4 on the use scale as compared to 5.8 for the blacks. The F value of 13.24 indicates that usage of facilities is significantly different for the two groups.

Information Use

Results from the oneway ANOVA's indicate there are significant differences between blacks and whites on all information sources. Blacks tend to see all sources of information as more useful for healthcare decisions than do whites. As the results in table 5 shows, in every case, the black segment relates a significantly higher usage worth of the information, whether the source be electronic, print or personal.

DISCUSSION

As the results show, older black individuals are more involved in information search about and use of healthcare programs/facilities than are their white counterparts. There are significant differences between the two groups on all the information source questions as well as the facility usage question.

An interesting finding which relates to this is that there are no differences reported between the two groups concerning the perceptions of personal health. Both groups view themselves at approximately the same level of health. Why then do blacks report being significantly higher users of healthcare services and believe more strongly in seeking information from all the various sources?

The answer may lie in the very essence of the white and black culture in the United States. That is, the traditional relationship of the two groups to the healthcare industry. It could be posited that whites have had a long history of interaction with the medical community. In other words, they have always had the "family doctor." Their parents essentially enculturated them with the healthcare concept when they grew up. Thus, the whites estabished a long running association with doctors and the healthcare community at large. As they entered into their later years they maintained a cognitive file on health services and did not see the need for extended information search for routine medical care.

Blacks, on the other hand, may have not established these personal connections with the medical community over the course of their lives. Therefore, they may not have established any sort of a health maintenance program that many of the whites may have. As a consequence, in their later years, they are not only in need of more medical services, but also in need of much more information to make decisions concerning those services.

These possible explanations are consistent with activation theory (Schiffren and Atkinson 1970), the "psychology of simplification" (Howard and Sheth 1969), and Johnson and Russo's (1981) contention that continued use within a product class diminishes the need for external information search (see Sirgy 1981 for a discussion

of product familiarity as it may relate here). However, the current higher usage of medical services by blacks would suggest this explanation should not hold. Once again, it may be the long term interaction which has caused the differences between the two groups.

This long term association with the healthcare community may also help explain the apparent lack of difference in perceived subjective health between whites and blacks and increased use of health facilities by blacks. Whites may be more aware of what constitutes "good health" since they may have maintained a long running association with the medical community. Blacks may simply perceive their health as "good" by default. That is, lacking a long term objective evaluation history of their health by the medical professional, blacks may make evaluations of their health compared to those around them.

They may then consider themselves as healthy compared to those they know and accept it as "being old." In reality they may be of lower health compared to the total population of their age group. Maddox and Douglass (1978) felt the subjective ratings were correlated highly with objective rating of health (i.e., by rating by professionals). However, if a segment has lacked interaction with the "objective rater" over time the correlation may be greatly diminished.

The results of this study and the following discussion have tried to provide some possible insight into the role of race in healthcare information search and usage. There are, however, a number of limitations which need to be considered, first of which is the exploratory nature of this research. The intent here was to explore the relationship between race and some of the healthcare variables in the elderly population. It was not the intent to seek full explanation of those relationships. Second, the low response rate may have yielded high non-response bias of the results. Future research may wish to seek means to increase response rate.

Additionally, as noted, the results may have been influenced by a number of extraneous variables. It has been noted that two demographics, income and education are significantly different for the two groups. These two may have played a major role in the outcome of other analyses. The study design did not measure other possible variables which may have influenced findings as well. An area for future research may be to try and assess the hypothesized effects of long term interaction between the elderly and the healthcare community on the variables presented in this research and others.

Overall, the results suggest certain relationships exist between race and healthcare behavior in the elderly population. As the preceding discussion imparts, however, there may be a number of explanations for these findings. Future research must decide which of the explanations is appropriate under much more controlled conditions. We are just beginning to try to understand the elderly population, and race is but one of the many interactive variables in this dynamic subculture.

REFERENCES

Ferber, R. (1981), "The Role of Response Rates in Evaluating Manuscripts for Publication," in K. B. Monroe, ed., Advances in Consumer Research - Volume III, Ann Arbor: Association for Consumer Research, 31-34.

Howard, J. and J. Sheth (1969), The Theory of Buyer Behavior, New York: Wiley and Sons.

Johnson, E. J. and J. Russo (1981), "Product Familiarity and Learning New Information," in K. B. Monroe, ed., Advances in Consumer Research - Volume VIII, Ann Arbor: Association for Consumer Research, 31-34.

Lazer, W. (1985), "Inside the Mature Market," American Demographics, (March), 23-25, 48-49.

Maddox, G. L. and E. B. Douglass (1978), "Self Assessment of Health: A Longitudinal Study of Elderly Subjects," Journal of Health and Social Behavior, 14, 87-93.

O'Hare, W. (1987), "Blacks and Whites: One Market or Two?, American Demographics, (March), 44-48.

Rahtz, D. and D. L. Moore (1986) "The Mature Direct Mail User: A Profile," in F. Feasley, ed., Proceedings of the 1987 Conference of the American Academy of Advertising, American Academy of Advertising, R87-91.

Schiffen, R. and R. Atkinson (1970) "Storage and Retrevial Processes in Long-Term Memory, Psychological Review, 76, 1979-83.

Sherman, E. (1987) "The Senior Market: Opportunities Abound, Direct Marketing, (June), 82-86, 119.

Sirgy, M. J. (1981) "Product Familiarity: Critical Comments on Selected Studies and Theoretical Extensions," in K. B. Monroe, ed., Advances in Consumer Research - Volume VIII, Ann Arbor: Association for Consumer Research, 156-60.

Swayne, L. and A. Greco (1987) "The Portrayal of Older Americans in Television Commercials," Journal of Advertising, 16, 1, 47-54.

FUNCTIONAL/DYSFUNCTIONAL CONSUMER BEHAVIOR:
A NORMATIVE FRAMEWORK FOR PUBLIC POLICY

M. Joseph Sirgy, Virginia Polytechnic Institute and State University
A. Coskun Samli, Virginia Polytechnic Institute and State University

Abstract

This paper develops a conceptual framework to (1) define functional/dysfunctional consumer behavior based on the medical concept of clinical adjustment and (2) classifies functional/dysfunctional consumer behaviors based on risk perception/risk reduction theory. A dysfunctional consumer behavior is conceptualized as a significant and negative deviation from the norm along a specific behavior dimension involving risk reduction. The concept of dysfunctional consumer behavior is operationalized as a z-formula in which a particular consumer score along a risk dimension is compared with the norm. The norm of the risk dimension is obtained from a large sample of consumers, and specification of the directionality of the scores (functional versus dysfunctional) is obtained from a sample of "educated" consumers. Public policy implications are discussed in the context of minority consumers.

Introduction

Marketing scolars (e.g., Bettman 1975; Capon and Lutz 1974; Cohen 1969; Wilkie and Gardner 1974) have long argued that consumer information and education programs have to be designed by studying consumer behavior. That is, marketing scientists concede that consumer information/education programs should not be based on policy makers' notion of what consumers ought to know (or how consumers should act like in the marketplace). Instead, policy makers should make consumer policy decisions based on a thorough understanding of consumer frailties. Thus, specific programs can be tailored to specific consumer groups in specific situations.

A number of conceptual frameworks have been developed in marketing to study consumer behavior for the purpose of designing consumer information/education programs. An example of a popular framework in marketing is the Capon and Lutz's (1979) framework. Capon and Lutz viewed consumer information as a marketing product. Thus information (as a product) has to be "marketed" in such a way to achieve a balance between information supply and information demand.

In this paper, we develop another conceptual framework to aid in the design of consumer information/education programs. The conceptual framework is based on the concept of clinical dysfunctionality propagated in clinical psychology and risk perception/risk reduction theory. It is maintained here that a large group of people in our society may be experiencing certain marketplace dysfunctionality. This is a critical minority group which may need help.

Functional/Dysfunctional Consumer Behavior

The practice of clinical psychology has long been dominated by the medical model (Reiff 1966; Maher 1966). Implicit in the medical model is the construal of psychological maladjustment as significant deviation from the statistical norm along clinical dimensions such as self-esteem, stress, coping behaviors, among others (Foley 1935). Many raise objections to the term "deviance" on the grounds that some deviances are desirable (high intelligence, great wealth) and modify their position to conclude that the term **deviant** should be applied only to behavior which seems inappropriate and disabling to the individual (Maher 1966). Hence, clinical psychologists and psychiatrists have distinguished between positive and negative deviancy. Negative deviance is behavior that is **dysfunctional** to the individual and others around him/her. Positive deviance, on the other hand, reflect optimal scores on mental health dimensions. We will use this medical analogy of conceptualizing dysfunctional, average, and functional behaviors to develop a framework to conceptualize functional/dysfunctional consumer behavior. Hence, consumers who maximize their utilities in the market place can be thought of as "informed consumers." Using the medical analogy, this behavior may be characterized as "functional." We also have the "average" consumer and by the same token, we have the "dysfunctional consumers." Dysfunctional consumer behavior is therefore viewed as **significant negative deviation** from a statistical central tendency along one or more consumer behavior dimensions.

This definition of consumer dysfunctionality may be more precisely viewed in terms of a Z-score model. In other words, the buying behavior of a particular consumer (or a consumer group) can be assessed with regard to its degree of functionality or dysfunctionality. Mathematically,

$$Z\text{-score}_k = (B_k - MB)/\sigma_B \qquad (1)$$

where $Z\text{-score}_k$ = consumer [group] (k) standard deviation score from mean

B_k = buying behavior score of consumer (k) for consumer group (k)]

MB = mean of buying behavior scores obtained from a large consumer sample

σ_B = standard error of the sample scores of behavior (B)

Using a Z-score model one can produce a score for each individual consumer (k) [or consumer group (k)] along a given behavior (B) and assess the extent to which this score is deviant or not deviant from the average (i.e., norm). A consumer's buying behavior (B) can be classified as "dysfunctional" if it produces a Z-score that is at least one standard deviation <u>below</u> the norm. Note the emphasis on the term "below." That is, we are not simply looking for significant deviations from the norm; we are looking for significant <u>negative deviations.</u>

But then how can we know what is positive and what is negative? That is, how can we distinguish "dysfunctional" consumer behavior (i.e., significant negative deviation) from "functional" consumer behavior (i.e., significant positive deviation). This is where the sample of <u>educated</u> consumers comes in. We can gather data about a given buying behavior phenomenon from a selected sample of "educated" consumers. "Educated" consumers can be selected based on the knowledge, disposition, and history of making "informed" decisions in the marketplace. Or, we can "educate" a sample of consumers in the context of a specific situation, thus creating an environment that allows the sample consumers to make "informed" decisions.

Once we get the average buying behavior score of the "educated" consumer sample, we can pinpoint the directionality of "functional" versus "dysfunctional" along the consumer behavior dimension. Using a clinical psychology example, we may measure aggressive behavior as the clinical behavioral dimension. Data are collected from a large sample of people using a valid measure of aggressive behavior. The data then are frequency tabulated, and converted to a normal distribution, i.e., a z-distribution. The mean score is treated as "average" score. The interval or +/-1 standard deviation scores from the average can be considered also as "average" aggression. However, <u>significant</u> deviations (> +1 or < -1 standard deviation scores) from the "average" aggressive behavior can be either "dysfunctional" or "functional." How do we assess the directionality of the normal distribution. That is, are > +1 standard deviation scores reflect "functional" or "dysfunctional" aggression? This can be done in different ways. One way may involve selecting a sample of clinically well-adjusted individuals and measure their aggression using the same measure administered to the original sample (the general population). The average aggression score derived from the "well-adjusted" sample, therefore, is used to indicate the directionality of the normal distribution of the measure in the general population.

For example, let us say that the average aggression score of the general population is 90 on a scale that has a range of 40 and 120. Now let us say that the standard deviation of the aggression data of the general population is 10. Hence, we can say that average aggression is defined as a score on the aggression measure between 80 and 100. A score below 80 is a score < -1 standard deviation and hence can be classified as either "dysfunctional" or "functional." Similarly, a score above 100 is a score > +1 standard deviation, which is viewed to reflect a "dysfunctional" or "functional" score. The question becomes what is the directionality of the distribution? Does a score above 100 reflect a dysfunctional or functional condition? Which is it? Does a score below 80 reflect a dysfunctional or functional condition? Again which is it? This is where the sample of the "well-adjusted" individuals come in. The average aggression score of the sample of the well-adjusted subjects may turn out to be, let's say, 60 on the aggression measure. Now we are in a position to say that scores below 80 reflect a "functional" condition, and scores above 100 reflect a "dysfunctional" condition.

Let us now apply the medical analogy of functionality and dysfunctionality to consumer behavior. To do this we first have to use some theoretical framework allowing us to derive a set of consumer behavior dimensions. Each of these consumer behavior dimensions, therefore, can be treated using the Z-model. But then what would these consumer behavior dimensions be? We can specify a number of consumer behavior dimensions using risk perception/risk reduction theory in consumer research.

Classifying Consumer Behaviors Normatively

Most developed applied disciplines have diagnostic schemata designed to deal with specific problems. For example, in clinical psychology and psychiatry, a standard nomenclature or diagnostic and statistical manual for mental diseases exists. These are referred to as the Diagnostic and Statistical Manuals (DSM-I, DSM-II, and DSM-III) (Zax and Cowen 1984).

Classification systems are usually developed deductively. That is, the researcher starts out with some hypothesis or theory involving one or more relationships. The categories making the variables involving the hypothesized relationships make up the taxonomy. We use risk perception/risk reduction theory to <u>illustrate an example</u> of a classification schema involving functional/dysfunctional consumer behaviors.

Most risk perception/risk reduction studies have involved subsets and/or combinations of five facets of risk believed to be connected with the purchasing process. These are: (1) performance risk, (2) financial risk, (3) physical risk, (4) social risk, and (5) psychological risk (e.g., Jacoby and Kaplan 1972; Perry and Hamm 1969; Roselius 1971; Schiffman 1972; Zikmund and Scott 1973; Brody and Cunningham 1968; Locander and Hermann 1979; Ferber and Lee 1974).

Many consumer behavior studies have focused on particular risk reducers. For example, Arndt (1967), Popielarz (1967), and Schiffman (1972) focused on the relationship between risk perception and delayed adoption of innovations as a risk reducer. Lutz and Reilly (1973) studied how consumers acquire and handle information to reduce their risk perceptions. Cunningham (1967) studied brand loyalty as a risk reducer. Roselius (1971) addressed the issue of risk reduction in a general way. He argued that when a buyer perceives risk in a purchase s/he could pursue one of four different strategies of risk resolution: (1) S/he could reduce perceived risk by either decreasing the probability that the purchase will fail, or by reducing the severity of real or imagined loss suffered if the purchase does fail; (2) s/he could shift from one type of perceived loss to another for which s/he has more tolerance; (3) s/he could postpone the purchase, in which case s/he would be shifting from one general risk type to another; or (4) s/he could make the purchase and absorb the unresolved risk.

These risk reduction strategies in a consumer setting are reflected in (1) buying that brand endorsed by celebrities or experts (endorsements), (2) buying that brand used before and have been satisfied with in the past (brand loyalty), (3) buying a major, well-known brand (major brand image), (4) buying whichever brand has been tested and approved by a private testing company (private testing), (5) buying the brand that is carried by a store which is perceived to be dependable and reputable (store image), (6) using a free sample of the product on a trial basis before buying (free sample), (7) buying whichever brand offers a money-back guarantee (money-back guarantee), (8) buying the brand that has been tested and approved by an official branch of the government (government testing), (9) shopping around and comparing product features on several brands in several stores (shopping around), (10) buying the most expensive and elaborate model of the product (expensive model), (11) asking friends or family for advice about the product (word-of-mouth), and (12) refraining from buying new products

until their reputation becomes well established (delayed adoption) (Roselius 1971; Bettman 1973; Schiffman and Kanuk 1978). Each of these risk relievers operate to relieve differential amounts of risks perceived. Also different consumers use different risk relievers depending upon the circumstances involved.

We can establish a taxonomy of functional/dysfunctional consumer behaviors by simply focusing on any one or more of the above hypothesized relationships. For the sake of illustration, we can define at least 12 dysfunctional behaviors from the list of 12 risk reduction behaviors suggested by Roselius (1971), Bettman (1973), and Schiffman and Kanuk (1978) (see Table 1).

We will use one example of risk reduction dimensions of consumer behavior to illustrate how the normative framework of consumer behavior can be used. This is the "Expensive Brand Syndrome."

An Illustration

Overreliance (or underreliance) on price to infer quality may be viewed as dysfunctional. This phenomenon may be referred to as the "Expensive Brand Syndrome" (see Table 1). A number of research studies support the view that consumers rely on price as an indicator of product quality (Monroe and Petroshius 1981). Since high quality products generally are less risky, consumers buy high priced items in an attempt to reduce the amount of perceived risk associated with a product. Such a perception may be biased since price decisions may not be based on quality control. For example, known (national) brands may be higher in price compared to private (or generic) brands, mainly because

TABLE 1

CONSUMER RISK REDUCTION DEVIANCES AS AN EXAMPLE OF A CLASSIFICATION
SYSTEM OF CONSUMER ABNORMAL BEHAVIORS

CONSUMER BEHAVIOR (RISK REDUCING BEHAVIORS)	CONSUMER BEHAVIOR ABNORMALITY
BUYING ENDORSED BRANDS	THE ENDORSEMENT SYNDROME
BUYING BRAND PREVIOUSLY USED	THE BRAND LOYALTY SYNDROME
BUYING MAJOR BRAND NAMES	THE BRAND NAME SYNDROME
BUYING BRANDS APPROVED BY PRIVATE TESTING FIRMS	THE PRIVATE TESTING SYNDROME
BUYING BRANDS CARRIED BY REPUTABLE STORES	THE STORE IMAGE SYNDROME
TRYING THE BRAND BEFORE PURCHASE	THE FREE SAMPLE SYNDROME
BUYING BRANDS THAT OFFER MONEY-BACK GUARANTEE	THE MONEY-BACK GUARANTEE SYNDROME
BUYING BRAND APPROVED BY GOVERNMENT	THE GOVERNMENT TESTING SYNDROME
SHOPPING AROUND	THE SHOPPING AROUND SYNDROME
BUYING MOST EXPENSIVE BRAND	THE EXPENSIVE BRAND SYNDROME
ASKING FAMILY/FRIENDS FOR ADVICE	THE WORK-OF-MOUTH SYNDROME
REFRAINING FROM BUYING NEW BRAND UNTIL ITS REPUTATION BECOMES ESTABLISHED	THE DELAYED ADOPTION SYNDROME

of promotion and distribution costs and not necessarily because of quality.

Hence, the Expensive Brand Syndrome may be defined as a perception of price-quality relationship that is significantly and negatively discrepant from the norm. In other words, this dysfunctionality can be operationalized as a significant negative deviation from the average perception price-quality relationship. The average score is the mean score (plus or minus one standard deviation) derived from a sample of large consumer population. The directionality of the scores can be attained by using a sample of educated consumers. The average score of the educated sample is employed to indicate the directionality of any subject's score. That is,

$$PQ_k = (PQS_k - MPQO)/\sigma_{PQO} \qquad (2)$$

where

PQ_k = z-score of price-quality perception of consumer [group] (k)

PQS_k = raw score of price-quality perception of consumer [group] (k)

MPQO = mean score of price-quality perception from sample of consumers

Significant negative discrepancies may represent dysfunctional misperception of price-quality relationship. But how do know the directionality of the deviation. This is where the sample of an educated consumer population comes in. We can "educate" a sample of consumers about the product category and the various characteristics of each brand in the product category. This can be done, for example, with consumer reports and other technical and trade information. Then, we administer the same price-quality perception measure to them, and get an average score of this sample. The average score thus is directly used to indicate the directionality aspect of any individual (or group) score.

Public Policy Implications

The concept of functional/dysfunctional consumer behavior can be appreciated from a public policy point-of-view, and not necessarily from a traditional business point-of-view. This is because policy makers are naturally interested in providing assistance to those consumers who need assistance. For a policy maker, certain consumer groups (e.g., minority consumers) may have problems in the market place that usually take some form of deviance, e.g., inability to recognize a deceptive advertisement, lured to purchase items on credit to the point of bankruptcy, over-reliance on brand image or high price to make judgments about the quality of the product.

The concept of functional/dysfunctional consumer behavior must be understood from a public policy point-of-view rather than from a traditional business point-of-view. In so doing, it would be possible to that dysfunctional consumer behavior in a remedial fashion.

From a public policy perspective, there are at least four policy alternatives which can be used to perhaps remedially treat dysfunctional consumer behavior. These four alternatives are not mutually exclusive. In fact it is quite likely that some combination of these four alternatives may enhance market demand and increase market opportunities for businesses too.

The four alternatives are: consumer information, consumer education, consumer protection and supplier protection.

Consumer Information: If dysfunctional consumer behavior is due to lack of information it may be rectified by providing the necessary information. As product complexity increases the necessary information to select, operate, care, or repair a product becomes more voluminous and urgent. Thus, making the necessary information available, by definition, would reduce the dysfunctionality in the behavior of certain consumers.

Consumer Education: In certain cases, availability of necessary information may not be sufficient, unless the information is assimilated and successfully used in product or service selection, use, care, or repair. Consumer education comes in different forms and shapes, from special brochures to workshops Society will not make particularly good use of consumer, education programs unless these programs are specifically directed to those consumers experiencing dysfunctional behavior.

Consumer Protection: The ever increasing complexity of society leads to the development of certain products which may be physically dangerous. Consumers who exhibit dysfunctional behavior may be particularly susceptible to the dangers of these products. In such cases, consumer protection has to be exercised. Consumer protection practices may vary from banning certain products such as Red Die No. 2 to specifying certain trade practices such as truth-in-lending. More protection should be aimed at those who are suffering from dysfunctional behavior.

Supplier Protection: This concept, in a sense, is a different version of caveat vendor. Manufacturers, producers and makers of goods and services may wish to take a proactive position to intercept and/or reverse the tendency on the part of the regulating authorities to legislate or establish rules and regulations to limit the practices so that no harm will come to the consumers. Many suppliers, on their own, can take the position that what is good for customers is good for them also. In such cases they will do their best not to take advantage of consumers who may exhibit dysfunctionality, but instead assist in the remedial treatment of dysfunctional consumer behavior.

Conclusions

Functional/dysfunctional behavior in an effort to determine its causation and consequences. The knowledge derived from such research can be utilized as the foundation for public policy to cope with consumer dysfunctionality. The research outcome would indicate which of the four remedial alternatives, (consumer information, consumer education, consumer protection, and seller protection) is likely to be emphasized in dealing with the minority of dysfunctional consumers. It is quite likely that all four may be required. In such cases the research outcome may indicate the proportions to which the four remedial alternatives are likely to be used.

References

Arndt, J. (1967), "Role of Product-Related Conversations in the Diffusion of a New Product," Journal of Marketing Research 4, 291-295.

Bettman, J. R. (1973), "Perceived Risk and Its Components: Model and Empirical Test," Journal of Marketing Research. 10, 184-190.

Bettman, J. R. (1975), "Issues in Designing Consumer Information Environment," Journal of Consumer Research. 2(December), 169-177.

Brody, R. P. and Cunningham, S. M. (1968), "Personality Variables and the Consumer Decision Process," Journal of Marketing Research. 5, 50-57.

Capon, Noel and Richard Lutz (1979), "A Model and Methodology for the Development of Consumer Information Programs," Journal of Marketing. 43 (January), 58-67.

Cohen, Dorothy (1969), "The Federal Trade Commission and the Regulation of Advertising vs. Consumers Interest," Journal of Marketing. 33 (January), 40-49.

Cunningham, S. (1967), "Major Dimensions of Perceived Risk." In D. F. Cox (ed.), Risk Taking and Information Handling in Consumer Behavior. Boston: Division of Research, Graduate School of Business, Harvard University.

Ferber, Robert and Lee, Lucy Chao (1974), "Husband-Wife Influence in Family Purchasing Behavior," Journal of Consumer Research. 1(June),43-50.

Foley, J. P. Jr. (1935), "The Criterion of Abnormality," Journal of Abnormal and Social Psychology. 30, 279-291.

Jacoby, J. and L. B. Kaplan (1972), "The Components of Perceived Risk," in M. Venkatesan (ed.), Proceedings of the Third Annual Conference of the Association for Consumer Research. University of Chicago, pp. 382-393.

Locander, W. B. and P. W. Herman (1979), "The Effect of Self-Confidence and Anxiety on Information Seeking in Consumer Risk Reduction," Journal of Marketing Research. 268-274.

Lutz, R. J. and P. J. Reilly (1973), "An Exploration of the Effects of Perceived Social and Performance Risk in Consumer Information Acquisition," in Scott Ward and Peter Wright (eds.), Advances in Consumer Research. vol. 4, pp. 393-405.

Maher, B. A. (1966), Principles of Psychopathology. New York: McGraw-Hill.

Monroe, K. B. and S. M. Petroshius (1981), "Buyers' Perception of Price: An Update of the Evidence," in Harold H. Kassarjian and Thomas S. Robertson (eds.), Perspectives in Consumer Behavior. 3rd edition. Glenview, Ill.: Scott, Foresman and Co.

Perry, M. and B. C. Hamm (1969), "Canonical Analysis of Relations Between Socio-Economic Risk and Personal Influence in Purchase Decisions," Journal of Marketing Research. 6, 352-358.

Popielarz, D. T. (1967), "An Exploration of Perceived Risk and Willingness to Try New Products," Journal of Marketing Research. 4, 368-372.

Reiff, R. (1966), "Mental Health Manpower and Institutional Change," American Psychologist. 21, 540-548.

Roselius, T. "Consumer Rankings of Risk Reduction Methods," Journal of Marketing. 1971, 35, 55-61.

Samuelson, P. A. (1972), Economics. ninth edition. N.Y. McGraw-Hill

Schiffman, L. and Kanuk, M. (1978), Consumer Behavior. Englewood Cliffs, N.J.: Prentice-Hall.

Schiffman, L. G. (1972), "Perceived Risk in New Product Trail by Elderly Consumers," Journal of Marketing Research. 9, 106-108.

Wilkie, William L. and David Gardner (1974), "The Role of Marketing Research in Public Policy Decision Making," Journal of Marketing. 38 (January), 38-47.

Zax, Melvin and Emory L. Cowen (1984), Abnormal Psychology. New York: Holt, Rinehart & Winston.

Zikmund, W. G. and Scott, J. E. (1973), A Multivariate Analysis of Perceived Risk, Self-Confidence, and Information Sources, In Scott Ward and Peter Wright (eds.), Advances in Consumer Research. vol. 1, Ann Arbor, MI: Association for Consumer Research.

CONSUMER BEHAVIOR PATTERNS OF THE OLD ORDER AMISH IN SOUTH-CENTRAL PENNSYLVANIA

Henry T. Wilkens and Margaretha M. Hsu, Shippensburg University

Abstract

The Old Order Amish are a distinct minority
subcultural group in the United States that has
cultivated and maintained a unique lifestyle
here for over 250 years. There is a paucity of
data about their consumer behavior patterns and
this research sheds some light in this area.

Introduction

The Amish trace their placid way of life,
physical and spiritual, to the late 17th
century, when Jacob Ammann led his followers
out of the Mennonite church. Those who have
most resisted change in worship and life style
are known as Old Order Amish (Lee 1984).

Since William Penn invited this sect to settle
in Pennsylvania over 250 years ago, they have
sought, and for the most part succeeded, to
remain secluded from outsiders. While some
accounts have been written about the Amish and
their secluded way of life, there is a paucity
of data on consumer behavior of this minority
group.

A search of the literature has provided little
information, other than about Amish cooking,
quilting, genetic and health concerns, and
farming. Nothing was discovered on the subject
of consumer behavior of the Old Order Amish.
To contribute data to this void became the goal
of these researchers.

Research Methodology

The researchers created an instrument that
would reflect data on demographics and consumer
behavior patterns. The questionnaire was
closed-ended and consisted of highly structured
questions that were dichotomous, multiple
choice, and rank-ordered in nature. It was
pre-tested with the religious leader of the Old
Order Amish, who held the title of Bishop of
the Cumberland Valley District in South-Central
Pennsylvania. Three revisions of the
instrument followed before actual respondent
visitation began.

The researchers collected the primary data for
this study directly from the respondents by
administering a survey instrument in person at
the home or work place or farm adjacent to the
home.

During interviewing, the researchers
administered the questionnaire to either the
husband or wife, whomever first answered our
initial visit. A statistically insignificant
number of wives asked us to speak with their
husbands, but this was so seldom encountered it
caused no concern regarding the validity of the
data. No children were interviewed and no
unmarried adults were interviewed. In the Old
Order Amish community, the children living at
home follow strict parental guidelines.
Single, older adults were rarely found because
this is a community that traces its beginning
to the early 1970's. Younger adult members
came to the area, and in fact, there were only
three "senior citizen" Old Order Amish that
were observed in this community during our
research. The oldest husband was 51 and the
oldest wife was 52 years of age.

The sequence of interviewing the membership was
random and 54% of the target population
actually participated, while 6% refused to
participate. Those non-participants brought
strong pressure on the Bishop to end the
research project. The Bishop then asked the
researchers to stop conducting the
investigation.

At this point, the interviews ended and
analysis of data began. Because of the random
sequence of interviewing and the high
percentage of participation, the researchers
believe the data well represents the whole
population.

Findings

Demographics

The Amish family in South-Central Pennsylvania
is one that can be described as young and
large. The age of husbands ranged from 23 to
51, with the average being 36 years of age.
Wives' ages ranged from 19 to 52, with the
average being 35. The number of children
ranged from 0 to 10; 33.3% of families had
three or less children, 29.6% of families had
four children, and 37.1% of families had more
than four children.

A commonly held stereotype among non-Amish is
that all Amish are farmers. However, the data

revealed that farming was indicated as the primary occupation for only 48% of the families, and the secondary occupation for 26% of the families interviewed. Furthermore, 44% of Amish families were not associated with farming activity at all. Among primary and secondary occupations mentioned were carpenter, shed maker, cabinet maker, furniture refinisher, operator of a health food store, blacksmith, painter, wholesale and retail florist, harness maker and leather tooling, operator of a dry goods store, shipping pallet maker, home builder, maker of ventilation louvers, and processor of horseradish grown by others.

All Old Order Amish families lived in sparsely populated, rural areas and had a barn structure where horses could be maintained to provide power for the buggy in which they ride. The land of the non-farming Amish was used by those who farmed, under agreement between the families.

Shopping Frequency

The data gathered showed that the Old Order Amish are not frequent shoppers. Table 1 shows that only 3.7% shop two or three times a week, with 33% shopping weekly, 44.4% shopping every two weeks, and 18.5% shopping once a month. Comments made while data was being gathered indicated that time was precious and a single shopping trip every week or two or three would have to suffice. In addition, no one indicated a willingness to shop on Sunday. One respondent did not shop on Monday because the shelves were not always stocked and thus time was wasted.

TABLE 1

Frequency of Shopping

Frequency	Percentage
Daily	0%
Two or three times a week	3.7%
Weekly	33.0%
About every two weeks	44.4%
Once a month	18.5%

Attitude Toward Returning Items

Table 2 shows that 85.2% of the Old Order Amish are reluctant to return items that do not give satisfaction, indicating that they return only "sometimes" or "never." Only 14.8% indicated that they frequently return items that fail to give satisfaction and no one indicated that they will always return an item. One respondent went so far as to comment that, "If your're dumb enough to pay for it, it's yours."

TABLE 2

Frequency of Returning Items
That Do Not Give Satisfaction

	Percentages
Never	25.9%
Sometimes	59.3%
Frequently	14.8%
Always	0%

Buying Decisions

The researchers felt that it would be interesting to explore who makes buying decisions within an Old Order Amish family. Accordingly, over seven categories the question was asked, "Who makes buying decisions on these items?" Respondents were shown the list and asked to choose which response was appropriate, the husband, wife, both, or family. Table 3 reflects data gathered over the seven categories.

The wife dominates decision making in groceries and clothing. The husband does not dominate in any buying decisions, with the exception of determining what might be appropriate for repairs to the property owned or for tools or occupation equipment. Husband and wife share decisions for furniture, shelter, reading materials, appliances, and home furnishings.

TABLE 3

Who Makes Buying Decisions

Items	Husband	Wife	Both	Family
Groceries		70.4%	25.9%	3.7%
Clothing		70.4%	22.2%	7.4%
*Furniture		18.5%	74.1%	
*Shelter	14.8%		81.5%	
Reading Materials	11.1%	11.1%	70.4%	7.4%
Appliances		3.7%	96.3%	
*Home Furnishings		22.2%	74.1%	

*3.7% of the respondents were younger couples who received these items from parents (or relatives) to start off married life.

Only two categories, shelter with 14.8% and reading materials with 11.1%, were decision making areas claimed by husbands. One husband made an interesting comment when responding to the category of reading materials when he replied "I censor that." Families with teen-aged children had their participation in buying decisions involving groceries, clothing, and reading materials.

Payment of Bills

The respondents were asked to indicate how they paid bills and given a choice of payment by cash, check, barter, or credit cards. Table 4 shows the percentage that pay bills by check. The data revealed that 77.7% pay by check at least 75% of the time.

No one used barter in the true sense of the word, although one respondent running a food store did receive some free products from her brother living in another community for stocking his health food products in her health food store.

TABLE 4

Percentage That Pay Bills By Check

% Paid by Check	25%	50%	60%	75%	80%	90%	100%
% of Families	7.4%	11.1%	3.7%	37.0%	7.4%	29.6%	3.7%

Although we found widespread use and interest in mail order activity with Sears, Roebuck and Company and J.C. Penney, only two respondents had charge plates with those firms. All the rest calculated the costs and sent their payment in the form of a check with the order.

Where are Goods Purchased?

Data from Table 5 indicates that 78% of Old Order Amish families bought most of their goods from supermarkets with Amish stores being their second choice of supply and small stores ranking third. A t-test showed that families which did not rank supermarkets as their first choice were farmers who grew practically all of the products they needed and would go to nearby Amish stores or small stores for minor items.

TABLE 5

Rank Order of Where Goods are Purchased

Where	Rank	Percentage of Families
Supermarkets	1	78.0%
	2	14.8%
	3	7.4%
Amish Stores	1	18.5%
	2	63.0%
	3	18.5%
Small Stores	1	3.7%
	2	22.2%
	3	74.1%

Who Goes Shopping?

Figure 1 shows that just under 75% of all shopping in an Old Order Amish family is done by the wife alone or with children. Only 3.7% is done by the husband alone or with children. The data shows that husband and wife shopping together amounted to 7.4%, and that shopping was a family experience for 14.8% of the respondents.

FIGURE 1

Who Goes Shopping?

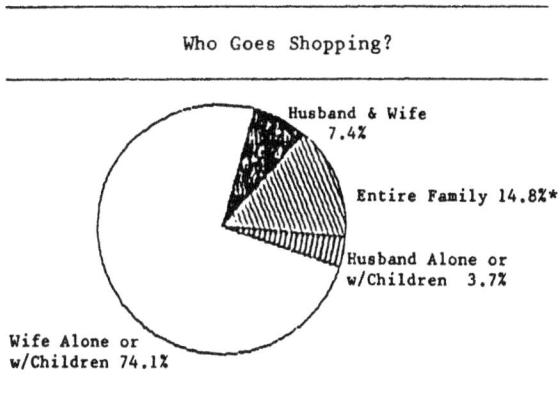

*Husbands and wives without children who shopped together were not counted here even though they constituted an "entire family."

Conclusions

Perhaps the most surprising finding from the data analysis was that 44% of the target population was not associated with farming at all. Equally surprising was the finding that 77.7% of the families pay bills by check (Table 4) at least 75% of the time (a t-test showed that non-farmers pay more often by check than farmers).

Another surprising result of data analysis was the heavy patronage of supermarkets vs Amish operated stores, shown in Table 5. An even 78% of the families interviewed indicated that supermarkets are their first preference in purchasing needed goods.

Data also showed the Old Order Amish to be extremely reluctant to return to merchants items that did not give satisfaction, and Table 2 reflects these attitudes.

A MANOVA test was conducted to determine the differences in consumer behavior for adults 30 or under, and those over 30. No significant differences were found.

Another MANOVA test showed no significant difference between farmers and non-farmers regarding store preference, who goes shopping and how often, their attitude toward returning items, and who makes buying decisions.

Even though the respondents showed a definite interest in buying at the lowest available price (37.0%), brand loyalty was evidenced by 63% indicating that they at least sometimes buy because of the brand name.

Religion precludes their purchase of goods on Sunday. All Amish-operated businesses known to the researchers were closed on that day. All other days were considered appropriate business days.

In addition to the surprising discoveries uncovered by our data analyses, we also feel that something else is evident. Male dominance is not total in Old Order Amish families, as shown by the strong participation by wives in decision making regarding purchase of the various items used in daily life and their lifestyle.

In summary, this effort represents a beginning point in examining the consumer behavior of the Old Order Amish.

References

1. Lee, Douglas (1984), "The Plain People of Pennsylvania," National Geographic, (April), pp. 492-519.

ASIAN AMERICANS: DEMOGRAPHIC OF
AN IGNORED TARGET MARKET

Monle Lee, Indiana University at South Bend
Ernest F. Cooke, Loyola College in Maryland

Abstract

Considerable research has been done on Black and Hispanic minority market segments. These markets are considered to be important, yet there is an untouched market, Asian Americans, waiting to be discovered by marketers. This group of consumers tend to be better educated and to have higher incomes than other minorities. The purpose of this paper is to examine this minority. Life insurance and real estate represent two markets where some firms have benefited by developing specific marketing mixes for the Asian-American market.

Introduction

Parker Pen, about 1984, decided to standardize their marketing mix for the entire world (Winski and Wentz, 1986). With one of the world's best known brand names they decided to centralize and standardize everything connected with the selling effort: packaging, pricing, promotional material and advertising. One look, one voice, Parker Pen's global marketing attempt failed, and failed fast. Pens were the same but markets were not. France and Italy fancied expensive pens, Scandinavia was a ballpoint pen market and so on. The successful companies know that marketing managers who are not native to the market they are in, have to learn about the foreign culture and adapt the marketing mix to different consumer needs and wants (Coleman et al, 1987, pp. 176-180). They have to check the way foreign consumers think about and use their products. However, American firms do not need to go abroad to face these problems. Consumers in this country belong to many different ethnic groups. They do not respond in the same way to a given marketing mix as do majority Americans or other minorities. Even the American majority is significantly different regionally. Most firms consider Blacks and Hispanics to be two important minority groups in the domestic market and they change their marketing mixes to reach these groups.

The Emerging Minority Group

In contrast to the American Black and Hispanic markets, the Asian-American market (over five million in 1986) has traditionally been considered to be too small to warrant a separate marketing effort (Paskowski, 1986, p. 76). Furthermore, the disparate make-up of this market (Chinese, Koreans, Filipinos, Vietnamese, Cambodians, Asian Indians and so on) has discouraged the national firms from launching a marketing campaign to target these groups. For the purposes of this paper, Asia includes Pakistan and the countries lying east of it in South Asia, Southeast Asia and East Asia, but not Soviet Asia. The term Asian American refers to immigrants and refugees from these countries and the U.S.-born descendants of the earlier arrivals in the U.S.. It also includes such people as students or businessmen from these countries whose primary residence is the U.S..

The 1980 census found 3.5 million Asian Americans living in the U.S., up from 1.4 million in 1970. This is a 141 percent increase in the Asian American population as opposed to 17 percent for Blacks and 39 percent for Hispanics (Gardner, et al. 1985, p. 3). It is estimated that the Asian American population reached 5.1 million as of September 30,1985 (Gardner, et al. 1985, p. 5). Tables 1, 2 and 3 show a break down of the Asian American population in 1970 and 1980 and the rate of increase in each category as compared to Blacks and Hispanics. These numbers affirm the Asian American's status as the fastest growing U.S. minority.

There are many other factors, however, that are more important than the size of the Asian-American market. The most important one is the purchasing power of this segment. As shown in Tables 4, 5,and 6, the income level of Asian-Americans is impressive when compared to that of the other segments of the population.

L3, A Chinese advertising agency in New York, surveyed a sample of Asian Americans. The company found that among 411 Asians in the New York metro area, some 40% reported household incomes over $30,000, 37% own their homes, and 52% attended college (Poltrack, 1987, p. 30).

As shown in Tables 7 and 8, the Asian Americans tend to be highly educated. College is considered a must for children in Asian families. The firm targeting this segment would be dealing with a more sophisticated group. This would in turn lead to an improved understanding of promotional messages. "Chinese see advertising as a personal invitation," explains Joseph Lem, one of L3 owners, "if you advertise, the Chinese customer thinks you want his business." (Paskowski, 1986, p. 73).

TABLE 1

ASIAN-AMERICAN POPULATION BY ETHNIC GROUP
(1980)

ETHNIC GROUP	POPULATION
Chinese	812,178
Filipino	781,894
Japanese	716,331
Asian Indian*	387,223
Korean	357,393
Vietnamese*	245,025
All other Asian	200,395
Black	26,495,025
Hispanic	14,608,673
Total Asian	3,500,439

* Note: In 1970 data on Asian Indians were included in the "white" category, while Vietnamese were put in a general "other" race classification.
Source: Population Bulletin, Population Reference Bureau, Inc., 1980 Census data.

TABLE 2

ASIAN-AMERICAN POPULATION BY ETHNIC GROUP
(1970)

ETHNIC GROUP	POPULATION
Chinese	431,583
Filipino	336,731
Japanese	588,324
Korean	69,510
All other Asian	112,573
Black	22,580,289
Hispanic	9,072,602
Total Asian	1,538,721

Source: Bureau of Census in U.S. Department of Commerce, 1970 Census data.

TABLE 3

POPULATION CHANGES (000)
1970 TO 1980

	1970	1980*	Percent Increase 1970 to 1980
White	177,749	188,372	6.0%
Black	22,580	26,495	17.3%
Hispanic	9,073	14,609	61.0%
Chinese	432	812	88.0%
Filipino	337	782	132.0%
Japanese	588	716	21.8%
Korean	70	357	410.0%
American Indian	827	1,420	71.7%
All Asians	1,537	3,500	127.4%

* Figures for Asian Indian and Vietnamese are not available for 1970 because these groups were so small in 1970. It is estimated that the population of both groups increased by at least a factor of five times.

TABLE 4

INCOME BY ETHNIC GROUP (1980)

ETHNIC GROUP	INCOME IN DOLLARS*	INDEX NUMBER**
Black	11,327	73
Vietnamese	11,641	75
Hispanic	11,650	75
Filipino	13,690	88
Korean	14,224	91
White	15,572	100
Chinese	15,753	101
Japanese	16,829	108
Asian Indian	18,707	120

*Full-time American workers, median annual income, 1980 Census data, Source: Population Reference Bureau, Inc.

**The index number is a better guide to relative income. White, $15,572 equals 100.

TABLE 5

INCOME BY ETHNIC GROUP (1970)

ETHNIC GROUP	INCOME IN DOLLARS	INDEX NUMBER
American Indian	5,832	59
Black	6,067	61
Hispanic	7,348	74
Filipino	9,318	94
White	9,961	100
Chinese	10,610	107
Japanese	12,515	126

Source: Bureau of Census in U. S. Department of Commerce, 1970 Census data.

TABLE 6

INCOME CHANGES
1970 TO 1980

	1970	1980	Percent Increase 1970 to 1980
Black	6,067	11,327	87%
Hispanic	7,348	11,650	59%
White	9,961	15,572	56%
Chinese	10,610	15,753	54%
Filipino	9,318	13,690	47%
Japanese	12,515	16,829	34%

Calculated from tables 4 and 5.

TABLE 7

PERCENT OF PERSONS COMPLETING HIGH SCHOOL
OR MORE AMONG WHITES, BLACKS, HISPANICS,
AND ASIAN AMERICANS AS OF 1980

ETHNIC GROUP	AGE 25-29	AGE 45-54	AGE 25-29	AGE 45-54
White	87.0%	68.7%	87.2%	70.1%
Black	73.8	42.9	76.5	45.9
Hispanic	58.4	38.4	59.2	35.5
Japanese	96.4	88.1	96.3	82.5
Chinese	90.2	68.7	87.4	57.7
Filipino	88.8	79.6	85.0	68.5
Korean	93.5	90.4	79.0	68.5
Asian Indian	93.5	86.1	87.9	62.0
Vietnamese	75.5	63.3	63.4	44.1

Source: Population Bulletin, Population
Reference Bureau, Inc., 1980 Census data.

TABLE 8

EDUCATION IN 1970
(Age 25 and over)

ETHNIC GROUP	HIGH SCHOOL	COLLEGE
White	54.5%	11.3%
Black	31.4	4.4
American Indian	33.3	3.8
Hispanic	28.7	3.4
Chinese	57.8	25.6
Filipino	54.7	22.5
Japanese	68.8	15.9
Korean	71.1	36.3

Source: Bureau of Census in U.S. Department of
Commerce, 1970 Census data.

All of these factors point to the need for a
separate marketing mix aimed at the Asian-
American community. This is particularly
relevant for those products that are targeted
toward higher income groups, such as luxury
consumers goods,professional services, and so
on. Rublin Lopez, market director of special
projects at Metropolitan Life, said "when you
look beyond the raw statistics (five million
people), the audience tends to be better
educated, have income 11% greater than the norm
and is growing fourteen times faster than the
general population" (Paskowski, 1986, p. 76).

The Companies Entering into This Market

Metropolitan Life is one of the pioneers among
national firms in marketing to Asian Americans.
For Metropolitan the impetus came from a report
by Judity Langer & Associates, a market research
firm. Previously, the insurer had experience
with Langer when the company approached the

Hispanic market in 1983. Metropolitan now leads
that market and is increasing its Hispanic
advertising budget to $2.4 million this year
(Schnorbus, 1987, p. 8). Since the company
succeeded with Hispanics, it decided to follow
the same steps it used for that market in
developing the Asian-American market. The
Langer report suggested that Metropolitan enter
the Asian-American market quickly. Lopez
further explained "...They are centered on
family and view education as a high priority.
Therefore, when you look at Asian Americans
across the board, they are the ideal prospect
for insurance products and services" (Paskowski,
1986, p. 76).

Metropolitan Life found out from the Langer
report that the Chinese were ideal candidates
for whole life and universal life policies
because they tend to purchase insurance both for
family member's protection and for children's
education (Paskowski, 1986, p. 76). In order to
learn more about Asian Americans and find
appropriate media buys, L3, the Chinese
advertising agency, designed an advertisement
with the slogan "Your child has the best
protection (from you)...How about yourself?"
This slogan seemed to work. Upon the advice of
L3, Metropolitan Life has spent $200,000 on
Chinese and Korean newspaper advertising in 1985
and has written up $17 million worth of new
premiums (Paskowski, 1986, p. 75). Recently
other insurance companies have followed the lead
of Metropolitan. New York Life, for example,
had a full page advertisement in The World
Journal-a Chinese language daily published in
New York-promoting its line of insurance and
investment services (The World Journal, 1987,
page 25).

Remy Martin, the cognac people, is another firm
that has entered the Asian-American market.
"Beautiful moon with nice wine to celebrate the
Chinese Moon Festival" is a rough translation of
the slogan developed by the L3 advertising
agency for Remy. This slogan was used in a full
page advertisement in The World Journal (1987,
p. 25). Remy's associate marketing manager, Pat
Prudhon,has high hopes for this campaign. He
says "The incidence of cognac consumption in the
general population is about 3%, but with Asians
it is much higher, so it makes plenty of sense
to target this group" (Paskowski, 1986, p. 75).
An L3 survey among all Asians in the New York
metro area showed that Remy Martin was the top-
of-mind liquor brand (Poltrack, 1987, p. 28).

Another reason behind Remy Martin's attempt to
market to the Chinese community, and the
subsequent competition from Schieffelin &
Somerset Company, importer of Hennessy Cognac,
is again the higher average income of the
Chinese community. Because of their higher
income, the Chinese are more inclined to buy
higher-priced liquor brands.

Another company to enter this market is Proctor
& Gamble who will not discuss their complete
marketing strategy for the Asian-American

market, but Chinese language advertisements for Tide detergent have been seen in New York subway stations.

The Zeckendorf family, one of the largest real estate developers in New York, recognizing the importance of the Asian-American market has used the appropriate media to sell real estates to this segment. Arthur Zeckendorf said that 30% of his sales are to Asians, especially Chinese. This percentage is far higher than the general population (Cheung, 1987, p. 57). Other real estate developers, Chinese or American owned, have also seen the potential of the Asian-Americans market and have had their representatives even go overseas to look for the buyers.

Media

Of 333 randomly chosen Asian-Americans in a L3's survey, 47% claim to accept English advertisements. However, Joe Lem, president of the agency, notes "Based on my observations of the community, I would say this is exaggerated" (Poltrack, 1987, p. 30). Whatever the ability of the Asian Americans in English, it is clear that most of them are more comfortable with their own language. Therefore, there is a need to advertise in the native language of the Asian-American community.

Among 411 Asians in the New York metro area interviewed by L3, 48% cited advertising as an important source of product information. Most indicated television as the most influential medium (71%), followed by newspapers (55%) and magazines (46%) (Poltrack, 1987, P. 28). Yet the survey found that most Asian Americans get their information from newspapers, business and commercial directories and 86% of the respondents are regular readers of Chinese-language newspapers and/or publications (Poltrack, 1987, pp. 28, 30). The Chinese are one of the largest and oldest Asian-American segments. Therefore, a study of the Chinese media available for advertising should provide a general guide fornational firms interested in this market.

Among the different advertising media, T.V., radio and newspapers are the most important. There is a Chinese T.V. station in New York, one in San Francisco, and more are coming . There are also many Chinese newspapers. In New York, for example, there are at least seven Chinese daily newspapers which accept advertising. The advertisers can find good local newspaper buys in most big cities. Currently, most of these newspapers carry local advertisements for Chinese shops and only a few national advertisers, such as Metropolitan Life. This is also true for Korean newspapers (Paskowski, 1986, p.77). The Zeckendorf family found their success in Chinese language newspaper advertising in New York. Although real estate in New York is expensive, $500 to $600 per square foot, they often find it is easy to sell to the Chinese. Zeckendorf says "They (The Chinese)

even bring a whole bag of cash!" (Cheung, 1987, p. 57). There is another way to reach the Asian-American market. Zeckendorf said his company has hired several Chinese and Asian Americans as sales representatives. This is also a conclusion in the Langer's report which notes that it is necessary to hire Asian Americans to develop the Asian-American market.

Joe Lem found that the respondents in his survey seem to appreciate special marketing efforts aimed at them. The respondents stated they shop at Macy's frequently, a store which has a well-known policy of hiring Chinese (Paskowski, 1986, p. 78). Not every Asian American speaks English and even many who do, feel more comfortable with a sales representative who can speak their language and appreciate their wants and needs.

Another advertising medium in Asian-American communities is the local yellow pages published in Chinese. There are Chinese yellow pages in both New York and San Francisco. Such companies as Charles Schwab and Aamco Transmission have used this medium to reach Chinese-American market.

Conclusion

Each year, some 40,000 Chinese are allowed to immigrate into the U.S.. The immigration Reform and Control Act of 1986 provides the opportunity for Chinese in Hong Kong to increase the quota from 600 to 5,000. The law also allows illegal aliens to apply for status as permanent residents.

Some 3 million to 5 million illegal aliens live in the U.S., according to the Bureau of Census. The Bureau of Census also estimated that ten percent of these illegal aliens came from Asia and 50% of these Asians stay in California and 11% in New York (Stengel; 1987, page 16). With the significant 1997 deadline, more Chinese in Hong Kong are expected to move overseas.

With this rich and fast-growing Asian-American market, especially Chinese and Koreans, concentrated in a few large cities, local and national advertisers can use specific media to reach this market. The advertisers should use the success of Metropolitan Life, or Zeckendorf as a model.

Newspapers seem to be the best way to reach this audience. As Lopez said, "You can almost get $10 worth of advertising for every dollar that you would spend in general media" (Paskowski, 1986, p.77). Metropolitan's success is not a secret and marketers should enter into Asian-American market without hesitation but with careful preparation.

References

Cheung, Hen-Lien (October 18-24, 1986), "The Rush to Hop on the Orient Express," China Times Weekly.

Coleman, Linda J., Ernest F. Cooke and Chandra M. Kochunny (1987) "What is Meant by Global Marketing?" Developments in Marketing Science Volume X, Jon M.Hawes, Ed., Akron, OH: Academy of Marketing Science.

Gardner, Robert W., Bryant Robey, and Peter C.Smith (1985), "Asian Americans: Growth, Change, and Diversity," Population Bulletin, Vol.40, No.4 Washington, DC: Population Reference Bureau, Inc.

Paskowski, Marianne (October, 1986), "Trailblazing in Asian America," Marketing & Media Decisions.

Poltrack, Terence, (June, 1987) "A Map of Chinatown," Marketing & Media Decisions.

Schnorbus, Paula (May, 1987), "Met Life's Official with Hispanic Businesses," Marketing & Media Decisions.

Stengel, Richard (May 4, 1987), "Out of the Shadows" Time.

The World Journal, (October 4 & 5, 1987).

Winski, Joseph M. and Laurel Wentz (June 2, 1986), "Parker Pen: What Went Wrong? Why Global Marketing Plan Floundered," Advertising Age.

THE ENGLISH AND NON FRENCH MARKET IN QUEBEC: ISSUES AND PROSPECTS[1]

Robert D. Tamilia, University of Quebec at Montreal
and
Stanley J. Shapiro, Simon Fraser University

Abstract

The status of the Quebec market is a minority one in North America but is in the majority within the Province. The anglophone and non French market is, however, a minority one within Quebec, but is in the majority outside the Province. This paper examines the current status of this minority market and discusses some of the marketing issues related to the impact of the Charter of the French Language on it.

Introduction

The Quebec market is probably one of the most unique markets in North America for a number of reasons. It is the only market whose population is dominated by a French-speaking majority. Other markets may also exhibit such a characteristic (e.g., Miami, Southwestern Texas and California). However, apart from its size of over 6.5 million individuals (25.8 percent of the Canadian population), its uniqueness comes from the presence of the French language which, over the last four centuries, has contributed to the history and richness of Canada (Rudin 1985).

It is also the only market in North America which is under the political control of a French-speaking majority. In other words, it is the only area in which the English language occupies a secondary role socially and politically. The implications of such a reality means that the French language is institutionalized at all levels in Quebec society (Arnopoulos and Clift 1984).

The purpose, then, of this paper is to examine the minority status of this anglophone market (and other non French-speaking consumers). We will try to seek answers to such questions as: how can this market be defined; what is happening to this market, especially since the passage of Bill 101; what is the marketing significance of the above questions. Is this market a disadvantaged one? Finally, what does the future hold for this market in Quebec society.

The Definition of an Anglophone or a Francophone Consumer

Defining a francophone or an anglophone consumer is not an easy task (Tamilia 1980). Numerous approaches have been used to define such consumers. Some of these are: (1) mother tongue (language first learned during childhood), (2) dominant language (language spoken at home; language most often used), (3) language of returned questionnaire, (4) geography (Quebec vs Ontario), and finally (5) surname of respondents.

Depending on the definition used, one study found that French and English consumers were misclassified ranging from a low of 12 percent to a high of 37 percent (Bergier and Rosenblatt 1982). The surprising finding of this study was that the misclassification rate was consistently higher for anglophones than for francophones.

How Important is the Non French Market in Quebec?

The 1981 census revealed that out of a total Quebec population of 6,438,405, 11 percent or 706,115 individuals had English as their mother tongue, and 6.6 percent or 425,280 had a mother tongue other than French and English, referred to as allophones. Thus, 82.4 percent of the population had French as its mother tongue.

The 1986 census for the first time made it possible for respondents to select more than one mother tongue. The 1981 data were readjusted to reflect this change. Based one a single mother tongue choice, there was a decrease of 61,520 individuals whose mother tongue was English (Tamilia 1987, Table 3). This decrease between 1981 and 1986 corroborates with the decrease of 94,565 English mother tongue individuals between 1976 and 1981 (Tamilia 1987, Table 4).

The actual decrease of English mother tongue individuals between 1976 and 1986 cannot be obtained due to the 1986 census change on the mother tongue question. Nevertheless, it is safe to assume that in the decade following the election of the PQ party in 1976, the Quebec anglophone population dropped by at least 100,000. Furthermore, the number of individuals whose mother tongue is neither French nor English also dropped by over 50,000 during this same period (Tamilia 1987). While it is true that events since 1976 have exacerbated the outflow of anglophones and others, the reality is that this market has actually been declining steadily over the last one hundred years (Bailey 1985).

The relative decline of the anglophone and non French market notwithstanding, it is still a market larger than the total provincial population of Manitoba, Saskatchewan, Nova Scotia, Newfoundland or Prince-Edward-Island.

---

1   Funds for this paper were provided by the Programme d'aide financière aux chercheurs et créateurs, UQAM.

More importantly, it is also a less expensive market to reach as 79 percent of them are to be found within Montreal CMA.

The last decade has seen an increase in the number of francophone viewers tuning in to English media, notably television (Beauchamp and Bouchard 1982). In fact, some English television programs in Montreal have up to 75 percent of the audience being francophones (Boychuk 1983). Hence, the anglophone and non French market in Quebec is actually much larger than based on figures derived from mother tongue statistics.

The Charter of the French Language

The Charter is a very complex law affecting every facet of living and working in this province. It is a powerful law whose intent is to make Quebec as French as the rest of Canada is English. The law has received worldwide news coverage and is constantly debated in the Quebec and Canadian news media.

It is a law of very important significance to Canadian marketers for it imposes strict rules on the use of the English language. For example, the use of English in outdoor and transit advertising is prohibited, and so are English-only product manuals, labels, catalogues, and other sale promotion material. The law permits the use of English or other languages only in certain cases (i.e., religious messages) and only on the condition that French is also prominently shown. The law disallows the use of English on all public signs, commercial or otherwise, as stated in article 58. For many, this article of the law is the most contentious one in Quebec. Due to its importance, more will be said about this section of the law later on.

The French Language Charter and Marketing Issues

The French Language Charter does not prohibit a customer from obtaining information (e.g., catalogues or correspondence) in English. A written request is usually sufficient to receive information in English; otherwise the information is automatically sent in French. Unfortunately, even when specifically asked, some Quebec firms or government agencies have not always responded favorably to English Quebecers' wishes (Montreal Gazette 1983, 1987). Yet the Official Languages Act of 1969 states that all federal services, correspondence, public signs, and so forth need to be in both languages in Quebec and elsewhere. Such past violations of a federal law in Quebec indicates that, perhaps, Bill 101 takes precedence over this federal act. Indeed, many other federal laws seem to be subordinate to Bill 101.

For example, the labelling provisions of the language law go beyond those under the federal act. Overlabels are not permitted on products sold in Quebec (i.e., sticker labels) even though the federal act allows every other province to use them for certain imported products (e.g., imported beer, ethnic foods, etc.). Instructional booklets, parts manuals, price lists, industrial and commercial catalogues, sales kits, training manuals, and so forth need to be in French before the product or service is allowed to be marketed here. Kucharsky (1985) reports that the introduction of wine coolers in Quebec may have been delayed due to its English-sounding name. This example demonstrates the impact of the language law on new product introductions. Unfortunately, no study has actually been done showing which products or services never made it to Quebec or had a delayed introduction due to the language law.

The law then acts as a trade barrier, a form of tariff for that market. The current Canada-United States free trade debate raises the question of whether or not products and services moving freely between the two borders will need to conform to the language law (Sparer 1986). Apparently, yes, according to a recent report (Warren 1987).

The federal packaging and labelling act specifies that consumer products sold in Canada need to satisfy bilingual informational requirements such as, the country in which the product is made, the name of product, its size or weight, expiration date, and so forth. However, not all information on the package needs to be bilingual. But with Bill 101, some Quebec-based firms and some provincial crown corporations have not continued this tradition. In other words, the bilingual requirements for labels and packages are conforming only to what is legally required under the federal law with some information printed in French only (Tamilia 1987).

The language law also goes beyond the federal agricultural and foodstuff act. Bill 101 can, in theory, prohibit the sale of imported agricultural products having an English sticker attached to them, as in the case of pineapple rather than the French equivalent word "ananas" (Aubin 1982; Blouin 1983). Obviously, no fruits and vegetables have yet been barred from entering the Quebec market. But the specificity of the law, nevertheless, gives it such power.

Until recently, bilingual catalogues were illegal in Quebec under Bill 101. However, the language law was challenged in the Quebec courts and as of April 1984, merchants can now freely distribute such promotional material (Laurent 1984). But the language victory may be no more than a moral one given that most firms had already switched to printing separate English and French catalogues at the time the law was passed.

The printing of separate French and English flyers and catalogues raises an important segmentation problem. How can a firm be sure that the unilingual English catalogue is reaching those who are anglophone or who desire such material? Given the difficulty of defining and reaching such consumers, as previously discussed, raises the possibility of such material falling into the wrong hands. Apparently, this happens (Montreal Gazette, November 20, 1987).

In such instances, the French consumer who has been "victimized" can complain to a special governmental agency, called the Commission de la protection de la langue française, the enforcement agency for Bill 101. Not surprisingly, its agents are colloquially referred to as "tongue troopers". Any francophone citizen can report violations and violators of Bill 101 to this agency without any fear of reprisal. The law protects the anonymity of those who complain. This agency has generated much criticism, especially among Quebec anglophones (Allen, 1982; Neal 1984). The very existence of this agency is testimony, according to these authors, of the disadvantaged status of Quebec's non French population.

An important case in which this agency was involved with not long ago is pertinent here. The marketing of kosher products in Quebec was threatened because their labels violated the French Language Charter. Apparently, the Commission received a number of complaints from the public about the so-called illegality of such products since they did not respect the language law. This case raises the important issue of who complained. Would a user of such products complain to the Commission knowing full well that such an action could result in kosher products being removed from store shelves? The answer is an obvious no. The religious nature of such products would almost disqualify users from voicing a complaint. In all probability, it was a nonuser, likely associated with one of the militant French language rights groups.

It took almost ten years to resolve the marketing dilemma of such products, since many of them were imported in small quantities from New York (Conseil de la langue française 1986). The lesson to be learned from this case is that under the law, a nonuser can potentially prohibit a user from buying a product or a service legally sold elsewhere in Canada.

This example is atypical in today's marketplace in which a nonuser tries to prevent a user from obtaining the product he or she wants. It is more typical for certain controversial products such as cigarettes, drugs or pornographic material. Yet the law has the potential of removing any product, controversial or not, from the market, if it does not conform to the language law requirements.

The Sign Provisions of Bill 101

Article 58 of the language law specifies that all signs need to be in French only. It disallows the use of bilingual or English-only signs. Given the 1.1 million non French residents of Quebec, it goes without saying that this article has created a lot of tension and controversies in Quebec society.

What is surprising about this article is that it has been successfully challenged in the Quebec courts as being unconstitutional. The present "illegality" of article 58 is now before the Supreme Court of Canada. The decision should be known by late 1988. Yet the current government refuses to amend the present law to bring it in line with recent court decisions. The argument used is that the law as it now stands has brought "social peace" which could be threatened if the law is modified.

Article 58 guarantees the French face of Quebec. After all, Quebec is a French-speaking society and the law permits that only French be visible. But the article also raises an important distributive justice question. To what extent can a majority prohibit a minority from displaying commercial signs in its language? After all, the Quebec anglophones are saying that it is allright for them to be heard but not seen! Similarly, to what extent should an anglophone be denied access to a product or service, or to consumer information because of the unavailability of such information in the language of the majority? Of course, the ultimate question we could ask is to what extent can a majority impose its will on a minority?

The politics of article 58 notwithstanding, what are the marketing implications of the sign provisions of the language law? We could say that French-language marketing communications are now more widespread. But to what extent do commercial signs in French only help consumers? After all, such signs do not provide much information, at least sufficiently to affect market behavior.

In a sense, all consumers, French and English, are now less knowledgeable of the types of merchants they may wish to patronize. In the past, a consumer could select a merchant on the basis of the language store sign. With all signs now being in French, a consumer can no longer make a store selection based on the language of the sign. We could argue that, all other things being equal, it tends to favor anglophone retailers since francophones no longer have the benefit of selecting a store on the basis of the store sign language. In theory, the market base of an anglophone retailer has been enlarged due to francophones becoming potential customers. Also, the market behavior consequences of the sign article would probably be more important for small anglophone retailers predominantly located in French-speaking sections of the market than for large ones such as department stores, chain stores or other large retailers

The Future of the Quebec Anglophone Market

The disadvantaged status of the Quebec non

French market is due to the fact that it is English-speaking. In addition, the market and social restrictions imposed upon it by Bill 101 contribute to its minority status (Caldwell and Waddel 1982). In all likelihood, it would be difficult to find an equivalent situation in the recent history of an industrialized democracy, in which a government has imposed such restrictions on freedom of speech, including commercial speech. First Amendment protection has been extended to commercial speech in the United States (Cohen 1978). The commercial prohibition of a language, as outlined in article 58, would surely be judged unconstitutional there. Perhaps the Supreme Court of Canada will follow suit.

Irrespective of the present legal status of Bill 101, the reality of Quebec anglophones is that they have been left mostly to themselves to fend for their rights without much help from Ottawa (Yalden 1983). Also, the present insignificant number of anglophones within the Quebec civil service or the federal one based in the province, is not helping the English cause (Mann 1983). Recent surveys indicate that an alarming proportion of anglophone youths (up to 50 percent) intend to leave this province upon graduation (Caldwell 1982; Caldwell and Obermeir 1978). On the political front, English-speaking Quebecers have lost the representation they once had at both the federal and provincial legislative assemblies.

Another harsh reality of the English market is that immigration policies are under provincial and not federal jurisdiction in Quebec (Simar 1983). In addition, English Quebec is reported to have a birth rate even lower than French Canada's, whose rate is considered to be one of the lowest in the world (Tamilia 1987). Bill 101 also imposes restrictions on the accessibility of English language education (excluding university) for children whose parents were educated in the English language. In fact, Seidman (1987) reports that the English student population in Quebec dropped by 53 percent between 1975 and 1986. Also, English-speaking professionals need to take French language competency tests in order to work in this Province. Finally, there are other laws, apart from Bill 101, which impinge upon the non French market (e.g., the Cinema Act, which restricts distribution of English films). It is obvious, then, that English Quebecers (and others) are being subjected to social, political, and regulatory forces whose impact will be felt well beyond the twenty-first century.

The recent debate on the Meech Lake accord which, if approved, will amend the Canadian Constitution and recognize Quebec as a distinct society within Canada. In essence, the distinct society clause will state that Quebec is not a province like the others, and accord it a form of special status it has sought since Confederation. Understandably, this clause is worrisome for English Quebec. While the legal status of the clause is ambiguous despite recent constitutional hearings, it will further strengthen the French-speaking majority status in Quebec. It will legitimize Bill 101, and it will provide Quebec with more "power" relative to the central government. But the extent to which it will do so is unknown at this time. Furthermore, will it impose the same restrictions or more of them on the non French segment of the population?

Conclusions

The language law presents a marketing dilemma for Quebec consumers. For francophones, they are not given the opportunity of either choosing between a product now available with English-only labels and instructions or delaying their purchase until such time as the product conforms to the language law. Without the law, would market forces prevail and offer such consumers all of the French language marketing information that they need and require? Apparently, the Royal Commission on the Status of the French Language in Quebec (1972) found a number of cases which showed that the market was not responding fully to the linguistic needs of its French-speaking consumers. French language requirements notwithstanding, what happens to the price of products after the language law has been satisfied? Are prices the same or higher? If they are higher, are consumers aware of it, and would they accept or reject the higher price if they had a choice? In essence, the language law removes such decisions from the marketplace.

Non availability of products or product delays may hurt more the industrial, commercial, and financial services markets (i.e., software, computers, medical, dental, and advanced engineering products) more than the consumer market.

Irrespective of the constitutionality of the language law or whether or not the distinct society clause will be approved, the non French market in Quebec has been subjected to regulatory forces unlike anywhere else in recent history. The anglophone exodus attests to that fact. However, the language law is also having an impact on the Quebec market system. Whether or not the evolution, growth, and direction assumed by the Quebec market in the years ahead will be in the interest of all Canadians, including non French Quebecers, remains to be seen.

References

Allen, Glen (1982),"What are the 'language cops' really like?", Montreal Gazette, (June 5), B-5.

Arnopoulos, Mcleod Sheila, and Dominique Clift (1984), The English Fact in Quebec, 2nd edition, Montreal and Kingston: McGill-Queen's University Press.

Aubin, Benoît (1982), "Cinq ans Après,", L'Actualité, 7 (August), 34-42.

Bailey, Donald (1985), "The French Presence in Canada: The Case for Optimism," Canadian Ethnic Studies, 17 (No. 3), 100-119.

Beauchamps, Sylvie and Pierre Bouchard (1982), Le français et les médias, les habitudes des Québécois, Conseil de la langue française, Éditeur officiel du Québec.

Bergier, Michel and Jerry Rosenblatt (1982), "A Critical Review of Past and Current Methodologies Used for Classifying English and French Consumers", in Marketing, 3, Michel Laroche, ed., Ottawa: ASAC Proceedings, 11-20.

Blouin, Jean (1983), "Les gardiens de la langue", L'Actualité, 8 (August), 49-56.

Boychunk, Ron (1983), "The Impact of English media on Francophones, " Marketing, (June 13), 22-25.

Caldwell, Gary (1982), "Anglo-Quebec on the verge of its history", Language and Society, 8 (Autumn), 3-6.

Caldwell, Gary and P. Obermeir (1978), "Emigration de la jeunesse anglophone au Quebec 1971-1976," Cahiers québécois de démographie, 7 (August), 3-24.

Caldwell, Gary and E. Waddell eds. (1982), The English of Quebec From Majority to Minority Status, Quebec City: Institut québécois de recherche sur la culture.

Cohen, Dorothy (1978), "Advertising and 1st Amendment", Journal of Marketing, 42 (July), 59-68.

Conseil de la langue française (1986), L'étiquetage des produits kosher, Rapport et Avis.

Fraser, Joan (1986), "Defining the problem: principles for action", Language and Society, 17 (March), 16-18.

Kucharsky, Daniel (1985), "Use of English word could delay 'hot' drink", Montreal Gazette, (October 1), A-5.

La Commission d'enquête sur la situation de la langue française et sur les droits linguistiques au Québec (1972), La langue de travail, Livre 1, l'Editeur officiel du Québec.

Laurent, René (1984), "Superior Court rules Quebec can't ban bilingual catalogues", Montreal Gazette, (April 5), A-1, A-2.

Mann, Jonathan (1983), "English-speaking Quebecers under one percent of civil service: Study", Montreal Gazette, (May 31), A-5.

Montreal Gazette (1983), "Use gas and essence both", (June 3), B-2.

Montreal Gazette (1987a), "Petro-Can and should", (March 7), B-2.

Montreal Gazette (1987b), "English-only chain-store flyers worry PQ", (November 20), A-4.

Neal, Christopher (1984), "Mentality of language watchdog created climate of fear: Alliance", Montreal Gazette, (January 6), A-3.

Ronald Rudin, (1985), Quebecers A History of English-Speaking Quebecers 1759-1980, Quebec City: Institut québécois de recherche sur la culture.

Seidman, Karen (1987), "Francophone tide flooding English school boards", Montreal Gazette, (December 12), B-1.

Sparer, Michel (1986), Libre-échange et droit linguistique, Notes et Documents 60, Conseil de la langue française.

Tamilia, Robert (1980), "Cultural Market Segmentation in a Bilingual and Bicultural Setting," European Journal of Marketing, 14 (No. 4), 223-231.

Tamilia, Robert (1987), "The Duality of Canadian Culture: Toward an Understanding of the Quebec and French Canadian Markets", Working paper no. 01-88, Centre de recherche en gestion, UQAM, Décembre.

Warren, Jack (1987), "Quebec's demands are being met in free-trade deal", Montreal Gazette, (November 30), B-3.

Yalden, Max (1983), "Federal attitudes to anglo-Quebec an ambiguous one," Montreal Gazette, (March 25), B-3.

PORTRAYAL OF BLACKS IN ADVERTISING: A CRITICAL REVIEW OF THE LITERATURE

Thelma L. Snuggs, Purdue University
William J. Qualls, University of Michigan

Introduction

As the largest minority group in the United States, black Americans with an annual purchasing power of over two billion dollars, are an attractive marketing segment (Joseph, 1986). The challenges confronting advertisers today revolve around two issues: (a) How should advertisers use black models in advertising in a way that appeals to the profitable and growing black segment? and, (b) How can advertisers appeal to the black segment in a way that retains or increases the favorable product perceptions of the white segment?

The purposes of this paper are 1) to review the research literature which has examined the portrayal of blacks in advertising over the past fifteen years, and 2) to identify key issues for future research regarding the representation and role of blacks in advertising. Nine major research journals in which advertising research is frequently published were selected for study over the fifteen year time period from 1970-1985. Relevant articles were reviewed from: Journal of Marketing, Journal of Marketing Research, Journal of Advertising, Journal of Advertising Research, Journal of Consumer Research, Journal of Communication, and Journalism Quarterly, Public Opinion Quarterly, and Current Issues & Research in Advertising.

Numerous research studies have been undertaken in an attempt to address the issue of the role of blacks in advertising (see Humphrey and Schuman 1984). The period of this review is particularly important, because of the number of studies which have been published since Kassarjian's (1969) critical piece.

In the sections to follow, a critique of research on the role of blacks in advertising is presented. For the purposes of this review, research studies have been divided into three major categories. Section I deals with research on the presence and role portrayal of blacks in advertising. Section II discusses studies conducted on the effects of the model's race on product evaluations, and/or attitudes toward the ad. Finally, Section III examines research on the perceptions of blacks in advertising. Limitations of the research in this area are also discussed and suggestions for future research are presented.

The Presence and Role Portrayal of Blacks in Advertising

One of the earliest studies to have investigated the portrayal of blacks in advertising was published by Shuey, King, and Griffith in 1953. They found that blacks were present in less than one percent of all the ads examined and were typically portrayed as porters, waiters, or servants. Some 15 years later Kassarjian (1969) and Cox (1970) conducted similar studies and found that blacks comprised less than one-third of one percent of the total pages printed in the magazines studied. In a replication of the Shuey, King and Griffith (1953) study, Cox (1970) attempted to determine whether the percentage of integrated ads and the occupational status of blacks in ads in magazines had changed during the last twenty years. A comparison of the findings of these two studies revealed a statistically significant increase in the number of blacks used in advertising, and also found a significant shift in the occupations portrayed by blacks in magazine advertising. More recently, Humphrey and Schuman (1984) found that while the occupational levels of blacks portrayed in ads had risen, blacks remain underrepresented in American advertising. These four studies are typical of the studies which had investigated the role of blacks in advertising.

Most studies concentrated on the use (presence) of black models and/or the role portrayed by blacks in commercial ads, and were mainly interested in determining whether a black face appeared in the ad and the role played by the model. For example, Dominick and Greenberg (1970) examined television commercials to determine trends with respect to the portrayal of blacks for three consecutive television seasons (1967-69). They found that blacks were used to sell actual products rather than used as background figures, but were rarely seen alone in an advertisement.

Several different research studies which arrive at similar findings and conclusions would generally be accepted as proof enough to validate the results. Yet, significant methodological problems exist in each of the studies lead one to question the method by which the results were obtained. For example, in a critique of Kassarjian's (1969) study, Wheatley (1971) questioned the method used by Kassarjian to estimate the number of blacks in ads relative to the total number of pages in a magazine. Wheatley contends that if Kassarjian had calculated the number of blacks as a function of the number of ads, the number of blacks in ads would be double. Further nonconfirming evidence is provided in a study by Colfax and Steinberg (1972), who concluded that although the number of blacks appearing in ads increased, the manner in which blacks were depicted tended to confirm and perpetuate racial stereotypes.

Thus, while the evidence suggests a clear increase in the number of blacks in ads over the years, the effect of this increase is not clearly understood. There is less of a consensus regarding the roles portrayed by black models in advertisements. Several authors found a significant shift in the stereotypical occupations portrayed by black models in advertising to less stereotypical occupations over time, (Cox 1970, Dominick and Greenberg 1970). Conversely, other researchers have found no appreciable shift in the stereotypical occupations portrayed by black models in advertising (Colfax and Steinberg 1972, Bloomquist and O'Kelly 1976). Thus while it appears that the actual number of black models in advertising has increased, the roles they play and the impact they have had is ambiguous and not fully understood. This would suggest that researchers have failed to address issues which would benefit managers in making marketing and promotion decisions. For example, it would be interesting to determine whether the patterns exhibited in magazine advertising extend to other types of media. Similarly, it would be helpful to determine whether the presence of black models inhibit or stimulate the purchase of a product or service to the majority or minority communities. The next section of the paper will examine the research that has addressed the first question.

Bloomquist and O'Kelly (1976) examined the presence of black models in television commercials for 28 hours over a 28-day period. Their findings suggest that 1) blacks tended to be greatly under represented in T.V. ads, and 2) blacks are still shown in stereotypical roles. Such findings would tend to provide support for results suggested by Colfax and Steinberg (1972) in an earlier study.

In a replication of the magazine study by Dominick and Greenberg (1970), Bush, Solomon, and Hair (1974) and Hair, Solomon, and Bush (1977) examined the role of blacks in television ads and compared their findings across cities in the South and West. They found: 1) an increase in the use of black models between 1967 and 1974, 2) no differences between the South and West in the use of black models, 3) black models were more likely to be portrayed in public service and promotion ads than in product ads, 4) blacks tended to be used to advertise personal products more than nonpersonal products and, 5) blacks were more often portrayed in major roles in national ads but were shown more frequently in minor and background roles in local ads.

Again, while such studies have been beneficial in helping to describe the phenomena of blacks in advertising, very little understanding about the dynamics of the phenomena or the impact it has upon buyer behavior is ever obtained. The reason that research has not advanced beyond the descriptive level of analysis is related to the lack of theory development or theory testing.

Effect of Models' Race on Audiences' Product and Advertising Evaluations

In an effort to understand how white and black consumers react to the use of black models in advertising, a second major stream of research has concentrated on examining of consumer product evaluations and attitudes toward the ad or sponsoring company. This section begins with a review of empirical studies that have investigated consumer reactions to the use of black models, and then reviews briefly.

Many of the studies on product evaluation based on the model's race were conducted because marketers and advertisers are concerned that they will alienate the white market by using black models in advertisements. For example, Cagley and Cardozo (1970) attempted to measure the attitudes of high- and low-prejudice whites to all-black and integrated ads for three products (Trim-line telephones, vodka, and men's suits). They hypothesized that highly prejudiced whites would evaluate ads with white models more favorably than ads with all black or with integrated models. In general they found that whites respond to blacks in advertisements according to the level of their prejudice.

However, a series of studies that followed Cagley and Cardozo (1970) revealed just the opposite in terms of consumer reactions, both white and black. That same year Guest (1970) reported results of an experiment on the use of black models in ads and attitudes toward the sponsoring company. Their findings suggest that there appeared to be a more positive attitude toward the company from respondents who were shown integrated advertisements and a overall neutral reaction toward all black ads. Guest concluded that there were no "clear-cut" differences found for consumer evaluations to the company, and that integrated ads appeared to attract greater attention than all-blacks ads alone.

Similar results were found in a study conducted by Stafford, Birdwell, and Van Tassel (1970). In an experimental study of one hundred white consumers (50 males and 50 females), they investigated the attitude of whites toward integrated advertising. Respondents from New York, Chicago, and Los Angeles were recruited from major shopping centers in each city, and placed in either a control group which viewed ads with all white models, or in the experimental groups to view ads with integrated models.

The results suggest that white consumers' reactions were quite similar for both the integrated and nonintegrated ads, with their verbal reactions to the ads and their corresponding intentions to purchase. The researchers found that the respondents were slightly less positive for a personal product ad (lipstick) than for a durable good (automobile). Differences in consumer responses were attributed to the products. They concluded that certain integrated ads may elicit negative responses, not as a function of race but as a result of poor creative advertising and execution, or of yet unidentified interactions.

Muse (1971) extended this stream of research on evaluations by white respondents on the use of black models to four products: cigarettes, vodka, feminine napkins, and beer. An experiment was designed which divided respondents into two groups, one which viewed ads with black models (control group) and a second which viewed ads with white models (experimental group). Findings from the study tended to support Muse's hypothesis that, ads with black models would be rated as favorably as duplicate ads with white models among white audiences.

However, variations in consumer reactions were found to exist across product categories. For example, there were no significant differences in consumer ratings for vodka and beer. Conversely, cigarette ads with black models received significantly lower rating than those with white models, while feminine napkin ads with black models received significantly lower consumer ratings than those with white models. Muse concluded that white college students tend to rate ads with black models as favorably as ads with white models. Finally, an unfavorable reaction to black models in ads appear to be product-related.

In a similar test of the same hypothesis, Tolley and Goett (1971), examined the reactions of 400 black and white, middle- and lower-class women (100 from each group) to the use of black models in newspaper ads. Results from the study indicate that the use of black models may create a competitive advantage for retailers. Ads with black models tend to receive greater visibility in the black community, while the use of black models did not detract from the product advertised, the store, or the creative treatment used in the ad. Secondly, the use of black models did not alienate white consumers as whites tended to overlook black models depicted in department store ads. When white respondents did notice black models in ads, the majority reacted favorably. The researchers concluded that black models should be placed "in a position of equality with white models and black models that are immediately perceived as black [should be used]."

A different medium was investigated by Schlinger and Plummer (1972) who investigated the reactions of 94 black and 192 white female consumers to identical all-black and all-white versions of a 50 second cigarette television commercial. In the commercial a man and woman, each of whom was smoking a cigarette, were shown in a home setting. Half of the respondents were shown the all black commercial and half viewed the all white version. Results indicate that black consumers tend to identify and react more favorably to commercials/advertisements with all black models rather than to ads with all white models. There was no evidence to suggest that black consumers might have negative reactions to the use of black models. Conversely, white consumers' reactions were quite different. White women tended to view the black version of

the commercial as less professional, less developed, and less sophisticated than the all white version of the ad.

Thus, research up until 1974 appeared to suggest very negative reactions to the use of black models by white or black consumers. The conclusion, when negative reactions were found to exist, centered on the interaction between the product and the race of the model. In a test of this proposition, Szybillo and Jacoby (1974) examined the reaction of 90 black and 90 white students to advertisements with varying levels of integration for six products (Irish whiskey, dress shirts, umbrellas, attache cases, deodorant, and underwear). The five levels of racial integration depicted in the ads were: 1) 100% black (4 black models), 2) 75% black (3 black, 1 white models), 3) 50% black (2 black, 2 white), and 5) 0% black (4 white models). Thus a 2x5x6 (2 racial groups x 5 levels of racial integration x 6 products) factorial design was tested in the study. The researcher found support for their hypothesis "that young blacks reacted negatively to integrated ads depicting tokenism (e.g., three whites to one black) and positively to ads depicting equality (e.g., two whites to two blacks)."

In an attempt to verify and extend the previous research in this area, Bush, Gwinner, and Solomon (1974) measured the responses of black and white consumers to black models in promotional materials which used black models in point-of-purchase displays for bars of bath soap. The study results indicated no differences in consumer response to the black, white, or integrated point-of-purchase displays by white consumers. The authors concluded that marketers need not be concerned about using black models in promotional materials because whites respond similarly to white and black models.

In a replication of the study by Cagley and Cardozo (1970), Bush, Hair, and Solomon (1979) examined the reaction of high- and low-prejudice white consumers to the use of black and black-and-white (integrated) models in ads for six products. Three versions of each of the six experimental ads were tested with only the model's race varying in each condition. Results of the 2x3 factorial design (high and low prejudice x all black, all white, both black and white models) again provided nonconfirming evidence of the Cagley and Cardozo hypothesis. The researchers found "that the level of prejudice held by consumers does not appear to affect "white consumers' responses to ads containing all white, all black, or black and white (integrated) models. They concluded that there is very little difference between white and black consumers' evaluations of the ad regardless of the race of the model depicted.

In general the major conclusion from the research in this area centers around three conflicting findings. First, it is suggested that white respondents evaluate ads with white models more favorably that ads with black models (Cagley and Cardozo 1970, Schlinger and Plummer 1972, Kerin 1979). Second, the research suggests that black respondents evaluate ads with black models more favorably than with white models (Tolley and Goett 1971, Schlinger and Plummer 1972, Szybillo and Jacoby 1974, Kerin 1979). Finally, there is a set of research that found that white respondents evaluate ads with black models as favorably as ads with white models (Guest 1970, Stafford, Birdwell, and Van Tassel 1970, Muse 1971, Tolley and Goett 1971, Bush, Hair, and Solomon 1974, 1979). There is a serious question regarding the physical characteristics of the black models used is several of the studies. It is believed that the black models may in fact resemble the majority population more so than its own racial group. In those studies that found an effect, it appears significant effects occurred only when the product was of a personal nature (i.e., deodorant, tampons, etc.). These issues are addressed in the next two sections of the paper.

Perceptions of Blackness: Physical Characteristics of Black Models in Ads

What constitutes "black advertising"? Does the mere presence of a black face constitute a black ad? This section of the review focuses on the characteristics of black models used in advertisements. The impetus for research in this area appears to have been driven by methodological concerns regarding biases found in previous research studies. Specifically, the major issue has been the degree in which black models are perceived as black through facial characteristics, skin color, and hair type. Not surprisingly, only a few studies have been published which examine this issue. These studies have examined such items as the physical features of the black model (skin tone, hair quality, facial features, etc.) and their effect on the type of product advertised.

Gitter, O'Connell and Mostofsky (1972) investigated the self-concepts of black Americans by examining the trends in the racial appearance of black male and female models in Ebony magazine over a 17-year period, 1952-68. Each model was evaluated and rated on three anthropological racial features: 1) physiognomy - thickness of lips and width of nose, 2) hair texture - straight smooth hair or kinky coarse hair, and 3) skin tone - light vs. dark skin. The researchers found that the facial appearance (lips, nose, hair texture, and skin color) of both black male and female models tended to be more white than black over the study period. In addition black males tended to portray more facial features associated with blacks, while black females tended to exhibit more white physical characteristics.

A replication of the above study was conducted by Chapko (1976) in a examination of ads in Ebony magazine for the years 1970, 1972, and 1974. Chapko reported a reduction in the number of advertised products to make blacks appear more white (e.g., skin lighteners, hair straighteners, and wigs), and an increase in the number of products directed towards black consumers (i.e., Afro products). Such results lead the researcher to conclude black consumers no longer desired to emulate whites, as reflected in 1) the reduction of ads with only white models and 2) an increase in the number of ads with black models only. In addition, Chapko found that while black male models had gotten darker, black female models had gotten lighter.

More recently Kerin (1979) examined the effect of a black models physical characteristics on consumer product evaluations. A 2x2x2 factorial experimental design manipulated the facial features (Negroid vs. Caucasian), hair style (Afro vs. wavy hair) and skin tone (dark vs. light skin) of black models featured in a proposed ad. Kerin found that the black model's physical appearance does affect consumers' perception of product quality. Further analysis revealed that the physical features of black models for personal use products impacted the perception of suitability of the product for white consumers. Based on these results Kerin concluded that blacks and whites tend to associate product quality with models possessing physical characteristics similar to theirs.

Methodological Limitations of Previous Research

While the limitations of research on blacks in advertising has been discussed throughout this review, it is important to highlight certain deficiencies before any generalizations or conclusions can be drawn from any of these studies. First many of the findings reported in previous research were not statistically evaluated, but were only submitted to qualitative analytic techniques, or relied upon frequencies or percentage distributions as the primary mode of analysis. This is shown in Table 1, which presents an overview of the data collected and the analytic techniques used in the research studies reported in this paper.

Methodological concerns regarding sample size and composition raise additional red flags about the reliability and validity of previous research findings. For example, in a number of these studies college students were used as subjects, making questionable any inferences that are drawn on the basis of the general consumer population. In far too many cases, implications or conclusions drawn from the studies' results by researchers appear to surpass their findings. In some instances, generalizations advanced by the researchers appear based upon their opinion rather than on the facts.

Furthermore, there are serious questions about the research design employed in several of the studies, e.g., altering the model's color but not his/her facial features; constructing and testing pseudo ads, rather than attempting to locate ads with black models; using white researchers to interview black respondents or to evaluate the skin coloring and hair texture of black models to be used in test ads. All the above examples represent possible sources of bias for survey respondents.

Finally and possibly the most serious limitation of this field of research is its lack of theory construction and testing. The lack of theory has probably been the reason that more is not known and understood about the use of black models in advertising. In general, research on the portrayal of blacks in advertising suffers from numerous methodological shortcomings which have inhibited development of this field of research. A major goal of this paper has been to cite some of the limitations of these studies so that future research in this area can avoid problem areas and improve present information.

Conclusions

This paper has attempted to provide an overview of the research on the portrayal of blacks in advertising. In spite of the number of studies which have been published advertisers are still not certain how to target the black market while retaining the white market because of the conflicting results of past research studies. There is a need for further theoretical development and empirical testing to resolve conflicting findings. Future research must overcome the problems and limitations discussed in this paper to gain an understanding of the dynamics of blacks in advertising or the consumer behavior resulting from the effects of minority models in advertising. The nature of the preceding discussion has been critical, but it should help guide thinking and serve as a basis for future research in this area. As the interest in marketing niches grows, and especially as marketers become interested in targeting minority groups (Hispanics, blacks, Asian-Americans), researchers will need to address the issues discussed above.

Further research studies should be concentrated on:

1. What constitutes black representation in advertising (physical characteristics, number of blacks, etc.).

2. Impact of stereotypical vs. non-stereo-typical roles for blacks. Examination of issues regarding the social consequences of black models in advertising. Do they perpetuate racial stereotypes or help to eliminate them.

3. Examination of the "product category inter-action" effect in regards to why some product categories get more favorable evaluations when they carry black models than others.

4. Development of theories that lead towards explanation and prediction. For example, perhaps theoretical frameworks from the racial stereotyping or attribution research might be appropriate in addressing the above issues.

5. Examination of how the representation of blacks affects consumers behavior (purchase intentions, consumption behavior). Are

differences in attitudes and/or evaluations in/significant to the extent we should ignore/acknowledge racial differences.

What have we learned about the role that blacks have had in the advertising and marketing of products as a result of the research to date? As we pointed out in the above discussion, the number of black models in advertising may have increased but our knowledge concerning the impact of their presence remains unchanged. The results of our critique support the general hypothesis that the research in this area has advanced very little beyond the descriptive level, and it lacks a theory or research structure to guide future research.

References

Barban, Arnold and Edward Cundiff (1964), "Negro and White Response to Advertising Stimuli," Journal of Marketing Research, Vol. 1 (November), 53-56.

Block, Carl (1972), "White Backlash to Negro Ads: Fact or Fantasy?, Journalism Quarterly, Vol. 49 (Summer), 258-262.

Bloomquist, Edwards, Linda and Charlotte G. O'Kelly (1976), "Equality in Advertising: Women and Blacks on TV," Journal of Communication, Vol. 26 (Autumn), 179-184.

Bush, Ronald, Paul Solomon, and Joseph Hair (1977), "There are More Blacks in TV Commercials," Journal of Advertising, Vol. 17 (January), 21-25.

_____ (1974), "A Content Analysis of the Portrayal of Black Models in Television Advertising," in Combined Proceedings of the American Marketing Association, Ronald C. Curhon, ed. Chicago: American Marketing Association, 427-430.

Bush, Ronald, Joseph Hair and Paul Solomon (1979), "Consumers Level of Prejudice and Response to Black Models in Advertisements," Journal of Marketing Research, Vol. 16, (August), 341-345.

Bush, R.F., R.F. Gwinner, J. Solomon (1974), "White Consumer Sales Response to Black Models," Journal of Marketing, Vol. 38 (April), 25-29.

Cagley, James W. and Richard Cardozo (1970), "White Response to Integrated Advertising," Journal of Advertising Research, Vol. 10 (April), 35-39.

Chapko, Michael K. (1976), "Black Ads Are Getting Blacker," Journal of Communication, Vol. 26 (Autumn), 175-178.

Choudhury, Pravat and Lawrence S. Schmid (1974), "Black Models in Advertising to Blacks," Journal of Advertising Research (June), 19-22.

Cohen, Dorothy (1970), "Advertising and the Black Community," Journal of Marketing, Vol. 34 (October), 3-11.

Colfax, David and Susan Steinberg (1972), "The Perpetuation of Racial Stereotypes: Blacks in Mass Circulation Magazine Advertisements," Public Opinion Quarterly (Spring), 8-18.

Cox, Keith K. (1970), "Social Effects of Integrated Advertising," Journal of Advertising Research, Vol. 10 (April), 41-44.

_____ (1969-70), "Changes in Stereotyping of Negroes and Whites in Magazine Advertisements," Public Opinion Quarterly, Vol. 33 (Winter), 603-606.

Culley, James and Rex Bennett (1976), "Equality in Advertising: Selling Women, Selling Blacks," Journal of Communication, Vol. 26 (Autumn), 160-174.

Dominick, Joseph and Bradley Greenberg (1970), "Three Seasons of Blacks on Television," Journal of Advertising Research, Vol. 10 (April), 21-27.

Gitter, A. George, Stephen M. O'Connell, and David Mostofsky (1972), "Trends in Appearance of Models in Ebony Ads Over 17 Years," Journalism Quarterly, Vol. 49 (Autumn), 547-550.

Guest, Lester (1970), "How Negro Models Affect Company Image", Journal of Advertising Research, Vol. 10 (Winter), 29-33.

Hair, Joseph, Paul J. Solomon, and Ronald R. Bush (1977), "A Factor Analytic Study of Black Models in Television Commercials", Journal of Business, Vol. 50, 208-215.

Humphrey, R. and H. Schuman (1984), "The Role Portrayal of Blacks in Magazine Advertisements: 1950-1982", Public Opinion Quarterly, Vol. 48, 551-563.

Joseph, W. Franklin (1986), "Despite Growth in Marketing, Strong Resistance Continues" in Special Report: Marketing to Blacks, Advertising Age, (August 25), S-2.

Kassarjian, Harold H. (1969), "The Negro and American Advertising 1946-1965", Journal of Marketing Research, Vol. 6 (February), 29-39.

Kerin, Roger (1979), "Black Model Appearance and Production Evaluation", Journal of Communication, Vol. 29 (Winter), 123-128.

Muse, William V. (1971), "Product-Related Response to Use of Black Model in Advertising", Journal of Marketing Research, Vol. 8 (February), 107-109.

"Printers Ink", Advertising Week, Vol. 282 (March 1, 1963), 11.

Schlinger, Mary J. and Joseph Plummer (1972), "Advertising in Black and White", Journal of Marketing Research, Vol. 9 (May), 149-153.

Shuey, Audred M., Nancy King and Barbara Griffith (1953), "Stereotyping of Negroes and Whites: An Analysis of Magazines Pictures", Public Opinion Quarterly, Vol. 17 (Summer), 281-287.

Solomon, Paul J., Ronald R. Bush and Joseph Hair (1976), "White and Black Consumer Sales Response to Black Models", Journal of Marketing Research, Vol. 13 (November), 431-434.

Stafford, James, Al Birdwell and Charles Van Tassel (1970), "Integrated Advertising-White Backlash", Journal of Advertising Research, Vol. 10 (April), 15-20.

TABLE 1

Classification of Research Studies by Medium Examined, Subject Used, Data Collection Procedures and Analysis

	Advertising Medium	Subjects	Data Collection	Data Analysis
Shuey, King and Griffith (1953)	Magazines	-	Content Analysis	Percentages
Kassarjian (1969)	Magazines	-	Content Analysis	Frequency, Chi-Square
Cox (1969-70)	Magazines	-	Content Analysis	Frequency & Percentages
Choudhury and Schmid (1970)	Magazine ads with black & white models	Black college students	Questionnaire	Chi-Square, Kolmogorov Smirnov tests, T-tests
Dominick and Greenberg (1970)	Television	-	Content Analysis	Percentages Chi-Square
Guest (1970)	Slides of print ads	582 white college students	Questionnaire	Percentages Chi-Square
Stafford, Birdwell and Van Tassel (1970)	Lipstick & car ads	100 white consumers	Questionnaire, eye camera interviews	T-test, Mann-Whitney U tests
Muse (1971)	Magazine ads for 4 products with black & white models	120 college students	Personal interview	T-tests, regression, correlation coefficients
Tolley and Goett (1971)	Newspaper	400 middle and lower income consumers (black and white)	Personal interviews	Percentages correlation coefficients
Wheatley (1971)	Magazines	-	Content Analysis	Percentages
Block (1972)	Magazine ads for 3 generic products (21 ads)	104 white adults	Interviews	Mann-Whitney U tests
Colfax and Steinberg (1972)	Magazines	-	Content Analysis	Frequency & Percentages
Gitter, O'Connell, and Mostofsky (1972)	Magazines	-	Content Analysis	Frequency, Percentages
Schlinger and Plummer (1972)	Created TV ads	192 white & 92 black women	Likert scale	F-tests
Bush, Gwinner & Solomon (1974)	End-aisle, point of purchase displays	443 white consumers	Observation	ANOVA, Chi-Square
Bush, Solomon, Hair (1974)	Television	-	Content Analysis	Percentages Chi-Square
Szybillo and Jacoby (1974)	Proposed ads	180 college students (90 white & 90 black)	Questionnaire	ANOVA Newman-Keuls
Chapko (1976)	Magazines	-	Content Analysis	Frequency & Percentages
Fox (1976)	Television, Magazines	-	Content Analysis	
Bloomquist & O'Kelly (1976)	Television	-	Content Analysis	Percentages Chi-Square
Bush, Solomon, Hair (1977)	Television	-	Content Analysis	Factor Analysis, F-tests
Bush, Hair, Solomon (1979)	Print ads	237 white adult shoppers	semantic differential scale	F-tests, Scheffe tests
Kerin (1979)	Created black and white print ads	180 black & 180 white female college students	Semantic differential scales	ANOVA

102

PERCEPTIONS AND BEHAVIOR OF MINORITY CONSUMERS TOWARD GENERIC CONSUMER PRODUCTS

Bhagaban Panigrahi, Norfolk State University
Jon C. Stuart, Norfolk State University

Abstract

This study reports the findings of a survey of ethnic consumers' perceptions toward no brand (i. e., generic brand) consumer products. Regarding the perceptions of generic's compared to manufacturer's brand, the data revealed that generics are viewed as moderately different with respect to various brand attributes. Implications from these findings are drawn for manufacturers and retailers.

Introduction

In the U.S., patterns of ethnic target markets are changing continuously. In the past ethnic segments have been well integrated to a large extent into the mainstream of the American society. Such groups include: Poles, Irish, Germans, Italians, Greeks, and the Jewish to name a few. In recent years, however, immigration from Europe to America is continually declining. Whereas new immigrants from South and Central America as well as Asian countries are increasing at a faster pace (Berkman 1980). This trend should encourage marketers to study the characteristics of new subcultural segments-particularly Asian Americans (i.e., Chinese, Filipinos, Vietnamese, and Asian Indians) in addition to Blacks and Mexican Americans. Because Asian American subcultures represent the third largest, and the most well-to-do segments of the U.S. population today.

Several different subcultural as well as ethnic groups in the U.S. have been studied widely by consumer analysts and marketing researchers. Many of these research studies are cross-cultural in nature in the sense that they have compared two or more subcultural groups. Often this comparison has been done between Whites, Blacks, and Mexican Americans (Alexis 1962, Dalrumple 1971, Hoyer 1982). However, very little information is available about Asian Americans in general, and Asian Americans as a consumer in particular. For instance, according to 1986 population figures, there are more than five-million Asians and Pacific Islanders living in the U.S. In addition, this particular subcultural segment of the American population is growing rapidly, and it is expected to reach a total of ten million by the turn of the century. The family income of these groups is at the top among all ethnic groups, exceeding the U.S. norms by 11 percent (Paskowski 1986). Therefore, this subcultural segment as a whole will be of great interest to marketers because of their background, tradition, customs, and socio-economic status.

Purpose

Generic brands are comparatively new to the U.S. retail industry. Even though generic brands were introduced about a decade ago, and there are still considerable debates on the offering of the generic products by retail dealers and the consumption pattern of the ultimate consumers. The primary objective of this study is to determine and to compare the attitudes of two ethnic groups; such as Blacks (the largest racial minority in the U.S.), and Asian Americans (the third largest, and the fastest growing minority in the U.S.) with regard to the purchase and consumption of generic consumer goods. Besides the size of the Asian American consumers in the U.S., very little is known about their decisions on brand choice, especially their generic brand purchase behavior.

More specifically, this paper examines the following: (1) How generic products are perceived among these two ethnic subcultures among: one (Black) which is very visible, and the other (Asian Americans) is less visible?; (2) How often, and what types of generic products are purchased by these two distinct subcultural groups? (3) How satisfied are these ethnic segments in consuming generic products? (4) What are their demographic characteristics?

Methodology

Data for this study were collected by a short questionnaire using a convenience sample of 200 Blacks and 200 Asians from the Hampton Roads Metropolitan Statistical Area (the 28th largest in the U.S. in 1987). The total usable sample received consisted of 125 respondents (i.e. 85 Blacks, a response rate of 42.5 percent and 40 Asian a response rate of 20 percent).

The structured questionnaire employed in the study consisted of eight comparative statements designed to be answered on a five-point, strongly agree and strongly disagree scale. Statements were chosen with an intention of obtaining a cross section of attitudes and perceptions of Black and Asian consumers toward generic brand products. In addition, a variety of demographic data; including information on income, marital status, formal education, age, occupation of respondents were collected. Furthermore, a few behavior related questions such as frequency of purchase, identification of the actual buyer, type of generic goods purchased, store preference, and the satisfaction level of generic products purchased were included.

Results and Discussions

To determine the relative perceptions toward generic brands and manufacturer's brands, a few brand attributes were compared among Black and Asian consumers. As can be expected, the manufacturer and generic brand attributes are widely ranged on value (price), prestige, quality, package, popularity, etc. (Wilkes 1985). Both groups of consumers indicated widely held perceptions to the first statement that generic brands have attributes that are similar to manufacturer's brands. For example, approximately 86 percent of Black consumers agree with the statement whereas only 62 percent of the Asian consumers agreed with this statement. With regard to the remaining seven attitudinal statements both groups of consumers showed similar perceptions toward generic and manufacturers' branded products and no significant difference were noted. (see Table 1). The results, in part, may be due to the relatively small sample of black and Asian consumers.

Table 1 shows the frequency distribution in percentages for all the attitudinal variables. Although the results indicated differences between the two groups to be insignificant, it appear that Asian are less enthusiastic and relatively little less concern toward generic brand products than Black respondents. In other words, Asian consumers showed less agreement to the statement such as generic brands carry prestige equal to manufacturers' brands. This may be attributed to the fact that many Asians have recently emigrated from poorer countries (i.e. India, Pakistan, China, Philippine Islands, Malyasia, Indonesia, etc.) and their desire for a better life means seeking out products that carries status symbols. In order to demonstrate that they are equal with average Americans, they purchase and consume more of established manufacturers' brands rather than generic brand products. However, respondents from both groups showed a great deal of agreement with each other to the statement #2, #4, #5, #6, #7, and #8. (see Table 1). Overall, the findings of this study showed relatively positive attitudes toward generic brands, but respondents seem skeptical about its popularity. This could be due to satisfaction with their current usage of name brand manufacturers' products, as well as imported generic products by Asian consumers that are made available to them through the ethnic stores. Furthermore, the differences between Blacks and Asians could be attributed to the fact that average Asian household income is higher than average Black household income and hence Asians can afford in purchase name brand goods more frequently than Blacks.

With respect to demographics, data showed no major differences between Blacks and Asian consumers in terms of age, marital status, education, and occupation. These difference are presented in Table II. It was anticipated that Asians would be different from Blacks in socio-economic characteristics and hence, attitudes toward generic brands would vary. The rational

was that Asian consumers would maintain their economic consciousness for survival and which would lead them to purchase and consume generic brand products more often than Black consumers (Dalrymple 1971). The results of this study, however, provide no support for this expectation.

In addition, Black and Asian consumers do not appear to be appreciably different in their shopping patterns of generic brands. Both groups were only marginally different with regard to the frequency of purchase, store preference, the amount spent on generics and the type of generic goods purchased. Table III presents the results on generic brand purchase behavior by both groups. The study indicated that both Blacks and Asians are spending a relatively small amount on generic brands. More than 60 percent Black and Asians, however, mentioned that they purchase generic brand products occasionally and about 88 percent of the respondents have tried generic product(s) at least once, while only 12 percent respondents have never bought generics. This represents a higher purchase rate for generic brand products than the findings of prior studies (Faria 1979) In terms of satisfaction received from the usage of generic brand products, a majority of the respondents stated that they are satisfied in their generic product consumption. From all these, it can be interpreted that as long as generic brands continue along with manufacturers' brands and reseller brands to meet the needs of average consumers whether they are ethnic or non-ethnic.

Conclusions and Implications

The primary focus of this paper was to investigate the perceptions of two groups of ethnic consumers (i.e., Blacks and Asians) toward generic brand products. The overall results of this study of 125 respondents indicated that Blacks and Asian consumers do not appear to be significantly different in their attitudes as well as their shopping habits. However, Black consumers perceive generic brands more favorably than do Asians. This finding support the conclusion reached by an earlier study (Wilkes 1985). Given the brand image, popularity, and attractiveness of manufacturers' brands and the taste for quality product which appear among middle-income consumers of this country, it is not surprising that minority consumers are unwilling to give up their status of using brand name goods. Although, the diffusion of innovation in the usage of generic products have a moderate effect on retailers as well as ultimate consumers, it does not appear that there have been any significant change in minority consumer behavior.

These findings have some important implications for manufacturers and producers of branded products and intermediaries, particularly retailers. The general implication for producers and distributors is that as the attitudes and perceptions of minority (i.e., ethnic) and majority (i.e, anglo) consumers do not vary substantially, classifying them as separate target markets based upon the purchase of generic products may not be necessary. Therefore, it can be concluded at this time that these attitudes are widely distributed throughout markets.

In addition, for national brand manufacturers, this study clearly suggests that consumers, whether Black, Asian, Mexican or any other ethnic group(s), instead of purchasing no brand products would prefer to purchase products with superior image, value, and attractiveness. Therefore, this strategic opportunity should not be overlooked by manufacturers, for example, manufacturers and producers of traditionally branded goods should promote heavily their brand name supermarket items to remind and reestablish brand loyalty among ethnic consumers.

From the perspective of retailers and other intermediaries, generic brand products present several valuable opportunities. As the growth rate is increasing year after year due to their low price and acceptable quality appeal, moderate promotional campaign emphasizing price differentials and consistent quality may generate further ethnic interest toward these brands.

The final implication of this study is that ethnicity has some influence on purchasing and consumption of generic brand products. Therefore, retailers may be particularly affected by ethnic influences on a community basis. Hence, they should be sensitive to purchasing pattern of each ethnic target market and may need to locate manufacturers and wholesalers who would be able to supply ethnic products to meet the needs of many ethnic segments present in the U.S.

In conclusion, given the exploratory nature of this study, the results are fascinating. Since the sample was not representative of the Hampton Roads MSA, the results are not conclusive however, and hence not projectable. A great deal of further studies are needed in this topic in order to obtain projectable and reliable findings.

TABLE 1

Question 1: Generic products have attributes that are similar to manufacturer's brands.

	Blacks %	Asian %	Total %
Strongly agree	12.94	5.26	10.57
Agree	72.94	57.89	68.29
Neither	2.53	10.53	5.69
Disagree	8.24	26.32	13.82
Strongly disagree	2.35	0.00	1.63

Question 2: Generic Brands have a value equal to a manufacturer's brand.

	Blacks %	Asian %	Total %
Strongly agree	5.88	5.26	5.69
Agree	42.35	47.37	43.90
Neither	11.76	10.53	11.38
Disagree	32.94	34.21	33.33
Strongly disagree	7.06	2.63	5.69

Question 3: Generic brands carry prestige equal to a manufacturer's brands.

	Blacks %	Asian %	Total %
Strongly agree	5.88	0.00	4.03
Agree	15.29	5.13	12.10
Neither	12.94	17.95	14.52
Disagree	45.88	61.54	50.01
Strongly disagree	20.00	15.38	18.55

TABLE 1 (Con't)

Question 4: Generic brands have quality that is as consistent as a manufacturer's brand.

	Blacks %	Asian %	Total %
Strongly agree	3.57	5.26	4.03
Agree	42.86	34.21	40.16
Neither	14.29	15.79	14.75
Disagree	34.52	42.11	36.89
Strongly disagree	4.76	5.26	4.92

Question 5: Generic brands have packages that are as attractive as a manufacturer's brand.

	Blacks %	Asian %	Total %
Strongly agree	1.18	0.00	0.81
Agree	9.41	15.32	11.29
Neither	7.06	5.13	5.65
Disagree	52.94	48.72	51.61
Strongly disagree	29.41	30.77	29.84

Question 6: Generic brands are as popular as manufacturer's brands.

	Blacks %	Asian %	Total %
Strongly agree	1.18	0.00	0.81
Agree	14.12	10.26	12.90
Neither	9.41	15.38	11.29
Disagree	57.65	66.67	60.48
Strongly disagree	17.65	7.69	14.52

Question 7: It is easier to make decisions to buy generic brands compared to a manufacturer's brand.

	Blacks %	Asian %	Total %
Strongly agree	3.61	2.56	3.31
Agree	26.51	23.68	25.62
Neither	12.05	13.16	10.75
Disagree	48.19	57.89	51.24
Strongly disagree	12.05	2.63	9.09

Question 8: There is a bright future for generic brands as more and more consumers develop a "no frills lifestyle".

	Blacks %	Asian %	Total %
Strongly agree	9.64	7.69	9.02
Agree	46.99	38.46	44.26
Neither	14.56	20.51	16.39
Disagree	22.89	28.21	24.59
Strongly disagree	6.02	5.13	5.74

TABLE II
Profile of Respondents

Marital Status	Blacks %	Asian %	Totals %
Single	50.3	0.0	43.0
Married	40.0	97.5	58.4
Other	9.4	2.5	7.2

Occupation	Blacks %	Asian %	Totals %
Mgr./Bus. Own./Profess.	36.9	75.0	49.2
Skilled	15.5	2.5	11.3
Non-skilled	35.7	20.0	30.6
Other	10.7	2.5	8.1
No Response	1.2	0.0	0.8

Spouse	Blacks %	Asian %	Totals %
Mgr./Bus. Own./Profess.	39.3	69.7	55.7
Skilled	32.1	9.1	19.7
Non-skilled	7.1	3.1	4.9
Other	21.5	18.1	19.7

Education	Blacks %	Asian %	Totals %
High school or less	9.6	10.0	9.7
College grad or some college	61.4	25.0	48.7
Grad. school/adv. degree	27.7	65.0	39.8
No response	1.2	0.0	0.8

Age	Blacks %	Asian %	Totals %
25 yrs. or less	38.1	2.5	26.6
26 yrs. to 45 yrs.	41.6	65.0	49.2
46 yrs. or more	19.1	32.5	23.4
No response	1.2	0.0	0.8

Income	Blacks %	Asian %	Totals %
$20,000 or less	25.9	5.4	19.7
$20,001 to $45,000	34.1	27.0	31.9
$45,001 and over	32.9	66.6	43.4
No response	7.1	0.0	5.0

Household head	Blacks %	Asian %	Totals %
Yes	59.6	78.1	67.1
No	39.4	21.9	31.9

TABLE II (Con't)
Profile of Respondents

Who is the primary purchaser of groceries?

	Blacks %	Asian %	Totals %
Wife	35.3	51.3	40.3
Husband	12.9	15.4	13.7
Both	28.2	30.8	29.0
Other	2.4	0.0	1.6
No response	21.2	2.6	15.3

TABLE III
Table of Respondents Generic Purchase Behavior

Question 9: How frequently do you purchase generic products.

	Blacks %	Asian %	Totals %
Regularly	7.1	7.5	7.2
Occasionally	60.0	62.5	60.8
Once	17.7	25.0	20.0
Never	15.3	5.0	12.0

Degree Satisfied

	Blacks %	Asian %	Totals %
Very Satisfied	21.2	18.0	20.2
Somewhat Satisfied	47.1	59.0	50.8
Somewhat Dissatisfied	4.7	7.7	5.6
Dissatisfied	2.4	2.6	2.4
No response	24.7	12.8	20.1

Shop at store without generic products?

	Blacks %	Asian %	Totals %
Yes	71.4	70.0	71.0
No	20.3	17.5	19.4
No response	8.3	12.5	9.6

What generic products do you purchase?

	Blacks #	Asian #	Totals #
Paper products	53	28	81
Plastic products	36	11	47
Canned foods	25	12	35
Laundry	25	10	35
Non-Alcohol Drinks	15	4	19
Frozen foods	12	6	18
Candy	10	0	10
Beauty products	4	3	7
Prescription drugs	4	3	7
Baked goods	2	4.	6
Alcoholic drinks	5	1	6
Cigarettes	4	0	4
Snacks	2	2	4

Of every $100 you spend in a supermarket, how much would be spent on generic products?

	Blacks %	Asian %	Totals %
$5 or less	20.0	35.0	24.8
$6 to $10	22.4	15.0	20.0
$11 to $25	12.9	7.5	11.2
$26 or more	16.5	15.0	16.0
No response	28.2	25.0	27.2

References

Alexis, Marcus, "Some Negro-White Differences in Consumption," American Journal of Economics and Sociology, Vol. 21 (January 1962).

Berkmean, Harold W. and Gilson, Christopher C., Consumer Behavior Concepts and Strategies, Dickenson Publishing Company, Inc., California, p. 123.

Dalrymple, Douglas J. and others, "Consumption Behavior Across Ethnic Categories," California Management Review, (Fall 1971), pp. 65-73.

Faria, Anthony J., "Generics: The New Marketing Revolution," Baylor Business Studies, Vol. 10, August 1979, pp. 63-79.

Hoyer, Wayne and Rohit Despande, "Cross-Cultural Influences on Buyer Behavior: The Impact of Hispanic Ethnicity," AMA Educators' Proceedings, Eds., Bruce J. Walker and Others, 1982, pp. 89-92

Paskowski, Marianne, "Trailblazing in Asian America," Marketing and Media Decisions, October 1986, pp. 74-80.

Wilkes, R. E. and H. Valencia, "A Note On Generic Purchasers Generalization and Subcultural Variations," Journal of Marketing, Vol. 49, Summer 1985, pp. 114-120.

EXAMINING THE EFFECTIVENESS OF CELEBRITY ADVERTISING TO MINORITIES: ENTERTAINERS VS. ATHLETES

Jerome D. Williams, The Pennsylvania State University

Introduction

Advertising testimonials are almost as old as advertising itself. Dating back at least to the time the first merchant added "by appointment to his Majesty" to his flyers, testimonial claims have been a favorite form of advertising (Starch 1984). Today testimonials through the use of product endorsers are still widely used. Much of this usage focuses on the celebrity endorser. For instance, estimates are that from one-third to three-fifths of prime-time television commercials use celebrity endorsements, while celebrity usage accounts for ten percent of all commercials (Forkan 1980).

According to a Wall Street Journal article by Alsop (1985), only a very few celebrities, such as Robert Redford, still refuse to appear in ads. Another one of the rare celebrity "virgins" is Diana Ross (Gayle 1981). ("Virgins" are celebrities who have never appeared as product endorsers.) For the most part, though, the use of celebrities has reached the point where practically every major show-business personality has endorsed at least one product. According to the Screen Actors Guild, its members rely on advertising jobs for about 48% of their income. In addition to entertainers, the sporting world is also a fertile breeding ground for celebrity endorsers. Table 1 provides a listing of recent product endorser examples that have been identified as successful campaigns by advertisers. As indicated, entertainers and athletes comprise most of these examples.

To further demonstrate how effective celebrity endorsers can be, during March of 1984, Pepsi Cola achieved nearly a 20% lead over Coke in brand awareness. That marked the first time Pepsi had moved ahead of Coke in brand awareness in several years. Responsibility for this significant gain was attributed directly to the use of a celebrity, Michael Jackson (Advertising Age 1984). As a counteroffensive, Coke quickly announced that more than a dozen celebrities would endorse Diet Coke (Montgomery 1984).

Despite such successes and continued wide usage, research indicates that celebrity effectiveness varies substantially. In one study (Alsop 1985) Video Storyboard Tests Inc. found that just 19% of the 1,000 consumers surveyed felt that celebrity endorsers increased their interest in products. And about half of those surveyed said celebrities do commercials only for money. Along the same lines, McCollum-Spielman, a marketing research organization specializing in analyzing celebrity impact, acknowledges that only 39% of celebrities achieve acceptable performance (Marketing News 1984). Recognizing this high degree of uncertainty surrounding the usage of celebrity endorsers, McCollum-Spielman developed a new testing service called "Star

TABLE 1
Examples of Celebrity Endorser Advertising

	Celebrity	Company/Product	Reference
1.	Michael Jackson (Singer)	Pepsi-Cola	Advertising Age (1984)
2.	Paul Anka (Singer) Robert Klein (Comedian) Shari Belafonte (Singer) Marcus Allen (Athlete) Ted Turner (Cable TV)	Diet Coke	Montgomery (1984)
3.	Lionel Richie (Singer)	Pepsi-Cola	Alsop (1986)
4.	James Coco (Actor) Chuck Yeager (Pilot) Christie Brinkley (Model)	Diet Coke	Alter (1984)
5.	John Houseman (Actor)	Smith Barney	Bernstein (1984)
6.	Barry Goldwater (Senator) Stansfield Turner (Former CIA Director) Arthur J. A. Clement Jr. (Civic Leader) Norman Cousins (Former Saturday Review Editor)	Christian Science Monitor	Marketing News (1983)
7.	Merlin Olsen (Athlete and Actor)	Florists Transworld Delivery (FTD)	Marketing News (1983a)
8.	Mary Lou Retton	McDonald's Wheaties Vidal Sassoon Energizer Batteries National Bowling Council Pony Athletic Shoes	Wall Street Journal (1986)
9.	Tina Turner (Singer) Cher (Singer) Carly Simon (Singer) Diane von Furstenburg (Designer)	McCall's	Elliott (1984)
10.	Bill Cosby (Actor and Comedian)	Coca Cola Texas Instruments Jell-O	Gayle (1981)
11.	Alan Alda (Actor)	Atari	Burstein (1984)
12.	Mr. T (Actor) Mr. Bill (Actor) Loretta Switt (Actress) Bruce Weitz (Actor) Emmanuel Lewis (Actor)	Burger King	Denver Post (1985)

Power" to get a better handle on measuring celebrity impact. These mixed results imply that celebrities can be highly successful in promoting products, but care must be exercised and marketing research must be employed to determine under which set of circumstances they are most effective.

One factor that could interact with the celebrity endorser, causing effectiveness to vary, is the demographic background of the receiver of the advertising message. For example, the ethnic background of a consumer can be a significant factor in the attitude toward celebrity endorsers. It has been suggested, though not based on empirical research, that advertisers can often get more mileage with advertising directed at Hispanics through the use of celebrities (Duga 1985).

Another factor that can interact with the celebrity endorser is the type of product. It has long been recognized that some types of products are more susceptible than others to source influences, such as celebrity endorsers. For example, Friedman and Friedman (1979) found that celebrities were more effective as endorsers for socially-oriented, value-expressive products. These types of products would involve higher degrees of psychological and social perceived risk. This research suggested, on the other hand, that celebrity endorsers may be less effective for products involving higher degrees of financial, performance, and physical risk. This may be due to the fact these latter products are more complex and require more explanation; and therefore, consumers may respond more favorable to an endorser with expertise about the product as opposed to a celebrity, who might be viewed as having less expert knowledge about these types of products.

Although the foregoing research would make it plausible to hypothesize that celebrities are less effective with high technology products, which are more complex and require more explanation, there are many situations where celebrities are used with high technology products (e.g., Alan Alda for Atari computers, Bill Cosby for Texas Instruments, and Charlie Chaplin portrayal for IBM computers). At the recent COMDEX Computer show in Las Vegas, several manufacturers employed advertising utilizing celebrities, including such examples as scantily clad model Lori Quint, and athletic personalities Gordie Howe, hockey's all-time leading scorer, Hank Aaron, baseball's top home-run hitter, and Terry Bradshaw, four-time Super Bowl quarterback (Lewyn and Hillkirk 1987). In a seemingly extreme example of incongruity in matching a celebrity spokesperson with a high technology product, a personal computer manufacturer ran a full-page advertisement in USA Today (November 4, 1987, page 5A) with "King Kong" Bundy, professional heavyweight wrestler, as the endorser.

The current study is designed to gain a better understanding of types of celebrity endorsers, such as athletes and entertainers, and how effective they are with different types of products, such as high and low technology, and whether this effectiveness varies among different ethnic groups, such as Blacks, Hispanics, and Anglos. First a review of some previous studies on celebrity advertising research will be given, followed by methodology, analysis and results, and finally a conclusion which will briefly discuss the implications for marketers.

Previous Research on Celebrity Advertising

Although there is not an overwhelming number of published studies on celebrity effectiveness, two general studies that provide some evidence to support continued use are reviewed here.

The first study was conducted by Starch (1984). The analysis is based on readership interviews in which 100 celebrity testimonials ads were matched with a non-testimonial ad of the same size and color for the same product or product of the same category. Products included clothing, cosmetics, flooring and furniture,

food, household equipment and supplies, pharmaceuticals, and toiletries. Most of the subjects were female.

The results showed that among women a celebrity testimonial advertisement usually produces higher readership scores than conventional advertisements. Celebrity advertisements are seen and remembered more than other types, and more of the text is read, according to this study.

In another study by McCollum-Spielman (1980), types of celebrities and types of products were analyzed. As shown in Table 2, entertainers and athletes, with the former holding a commanding lead, comprised most celebrity endorsers. This research also showed that most celebrities are male (seven out of ten).

TABLE 2
Types of Celebrity Endorsers

Male Entertainers	67%	Female Entertainers	82%
Dramatic Actors	27	Models, Actresses	53
Comedians	22	Comediennes	10
Singers, Musicians	12	Singers	11
MC's/Hosts	6	Veteran Actresses	8
Male Non-Entertainers	33%	Female Non-Entertainers	18%
Athletes	23	Athletes	15
Others	10	Others	3

In addition to being more frequently used, male celebrities have been used to promote a wider variety of products, as shown in Table 3. Just considering male celebrities, the major product categories are food and beverage (28%), televisions, stereos, and cameras (12%), automotive and petroleum products (8%), and beer and wine (6%). This tends to support the Friedman and Friedman (1979) study on the use of celebrities for socially-oriented, value-expressive products.

TABLE 3
Types of Products Endorsed by Celebrities

Male		Female	
Food and Beverage	28%	Women's Beauty Aids	41%
TV, Stereos, Cameras	12	Food and Beverage	21
Cars, Automotive,		TV, Stereos, Cameras	13
Petroleum	8	Household Appliances	
Beer and Wine	6	and Products, etc.	5
Men's Toiletries	6	Drugs, Remedies, etc.	5
Women's Beauty Aids	5	Others	15
Household Appliances	5		
Financial Services, Real	5		
Estate, Insurance			
Travel, Car Rental,			
Hotels, Motels	5		
Public Service	4		
Household Products	3		
Others	13		

In terms of effectiveness, the study concluded that only 41% of all celebrity commercials tested obtained above-average scores on individual measurements of clutter/awareness and attitude shift. Among male celebrities, athletes and veteran actors were quite strong, while other types (cooking experts, astronauts, journalists, politicians, corporate executives, etc.) performed comparatively poorly. Although fewer in number, women celebrities were more likely to achieve a higher level of effectiveness.

There are three studies that shed some light on celebrity effectiveness and ethnic background of the message receiver that are reviewed here.

The first study by SRI Research Center (Hume 1983) measured the reaction of Blacks, Hispanics, and Anglos to celebrity endorsers and found that Blacks and Hispanics were at least twice as likely as Anglos to rate celebrities as being "more believable" than non-celebrity endorsers. However, the same study also indicated that celebrities are "less believable" compared to "more believable" for all three ethnic groups.

In a second study reported in Marketing News (1981) by Data Black Opinion Polls, Inc. of New York, Blacks were asked what types of spokespersons were most likely to cause them to buy a product. Celebrity athletes lead the list with celebrity entertainers second.

In a third study, Marketing Evaluations Inc., a company that measures how well-liked celebrities are, began to include Hispanics in their survey. As a result, their findings showed that, on the average, the Performer Q-ratings for celebrity appeal were higher for Hispanics than for the general market. This was true regardless of whether the celebrity was Hispanic or not. For example, the highest Q-rating among Hispanics was a 59 for Clint Eastwood, while the highest among the general population was a 50 for Alan Alda. The study concluded that Hispanics tend to rate people they like higher than the intensity of liking among the rest of the population (Duga 1985).

Methodology

The purpose of this study is to examine the effectiveness of entertainer and athlete celebrities with high and low technology products among consumers with different ethnic backgrounds, in an advertising context. To address the primary areas of interest, a laboratory experiment is conducted among 160 Black, 160 Hispanic, and 160 Anglo consumers. Subjects view advertisements in which the type of celebrity and product are manipulated. They are asked to complete a questionnaire whereby they indicate their attitudes toward the celebrity spokesperson, the product, and the overall advertisement.

To manipulate the celebrity component, two spokespersons are used: a celebrity athlete (Sugar Ray Leonard) and a celebrity entertainer (Bill Cosby). These two celebrities are selected based on a pre-test from among sixteen celebrities. These were the only two that met the study's criterion of being fairly close on recognition, familiarity, and likeability among all three ethnic groups. Table 4 provides the means for these measurements for the three ethnic groups.

The product is manipulated by using four products: two high-technology products (solar energy systems and a home computer) and two low-technology products (shoes and toothpaste). These products are chosen from among sixteen

TABLE 4
Mean Values for Selected Celebrities:
Recognition, Familiarity, and Likeability

	Bill Cosby:				Sugar Ray Leonard:			
	B	H	A	I	B	H	A	I
Recognition (% Recognizing)	100	97.2	100	93.9	100	97.2	100	92.8
Familiarity (Scale 1-5)	4.66	4.25	4.49	4.21	4.53	4.33	3.86	4.05
Likeability (Scale 1-5)	4.69	3.78	4.51	4.14	4.31	3.42	3.43	3.61

n = 197
B: Blacks; H: Hispanics; A: Anglos; T: Total Mean for Entire Sample

products in a pre-test to determine the level of low and high technology as applied to different types of products. Each endorser is coupled with each of the four products. This combination of two types of endorsers, athlete and entertainer, and four products, two high technology and two low technology, results in eight different advertisements (two spokespersons x four products).

The dependent variables consist of four attitudinal measures toward the source (believability, attractiveness, competence, persuasiveness), six toward the product (likeability, superiority, reliability, pleasantness, overall attitude, and behavioral intention), and five toward the advertisement (convincingness, informativeness, interestingness, effectiveness, and overall attitude). This results in a total of fifteen dependent variables.

With two levels of the celebrity endorser (entertainer and athlete), two levels of the product (high and low technology), and three levels of the ethnic group (Blacks, Hispanics, and Anglos), this results in a 2 x 2 x 3 factorial, between-subjects design.

The two major hypotheses of interest are based on the main effects:

H1: Celebrity advertising (both athlete and entertainer) will be more effective among Blacks and Hispanics than among Anglos.

H2: Celebrity advertising (both athlete and entertainer) will be more effective for low technology products than for high technology products.

Analysis and Results

To analyze the data, and to test the hypotheses, the technique of multivariate analysis of variance (MANOVA) is used. Table 5 provides the means for the four treatment conditions (two types of celebrities x two types of products) for all subjects combined. (Separate tables for each of the three ethnic groups are available from the author if desired.) Table 5 also gives the univariate Analysis of Variance (ANOVA) results for the fifteen dependent measures for the two hypothesized main effects: ethnic background and product type.

TABLE 5
Results

	Means for Four Treatment Conditions				Univariate ANOVA for Two Hypothesized Main Effects (F-Tests, df = 1,396)	
	High Technology		Low Technology		Ethnic Background (Blacks, Hispanics, and Anglos) F	Product Type (High and Low Technology) F
	Entertainer Bill Cosby [**] (n=120)	Athlete Sugar Ray Leonard [**] (n=120)	Entertainer Bill Cosby [**] (n=120)	Athlete Sugar Ray Leonard [**] (n=120)		
Spokesperson						
Believability	6.6	5.7	7.6	6.9	14.0[*]	22.9[*]
Attractiveness	6.9	7.0	7.7	7.3	9.3[*]	6.9[*]
Competency	7.2	5.9	7.9	7.2	26.5[*]	25.8[*]
Persuasiveness	7.0	5.7	7.8	7.0	19.7[*]	24.5[*]
Product						
Likeability	6.7	6.8	6.8	6.9	9.3[*]	3.5
Superiority	6.3	6.5	6.9	6.8	10.1[*]	13.1[*]
Reliability	6.4	6.5	7.2	7.2	9.1[*]	24.6[*]
Pleasantness	7.0	6.9	7.4	7.3	4.1	9.2[*]
Overall Rating	3.6	3.7	3.9	3.9	14.5[*]	9.0[*]
Purchase Likelihood	4.7	4.9	6.1	5.9	15.7[*]	24.4[*]
Advertisement						
Convincingness	6.1	5.8	6.9	6.7	14.6[*]	21.3[*]
Informativeness	6.5	6.2	7.3	7.2	11.7[*]	24.3[*]
Interestingness	6.6	6.4	6.7	6.8	14.9[*]	4.3
Effectiveness	6.3	6.0	7.0	6.9	19.6[*]	16.5[*]
Overall Rating	3.4	3.3	3.7	3.6	21.6[*]	16.5[*]

[*] p < .01
[**] n = 120 = 40 Blacks + 40 Hispanics + 40 Anglos for each treatment.

Before analyzing main effects in a factorial design, it is appropriate to examine the inter-action effects first to determine if they are significant. If any are significant, then main effects must be analyzed and interpreted in the context of the higher order significant interactions (Kirk 1982).

Results of the MANOVA using the Wilks' lambda statistic, for the three-way ethnic group x product type x celebrity type interaction indicate no significance. Proceeding to the two way interactions, results of the MANOVA indicate that the two-way product type x celebrity type and the ethnic group celebrity type interactions also are not significant.

However, the two-way ethnic group x product type interaction is significant, $F(30,762)$ = 2.25, p < .01. Also, the univariate tests show there is significant ethnic group x product type inter-action effects for all fifteen dependent variables. An examination of the means shows the direction of the effect to be such that Blacks and Hispanics have more favorable attitudes towards low technology products while Anglos tend to have more favorable attitudes toward high technology products. One possible explanation based on previous research is that the low technology products of shoes and tooth-paste represent more socially-oriented products which are reflective of the cultural script of minorities (Williams 1986).

In examining the main effects, the major area of interest for this study, the results indicate that all three MANOVA main effects are signifi-cant: 1) celebrity type, $F(15,381)$ = 3.47, p < .01, 2) product type, $F(15,381)$ = 4.94, p < .01, and 3) ethnic group, $F(30,764)$ = 4.20, p < .01.

As indicated earlier, Table 5 gives the uni-variate main effects for the fifteen dependent variables for the two hypotheses. They are significant for all of the dependent variables at the .01 level, except for product pleasant-ness under the ethnic background main effect and product likeability and advertising interesting-ness under the product type main effect.

Although a main effect for celebrity type was not hypothesized, it is interesting to note that the entertainer celebrity was preferred over the athlete celebrity based on an examination of the means. However, this may be due to an idio-syncratic effect of Bill Cosby over Sugar Ray Leonard. According to a Denver Post (1985a) article, Bill Cosby was the most popular American celebrity, scoring higher than anyone in the past twelve years. It may be that subjects were responding to Bill Cosby's extreme popularity as opposed to just any entertainer celebrity. Perhaps with multiple operational-izations of the two types of celebrities, the results may have been different.

For the two hypotheses of interest, an examina-tion of the means indicates that the direction of the effects are as hypothesized. Blacks and Hispanics tend to rate both athlete and enter-tainer celebrities higher than Anglos. Also, athlete and entertainer celebrities when used with low technology products tend to be rated higher than when used with high technology products. Both hypotheses are supported based on this study.

Conclusion

The results of this study has a number of implications for marketers. It suggests that celebrity advertising, when targeted to Blacks and Hispanics in comparison with Anglos, can achieve extra mileage. This would be true with either an entertainer or athlete celebrity and whether the product is a high or low technology product. However, with low technology products, celebrity endorsers would be more effective than with high technology products, and this would be true for all three ethnic groups.

While some advertisers have used certain celebrities for everything from computers to Jell-O, this research suggests that perhaps they should be more selective in matching endorsers with product types. Also, as marketers more aggressively develop strategies to tap the growing purchasing power of Blacks (over $200 billion) and Hispanics (approaching $100 billion) through more effective advertising, celebrity endorsers can play a major role.

References

Advertising Age (1984), "Observations: Leaping Ahead with Pepsi," (May 7), 16.

Alsop, Ronald (1986), "Lionel Richie Has No. 1 Hit, But It Isn't on Record Charts, Wall Street Journal, (March 13), 27.

_____ (1985), "Jaded TV Viewers Tune Out Glut of Celebrity Commercials, Wall Street Journal, (February 7).

Alter, Stewart (1984), "Diet Coke Broadens Its Reach: New Strategy Uses 'Pop' Celebrities," Advertising Age, (April 30), 1.

Bernstein, Sid (1984), "Celebrities Lose Glamor," Advertising Age, (September 10).

Burstein, Daniel (1984), "Computer Marketing: No Longer Fun and Games," Advertising Age, (March 5), M12.

Denver Post (1985), "Burger King Cooks Up Whopping Ad Blitz," (June 13).

_____ (1985a), "People: Most Popular," (July 31).

Duga, Christine (1985), "Marketers Find Celebrity Endorsers Sell en Espanol," Ad Forum, 6 (March), 13-20.

Elliot, Stuart J. (1984), "Celebrities Dress Up 'McCall's' Trade Ads," Advertising Age, (October 8), 6.

Forkan, James P. (1980), "Product Matchup Key to Effective Star Presenters," Advertising Age (October 6), 42.

Friedman, Hershey, and Linda Friedman (1979), "Endorser Effectiveness by Product Type," Journal of Advertising Research, 19 (October), 63-71.

Gayle, Stephen (1981), "Commercial Success," Black Enterprise, (December), 51-56.

Hume, Scott (1983), "Stars Are Lacking Luster as Ad Presenters," Advertising Age, (November 7), 3.

Kirk, R. E. (1982), Experimental Design, Belmont, CA: Brooks/Cole.

Lewyn, Mark, and John Hillkirk (1987), "Disk Makers Try New Spin to Drive Sales," USA Today, (November 4).

Marketing News (1981), "Survey Measures Blacks' Media, Product, Ad Preferences," (August 21), 6.

_____ (1983), "Newspaper Uses Testimonial Ads, Format Revisions in Readership Bid," (November), 16 (Student Edition).

_____ (1983), "Research Suggests Using Celebrity Spokesman as Focal Point fop Floral Group's Consumer, Trade Ads," (November), 12 (Student Edition).

_____ (1984), "Marketing Research Briefs: A New Testing Service Called 'Star Power'," (March), 2 (Student Edition).

McCollum-Spielman (1980), "Star Power: Will the Force Be With You?" McCollum-Spielman Topline, 2 (August), Great Neck, New York: McCollum-Spielman

Montgomery, Jim (1984), "Coca-Cola Is Seen Claiming Diet Coke Has Passed 7-Up as the No. 3 Soft Drink," Wall Street Journal, (March 7), 12.

Starch (1984), "Celebrity Testimonials Still Effective," Starch Tested Copy, 1 (No. 10), Mamaroneck, NY: Starch Inra Hooper.

Wall Street Journal (1986), "Is America Fed Up with Olympic Sweetheart and Super Saleswoman Mary Lou Retton?" (March 6).

Williams, Jerome D., James E. Nelson, and Calvin P. Duncan (1986), "Referent and Expert Social Power Effectiveness in Advertising High and Low Technology Products to Hispanics," in Robert E. Pitts, ed., Cultural and Subcultural Influences Conference Proceedings, Chicago, IL: American Marketing Association.

RETAILING, PARTICULARLY MULTI-LEVEL DIRECT SELLING, THE EASE-OF-ENTRY OPPORTUNITY

Ernest F. Cooke, Loyola College in Maryland
Monle Lee, Indiana University at South Bend
Richard Baxter, Belmont College

Abstract

In this paper potential business opportunities for minorities in retailing are examined with an emphasis on multi-level direct selling. This is done by first discussing all forms of retailing, showing where multi-level direct selling fits and discussing the possibilities for minorities.

Introduction

Minorities have always gone into retailing as a means of attaining majority status at least as far as joining the affluent majority. This goes back to well before the familiar York immigrant push cart peddlar. Today Blacks, Asians and Hispanics are familiar sights as owners of gasoline stations, restaurants, grocery stores and today's version of the push cart, the sidewalk vendor. Multi-level direct selling presented here as an easy field to enter since it provides a favorable balance of several factors: the ability to start part-time which means a small initial labor investment, little or no cash required, because of these two factors low down-side risk and finally the possibility of substantial rewards. The reason for this paper is to examine retailing in general and multi-level direct selling specifically as a business opportunity for people with limited resources. Another reason for this paper is that little, if anything is found in the academic literature on multi-level direct selling. There is nothing new here, just a basic look at an important subject.

Types of Retailing

In developing this theme, the first step is to outline the different types of retailing (Cooke, 1985). Such an outline is shown in Table 1 and is based on this definition of retailing activities involved in the sale of goods and/or services to the final consumer. This definition implies that any customer purchase is a retail purchase, and this concept is followed in Table-1.

Services can include transportation, insurance, financial services, repairs, medical services, education and so on. Most goods and many services are sold through retail stores (well over 90% for goods). Many services such as insurance, financial services and real estate (the agent sells a service-the owner sells a house) do not involve a store. Traditionally these are not considered retail sales. These non-store service sales are also changing slightly. For example, Sears is selling insurance, securities and real estate in some stores. The point could be made here that just as most goods will continue to be sold through stores, many services will continue to be sold outside of a store. Although not called a store services such as movies, lodging and banking involve a fixed location which could be considered a store.

Examples of II.1.b (in Table 1) are conventional department stores such as Macy's. Sears is an example of II.1.a. Sears and Macy's are of course, also examples of I (regular, full-line). Real estate and insurance would be included in IV.2 and conventional stock brokers would be VI but not telemarketing On the other hand, a boiler-room stock operation could be considered telemarketing (also VI). Gypsy retailers (X) frequently sell out of their vehicle and include fruits and vegetables, clothing, velvet paintings and so on. Push carts and sidewalk vendors are also included here. Category III includes the home-shopping services on television which are being touted as a new form of retailing but are just another form of direct response advertising with television the promotional medium and UPS usually the delivery medium.

As with any classification scheme there are problems, for example, automatic bank tellers would be examples of V.2 but certainly could also be considered to be a type of vending machine (VII).

Some firms use a combination of these methods and as already noted these methods are used to sell services that are not traditionally considered retailing such as direct marketing (III) for insurance and charities.

TABLE 1

DIFFERENT METHODS OF RETAILING

Definition: Retailing comprises those activities involved in the sale of goods and/or services to the final consumer.

- I. Conventional (store) Retailers
    1. Regular or Discount
    2. Full-line, Limited-line, Single-line

- II. Catalog Retailers
    1. Conventional (store) Retailers
        a. Separate Merchandise
        b. In-store Merchandise
    2. Direct Response Advertisers

- III. Direct Response Advertisers(except catalog) frequently called direct marketing (mail order?*).

- IV. Direct Selling (door-to-door or in-the-field selling)
    1. Multi-level or single-level
    2. Seller's Salespeople (employee or agent) or Independent Contractor.
    3. Party Plan
    4. Other

- V. Computerized Retailing
    1. Video Catalogs
        a. In-home
        b. Other locations
    2. Automatic Financial Services

- VI. Telemarketing and other sellers who rely primarily on telephone contact with the customer.

- VII. Automatic Vending Machines

- VIII. Auctions

- IX. Markets (Flea, Farmer's)

- X. Gypsy Retailers (Vehicle, Pushcart, Sidewalk Vendor)

*Direct Response Advertising is not a type of advertising, it is a type of retailing. Mail Order (and Direct Mail) are either obsolete terms or are misused. Mail order is just one form of direct response advertising (retailing). Today the direct response offer can be made by any promotional medium and the post office is no longer the only means of completing the offer. Direct mail is just a promotional medium as are magazines, newspapers, television, and radio.

For these two reasons there is some confusion as to how big (or small) any one of these methods is. Multi-level direct selling (IV.1) is basically goods retailing (household products, cosmetics, health products and so on). Over ninety percent of all goods retailing is done by conventional store retailers including automobile dealers, gas stations and eating places. Multi-level and other types of non-store goods retailers, including catalogs (II.1.a and II.2 but not II.1.b), direct response advertisers (II.2 and III), direct sellers (IV.2, IV.3 and IV.4), video catalogs (V.1), some sellers who use the telephone (VI), vending machines (VII), auctions (VIII), farmer's and flea markets (IX) and gypsy retailers (X) together probably account for less than ten percent of all goods retailing.

Store retailing is and will continue to be the dominant form of retailing because, despite the so-called inconvenience, people like to see, touch, smell and feel basically at a time and place of their choosing, and the store provides all of this more effectively than any other method of retailing. In store retailing there is also a socialization factor, an entertainment factor (people like to shop) and it is easier to return unsatisfactory merchandise. For example, in catalog sales the buyer can not see, touch and feel, and if not satisfied with the purchase, must go through the bother of returning it through some delivery service. Sears stores represent a convenient method of returning catalog merchandise which help explain the success of their catalog operation and justifies calling this store-type retailing (II.1.a and II.1.b).

In direct selling, the buyer loses some control over time and place. The buyer may not want to see the salesperson when they show up and because they are at home, they may find it difficult to "walk away" from the salesperson. Telemarketing for some buyers combine all these disadvantages.

Multi-Level Sales Organizations

The concept of several levels of personnel and managers is a standard part of the sales management (Baxter & Cooke, 1985) and/or channel of distribution literature as it applies to all types of organizations, but the subject here is basically limited to organizations using the direct selling method of retailing and building successive external independent levels. Since these levels are usually occupied by independent business people, there is a great deal of similarity here to the typical channel for packaged grocery products-food broker to grocery wholesaler to grocery retailer, which is three levels. The difference is that the multi-level sales organization represents one manufacturer and since there is no store or traditional retailer or wholesaler, it is called direct selling. Within a large sales organization several levels can be seen ranging from the sales manager to regional sales managers to district sales managers to branch sales managers to sales- people depending on the size of the organization. A comparison of two different multi-level marketing organizations with a typical multi-level direct selling organization is shown in Table 2.

It is important to note a difference between multi-level direct selling and typical channels of distribution. With a normal channel of distibution the actual movement of goods from manufacturer to consumer is through the channel. In the multi-level organizations the handling and movement of the product or the transfer of ownership is not a major factor. It is the recruitment of new dealers that is emphasized. The product channel does not necessarily parallel the organization channel and the two frequently have little relationship. It is the various commissions that follow the organizational lines of the multi-level system.

Pyramiding

Multi-level direct selling has, at times, a poor image. One reason is the pyramiding aspect which is a questionable form of the multi-level direct-selling system. Profits do not necessarily come from selling the product. The significant profits come from encouraging other people to join the organization as distributors or dealers.

There are three income sources at the upper levels in these pyramids. The first is the commission on products sold directly to the ultimate consumer by people in these upper levels, the second is the over-ride on all product sales made by their distributors or dealers to the ultimate consumer. The third source is in the selling of titles, ranks, motivational and inspirational products or services. The problems exist because the upper-level entrepreneurs in these pyramids find the second and third income source more profitable than the first. The legal, ethical and image problems come from some aspects of this third income source. It is specifically the emphasis on recruiting dealers which separate-and sometimes only on very fine lines-the legitimate multi-level organizations from the questionable pyramid organizations. Of course, when these distributorship or titles are sold, this is clearly illegal but recruiting for the purpose of loading up the lower levels is also questionable. As an example, the current "success story" in multi-level direct selling (Herbalife) has been called a pyramid by the state of California (Carey, 1985).

Motivation

The value of recognition as a motivator in many multi-level organizations is apparent in the fact that some of the levels involve recognition and only recognition. As far as duties or functions or authority or responsibility or payments

TABLE 2

EXAMPLES OF MULTI-LEVEL DISTRIBUTION AND/OR SALES ORGANIZATIONS

Traditional Channel of Distribution for Packaged Grocery Products	Large Grocery Manufacturer's	Multi-Level Direct Selling Organization
1. Manufacturer 2. Food Broker 3. Grocery Wholesaler* 4. Grocery Retailer*	1. Marketing Vice-President 2. National Sales Manager 3. Area or Regional Sales Manager 4. District or Branch Sales Manager 5. Salespeople	1. Manufacturer 2. Super Distributor 3. Qualified Distributor 4. Distributor 5. Dealer
Characteristics: Independent business people who carry the products of more than one principal.	Characteristics: Employees selling only the Manufacturer's own products to grocery wholesalers and/ or retailers.	Characteristics: Number of levels and the names of the levels vary. Each level is an independent businessperson.**

* Carries substantial inventory.
** In most cases merchandise is shipped from the manufacturer to the level selling to the ultimate consumer. A grocery product is used to illustrate this table because most multi-level direct selling organizations sell products that also move through the grocery product channel of distribution.

TABLE 3

EXAMPLES OF A MULTI-LEVEL DIRECT SELLING ORGANIZATION

Names and numbers have been frabricated-actual firms vary from
less complicated to more complicated than that shown below.

THE MANUFACTURER

LEVEL FOUR:

NAME	DIAMOND PRODUCER	GOLD PRODUCER	SILVER PRODUCER	BRONZE PRODUCER
Number of Super Producers (Level Three) Sponsored	20	15	10	5
Override on Gross Sales	3%	3%	3%	3%

LEVEL THREE:

SUPER PRODUCER

The level one and two people recruited by the Super Producers must sell, in total, $10,000.00 per month gross-the Super Producer receives a 10% override on these sales. Sales by the Super Producer direct to the ultimate consumer and to level one are included and also earn the corresponding level two and/or level one commissions.

LEVEL TWO:

Name	ADMIRAL	COMMANDER	CAPTAIN
Gross Sales (Personal Sales and/or Level One Sales)	$7,500.00	$5,000.00	$1,000.00
Override on Gross Sales	15%	10%	5%

LEVEL ONE:

DEALER

The dealer buys from someone in level two. The dealer is the only person who can not buy direct from the manufacturer. To buy direct, the dealer has to sell at least $1,000 per month at which point the dealer becomes a distributor, buys direct and sponsors other dealers while continuing to be sponsored by whoever brought the dealer into the organization. The dealer gets a 20% commission.

ULTIMATE CONSUMER

Level two does not stock the product but places orders for level one. This example might be considered a nine level organization (not counting the manufacturer and the ultimate consumer) but in reality there are only four levels. Within level four the differences are in name only (a motivational or recognition factor). Within level two the differences can be considered a quantity discount.

(margin, override commission) is concerned there may be only two levels in one of these multi-level organizations.

But, through a combination of recognition by special designation (such as SUPER DISTRIBUTOR) and a quantity discount (progressive commission rate) there may be a dozen so-called levels (see Table 3 for an example).

Distinguishing Characteristics

There are three key factors which distinguish the type of operation being described in this paper from other methods of distributing a product or service. These three characteristics of the multi-level direct selling organization are:

1. Emphasis on building a multi-level sales organization by recruiting people to be part of the direct-selling organization. To be really successful, you must recruit other people to work for you.

2. An evangelical attitude toward both the concept of multi-level direct selling and the product itself. To be successful you must really believe in the concept and the product.

3. Motivation through levels of recognition. The more people you recruit and the more levels through which you sell, the better your title.

Members of the various levels in these organizations are, by Federal Law, independent contractors. For the manufacturer this can be an effective method of distribution. For the independent contractor this can be a method of starting in business with minimum investment because costs are basically variable with low inventory requirements and essentially no fixed costs. Concerning the question of the best distribution channel to use for the sales of these relatively low-price packaged consumer products, theory would indicate mass advertising and long channels, not direct personal selling. One or few companies may try and succeed using direct personal selling contrary to theory, but all companies would not be thought to do this successfully and efficiently.

In direct selling as in other forms of selling, it is important to generate enthusiasm within the sales force to achieve sales goals. The challenge is how to motivate the individual sales representatives. For some people the potential to earn a large income and the recognition, success, and security that income brings plus the recognition inherent in titles appear to be a strong motivator.

Conclusion

Little or no research has been done on the business opportunities for minorities in retailing although it is obvious that this field has traditionally presented a chance for the disadvantaged to succeed in this country. Multi-level direct selling should combine all of the advantages of conventional retailing plus the added advantage of minimal investment but again there is no research to support this position.

It has been said over and over again that employment opportunities are created primarily by new small businesses. If the points being made in this paper concerning the advantages to the minority entrepreneur of multi-level direct selling are correct then there would be opportunities for the disadvantaged at all levels in the multi-level system with the leadership roles taken by the more entrepreneurial members of the community. To what extent this is occurring is a subject for research. Although retailing, especially multi-level direct selling, is easy to get into it is also easy to fail. The failure rate in retailing is higher than in any other broad business category. In addition someone who has the ability to succeed in multilevel direct selling might do much better in some other field. This would indicate that the major reasons for the disadvantaged going into multi-level direct selling would not be that it is such a great opportunity but that it is a great opportunity for someone who has one or more of the following problems:

1. Inferior education despite superior ability.

2. Lack of opportunity due to prejudice.

3. Need to start the new activity part-time or to have some flexibility in working hours.

4. Inexperience with the American culture and/or language.

References

Baxter, Richard P. and Ernest F. Cooke (1985), "Multi-Level Direct Sales Organizations-An Overview", Professional Sales and Sales Management in the 1980's, E. J. Randall, Ed., Statesboro, GA: Georgia Southern College, pp. 37-41.

Carey, John (April 8, 1985), "Selling Herbalife's Way", Newsweek, p. 89.

Cooke, Ernest F. (1985), "Why Has Multi-Level Direct Selling Reached the Saturation Stage in Its Life Cycle-A lesson for Other 'New Types of Retailing'", Retailing: Theory and Practice for the 21st Century, R. L. King, Ed., Charleston, SC: The Academy of Marketing Science, Special Conference Series Vol. 1, pp 26-30.

THE ROLLER COASTER THEORY OF RETAILING
AND
IMPLICATION FOR MINORITY ENTERPRISES

Walter E. Greene, Pan American University, Edinburg, Texas 78539

INTRODUCTION

The purpose of this research paper is to develop a model based on the theories of retail life cycle, wheel of retailing and market share. The author has constructed such a model, called the "Roller Coaster" Theory of Retailing. The name of the theory implies that the model is based on the shape of the roller coastal and momentum needed to keep going. In other words, the "Roller Coaster" theory calls for the identification of strategies or actions that can provide the "momentum" to push the declining whell back to the top of the life cycle and maintain or enlarge to market shares. The objective of this paper is to provide a new way of studying a retailer's position in the marketplace.

Importance of Retailing

The retailing sector is getting bigger. There are over two million retailing institutions in the United States in 1982-83 period accounting for almost $1 trillion is sales [14; 810]. A retail firm attracts customers because of its particular way of doing business, its merchandise, or its locations. Major factors that are considered by customers are usually price, convenience, quality, variety, and service offered. When these patronage factors are not sufficiently satisfied by existing retailers, the door is open for an innovator who can fulfill that market niche. In short, retailing is a vital business activity in the United States and many parts of the world.

Nature of Institutional Innovations

Retailing institutions change as time passes. Retailing is dynamic, and retail insitutuions evolve constantly. It is generally accepted that many of the new retailing institutions have penetrated the retail system on the basis of price appeal; that is, they have been able to compete against the existing store types by offering lower prices. The lower price usually reflects the lower gross margins of these stores. However, not all have entered in a nonservice and low-status profile [3; 62].

Retail innovations of importance and their periods of establishment have been; the early forms of the traditional department stores from 1870 to 1890; general merchandise mail-order selling from 1980 to 1910; variety, general merchandise, and food chain store from 1900 to 1930; the food supermarket after 1930; and the discount department stores beginning around 1955. Each of these new retail forms had a major impact on the existing retail structure; each offered the consumer something which had been lacking in the original structure [1].

Theories of Retail Institutional Change

A number of authors have explored retail changes (4, 5, 8, 9, 13). This paper will concentrate on two theories, namely, the wheel of retailing and retail life cycle to show that the cycle continues to exist.

Wheel of Retailing

According to this theory, new types of retailers enter the market as low-status, low-markup, low-price operations. As they become successful, they move into more elaborate buildings, offer more services, and generate higher operating costs and higher prices as a result. Eventually they become vulnerable to new low-status, low-markup, low-price retailers, and the cycle begins again. Figure 1 illustrates how in the late 1950s department stores like Sears, had moved up on the price and service scale, leaving room for discount stores like Wal-Mart or minority entreprenuers to enter the marketplace with few services and much lower prices.

Figure 1

WHEEL OF RETAILING THEORY

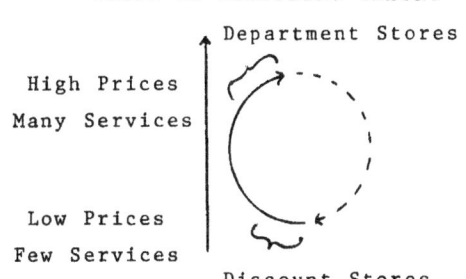

In any event, McNair proposed that their are four cycles that the wheel goes through. Each time when a innovator comes into the marketplace, the wheel revolves [9]. Sears, Penneys and Wards, for example, all have attempted to position themselves in various market niches as the retail wheel has revolved. Therefore, minorities should always be alert for any market niche they can fill because the market place is not one homogeneous market but rather a multi-series of hetrogenious markets waiting for the right entrepreneurs.

Retail Life Cycle

The retail life cycle concept parallels the product life cycle concept. Retail institutions are presumed to pass through introduction-growth-maturity-decline phases. Figure 2 shows the institutional life cycle in retailing. The cycle for its market share and profitability share the same shape and both pass through the four stages. According to Davidson, a confounder of Management Horizons, Inc., the retail life cycle concept provides retailers with opportunities to sustain profits [2; 89].

FIGURE 2

THE INSTITUTIONAL LIFE CYCLE
IN RETAILING

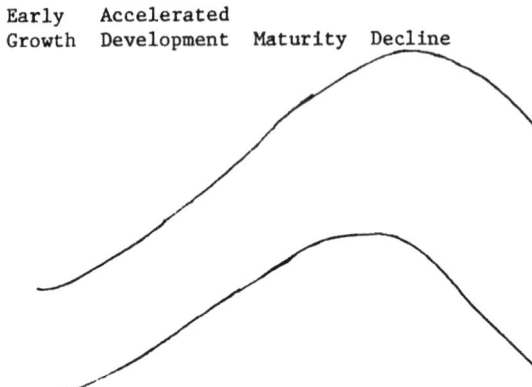

Early   Accelerated
Growth   Development   Maturity   Decline

Source: Davidson, Bill & Assoc., "The Retail Life Cycle," *Harvard Business Review* Nov-Dec 1976, p. 91

Development of Roller Coaster Theory of Retailing Basic Assumptions

First of all, the model assumes that each institution or product passes through the life cycle environment and evolves from the wheel. Secondly, this model also assumes that there is a possibility of enhancing a product's or

an institution's life by discovering new market niches for as long as possible if the appropriate action is taken by the retailer. Unfortunately, the duration in each stage of the life cycle or in the wheel remains unknown.

Tentative Explanations of the Model

The development of this model is mainly based on both the wheel of retailing theory and life cycle theory. The purpose of this model is to aid retailers identify where they stand in terms if life cycle stages and status in the wheel. In this way, appropriate strategies can be identified and used by the retailers. Figure 3 shows a conceptual picture of the wheel. As it is shown, the wheel is divided into four cycles: I, II, III, and IV. It is the objective of this article to superimpose these two models to produce a third model based on the two theories mentioned.

FIGURE 3

THE FOUR CYCLES OF THE WHEEL OF
RETAILING-McNair

Increase share Also attract competition	Trading up increase cost increase prices
II	III
I	IV
Low prices Low margin Low share	High Costs High Prices Become Traditional Retailer

The third model (new model) is shown in Figure 4, and the author has named it "Roller Coaster Theory of Retailing". As it is shown in the figure, cycle I of the wheel corresponds to stage I of the life cycle; cycle II of the wheel corresponds to stage III of the life cycle; and cycle IV of the wheel corresponds to stage IV of the life cycle. The solid wheels are the desired wheels in which they travel from one stage III to the stage II of the next life cycle. The dotted wheels are to be avoided so that each maturity stage of a life cycle can be prolonged. The goal of the Roller Coaster theory is to warn those retailers who are in cycle III of the wheel to change to cycle II of the next life cycle if possible (i.e., the concept of milking the cow in the Boston constantly group model). Again, the possibility lies in strategies or actions used by the retailer to discover new market niches.

FIGURE 4

"ROLLER COASTER" THEORY OF RETAILING-
NEW MODEL

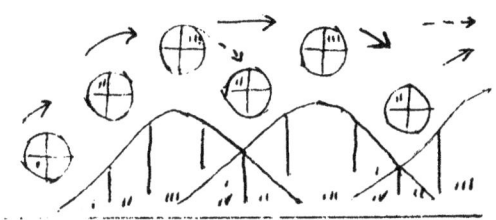

Roller Coaster Theory of Retailing implies that the retail wheel needs to use the "momentum" to roll back up to the next maturity stage as soon as possible. In this way, the retailer (minority entrepreneur) can be assured of his/her position in the marketplace. The ultimate goal of the theory is to roll flatly or to increase sales in the growth or maturity stage, avoiding the decline stage. Figure 5 illustrates such an ideal situation for a retail institution for a retail institution or retailer.

FIGURE 5

ROLLER COASTER THEORY OF RETAILING

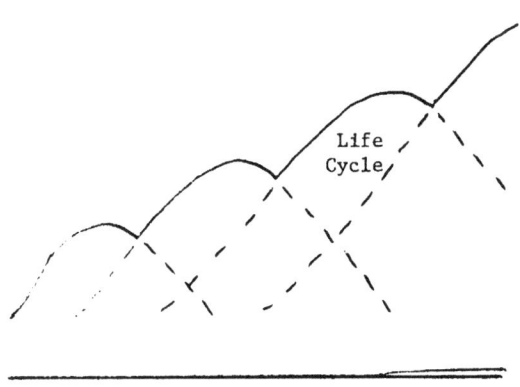

THE IDEAL SITUATION
(Stage III to II to III to II etc)

Implications and Opportunities

The Roller Coaster Theory of Retailing represents another way to conceptualdize changes in retailer behavior and profitability patterns. It can be quite useful in projecting retail developments and planning marketing strategy. An analysis of where a retail institution stands is vital for management and policy decision makers be they minority entrepreneurs or not.

The ultimate goal of the model is to guide retail executives to extend the duration of the third or maturity stage by finding new market niches to roll up to a new and higher stage II, or at least prolonging their current stage III. As recognition of this theory grows, more retail executives can be expected to devote more attention to developing differnet ways to build new market niches and attract new customers. In short, with this model, decision makers should work on ways of renewing and recapturing the interest of their existing customers or finding new hetergeneous portions of the current market (i.e., market niches) so as to keep their loyalty in the face of new forms of competition, by recognizing the problem.

Recommendations

Retail executives should know about the "wheel of retailing" concept, the notion of the products mix, the life cycle concept and market share. The retail/product life cycle has a long and rich history in marketing and serves as a basis for making product line decisions. The wheel of retailing explains the cylces a typical retailer may go through. In essence, each has proved to be helpful in understanding business success in retailing. For many retailers, turbulence and uncertainty are going to continue for some time to come, thus they should understand and apply several theories instead of just one or two concepts in making major decisions.

Roller Coaster Theory of Retailing now represents a new way of viewing the retailing development in the business world. One may study a retail institutions's position based on the life cycle concept, the wheel of retailing theory or both simultaneously as in this model. By utilizing different strategies at different stages of the life cycle development, at different cycles of the wheel, and by anticipating shifts from one stage to the next, retailers can maintain adequate profit levels. At maturity, retailers can develop sophisticated inventory control procedures, employ other modern management concepts, and seek new market niches. A sophisticated management group can slow the pace of its company's evolution, and it can hold profitability at adequate levels for an extended period of time. However, return to exceptional levels of profitability can be achieved only by converting to new forms of distribution or by entering new lines of trade. To cope with continued change, retailers must consider the use of different management styles or even different management groups to find new market niches during succeeding stages of development. By developing the Roller Coaster Theory of Retailing, it is hoped that the Roller Coaster model can be of great help to today's retail executives especially minority entreprenuers in planning and making decisions.

References

Davidson, William R., "Changes in Distributive Institutions," Journal of Marketing (Jan 1970), pp. 8-9.

Davidson, William R. and associates, "The Retail Life Cycle," Harvard Business Review, Nov-Dec 1976, pp. 89-96.

Goldman, Arieh, "The Role of Trading-up in the Development of the Retailing System," Journal of Marketing, (Jan 1975), pp. 54-62.
Hollander, Stanley C., "The Wheel of Retailing," Journal of Marketing, July 1960, pp. 37-42.

Kinnear, Thomas and associate. Principles of Marketing (Glenview: Scott, Foresman & Company, 1983).

Main, Jeremy, "K-Mart's Plan to be Born again, again," Fortune, September 21, 1981. pp. 74-85.

Marken, Rom and associate, "The Transformation of Retailing Institutions: Beyond the wheel of retailing and life-cycle theories," Journal of Macromarketing (Spring 1981), p. 58-59.)

Mason, Joseph B. and associate, Modern Retailing: Theory and Practice (Business Publications, Inc. 1978)

McNair, Malcom, Significant Trends and Developments in the Post War Period," in A.B. Smith ed. Competitive Distribution in a Free, High Level economy and its implications for university (Pittsburgh, Pa.: University of Pittsburgh Press, 1958), pp. 1-25.

Neiman, Janet, "Retailers should know their place," Advertising Age, November 1, 1982, pp. m-22+.

Pessemier, Edgar, "Store Image and Positioning," Journal of Retailing, Spring 1980, pp. 96-97.

"Retailing's Golden Age," Sales & Marketing Management, August 7, 1976, pp. 41-42.

Rosenberg, Larry J. & associates, "Retailing without stores," Harvard Business Review, July-August 1980, pp. 103-112.

Statistical Abstract of the United States, 1982-83 103rd ed. (Washington, D.C.: U.S. Department of Commerce, Bureau of the Census), p. 810.

Tinsley, D.B. and associate, "Will the wheel of Retailing Stop Turning?" Akron Business and Economic Review, Summer 1978.

THE ROLE OF BLACK ENTREPRENEURSHIP
IN THE SELF ACTUALIZATION OF BLACKS IN THE LABOR FORCE

William T. Ryan, Florida Atlantic University

Abstract

The history of the acceptance of blacks into the mainstream of corporate America reflects little optimism that change will be forthcoming. Black entrepreneurship, targeted toward the large populous black concentrations, would appear one technique for developing business skills and economic self-sufficiency. Minorities other than blacks have persevered in developing business acumen and economic independence. Why not blacks? The search for an answer to this question is the focus of this research.

Economic Vitality

Importance of Minorities

Economically, it is believed that the development of minority entrepreneurs is vital for maintaining the economic health of urban settings with large minority populations. Surveys in 1977 and 1982 of Minority-Owned Enterprises show that minority interest in business ownership is increasing, but - the data reveal a dramatic lack of growth of black-owned business in both real terms and relative to Hispanic- and Asian-owned firms (Aguirre 1986).

Lack of Black Representation

Hispanics are twice as likely to develop small businesses than are blacks. A program to stimulate black enterprise in Dade County, Florida found that the average Hispanic small business in Miami has revenues nearly twice that of comparable black firms. Median family income for Hispanics was 80 percent that of whites, while 63 percent for blacks. In 1980, Hispanics owned 48 percent of all service stations, up from 12 percent in 1960, while blacks, who owned 25 percent of the stations in 1960 fell to 12 percent by 1980. Blacks in Dade County control one bank, while Hispanics control 30 representing more combined assets than the nine largest black-owned banks in the United States (Mescon 1987).

Socio-Economic Characteristics

B-School Enrollments

Business school enrollments for the early 1970's show about 10 percent female, 5 percent black and scattered other minority groups. Depending on the size of the business school, enrollments of females range from 25 to 45 percent, other minorities, particularly Hispanics and Asians, have increased significantly, while black percentages have remained constant - or declined. Table 1 is a selected sample of college enrollments from 1965 to 1985.

Shifts in Minority Populations

In New York City, Hispanics are about to become the largest minority group, surpassing blacks, while in such cities as Miami, San Antonio and El Paso, they already constitute an absolute majority. In San Francisco and Los Angeles, a hodge-podge of ethnic and racial minorities outnumber residents of European descent. Given this scenario, where is the black business person's future? Why should the black minority fare worse than other minorities that have followed?

Minority Conditions

Like Asians, like Indians, like Hispanics, or females in general, blacks often have to outperform their white counterparts to achieve similar recognition or rewards. Blacks have traditionally filled low status positions in the hospitality, personnel, school administration and government sectors. Although some of these positions pay well, they are considered by aspiring managers to be positions of high-visibility and little upward mobility. Once placed in these public display jobs, promotions are often slowed down or stopped and layoffs imminent during recessionary periods.

Implications of Theories X, Y and Z

McGregor's X and Y

A Theory X approach assumes that workers are basically lazy, intellectually deficient and require constant supervision. A prototype that has traditionally characterized the black worker. Theory Y portends that workers can be motivated by positive incentives, bonus reward systems and some degree of involvement in how the work should be done. Neither has much faith in the intrinsic value of a human being.

Theory Z

The Japanese "Theory Z", popularized by Ouchi's book of the same name, portrays the effectiveness of the quality circle or productivity through team effectiveness. This approach implicitly stresses uniformity of standards, norms, appearance and behavior, within a structured format of "informality" and intimacy. Caring, unselfishness and a desire to ensure the

TABLE 1

College Enrollment of Persons 14 to 34 Years Old, by Sex, Race, and Spanish Origin:
October 1965 to 1985

(In thousands. Civilian noninstitutional population. For meaning of symbols, see text)

Sex, race, and Spanish origin	1985	1984	1983	1982	1981[1]	1981[2]	1980	1979	1978	1977	1976	1975	1970	1965
ALL RACES														
Total, enrolled in college..	10,863	10,859	10,825	10,919	10,734	10,437	10,180	9,978	9,838	10,217	9,950	9,697	7,413	5,675
Male..........................	5,345	5,513	5,504	5,409	5,372	5,193	5,025	4,993	5,124	5,369	5,296	5,342	4,401	3,503
Female........................	5,518	5,347	5,321	5,510	5,363	5,244	5,155	4,986	4,714	4,848	4,654	4,355	3,013	2,172
Year of college:														
First year....................	2,956	3,024	2,987	2,990	3,096	3,032	2,957	2,885	2,766	2,936	2,632	2,886	2,212	1,861
Second year...................	2,585	2,454	2,624	2,617	2,560	2,500	2,411	2,291	2,286	2,364	2,535	2,376	1,739	1,256
Third year....................	1,931	1,981	1,805	1,815	1,799	1,744	1,716	1,653	1,658	1,681	1,748	1,492	1,248	896
Fourth year...................	1,642	1,599	1,595	1,688	1,598	1,543	1,403	1,458	1,445	1,427	1,356	1,354	1,074	803
Fifth year or higher..........	1,749	1,802	1,814	1,810	1,682	1,618	1,692	1,691	1,681	1,810	1,680	1,589	1,140	859
WHITE														
Total, enrolled in college...	9,334	9,269	9,242	9,328	9,162	8,983	8,875	8,709	8,514	8,812	8,644	8,516	6,759	5,317
Male..........................	4,633	4,709	4,718	4,650	4,620	4,514	4,438	4,400	4,508	4,717	4,658	4,771	4,066	3,326
Female........................	4,701	4,559	4,524	4,679	4,543	4,469	4,437	4,309	4,006	4,095	3,986	3,743	2,693	1,991
BLACK														
Total, enrolled in college...	1,049	1,138	1,102	1,127	1,133	1,080	1,007	1,002	1,020	1,103	1,062	948	522	274
Male..........................	458	544	497	482	505	474	437	434	452	490	489	442	253	126
Female........................	591	594	605	645	628	606	570	568	569	614	573	506	269	148
SPANISH ORIGIN[3]														
Total, enrolled in college...	579	524	523	493	510	486	443	440	377	418	427	411	(NA)	(NA)
Male..........................	280	232	253	216	258	243	222	226	196	223	223	219	(NA)	(NA)
Female........................	299	292	270	278	252	243	221	214	181	194	204	192	(NA)	(NA)

[1] Controlled to 1980 census base.
[2] Controlled to 1970 census base.
[3] Persons of Spanish origin may be of any race.

Source: U.S. Department of Commerce, Bureau of the Census. 1985 Advance Annual Population Reports, No. 409, Series p. 20 (Sept. 1986), Table 3.

---

success of the group is a primary consideration. Given an American firm, this format would represent the most culturally, sexually and racially biased grouping possible.

Heterogeneity

New demographics portray America as a nation that continues to admit more immigrants each year than all other countries of the world combined. Japan, by comparison, is over 98 percent Japanese. Nationalism and resentment of foreigners has increased to the point that IBM is moving its Asian division to Hong Kong. Americans are the brunt of Polish-style jokes and typical anti-minority resentment.

"Mirror, Mirror on the Business Wall..."

Homogeneity

Japan's key to productivity and profit through quality circles is homogeneity. The blacks' uniqueness is their difference and homogeneity. Pariah groups, i.e. Chinese, Indian, Bangladesh, Amerasians, have followed a pattern of Theory Z business behavior. The Vietnamese and Chinese have carved out certain industries where

they eventually dominate or control. Jews have traditionally migrated toward the professions based on educational expertise. The Irish cop and Italian or Greek restauranteurs are ethnic stereotypes. In all this homogeneous identification, where is the black as a business entity?

Corporate Reflections

Blacks avoid the business school. One black attitude reflects the idea that even if U.S. firms used a Theory Z approach of lifetime employment, that minorities and women would be immediately classified as temporary work force members. They would become a "variable cost" that could be removed quickly to keep corporations competitive during harsh economic times.

Blacks understand that in Japan, those who eventually occupy the upper management positions are always chosen from the "better schools". Fierce competition exists to gain entry for one's child, even in the early years of kindergarten. Substantial sums of money are spent to prepare the young with the necessary skills to meet rigid entrance requirements. Business schools, due to high demand for their services, have begun to increase GPA requirements. Many now require a 2.5 or 3.0 GPA in the first two years of college for admission. Appendix 1 gives

three separate breakdowns of college enrollments.

The Trauma of Trying

Why Try?

Blacks who enjoy responsible corporate positioms
find that prejudice still exists and impedes
their climb to the top. In 1970, one major
retail chain had five blacks in senior buyer
positions. This number has remained constant.

Blacks who are unable to justify their positions
in the workplace to those who hold unfounded
biases against them feel cut off from important
social circles. This isolation hinders peer and
subordinate relationships and keeps blacks out
of the "good ole boy" network. Manifestations
of the invisible hand of corporate racism are
apparent in things like the memo with too little
information to make a decision and enough information to make it apparent a decision must be
made. The "whites only" sign hangs over the
doors that lead to the higher level corporate
decisions. In addition to the issues of racism,
black managers say they experience various
levels of culture shock, alienation, isolation
and a substantial loss of corporate identity.

Forced to abandon black English, accents, tastes
and mannerisms, blacks are isolated from black
culture but never fully accepted by the white.
A "no man's" land of identity. One black
grandfather told his nephew, who was enrolled in
business school, that "White men do not hire
black men to tell white men what to do and they
don't allow a black man to handle their money."
The devastating effects of racism, isolation and
alienation are even greater in the lives of
black female executives.

Is This What It Takes?

A new generation of black managers are being
graduated from the best white business schools
in the nation. They know very little about
black culture and the only real difference between them and their white counterpart is their
complexion. They have been taught next to white
kids from kindergarten and they talk just like
white guys. They have developed a "negative
racial conciousness". If they encountered two
guys in the hallway, one black and one white,
they would speak to the white guy and generally
ignore the black one. One researcher, after
interviewing a few of them, referred to them as
"new niggers". Incredibly well-focused, incredibly aware of what personal qualities have to be
cultivated to make it (Davis 1982).

Minority to Minority

The Black Business Rate

Divide the black-owned businesses in a community
by the black population and you get what demo-
grapher William O'Hare calls the "black business
rate". The importance of this figure is that it
could serve as a rough indicator of local business climates for black entrepreneurs. Fast-
growing communities have the highest rates,
indicating that minority-owned businesses do
relatively better where local economies are
surging.

Los Angeles has 25 black-owned businesses per
1,000 black citizens, tops in the nation. Next
are San Francisco, Houston, Washington and San
Diego. At the bottom of the list: Philadelphia; Chicago; Shreveport, La.; Newark, N.J.;
Buffalo, N.Y.; and Mobile and Birmingham, Ala
(O'Hare 1986).

Minority Targeting

Blacks do not have to sell only to blacks.
Examples of this are the Jewish dentist in San
Francisco who purchased a VW dealership going
nowhere and targeted the 70 percent Asian population as his market. Using market segmentation
and promotional techniques, he increased his
sales from 20 to 100 cars in a month and in 1986
was the sixth largest dealer in the U.S. Mark
Roth, a Californian, took a failing supermarket
in a newly Hispanic area and in a matter of
months began earning profits in excess of industry averages (Kotkin 1987).

The lessons here are that the minority markets
of today are the majority markets of the future.
A view that says "These are not undocumented
aliens, but undocumented consumers." It is the
story of pita pouches and pizza, of the bagel
and the croissant, of sushi and chow mein, and
Corona beer (Woolf 1986).

Planning a Strategy

Support Groups

A small, nearly constant, percentage of business
school graduates are black. Even this "successful" minority have monumental problems in coping
with a white corporate power structure. Black
entrepreneurship can utilize the efficient techniques of homogeneous groupings, as per the
Japanese, to maximize employment for blacks and
profitability of their enterprises.

This organizational strategy does not umply
blacks only selling to (or doing business with)
blacks. In South Florida, with the support of
the SBA's Small Business Development Centers,
black business people could be taught Spanish as
a tool for doing business in an area predominantly Hispanic. Not everyone in a firm would
need language training. When one calls a Hispanic business in Miami, they usually have at
least one person who speaks English. There are
also many black Hispanics, so short cuts are
possible.

Construction is one of the major sectors of
business activity in South Florida. Yet, blacks
have had little participation in this industry.

Government requirements that a percentage of public contracts go to minorities is a beginning. However, the "catch-22" is that without a track record, blacks have difficulty obtaining financing or bonding, and without them - no track record. One public sector goal must focus on breaking this cycle.

Target Areas

Those cities with large black and/or minority populations should be targeted for black entrepreneur programs and using the black business rate formula cited earlier, set goals for increasing the numbers of black businesses per 1,000 black citizens. Lacking a benchmark, public programs come and go with the winds of politics and leave little evidence of results to show for the expenditure. A pacifier is no substitute for real nourishment (Ando 1986).

Incubators for Entrepreneurs

One possible source of nourishment may be available in the form of business development incubators. Incubators can provide assistance in the areas of venture capital formation and business plan development. Minority entrepreneurs become tenants in a physical facility offering below-market rent, on-site business assistance, flexible leases and space arrangements and they have support services at low or no cost. Some incubators have a graduation policy specifying the length of time an entrepreneur may remain a tenant.

Incubators usually contain a variety of businesses and, depending on the sponsorship, they will have varying objectives. Business incubator sponsorship includes (1) publicly sponsored, (2) industrial development agencies, (3) non-profit, community-based, (4) university related, and (5) private corporate incubators.

The incubator concept, in conjunction with a public commitment to increasing the black business rate, may afford a viable alternative to one shot programs lacking specific support systems, constant monitoring and follow-up procedures (Ellis 1987).

Conclusion

The history of the acceptance of blacks into the mainstream of corporate America reflects little optimism that change will be forthcoming. A small number of blacks graduate from B-schools, but even their scenario is bleak. Black entrepreneurship, targeted toward the large populous black concentrations and including concepts like incubation for minority business development, are examples of techniques for developing business skills and economic self-sufficiency. Minorities other than blacks have persevered in developing business acumen and economic independence. Why not blacks?

A haunting possibility to the previous question may exist. Do blacks want "white acceptance" or individual financial/economic achievement? The two may not be compatible within the realities of America's socio-economic framework.

Appendix 2 contains a checklist for potential entrepreneurs.

APPENDIX 1

Graduates - College Enrollment

No. 230. HIGH SCHOOL AND COLLEGE GRADUATES, BY SEX AND CONTROL: 1950 TO 1983

[In thousands, except percent. Prior to 1960, excludes Alaska and Hawaii. See also table 252; Appendix III; and *Historical Statistics, Colonial Times to 1970*, series H 598-601 and H 752-756]

| YEAR OF GRADUATION | HIGH SCHOOL GRADUATES [1] | | | | | | COLLEGE GRADUATES [2] | | | | |
| | Total | | Sex | | Control | | Bachelor's degrees [4] | | | | Master's and doctor's degrees [5] |
	Number	Percent of persons 18 years old [3]	Male	Female	Public	Private, est.	Total	Per 100 high school graduates 4 yrs. earlier	Male	Female	
1950	1,200	56.0	571	629	(NA)	(NA)	432	40	329	103	58
1960	1,864	72.4	898	966	1,633	231	392	28	254	138	84
1965	2,665	70.8	1,314	1,351	2,366	298	501	25	289	213	162
1970	2,896	77.1	1,433	1,463	2,596	300	793	30	451	341	273
1975	3,133	73.6	1,542	1,591	2,823	310	923	31	505	418	362
1980	3,043	71.5	1,491	1,552	2,748	295	929	29	474	456	401
1981	3,020	71.2	1,483	1,537	2,725	295	935	30	470	465	401
1982	3,001	71.6	1,474	1,527	2,711	290	953	30	473	480	400
1983, prel.	2,890	71.6	1,438	1,452	2,600	290	970	31	479	490	400

NA Not available. [1] Data for 1950-1970 include about 7,000 graduates of subcollegiate departments of institutions of higher education, Federal schools for Indians and on Federal installations, and residential schools for exceptional children. [3] Based on estimated resident population as of July 1. [2] Data cover public and private institutions. [4] Through 1960, bachelor's or first professional degree; thereafter, bachelor's degree only. [5] Beginning 1965, includes first professional degrees.

Source: U.S. Dept. of Education, Center for Statistics, *Condition of Education*, annual.

124

No. 231. College Enrollment and Percent of High School Graduates Enrolled In, or Completed One or More Years of College, by Sex and Race: 1960 to 1985

[As of October, except as noted. Covers civilian noninstitutional population 14 to 24 years old]

ITEM AND YEAR	ALL PERSONS			MALE			FEMALE		
	Total¹	White	Black	Total¹	White	Black	Total¹	White	Black
College enrollment (1,000):									
1960*	2,279	2,138	*141	1,365	1,297	*68	914	841	*73
1970	6,065	5,535	437	3,461	3,213	202	2,604	2,322	236
1975	7,226	6,368	699	3,821	3,437	308	3,407	2,931	392
1980	7,475	6,546	716	3,700	3,303	292	3,778	3,243	426
1984	7,844	6,735	826	4,020	3,479	383	3,823	3,256	443
1985	7,799	6,729	755	3,880	3,374	355	3,917	3,357	400
Percent of high school graduates enrolled:									
1960*	23.6	24.3	*18.7	30.4	31.1	*21.1	18.0	18.1	*16.9
1970	33.3	33.9	26.7	41.8	42.9	29.5	26.3	26.3	24.7
1975	33.1	33.0	32.5	36.7	36.9	33.4	29.9	29.4	32.0
1980	32.3	32.5	28.3	33.8	34.3	27.0	30.9	30.9	29.2
1984	33.7	34.2	28.0	36.4	36.8	29.6	31.3	31.8	26.8
1985	34.3	35.0	26.5	36.0	36.6	28.2	32.8	33.6	25.1
Percent of high school graduates enrolled in college or completed 1 or more years of college:									
1960*	40.4	41.0	*32.5	46.1	47.1	*33.5	35.3	35.6	*31.8
1970	52.3	53.4	40.0	59.2	60.8	41.2	46.5	47.1	39.0
1975	52.5	52.7	48.0	56.1	56.6	50.3	49.2	49.1	46.4
1980	51.1	51.4	46.2	51.4	51.8	44.4	51.0	51.0	47.8
1984	53.0	53.8	45.2	53.6	54.2	45.2	52.4	53.4	45.0
1985	54.3	55.3	43.8	54.6	55.5	43.5	54.0	55.2	43.9

APPENDIX 2

A Checklist for Potential Entrepreneurs

Possible Attitudes/Feelings

*I can't find a job I like.
*I want to be my own boss more than anything.
*I want more money for necessities and luxuries than I can make at a fixed rate.
*I've helped someone else make money for years - now it's my turn.
*I want to avoid being laid off, fired or passed over for promotion because of company politics.
*No one will give me the chance to prove myself because of my background; I'll have to do it on my own.
*I come from a family of small business owners - it's in my genes.

Possible Traits

*Are you a self-starter?
*Do you have a positive, friendly interest in others?
*Are you a leader?
*Can you handle responsibility?
*Are you a good organizer?
*Are you prepared to put in long hours?
*Do you make up your mind quickly?
*Can people rely on you?
*Are you capable of running all day and night?
*Can you withstand reversals without quitting?
*Can you adapt to changing situations?

Source: Adapted from Feingold, Norman S. and Leonard G. Perlman, "A Quiz For Would-Be Entrepreneurs," Nation's Business, Vol.LXXIV, (March 1986), pp. 26-27.

References

Aguirre, A. and T. Sowell (Nov.1986), "Markets and Minorities," Annals of the American Academy of Political and Social Science, Vol.LXXXVIII, pp. 217-28.

Ando, F.H. (1986), "An Analysis of the Formation and Failure of Minority-Owned Firms," Review of Black Political Economy, Vol.XV, pp. 51-71.

Concept adapted from: Ellis, Richard (Nov.12-15, 1987), "Incubators for Minority Entrepreneurs," A paper delivered at the First Conference on Minority Marketing: Issues and Prospects, Greensboro, N.C.

Davis, George and Glegg Watson (1982), "Black Life in Corporate America: Swimming in the Mainstream, Garden City, N.J.:Anchor Press/ Doubleday, First Ed.

Kotkin, Joel (July 1987), "Selling to the New America," Inc., Vol.IX, No.8, pp. 44-52.

Mescon, Timothy S. (Jan.1987), "The Entrepreneurial Institute: Education and Training for Minority Small Business Owners," Journal of Small Business Management, Vol.XXV, No.1, pp. 61-71.

O'Hare, William (July 1986), "New Demographics," American Demographic Magazine, Vol.VIII, No.7, pp. 27-33.

Woolf, A.G. (1986), "Market Structure and Minority Presence: Black-Owned Firms in Manufacturing," Review of Black Political Economy, Vol. IV, pp. 79-89.

BLACK ENTREPRENEURS AND USE OF SBA LOANS FOR BUSINESS START-UPS: A FIELD STUDY

Vicki L. Bolden, Southern University
Winston Awadzi, Southern University

Abstract

This study presents the results of a field study on the sources of financing used by black entrepreneurs to finance their business start-ups. The results of the study indicate that most entrepreneurs do not use the loan services of the SBA. Specifically, only three (14 percent) of the twenty-two black entrepreneurs interviewed for this study used the Small Business Administration (SBA) as a means of financing their business start-ups. The findings also indicate that the non-use derives partly from the cumbersomeness of the SBA's loan procedure.

Introduction

As a nation, the United States has always depended on the small business sector to provide the necessary growth in the economy. According to the President's report on the State of Small Business (1984), small business provided two out of three workers with their first jobs. In 1982, small enterprises (with 500 or less employees) accounted for 47.8 percent of the total employment in the economy and 41.7 percent of sales in the non-government, non-farm economy. This implies that the small business sector has an important role to play in providing blacks (and other minorities) with both jobs and access into the mainstream of American society.

In recognition of the important role of small business the Small Business Administration (SBA) was set up to foster the creation of small businesses. Blacks, women and other minorities who have typically been left out of the mainstream of American business saw the creation of the SBA as an important means of gaining access into the more traditional areas of American business. There remain questions, however, as to the extent the SBA and its ancilliary sub-units, the MESBICS, have been instrumental in enabling minorities, especially black entrepreneurs to start and operate their own businesses.

This study, therefore, examines the sources of financing used by the more successful type of Black entrepreneurs whose annual gross sales range from a quarter of million dollars ($250,000) to more than fifteen million dollars.

Financing was chosen as the focus of this study because it has been identified as one of the greatest stumbling blocks to entrepreneural endeavors by blacks.

Minority Business and SBA Loans

A number of studies have found that blacks have lower participation in business rates than both non-minorities and other minorities. For example, the Minority Business Development Agency (MBDA) found in a 1982 study that the participation in business ownership rate for blacks was only 9 per 1,000 persons compared to 20 for Hispanics and 29 for Asian-Americans. However, Stevens (1984) found that while the participation rates were different the failure rates were similar. This implies that once formed, black businesses do just as well as others. This also points to the need to reduce and/or remove obstacles facing black entrepreneurs.

One of the most significant constraints facing the black entrepreneur is access to capital [Markwalder 1981; Tabb 1979; Yancy 1974; Bates and Bradford 1975]. More recently, Handy and Swindon [1984] found a positive relationship between the level of SBA loan activity and the growth of receipts of black businesses between 1972 and 1977. Handy and Swindon's finding would imply that access to SBA loans is an important factor in the performance of black businesses. However, while the Handy and Swindon study points to a relationship between SBA loans and black business receipts, it does not indicate the extent of usage of SBA loans by the sample of black entrepreneurs they studied. It is the objective of this study, therefore, to examine the extent to which black businesses use SBA loans.

Such examination is important in light of the findings of the 1984 National Chamber Foundation study of the strategies for Hispanic business development. The results indicate that only two (six percent) of the thirty-three established Hispanic enterprises located in or near eight major U.S. metropolitan areas utilized SBA loans for their business start-ups. Additionally, only three (9 percent) used SBA loans for subsequent financial requirements. Moreover, the results also indicate that where SBA loans were taken, they were used in conjunction with financing from other sources.

The pertinent question this study seeks to answer is, therefore, to what extent do black entrepreneurs use SBA loans? The answer to this question would indicate whether the SBA is providing black entrepreneurs the opportunity to move from the traditional "mom and pop" form of operation into the mainstream of American business.

Research Methodology

Sample Selection

The population of this study consists of Black-owned manufacturing companies with gross sales in excess of a quarter of a million dollars ($250,000). For the purposes of this stage of the study a sample of Black-owned businesses was selected from nine states east of the Mississippi River. These states were Michigan, Illinois, Maryland, Virginia, North Carolina, South Carolina, Alabama, Mississippi and Texas.

Data Collection

A two-stage process of data collection was used to elicit data from the respondents. First, a questionnaire was sent to 150 Black-owned businesses selected from the 1985 edition of TRY US. Seventy-five of the questionnaires were returned for a response rate of 50 percent. However, many of the respondents did not provide the financial data requested.

In the next step, therefore, efforts were made to elicit the desired financial information through personal interviews. Because of time and resource constraints, it was decided to interview the respondents in two stages starting with twenty-two entrepreneurs located in states east of the Mississippi River. The results reported in this study, therefore, pertain to these twenty-two interviews.

Research Results

The results of the study indicate that most black entrepreneurs do not use the SBA as a source of financing their business start-ups. Specifically, only three of the twenty-two entrepreneurs interviewed for this study (14 percent) took loans from the SBA. Twenty-eight percent used commercial (bank) loans, twenty-six percent used personal funds and thirty-two percent used private investors. Additionally, ninety-one percent of the entrepreneurs had to supplement whatever financing they got with personal funds. Only two firms in the sample did not use any personal funds.

TABLE 1
Number of Financing Sources Used

ONE SOURCE		32%
TWO SOURCES		36%
THREE SOURCES		32%
		100%

TABLE 2
Specific Methods of Financing as Percentage of Total

SBA	3	14%
MESBIC	1	.05%
COMMERCIAL BANKS	6	27%
PRIVATE INVESTORS	7	32%
PERSONAL FUNDS	20	91%
STOCK SALES	2	10%
PARENT COMPANY	1	.05%
RELATIVES	2	10%
SECOND MORTGAGES/ CREDIT CARDS	1	.05%

Table 1 shows the number of sources used for financing the initial business start-ups. Thirty-two percent of the respondents used only one source. Thirty-six percent used two sources while thirty-two percent used three or more sources of financing. Table 2 indicates the different forms of financing used. Ninety-one percent of the respondents used personal funds. The personal funds used included monies from sources such as credit cards, second mortgages and borrowings against life insurance policies. Twenty-seven percent of the entrepreneurs got commercial (bank) loans.

The above findings point to the diversity of financing sources but do not explain the lack of usage of SBA financing. The responses of the entrepreneurs interviwed indicate that SBA financing was used mainly because the entrepreneurs could not secure other financing. On the other hand, several reasons were given for not using SBA financing. Among these were:

* excessive bureaucratic redtape

* lack of responsiveness to the problems of small entrepreneurs

127

* lack of interest in business proposals presented

* inadequate levels of financing. One respondent felt the SBA program was self-defeating because SBA generally made available less funding than was required for successful operation of the business

* SBA staffers short on practical business expertise

* political considerations (need political clout to get loan approved)

* SBA interest rates too high

* amount of control SBA acquires over business operations

* application process takes too long (90-180 days)

* loss of independence

* excessive reporting requirements

* excessive collateral requirements leading to the tying up all personal assets. In the words of one entrepreneur, "I refused to tie up all available collateral of the business since it left (me with) no means of acquiring additional capital"

* overly cumbersome and lengthy application process

* SBA's inaccurate assessment of businesses and their financial needs.

* fear cannot get follow-up financing from SBA for subsequent expansion.

Almost all the complaints and comments made by the black entrepreneurs interviewed for this study were echoes of the complaints and comments made by hispanic entrepreneurs in the 1984 study by the National Chamber Foundation. This would imply that there is some validity to these complaints and that administrative actions may be required to make the SBA program more effective.

Implications

The findings of this study clearly indicate that SBA loan programs are not reaching black entrepreneurs (and other minorities) who need financing for business start-ups that would move them from the traditional mom and pop operation into the mainstream of American business. Although some of the reasons given for not using SBA loans may not be valid, it is still apparent that the SBA needs to re-evaluate its procedures for granting loans if the objective of creating more small and minority businesses is to be realized. Specifically, there may be a need to improve the administration of the existing program to make it more amenable to the needs of entrepreneurs. If small business is to continue to provide the engine of growth to power the economy, then there is a great need to nurture the development of black and other minority entrepreneurs.

In terms of further research, this study could be extended to cover a much wider sample of respondents throughout the United States. The reasons for non-usage of SBA loans could then be cataloged and policy changes made to make the SBA more responsive to the needs of entrepreneurs requiring its loan services.

References

Arellano, Richard G. (1984) Strategies for Hispanic Business Development: Trends and Implications, Washington, DC.: National Chamber Foundation.

Arellano, Richard and Allen E. Abrahams (1984), Strategies for Hispanic Business Development: Paths of Success, Washington, DC.: National Chamber Foundation.

Bates, Timothy (1984), "Urban Economic Transformation and Minority Business Opportunities," The Review of Black Political Economy, Fall, pp. 21-36.

Bates, Timothy and William Bradford (1975), "An Evaluation of Alternative Strategies for Expanding the Number of Black-Owned Businesses," The Review of Black Political Economy, #5, pp.376-385.

Handy, John and David H. Swindon (1984), "The Determinants of the Rate of Growth of Black-Owned Businesses: A Preliminary Analysis," The Review of Black Political Economy, pp. 85-110.

Markwalder, D (1981), "The Potential for Black Business," The Review of Black Business Political Economy, 2, #3, pp. 303-312.

Stevens, Richard, L. (1984), "Measuring Minority
Business Formation and   Failure, The Review of
Black Political Economy, Spring, pp. 71-83.

Tabb, W. (1979), What Happened to Black Economic
Development?" The   Review of Black Political
Economy, 9, #4, pp. 392-415.

TRY US (1985),   Minneapolis,   MN: National
Minority Business   Directories.

United States Government Printing Office (1984),
The State of Small Business: A Report of the
President.

Yancy, R.S. (1974), Federal Government Policy
and Black Business Enterprises.
Cambridge, MA: Ballinger.

INCUBATORS FOR MINORITY ENTREPRENEURS

Richard Ellis
North Carolina Agricultural and Technical State University

Abstract

This paper describes the types of incubators, their goals, and the characteristics of incubators that are affiliated with academic institutions.

A section of the paper is devoted to the benefits to the minority entrepreneur of tenancy in an incubator.

The recommendations are that minority entrepreneurs should investigate becoming tenants in an incubator and that The School of Business at A & T should develop an action plan to establish an incubator.

Introduction

An incubator is one way to improve the success rate of minority owned new businesses because the incubator offers the entrepreneur professional advice, low overhead, and centralized service.

This report will examine the purposes and types of incubators including the characteristics of incubators that are affiliated with educational institutions. The reader will learn the benefits that several entrepreneurs have received from incubator tenancy and the goals of the director of a Charlotte based incubator.

The principal sources for this report are Business Incubators Profiles: "A National Survey" by Temali and Campbell, "Incubators for Baby Businesses" by Nelton, "Incubators that Hatch Entrepreneurs" by Rachlin, "Hatching Promises" by Murphy, "Bring up Businesses" in Newsweek, "Central State Successfully Launches Incubator Center" in The IABBE Newsletter, and an interview with the director of the Metrolina Entrepreneurial Council's incubator.

The Purposes of Incubators

Incubators have been in existence for about 20 years. Nelton stated that "of the estimated 50 across the country, 90 percent have come into being since 1980." Temali & Campbell explained that the purpose of a business incubator was "Business Incubators are designed to meet the needs of entrepreneurs -- coordinating services and financial resources and reducing the costs and risks which all new business face."

Incubators can improve the viability of minority owned businesses by providing assistance in two areas. First the incubators can provide an introduction to a venture capital team. Second the staff of the incubator can provide a business plan for a promising entrepreneur.

In a study of 31 incubators Temali & Campbell listed the following characteristics and purposes of incubators:

---located in a large multiple-tenant building
---below market rate rents
---on-site business assistance at low or no cost
---assistance obtaining financing
---shared support services at low or no cost
---flexible leases
---flexible space arrangements
---a "graduation policy" sometimes requiring firms to leave after 3-5 years in this subsidized, nurturing environment
---employee training and placement services

Some incubators have a graduation policy which specifies the number of years that an entrepreneur may remain a tenant in the incubator.

Types of Incubators

In their assessment of business incubator profiles, Temali & Campbell listed the following types of business incubators:

---publicly sponsored incubators
---industrial development agency incubators
---non profit community-based incubators
---university related incubators
---private corporation incubators

The goals of an incubator are related to the type of the incubator. A non profit community-based incubator usually has the goals of creating jobs for unemployed residents, creating more consumer traffic and improving the community. An academic affiliated incubator can have the goals of providing training facilities for the students and a research laboratory for the faculty. A privately owned incubator can exist to provide jobs for under-employed workers and to utilize vacant facilities.

Incubators usually contain a variety of businesses. Newsweek reported that "The Fulton-Carrol Center in Chicago is home to 27 enterprises, including a metal fabricator and trade show exhibit designer." Miller stated that "the Duluth, Minnesota incubator has five firms that employ 200 workers in different industries." The Dayton, Ohio incubator that was initiated by Central State University has nine different firms.

Characteristics of Incubators with Academic Affiliations

A university related incubator can be mutually beneficial to the entrepreneurs, students and faculty. Murphy stated that: "University incubabors can provide a smorgasboard of services including business & engineering faculty for research and problem solving; and students for 'cheap slave labor'."

The Central State Incubabor Project has 60,000 square feet. The incubator has the purposes of 1) providing adequate service to the businesses participating in the facility, and of providing students with actual hands on experience in dealing with the day to day operations of a small business.

The University City Science Center (UCSC) in Philadelphia was started in 1963, and occupies 1.2 million square feet. UCSC offers leases up to five years. UCSC tenant selection criteria precludes those firms not engaged in scientific research. The faculty and other services in the 28 universities, colleges and medical schools is available to the tenants.

The Center for Entrepreneurial Development in Pittsburg attracts people who are interested in starting a business and need training and assistance. It was started in 1971 and has created over 200 jobs. Its support services include university computers, laboratories and role model workshops.

The Renesselear Polytechnic Institute (RPI) Incubator Program opened in June 1982, features 25,000 square feet. It offers a one year lease, an RPI does not have a graduation policy. The incubator has created 140 new jobs. Its support services include access to the university's computer, laboratories, business planning and loan packaging assistance.

The Advanced Technology Development Center (ATDC) is a unit of the University System of Georgia. It started in 1981 and has 28 companies. ATDC provides space, equipment, computer access, and business development services. The incubator has graduated two firms and has created some 200 new jobs. ATDC has a graduation policy of 3 years.

The Science Park Incubator in New Haven was opened in May, 1983 as a joint venture of Yale University, the Olin Corporation, the State of Connecticut and the city of New Haven. The facility will have 120,000 square feet. The incubator does not have a graduation policy and offers secretarial support services, data processing, and access to the Yale University Card Catalog.

The Ohio University Innovation Center opened in July 1983. Services include a variety of secrretarial services, bookkeeping, shipping and receiving, technical feasibility studies, market analyses, cash flow assessments and financial planning. The center focuses on product oriented firms that are spin-offs of basic research in high technology fields like avionics, bio-engineering, chemistry, and physics. Housed within the center is an SBA sponsored Small Business Enterprise Center.

The biotechnolgy Development Center of the University of Illinois offers 90,000 aquare feet and a $2 million Venture Capital Fund which is available only to people in the incubator. There are forty firms interested in the facility. The support services include academic and business support systems.

The University of North Carolina in Charlotte (UNCC) opened an incubator on September 23, 1986. The incubabor is a joint effort between UNCC and the Carley Capital Group. The facility contains 20,000 square feet and has the policies of 1) looking for early stage high growth companies, 2) providing space, a security system, receptionist, conference room, business and management advice, and secretarial services, and 3) giving each tenant a 4 person advisory committee composed of members of the board of directors. The incubator has a two year exit policy. The director, Dr. Jon Binson, stated that he expects employment opportunities for UNCC students from the tenants and the incubator will provide a laboratory for the students and faculty to prepare case studies. The incubator expects to become self-sustaining from leases and shared secretarial services income. The Director's five year goal is to build a 100,000 square feet facility.

How an Entrepreneur Can Find an Incubator

An entrepreneur can find an incubator by contacting the local office of the Small Business Administration or the small business loan department of his or her personal bank.

Benefits to the Entrepreneur

Anne Bergl, a tenant in Chicago's Fulton-Carroll Center has had $250,000 in revenues from her modular furniture business. She stated that she may not have been able to maintain 100% ownership of her firm without the incubator's discount services and low rent.

Alain Krayo is a tenant in the Bennington County Industrial incubator. His business buys partially finished beakers from manufacturers and then remodels them into cookware that retails for twice the price of his competition. In 1985 he had a $10,000 profit on $400,000 in sales. His initial rent in the incubator was about 25% less than the market rate. Krayo stated, "There was no lease or security deposit, and at one point when I got $1,800 behind on the rent, they went along with me."

William E. Murphy is also a tenant in Chicago's Fulton-Carroll Center. Murphy designs and builds large exhibits for trade shows. His business is profitable, and he anticipates revenues of $500,000 in 1986. Murphy's rent is very low, he pays $1.56 a square foot for his 15,000 square feet and he said "isn't that wonderful? That is what helps you make it."

Robert H. Beckett, the founder of Robec Distributors, a firm that distributes microcomputers and periphials, left the Technology Centes International Incubator after four years. He left because, "our organization was growing and we wanted to stand on our own two feet" Robec has 40 employees and does nearly $30 million worth of business annually.

Recommendations

1) I recommend incubator tenancy to potential
    minority business owners and potential small
    business entrepreneurs because:
    a)   the low rent
    b)   the availability of inexpensive sercre-
         tarial services
    c)   the professional management advice
    d)   the psychological support from peers
    e)   the entre to venture capital sources
2) The School of Business and Economics of North
    Carolina A & T State University should deve-
    lop an action plan to establish a local incu-
    bator because:
    a)   it will improve the viability of minority
         owned businesses.
    b)   it will provide a source of employment
         for the students
    c)   it will serve as a laboratory for case
         studies for the faculty to publish
    d)   it will foster better ties with the busi-
         ness community.

References

Binson, Jon Interview with on October 29, 1986.

"Bringing up Businesses", Newsweek, October,
1980, p.18.

"Central State Successfully Launches Incubator
Center" This is the International Association of
Black Business Educator's Newsletter, Summer,
1986, p. 13.

Miller, Annetta "Jeno's Economic Ego" Newsweek,
March 17, 1986, p. 52.

Murphy, Thomas P. "Hatching Promises", Forbes,
June 4, 1984, p. 232.

Nelton, Sharon "Incubators for Baby Businesses,"
Nation's Business, November, 1984 p. 40.

Pearsall, Thomas E. & D.H. Cunningham, How to
Write for the World of Work New York: Holt,
Rinehart and Winston, 1982.

Rachlin, Jill "Incubators That Hatch Entrepreneurs", Money January, 1986, p. 27.

Temali, Mihailo and Candace Campbell, Business
Incubators Profiles: A National Survey (Minneapolis, Minnesota: Hubert H. Humphrey Institute
of Public Affairs, 1984), p. 2.

MARKETING EFFECTIVENESS OF THE NATIONAL FUNERAL DIRECTORS
AND MORTICIANS ASSOCIATION (NFDMA)

Alexander M. Okrah
Associate Professor of Marketing
School of Business
North Carolina Central University

And

Tyronza R. Richmond
Chancellor and Professor of Decision Sciences
North Carolina Central University

Introduction

The purpose of this study was to investigate the role of marketing effectiveness in the NFDMA. NFDMA is a predominantly black organization composed of funeral directors and morticians. The marketing activities of the NFDMA were studied because the by-laws and code of ethics of the NFDMA stress that all state associations should conduct an annual intensified membership drive, and an annual report of this effort should be transmitted to the National Association. Although the national office had made concerted efforts to comply with the spirit of the by-laws and code of ethics, the membership had not been growing, and the national office continued to experience marketing and management difficulties. There is no unanimity of values, goals, and objectives of the membership of this august body.

The belief was that marketing research would unfold the needs and activities of members, and subsequently the National Association would integrate the findings in its strategic planning.

Purpose of Study

The purpose of the study is four-fold: (1) to assess the general needs of both members and non-members; (2) to determine the image of NFDMA among both members and non-members in order to take corrective action, if changes are needed; (3) to describe marketing of funeral homes in the economic structure of the country; and (4) to contribute to the improvement of marketing practices among NFDMA membership.

Methodology of Data Collection

Data collection methods can be categorized by degree of their directness. This survey sought information from individual respondents, and utilized the mail questionnaire rather than personal interview techniques. Information from secondary sources and knowledgeable funeral directors and morticians was sought.

The Survey

Two sets of questionnaires were drawn up; one set for members and the other for non-members.

A 1985/86 directory of funeral directors and morticians compiled by NFDMA was used to generate the sample size. The directory indicated that there were 590 members and 2,161 non-members scattered over 38 states including the District of Columbia. NFDMA members constituted 21 percent of all black funeral directors and morticians in the country.

The Sample Size

The 500 members and 2,000 non-members who were sent questionnaires were chosen through the use of random sampling.

Questionnaire Returns

Sixty-six questionnaires from member respondents representing 13.2 percent of the questionnaires sent to members were returned. Usable questionnaires for members numbered only sixty-one, representing 12.2 percent of all questionnaires sent to members.

One hundred and fifty-eight or 31.6 percent of the members moved and the post office returned their questionnaires.

In effect, errors in the directory reduced the sample size for members to 342. Based on the 342 questionnaires, the usable questionnaires represented 17.8 percent of questionnaires that reached members.

Out of 2,000 questionnaires sent to non-members, only 170 were completed and returned. The post office returned 162 questionnaires for non-delivery due to address changes. Again, the sample size for non-members was reduced to 1,838.

Among the 170 completed questionnaires from non-members, 16 were found to be from members. Five other questionnaires were returned unanswered. Thus, the usable questionnaires for non-members numbered 149, representing 7.5 percent of questionnaires sent to all members. Based on 1,838, usable questionnaires represented 12.3 percent of the questionnaires that reached non-members.

Analysis and results of this study are presented

in the following sections: I. Theoretical Framework; II. Findings--Members; III. Findings--Non-Members; and IV. Conclusions and Recommendations.

I. Theoretical Framework

Numerous writings relating to different aspects of the funeral industry exist. A few of the writings that are pertinent to this study are reviewed here.

Talarzyk summarizes the work of the funeral director by stating that the funeral director serves the living and assists and counsels survivors. He asserts that "today the funeral director must also provide comfortable facilities for the survivors, develop sound technical skill for the restorative process and have legal knowledge to cut through government and insurance red tape."[1]

Jean Rosenblatt points out the high cost of funerals. She states that Americans spend more than $6 billion a year on funeral related expenses, at an average burial cost that exceeds $2,571.[2]

Undertaking came under fire about two decades ago with the publication of such books as Jessica Mitford's "The American Way of Death" and Ruth Mulvey Harmen's "The High Cost of Dying," followed by the "death and dying movement" in which people were urged among other things to simplify burial ceremonies which often meant transferring planning from the undertaker to the family.[3]

A decade later, the FTC began investigation into alleged abuses in the funeral business which had been called to public attention. The FTC issued a report critical of many practices and imposed federal regulations on the industry to be effective in 1983.[4] The FTC's regulations required funeral directors to provide customers with itemized price lists of goods and services and to disclose prices over the telephone on request. Regulations also bar funeral directors from falsely claiming that state laws require embalming on the purchase of a casket for cremation.[5]

Consumer groups have lobbied vigorously for, and funeral directors against, regulation. The industry argues that the evidence does not support federal regulation, and besides, state regulation is adequate to deal with abuses. However, according to Thomas Nelson, "state boards that regulate undertaking have, historically, been made up of undertakers, so in effect, the industry is regulating itself."[6]

Jessica Mitford said in 1982 that "the funeral industry is actually experiencing its own funeral" and some industry specialists and sociologists agree. The number of morticians has declined from 24,000 in the 1960's to between 20,000 and 22,000 today and experts expect the decline to continue.[7] In a 1974 survey done by the Casket Manufacturers Association on American attitudes toward death, almost 30 percent of the respondents said they would prefer to by-pass funeral directors altogether.[8] Ebeling advises funeral directors and members of the funeral industry to demonstrate the values to be gained from providing total funeral services.[9] The Mortuary Management discusses how the funeral director can rebut articles critical of the funeral industry.[10]

Greer suggests that the funeral director's image can be improved by being active in the community, showing interest in public concerns and members of the local community, and joining churches, service clubs, or civic groups.[11] Matthews challenges funeral directors to realize their potential to become one of the foremost caretaking professions in the United States through research and publications that link funeral services to psychological, sociological, and theological values which have given the funeral industry the opportunity to exist.[12]

The New England Funeral Director focused attention on competition and the need for funeral directors' regular meetings to up-grade their profession, solve mutual problems, and provide better service to their patrons.[13] Kates, in a commencement address, reminded the graduates that "they must continue to pursue knowledge and excellence all their days, and that upon them rests the future of their craft." He further said "in the years to come they should never stray the slightest step away from the path of professional righteousness."[14]

1. W. Wayne Talarzyk, "Gistner Funeral Home," Contemporary Cases in Marketing, Hinsdale, Illinois, The Dryden Press, 1974, p. 174.

2. Jean Rosenblatt, Brief Report Issued November 5, 1952 in the Editorial Research Reports, Washington, D. C., 1982, Vol. 11, No. 17.

3. Ibid.

4. Ibid.

5. Ibid.

6. Ibid.

7. Jessica Mitford, The American Way of Death, New York, Simon and Schuster, 1963.

8. Ibid.

9. R. A. Ebeling, "Era of Accountability," Mortuary Management, Vol. 59, No. 2, p. 8, 1972.

10. Ebeling, "Some Syndicated Writers Pollute the Public Mind," Mortuary Management, Vol. 58, No. 12, p. 8, August, 1973.

11. John C. Greer, "Tips to Help You Build a Better Image," Casket and Sunnyside, Vol. 103, No. 7, p. 18+ (1971).

12. William F. Matthews, "Funeral--Funeral Director the Future," Mortuary Management, Vol. 58 No. 12, pp. 12-15 (1971).

13. "Competitors Helping Each Other," The New England Funeral Director, Vol. 1, No. 5, p. 19,, August, 1975.

14. Charles O. Kates, "Commencement Speakers Talk to the Wrong People," (Editorial) The American Funeral Director, Vol. 98, No. 8, p. 29, August, 1975.

The Goldfarb's case (1975) and subsequent cases on collusion by professional organizations have forced professionals such as lawyers, doctors, architects, and engineers and others to advertise their fees for services.[15] Therefore, NFDMA cannot afford to engage in any activities that suggest collusion on its part. The suggestion by some of the respondents that NFDMA have uniform prices is unacceptable in view of the foregone explanation.

Despite the interest that has been shown in the development of the funeral industry, there is at present a lack of specific data about marketing management practices, strategies, and attitudes. More tightly structured research studies based on survey research are needed to meet the need for a better understanding of marketing in the funeral industry. The sections that follow constitute such a research study in the context of the funeral industry, and in particular, of the NFDMA marketing system.

II. Findings--Members

From the study of marketing practices of members and non-members of NFDMA, the following conclusions were reached:

Members

There were sixty-one usable questionnaires from members who were asked to indicate their opinions towards NFDMA. Almost 77 percent of the respondents thought NFDMA was dedicated to promoting professional and business interests of its members. An overwhelming majority of members did not find any inconsistencies in NFDMA's activities and objectives. The few who found faults charged that the organization did not keep up with FTC rules, policies and regulations and that management did not truthfully carry out certain policies.

Seventy-three percent of the members had a positive view of the organization; NFDMA presented a social body whose members assembled to socialize and to conduct business as prescribed by the by-laws. However, the four percent that had negative opinions of NFDMA saw the organization as a social body which attended meetings solely to socialize and to self personify some members.

Two-thirds of the members found the management to be adequate and efficient. Most members had recently seen improvement in the financial management of the organization. Nevertheless, about forty-two percent of the members were not aware of the services provided by NFDMA.

Members rated as "very important" factors such as keeping abreast with laws and policies, educational exposure, dissemination of information through the newly founded newspaper, fellowship, financial knowledge, and general administrative

15. FTC News Summary, Vol. 39-80 (July 4, 1980), p. 2.

management, in that order. This response disproves the notion that fellowship or meeting other people is of utmost importance to the membership.

About 78 percent of the members were willing to pay between $200 and $1,000 each towards the building of the national seat in Washington, D.C. An overwhelming majority of the members would like to have a full-time paid executive director at the national office. The majority of them, about 57.4 percent, agreed to pay dues in March and April. However, about 20 percent would still like to make payment in July and August.

Members would like institutes to be held at the district level (39 percent), national meetings (21 percent), and both district and national meetings (14 percent). The majority of the members are also members of or are affiliated with other predominantly white funeral directors and morticians' organizations. However, they attached importance to NFDMA national, district and state, or local meetings.

Almost all of the members saw the need for more exposure of NFDMA to the public. While some members agreed there is representation of funeral directors and morticians, it is quite evident that the funeral business as a whole is not well represented in Congress, state legislatures, and in local governments.

About half of the members had not heard of the proposed NFDMA newspaper. Most of them believed the newspaper would be used mainly to disseminate general information to advertise NFDMA activities, and to announce NFDMA meetings.

An overwhelming majority of the members stressed quality merchandise, good services and reasonable prices in promoting their services and products. Most of the funeral homes relied on both advertising and word of mouth in promoting services and products. Newspapers are very important to funeral homes, followed by radio and television.

The majority of members made between $20,000 and $500,000 a year. Most of the members can be classified as small businesses. Slightly over half of the members would like NFDMA to reduce fees for members whose firms were marginal (based on income and number of people employed).

Almost all the members shipped corpses to both NFDMA members and non-members. They explained that the choice of funeral homes outside their cities and state was left to the bereaved family. However, the resources and qualifications of a funeral home were taken into consideration when deciding to which funeral home a dead body would be shipped. This illustrates the non-cooperation among NFDMA members.

III. Findings--Non-Members

An overwhelming majority of the non-members were aware of the existence of NFDMA. Almost 80 percent thought NFDMA was a national organization dedicated to promoting the common professional and business interests of its members.

Again, an overwhelming majority of the respondents indicated NFDMA's need for a lot of exposure to the outside world. They would like the organization to have a very strong cooperation with the NAACP, the Black Congressional Caucus, white funeral organizations, and Operation PUSH.

Slightly over half of the non-members felt they were not adequately represented as funeral directors or morticians in Congress and on the state level. This suggests that the funeral industry is not in touch with law makers which in turn partly explains why some industry members do not understand the laws that affect the funeral industry.

Non-members unanimously wanted legal representation at the local level. Most of them wanted a national officer to be present at both state and district meetings. Forty-one percent of non-members thought the organization did not present a positive image before law makers on the local, state and federal levels. However, most of the non-members did not find NFDMA to be engaged in any activities that were inconsistent with the objectives of the organization.

Over half of the non-members perceived NFDMA as a social body whose members attended meetings to socialize and to conduct business as perscribed by the by-laws of the organization. About half of them viewed the management of NFDMA to be sufficiently efficient.

A great majority of non-members stated they engaged in promoting their services and merchandise. About half of the respondents indicated they stressed quality merchandise, good services, and reasonable prices. A vast number of non-members relied on both advertising and personal reputation to promote their funeral homes. Radio was the medium mostly used to promote their services, merchandise, and firms. Newspapers came second while television came third as media for promotion.

Financing was the main problem facing non-members. Half of them favored the prorating of fees based on income and number of people employed. Most of the non=members, as a group, were either affiliated with, or members of, at least a total of sixty-five other associations in the funeral industry.

IV. Conclusions and Recommendations

Conclusions

The purpose of this study was to investigate the role of marketing within the management of NFDMA through the study of marketing research of both non-members and members of NFDMA.

The data were elicited through a literature search and a mail survey of 149 non-members and 61 NFDMA members. Marketing means several things to funeral directors and morticians. To most of the members and non-members marketing is

buying and selling. The next popular answer is that marketing is projecting the concept of traditional funeral service through advertising and exposing the firm to the public.

NFDMA has the usual management characteristics and image of a disorganized organization; low membership, lack of visibility, financial problems, lack of competent managers, and lack of professionalism among the membership. Poor (or lack of) strategic planning has exacerbated NFDMA's marketing management problems.

Marketing provides a link between resources and development. Inefficiences and wastes are reduced through efficient marketing. An efficient on-going marketing research can unfold the needs and activities of both members and non-members which will help the National Association to integrate the findings in its strategic planning. Both members and non-members of NFDMA understand and can cause positive management development.

The marketing system of NFDMA is in a very precarious situation. The organization is unable to sell itself. As such, out of the 2,851 black funeral directors and morticians in the country, only 590 are members of NFDMA. However, NFDMA is very well known among the black funeral directors and morticians. Both members and non-members are aware of NFDMA's objectives. Only six percent of members and eight percent of non-members saw some departure of the organization's activities from its objectives. The question then that arises is how effective is NFDMA in holding to its objectives?

Apparently, the objectives are either not truthfully carried out or are not widely known as explained by both members and non-members. NFDMA does not have any political clout due to its non-recognition by lawmakers on the federal, state, and local levels. A few black funeral directors and morticians have characterized NFDMA as an organization that meets to socialize. Though this poor image seems to stem from a few people, nevertheless, it has tarnished the reputation of the top management and the organization as a whole. Therefore, the attempt to increase membership has been a painful experience for NFDMA.

The management of NFDMA has performed poorly since its inception, largely because of inept management under seemingly incompetent managers. A few members and non-members would like to see a paid professional chief executive. In order to create a climate where desperately needed non-members can be attracted, a complete turn in the management and a change in the organization's image as a whole is a sin qua non. The spirit of favorable objectives stated in the by-laws has been negated by the incompetetent management through disagreement and bickering among the general membership. Attitudes of members and non-members toward NFDMA have been positive except for a few who disagree with top management and some members. Changes in these attitudes have been realized by both members and non-members.

Very few members saw NFDMA, as a whole, to be inefficient. Nevertheless, most of them realized the need for top management to identify and address the professional needs of funeral directors and morticians.

Marketing practices within NFDMA are inefficient, and no significant changes have emerged with increased productivity on the part of management in recent years, and marketing, as a whole, has not had any great impact on NFDMA's development.

Recommendations

These recommendations are made on the basis of the data reported in this study, observations, and conferences with knowledgeable individuals. (1) The Directory must be made current to ensure the status of members and non-members. This would help eliminate mail being returned by the post office. (2) A full-time staff must be employed at the national office and should be headed by a business manager. The appointment of a business manager will help cut down on the frequent travels made by top management. (3) A strong accounting department is necessary to convince members who have not seen any changes in the financial management, that management is being improved. (4) The date for paying annual fees should be changed from October 1 to March 1 of each year. Charter fees paid by March and April will enable the House of Representatives, which meets in September, to know how much revenue has been collected in considering budgets for the ensuing fiscal year which starts on October 1. (5) Payment of the annual fee should include fees for membership at both local and national levels as well as the price of the newspaper. Thus, all payments will be consolidated into one payment. (6) Currently, NFDMA refunds registration fees paid in advance to members who are unable to attend meetings and who petition the Executive Director for a refund. Only about half of the members and very few non-members knew of this policy. This refund-of-fees' policy must be extensively publicized in the NFDMA newspaper for members to take advantage of the policy. (7) A complete disclosure of income and number of people employed must be made in order to prorate fees for members whose firms are marginal. Members who would like to benefit from this must apply to the association for consideration. (8) In order to better serve the needs of members the association has proposed to erect a national building in Washington, D. C. A campaign should be launched to collect pledges or the $200 that 72 percent of the members agreed to pay towards the erection of the national seat. (9) Both members and non-members would like to have legal representation on the local level to explain laws and regulations that affect the funeral industry. NFDMA should send national officers such as legal counsel to financially strong local chapters that are willing to meet the expenditure involved while maintaining officers at national meetings. This may attract more members and non-members to NFDMA meetings. (10) NFDMA should be able to influence the enactment of laws and regulations that affect funeral directors and morticians through the use of the legal counsel at headquarters. This action will dispel the notion that the funeral industry is not adequately represented at the local, state and federal legislatures, and will help foster better understanding of funeral laws and regulations. (11) Small Business Administration officials and college professors should be invited by NFDMA to address members and non-members on the various aspects of small business management. Most of the black funeral homes are small businesses and will benefit from this needed education. (12) Marketing research in the funeral industry should be continuously carried out. Publicized research findings will enable members and non-members alike to become more knowledgeable of their industry and profession. (13) The needs of both members and non-members must be identified and addressed through the submission of ideas, suggestions, complaints and through on-going research. These ideas, suggestions and complaints can be turned into opportunities for NFDMA. (14) NFDMA could seek exposure from the outside world by inviting lawmakers on all levels as guest speakers at national meetings. Invitations should also be sent to NAACP, the Black Congressional Caucus, predominantly white funeral organizations, PUSH, and other bodies and organizations, as well as FTC officials to speak to members on current issues that affect the funeral industry. (15) NFDMA must design some minimum qualifications for applicants who seek admission into the association. Such qualifications could be a minimum academic qualification coupled with state certification as a funeral director or mortician. A high standard for entry into the association will dispel the general belief that funeral professionals are not highly educated. High standards may exclude some potential members but will portray increased credibility of NFDMA. (16) Bickering and non-cooperativeness among the membership must be reduced. One way to achieve this objective is to encourage members to ship corpses to one another. The distrust and friction among the members will dissipate when they communicate with each other more often. (17) Whatever socializing that is done at national meetings should be carried out at a minimum so as to dispel the notion that NFDMA's members meet mainly to socialize. (18) Ad hoc committees which have been extensively used in the past must now be sparingly used. Instead, standing committees must be instituted. Members would serve for periods of one year, two years and three years. Committee members whose terms expire each year must be replaced. This will ensure continuity of activities. (19) The president of NFDMA should be elected to office for more than one year. The term should be decided by the membership. This will enable the president to have sufficient time to carry out his or her plan for the organization. (20) NFDMA must draw up a strategic plan. The plan should embody both short-run and long-run goals and objectives which when properly executed can lead to improved management and marketing performances.

References

"Competitors Helping Each Other," The New England Funeral Director, Vol. 1, No. 5, p. 19, August, 1975.

Ebeling, R. A. (1971), Some Syndicated Writers

Pollute the Public Mind," Mortuary Management, Vol. 58, No. 12, p. 8.

_____ (1972), "Era of Accountability," Mortuary Management, Vol. 59, No. 2, p. 8.

FTC News Summary (July 4, 1980), Vol. 39-80, p. 2.

Greer, John C. (1983), "Tips to Help You Build a Better Image," Casket and Sunnyside, Vol. 103, No. 7, p. 18+.

Kates, Charles O. (1975), "Commencement Speakers Talk to the Wrong People," (Editorial) The American Funeral Director, Vol. 98, No. 8, p. 29.

Matthews, William F. (1971), "Funeral--Funeral Director the Future," Mortuary Management, Vol. 58, No. 12, pp. 12-15.

Mitford, Jessica (1963), The American Way of Death, New York, Simon and Schuster.

Rosenblatt, Jean (1982), Brief Report Issued November 5, 1982 in the Editorial Research Reports, Washington, D. C., Vol. 11, No. 17.

Talarzyk, W. Wayne (1974), "Gistner Funeral Home," Contemporary Cases in Marketing, Hindsdale, Illinois: The Dryden Press, p. 174.

BLACK CONSUMERS AND BLACK BUSINESS:
INCOME, SPENDING AND SALES RELATIONSHIPS

Thaddeus H. Spratlen, University of Washington

Abstract

The fundamental importance of Black customers in the survival and success of Black business is explored in this paper. Aggregate cross-section data are used to analyze Black consumer income, spending and their relationships to the receipts of Black-owned business. Comparisons are made for selected years of the patterns of and trends in the income and spending of Blacks relative to receipts of Black-owned business. The size, locations and composition of the Black busines sector are considered to be the most important determinants of the extent of Black consumer patronage of Black-owned businesses. It is concluded that unless and until major structural changes occur in the Black business sector, it will continue to receive a small and gradually decreasing proportion of Black consumer spending. Its share of total business receipts will also continue to decline.

Introduction

Most Black businesses serve a Black clientele almost exclusively. Their racially-defined customer base parallels the historic, geographic and other forms of racial segregation in the U.S. economy and society. Such a pattern can be found to a lesser extent in most ethnic- or racially-based ownership of business. Generally, this phrase refers to business firms owned by people of color or those who differ from the dominant groups of European heritage in the United States[1]. Thus, retail and personal service businesses in predominantly Korean, Vietnamese, Filipino or other Asian and Pacific Island communities are likely to serve customers who are similar in racial, ethnic and/or national origin to the business owners. Language, customs and other cultural factors can explain most of this pattern. To some extent there are distinct competitive advantages for both business owners and their customers in such a situation. However, when the pattern is so restrictive that it prevents growth and limits the exchange process for ethnic enterprise, the negative consequences should be recognized. Business and economic relationships must then be examined to determined desired policies and programs aimed at increasing business opportunities and improving the functioning of the business system.

This discussion is based on the premise that Black-owned business enterprise tends to be more restricted than other groups of owners among people of color in the United States. This notion is supported by several factors. Blacks are more segregated in terms of residence than others. Retail and service markets are commonly and closely linked to residential patterns. By structure and location, Black businesses tend to be narrowly circumscribed in these terms. Beyond housing there are also racial attitudes that further limit the clientele of Black businesses. For example, except for an occasional visit by Whites to a Black-owned cocktail lounge or club featuring well-known recording artists, or patronage of a "soul food" restaurant located in an integrated neighborhood or near downtown, it is rare for Black-owned retail and service firms to attract very many White customers. Indeed, it has become unusual for even all-Black music groups to achieve much success. White musicians are usually considered to be essential for appealing to a "crossover" (meaning a substantially White) audience. To worsen the situation for Black-owned business, in recent years Black consumers have become patrons of White business firms from which they were historically excluded. Examples include beauty salons, funeral service firms and tailoring shops. Even in the case of some franchised businesses, charges have been made that Black franchisees have not been permitted to acquire units in predominantly White areas.

Unfortunately, there is mostly anecdotal support for such examples. This paper represents an attempt to provide a comprehensive and systematic examination of patronage relationships involving Black business enterprise. Its main purpose is to document relationships between Black consumers as a group and Black business enterprise. The intent is to illustrate the inherent limitations of business or marketing opportunities when the exchange process limits the participation of Black enterprise in the broader markets beyond the geographic and race-ethnic boundaries of Black communities.

Research Methods

Secondary and cross-section data are used to analyze relationships between Black consumers income and spending, and the sales of Black businesses. the most comprehensive data available are provided in the periodic surveys of minority businesses conducted since 1969 by the U.S. Department of Commerce (Bureau of the Census 1984 and prior years). Surveys have been conducted for 1969, 1972, 1977 and 1982. Business receipts by ethnic categories (i.e., Blacks, Hispanics and "Asian Americans, American Indians and Others") and types of business are reported. Data from other government sources are also used to compare income and spending characteristics as well as sales/receipts data for the economy as a whole.

---

[1] The term "people of color" is more accurate than "minority" which obviously includes groups of individuals who differ in many recognizable ways other than race and ethnicity from a majority of the U.S. population. European-heritage refers to Whites or Caucasians.

Descriptive statistics are applied. More precise multivariate statistics and relationships are not available for analysis in this initial effort. Primary emphasis is on judgmental interpretations and general observations based on such aggregate and cross-section relationships. Possibly more complex research approaches will emerge following the presentation of this paper.

Data Analysis and Relationships

Several assumptions underlie the analysis that is presented. They are outlined below along with some comments on the structure of Black enterprise when compared to the U.S. economy as a whole. This is followed by a discussion of the comparative income and spending flows of Black consumers relative to Black business. Several important structural, operating and environmental characteristics of Black business are presented in the third topic of this section.

A Basic Structural Comparison

Retailing and service enterprises represent a substantially greater part of Black business than is true of U.S. business as a whole. In an anecdotal form this is illustrated by the fact that local retail firms (especially automobile dealerships) are included among the 100 largest Black enterprises (Black Enterprise 1987). Yet in the U.S. national business sector major retail corporations such as Sears and K-Mart would have such rankings.

But a more general descriptive measure from the data in Table 1 illustrates the point. Black retail firms had just over one-third of the receipts of all Black business. For business as a whole the proprotion was less than one-seventh: 33% v. 14%. In the case of services, the proportions are even more disparate: 26% v. 6%.

For Black business, then, 58.9% or nearly three-fifths of all business receipts come from retail and service busiensses. For the nation as a whole it is only 19.2%. Thus, the overall proportion of retail and service businesses in the Black sector is more than three times as great as it is for the economy as a whole.

This very substantial concentration of Black businesses in retailing and services highlights a special importance of Black consumers as the primary customer base for Black business. Since retailing and services are predominantly localized, their markets in residential terms are largely segregated. This makes reaching the larger market beyond the Black community quite difficult. Yet as noted in subsequent analysis, Black consumers have sufficient mobility to satisfy their demands for goods and services mostly in the larger marketplace. Thus, only a relatively small part of the Black consumer's dollar is spent in the patronage of Black firms.

The Flow of Black Consumer Income and Spending

At the time of the first survey of Black-owned business in 1969, their gross receipts amounted to $4.5 billion. This was about 11%-12% of Black

household income. However, note that these receipts include sales to businesses as well.

TABLE 1

Comparisons of Black Business Enterprise and U.S. Business Enterprise, 1982

Category/ Type of Comparison	Amount (Billions)	Percent
All business receipts[a]	$ 7,755.0	–
All Black business[b] receipts	12.4	–
All retail business[c] receipts	1,065.9	–
All Black retail business receipts[b]	4.1	–
All selected services[d] receipts	427.0	–
All Black selected services receipts[b]	3.2	–
All retail sales receipts as % total business receipts		13.7%
All Black retail sales receipts as % total Black business receipts		33.1
All selected services receipts as % total of all services receipts		5.5
All Black selected services receipts as % total Black business receipts		25.8

Source Notes:

[a]Statistical Abstract of the United States 1987, p. 503.

[b]1982 Survey of Minority-Owned Business Enterprises -- Black, p. 4.

[c]1982 Census of Retail Trade, United States, p.3.

[d]1982 Census of Service Industries, United States, p. 3.

More detailed comparisons of the changes in business receipts and Black income over time are shown in Table 2. Note that Black business receipts represent a declining proportion of all business receipts. In the survey years, the proportions have changed as follows: 0.29%, 0.25%, 0.18% and 0.16%, respectively. Yet Black income has risen during the same period from 6.3% of total income in 1969 to 6.9% in 1982 -- a larpercent of a larger income base.

But it is also of interest to note that Black income (in terms of the median) has declined relative to White median income. The decline was from 61.3% in 1970 to 55.3% in 1982.

The one other measure that is needed to show the bind that Black business generally is in relates to the estimated portion of Black income spent

TABLE 2

Gross Receipts of All Firms and Black-Owned Firms
Selected Survey Years, 1969-1982
(Millions of Dollars)

Year	Receipts	Average Annual Percentage Increase from Previous Survey Year	Receipts	Average Annual Percentage Increase from Previous Survey Year	Receipts of Black-Owned Firms as % of All Firms
1982	$ 7,755,000	13.0%	$ 12,444	8.8%	0.16%
1977	4,699,000	12.6	8,645	4.1	0.18
1972	2,883,500	30.8	7,168	20.1	0.25
1969	1,497,969	-	4,474	-	0.29

Source: Statistical Abstract of the United States 1987; U.S. Department of Commerce, Bureau of the Census, Survey of Minority-Owned Busienss Enterprise, 1969, 1972, 1977, 1982.

in Black business. Despite the importance of such a measure there are few estimates available as to its size. In the early 1970's Spratlen (1973) estimated that the proportion was 10%. More recently, quoting economist Andrew Brimmer, the Wall Street Journal (1985) indicated that the proportion had declined to 7%. Even this percentage could be considered somewhat high based on receipts of Black retail and service firms in 1982.[2]

Explanations of Black Patronage of Black Business

Black business generally has not shared fully in the increasing prosperity of Black consumers over the past two or three decades. There are several reasons why this is true. Most of the structural aspects of the explanation are related to the characteristics of Black business outlined in Exhibit 1. In marketing terms, it could be said that Black business is not positioned to meet most of the needs/pruchases of Black consumers. Based on business size, location and merchandise selection as well as other characterisitcs, Black business enterprise can meet only a very small portion of Black consumer demand for goods and services.

Note also the interrelationships among various characteristics in Exhibit 1 and the relationships summarized in Table 3. Small size and limited resources place severe restrictions on their ability to compete. Thus, growth potential as well as competitive strength and merchandise assortments are all quite limited. Such conditions are reflected in the fact that Black firms are capturing only small portions of Black consumer spending in their local and primary target markets.

Limitations

At this time mainly descriptive statements and relationships have been explored regarding Black business and their almost total dependence on Black consumers as a customer base. Estimates of the amount of Black consumer income spent in Black businesses are based largely on crude and somewhat arbitrary procedures. The emphasis is still on general judgment and observations. Yet the patterns described have persisted over a long period of time. Thus, more comprehensive and rigorous research efforts are needed to explore various dimensions of this important subject.

Research Needs and Policy Implications

The issues raised by this analysis require more extensive and complex research, if they are to be better understood, and eventually resolved. The following topics seem to deserve a high priority for future research:

°°°Nature and extent of Black consumer patronage of Black business;

°°°Market structure and environment as they affect Black consumer choice and Black consumer patronage of Black business;

°°°Micro- and macro-level problems and the need for major policy changes in order to increase the size and resource base of Black business;

°°°Strategies which have the potential to icnrease the success of Black business ownership and management.

In order to expand the market and growth potential of Black business, attempts should be made to explore opportunities for reaching and serving markets outside the Black community. Although such opportunities will be difficult to find and exploit, the benefits would seem to warrant significant business development program resources. Research into such new policy and program directions

---

[2]A gross percentage comparison of Black business receipts and Black consumer income amounted to 8.9% for 1982. However, using only the receipts of retail and service firms the percentage was only 5.2%. A rigorously developed estimate does not appear to be available at this time.

EXHIBIT 1

Characteristics of Black Business Enterprise

1. Size: See Table 3-- $27,448 annual sales	Small; self-employment as the typical pattern rather than direct and multiple job creation and income generation.
	In 1969 just over three-fourths had no paid employees. By 1982 this _increased_ to 89%!
2. Kinds of Business--	Mostly retail convenience goods and personal services.
3. Pattern of Location--	Mainly in the Black community.
4. Type of Ownership/ Management	Single proprietorships.
5. Merchandise Selection	Limited by size and type of business.
6. Operating Constraints	Frequently undercapitalized with limited resources for credit and quantity buying; limited specialization and management skills.
7. Other Constraints:	Generally location-bound in the Black community; serving a severely constrained market environment.

TABLE 3

Number and Average Size of Firms
Selected Survey Years, 1969-1982

(Number of Firms in Thousands)

All Firms	1969	1972	1977	1982
Number	**7**,489	12,990	14,741	14,546
Average Annual Percentage Increase from Previous Survey Year	--	24.5%	2.7%	(-1.3%)
Average Annual Receipts per Firm	$200,023	$221,978	$318,771	$533,136

Black Firms				
Number	163	195	231	339
Average Annual Percentage Increase from Previous Survey Year	--	6.5%	3.7%	9.3%
Average Annual Receipts per Firm	$ 27,448	$ 36,762	$ 37,391	$ 36,682
Size Relative to All Firms	One-Seventh	One-Sixth	One Eighth	One-Fourteenth
Percentage of all Firms	2.2%	2.2%	1.5%	2.3%

Source: _Statistal Abstract of the United States 1987_; U.S. Department of Commerce, Bureau of the Census, _Survey of Minority-Owned Business Enterprises_, 1969, 1972, 1977, 1982.

would lead to our better understanding of competitive and racial barriers to entry which face Black firms in the larger urban, regional and national marketplace. Successful applications of such program and policy directions would also lead to expansions in the stake and contributions of Blacks in the ownership and management of business enterprise generally.

Conclusions

Black business is severely limited by a number of constraints. They serve one group of consumers-- Blacks--almost exclusively. This group has relatively less income in comparison with the population as a whole. Moreover, they are generally not in a position to attract customers from the larger marketplace beyond the Black community. This is mainly ldue to geographic and type-of-business limitations. But historic patterns and attitudes of limited acceptance are also significant constraints facing Black business firms. In addition, there are structural and environmental barriers to their greater market exposure and acceptance.

At the present time increased sales to Blacks represent the primary and most accessible source of demand and growth for Black business. However, continued exclusive reliance on the present customer base will yield less potential for growth in the coming decades. Although not explored in this discussion, macro-level policies are needed to adequately address the numerous and complex macro-level problems facing both Black consumers and the Black business sector. Unless and until this policy and program connection can be made, Black business seems likely to remain marginal and quite limited with respect to both Black consumers and the overall market economy as well.

References

Becker, Gary S. (1986) "The American Dream May Be Coming Closer for Blacks," Business Week (April 21), p. 11.

Cohen, Richard (1981) "Black Concerns: Is Anybody Listening?," The Washington Post (October 17), p. A23.

Brimmer, Andrew F. (1986) Trends, Prospects, and Strategies for Black Economic Progress," The Review of Black Political Economy, (Spring) 14, pp. 91-97.

Hatchett, David (1986) "The Push for Economic Development," The Crisis (May) 93, pp. 17-19, 39-40.

Kotkin, Joel (1986) "Why Blacks Are Out of Business," The Washington Post, (September 7), pp. Cl, C4.

Spratlen, Thaddeus H. (1973) "The Black Consumer Response to Black Business," The Review of Black Political Economy (Fall) 4, pp. 73-105.

Black Enterprise (1987) "Top 100 Black Business Firms," (June), p. 129.

Statistical Abstract of the United States 1987, U.S. Department of Comemrce, Bureau of the Census December 1986.

U.S. Department of Commerce (various years). Survey of Minority Owned Business Enterprises-- Black. Washington, D.C.: U.S. Government Printing Office, 1969, 1972, 1977, 1982.

U.S. Department of Commerce (1984) 1982 Census of Retail Trade. - United States. Washington, D.C.: U.S. Government Printing Office.

_____. 1982 Census of Service Industries. United States. Washington, D.C.: U.S. Government Printing Office.

Wall Street Journal (1985) "Business Bulletin," (February 28), p. 1.

ADVERTISING BY ACCOUNTANTS: IMPLICATIONS FOR MINORITIES

Sarah Dunn, North Carolina Agricultural and Technical State University
William Cooper, North Carolina Agricultural and Technical State University
Mark Kiel, North Carolina Agricultural and Technical State University
Benton Miles, University of North Carolina at Greensboro

Abstract

Since the Supreme Court ruling authorizing advertising by professionals, accountants have had to reevaluate their advertising effort. Little research has been conducted codifying reactions to advertising by CPA firms. The authors paid particular attention to the advertising efforts of minority firms with reference to expenditures, media, and future expectations.

Introduction

Since the 1978 Supreme Court ruling authorizing accountants, as well as other professionals, to advertise their services, accountants have had to adapt to a changing environment. Prior to that decision, accountants were prohibited from advertising and thus had to rely on other indirect methods of promotion. Though slowly at first, accountants have increasingly adapted to the demands associated with advertising. This change toward advertising was nowhere more evident than in small or minority accounting firms. The objective of this study is to evaluate how small or minority accounting firms react to questions concerning advertising expenditures. The results will then be related to the rest of the accounting profession. Moreover, the researchers felt that by combining small and minority firms a more meaningful analysis could be obtained.

Methodology

The study focuses on the AICPA (American Institute of Certified Public Accountants) 1986 publication entitled Accounting Firms and Practitioners. This publication, published yearly, lists all accounting firms and practitioners in the United States which are members of the AICPA. The directory lists the individual accounting practitioners and accounting firms and professional corporations alphabetically by city within each state. A random sample of 523 questionnaires was sent to selected accountants. The results from the questionnaire are analyzed later.

Construction of Questionnaire

The questionnaire was divided into two parts. Part 1 consisted of logistical questions such as number of professionals employed, perceptions concerning competitors' advertising, and whether the firm currently advertises. Part II was filled out by firms that did advertise and concerned reasons why they advertise and the advertising media used.

Results of Study

Logistical Considerations

Of importance to the researchers was whether the size of the accounting firm had any impact on the desire to advertise. Table I does reflect the fact that there is a difference.

TABLE I
The Size of the Firm and Advertising Effort

Count Row Pct Col Pct Tot Pct	Yes 1	No 2	Row Total
1	29 19.7 70.7 16.0	118 80.3 84.3 65.2	147 81.2
2	12 35.3 29.3 6.6	22 64.7 15.7 12.2	34 18.8
Column Total	41 22.7	140 77.3	181 100.0

Of the 183 accountants who responded, 181 of them answered the question as to whether they advertised by indicating "yes" or "no." Of the 181 respondents, 147 indicated that they had less than 10 professionals working for them and thus were classified as "small" - Row 1. The remaining 34 firms were classified as large, or probably more accurately, "larger firms," and grouped in Row 2. The actual frequency or count for Row 1, small accounting firms, was twenty-nine "yes" that they advertised and one hundred and eighteen "no" that they did not advertise. The row percentages are presented in Table I at 19.7% and 80.3% respectively. In addition, Row 2, or larger accounting firms had twelve firms who did advertise or 35.3% of the population. This was expected by the researchers for it was felt that smaller firms were more conservative and had limited financial resources. Table II analyzed those firms who currently did and did not advertise with the respondents' perception of their firms' competitors' increases in advertising expenditures. Of the forty-one respondents who did advertise, twenty-six or 63.4% indicated that they feel their competitors are increasing advertising expenditures while of the one-hundred and forty who do not advertise, fifty-five or 39.3% indicated an increase in advertising expenditures by their competitors. It would appear that the greater the perception that competitors are increasing advertising expenditures, can lead the firm to favorably consider advertising.

TABLE II
The Relationship Between the Firms Advertising Effort and Expenditures by Their Competitors

Count Row Pct Col Pct Tot Pct		Agree 1	Unsure 2	Disagree 3	Row Total
Yes	1	26 63.4 32.1 14.4	9 22.0 16.7 5.0	6 14.6 13.0 3.3	41 22.7
No	2	55 39.3 67.9 30.4	45 32.1 83.3 24.9	40 28.6 87.0 22.1	140 77.3
Column Total		81 44.8	54 29.8	46 25.4	181 100.0

Firms Who Do Advertise

The researchers asked the question as to the accountants reasons for advertising. Table III reflects the results of the question categorized by large or small firms.

TABLE III
Reasons Why Firms Advertise

	Small Firms	Larger Firms
To gain new customers	13	6
To hold markets previously established	7	4
To combat competitors advertising	7	4
Other	4	3

The results revealed in Table III indicate that smaller firms are very interested in gaining new customers and perceived that advertising is a method to accomplish that goal. On the other hand, larger firms, while interested in gaining new markets, are concerned with maintaining what they already have. Smaller firms that advertise thus can be classified as taking a more aggressive position while larger firms are taking a more defensive or hold the line posture, a situation that in the long run may dramatically effect the future size of the firms.

The last table, Table IV, reveals what advertising media used by the larger and smaller accounting firms.

The last table, Table IV, reveals the advertising media used by large and small accounting firms surveyed.

TABLE IV
Advertising Media Used

Magazine	Small Firms	Large Firms
Professional	4	6
General Public	6	6
Direct Mail	10	8
Newspaper	13	8
Radio	8	3
Television	4	3
Other	22	7
	67	41

Findings

The researchers were able to draw four important observations concerning small or minority firms and the accounting profession.

1. Smaller accounting firms tend not to advertise as much as larger firms. The reasons given centered around the conservative nature of the practitioner, (advertising is not perceived to be "professional"), with many noting that they had severe financial limitation.

2. The more the accountants, small and large, perceive that their competitors were increasing advertising expenditures, the greater the likelihood they would advertise. Nothing stimulates the spirit of competition more than the actions of one's competitors.

3. Smaller accounting firms who do advertise have a great interest in gaining new customers. Larger firms, while interested in gaining new customers, feel that maintaining previously established markets and combating competitors were equally important.

4. The reasons given centered around a desire to be cautious with their financial resources. This cautious attitude would allow them to purchase more advertising space or time.

References

Block, Max. 1980. "Any Limits to 'Marketing' CPA Services?" CPA Journal, Vol. 50 (August) 35-40.

Hanggi, Gerald A. 1980. "Media Advertising As a Practice Development Tool." Journal of Accountancy, Vol. 149 (January) 54-58.

Keane, John G. 1980. "The Marketing Perspective: The CPA's New Image." Journal of Accountancy, Vol. 149 (January) 60-66.

Pollock, John M. 1981. "Benefits of Practice Advertising," Advertising, Vol. 92 (October) 59-60.

Smith, Bradford E. 1980. "Reaching the Public:
The CPA's New Image." Journal of Accountancy,
Vol. 149 (January) 47-52.

Traynor, Kenneth. 1983-84. "Accountant Advertising: Perceptions, Attitudes, and Behaviors."
Journal of Advertising Research, Vol. 23 (December-January) 35-40.

FOR THE SMALL, MINORITY BUSINESS:
A TRADE SHOW MAY BE YOUR BEST MARKETING ALTERNATIVE

M. Grant Cunningham, Clemson University
Brian J. Mihalik, Clemson University

Abstract

Small, minority businesses faced with budget limitations have traditionally avoided trade shows as a marketing alternative. However, close examination of factors such as cost-per-contact, large audiences, immediate reaction and competitive product comparisons, suggests that a trade show offers a small, minority business greater latitude in its marketing effort despite a limited budget. A trade show combines effective personal selling techniques with a shopping mall atmosphere. Probably, the greatest problem to solve before participating is obtaining adequate background information about a trade show and its operation. This paper is an attempt to initiate the interest of small, minority businesses in trade shows as a marketing alternative.

Introduction: The Problem

The minority businessperson faces a competitive marketplace that is both similar and dissimilar to the marketplace of the dominate and established business entities. The similarities are apparent if the product offered is similar to other products present in a particular market. Obviously, a comb can be used by those with either curly or straight hair. And, regardless of the manufacturer, the only differences apparent between combs are physical qualities such as the material composition, durability, size and price.

However, if the product is not just a comb but an afro-comb, then dissimilarities from the mainstream product abound. In fact, a different market (or submarket) is created.

While a product itself may have markets based on ethnic or racial background, this paper offers an alternative to minority business people who have products that could be competitive within and/or across several markets. Imagine this scenario: suppose a minority inventor has developed a widget in a garage workshop. Suppose the inventor shows the widget to the spouse of the house, who finds it fascinating but doesn't quite understand its purpose.

Now, suppose friends in the neighborhood find it fascinating -- a revolutionary invention ahead of its time. Joe, a friend and neighbor who works for XYZ, thinks this widget could solve some production problems at his plant. Joe takes it to work, introduces it in the workplace as an experiment, and it works wonders. The subordinate workers like it; the managers and supervisors like it; and the boss loves it. The boss wants 100 just like it immediately.

While obtaining a patent, work to produce the order begins based on an advance from Joe's company. Soon, the order is completed, but few additional orders have arrived. Obviously, with this widget being such a fascinating but undiscovered product, there is a need to begin a marketing program. Larry, who is a market researcher for CDE, gives several alternatives to pursue -- few that are really affordable at the time. One alternative is intriguing, however. It permits demonstrating the product firsthand to a potential 35,000 to 40,000 business people within a four- to five-day period.

Factors to Consider

The cost is relatively inexpensive on a cost-per-contact basis. All that is needed is $4,000 to $5,000 cash, and the widget can be exhibited in nearby Atlanta. Is it worth it? Is that a fair estimate of the cost? Can exhibiting in a trade show guarantee results, specifically a sale? How does one go about exhibiting? Which is the right trade show for exhibiting widgets?

After deciding to participate in a trade show, one must create an exhibit. There are numerous questions to be answered about the exhibit that is right for a particular product. Cost is always a consideration, and a string of other questions ensue. Where do you get an exhibit? How do you get the exhibit to the show? Here is a simple, explanatory guide for small, minority businesses to use in answering some management questions.

What is a Trade Show?

Trade shows are industrial exhibitions whose titles are based on the most popular and facile market classification of consumer goods and industrial goods. The division is unambiguous for such goods as motors or handicrafts, but it loses its identity when the exhibition or show combines two kinds of goods and for goods on the borderline of the division or those straddling it or changing from one sector to another depending upon application. Some trade shows operate on a semi-annual basis devoting one show in the spring to consumer goods and the one show in the fall to industrial products or vice versa. However, at the so-called consumer durables end of the spectrum, the division between consumer goods and industrial becomes obscured. Some products can make their way from one division to the other. The same is true for

industrial products, like hand tools which are
more consumable than industrial (Alles 1973).

Some examples of the types of product categories
that can be exhibited at a trade show include
manufacturing innovations, such as textile
production equipment, and consumer goods ranging
from personal computers to ski equipment to
fishing boats. Also capable of being exhibited
are food products displayed and sold by the
grocery market chains, equipment and supplies
affiliated and displayed in conjunction with
professional association meetings such as
optical supplies and turf care equipment, and
drugs and chemical advances exhibited by leading
pharmaceutical companies.

Current Statistics

The proliferation of trade shows has continued
through the years because many different types
of products can be displayed at trade shows.
Some current statistics about trade shows are:
- More than 9,300 trade shows take place each
  year.
- Over 40 million people a year attend trade
  shows and expositions.
- Over 60,000 companies exhibit at least once
  a year.
- Exhibitors spend more than $1.5 billion to
  attend shows.
- More than 100 major cities have modern
  convention facilities (Rice 1982).
- Today, trade shows are a $58 billion a year
  business (Alpern and Blumenfeld 1987).

What are Advantages of Participating
in a Trade Show?

For the small, minority business or manufacturer, a trade show may boost the marketing
plan. A trade show can offer:
1) An opportunity for the seller and the buyer
   to meet person-to-person where the products
   being shown can be demonstrated in a way
   that may not be duplicated by other
   mediums.
2) A pre-scheduled audience with specified
   interests who are at the show for the
   purpose of learning about new products,
   hopefully, regardless of minority ownership.
3) An opportunity to reach people who ordinarily may not be accessible to a minority
   business's smaller sales force and to
   uncover buying interests.
4) A place where buyers can do comparative
   shopping and discuss their problems with
   many technical people, and thus, a place
   where the buying process can be shortened
   (Konikow 1982).
5) Trade shows combine the selling powers of
   the internal sales force and the distributed promotional literature. This can be a
   more effective type of promotion effort
   than that offered by these sales tools
   singly.
6) The trade show is a visual, three-
   dimensional medium. The very size of the
   exhibit can give it immediate impact.

7) The trade show offers an interchange
   between peers, to up-date themselves and to
   compare themselves with their competitors.
8) The trade show allows the minority business
   person to get immediate reaction for
   relatively little expense and to evaluate
   it faster.
9) The trade show permits the minority business person to shorten the time involved in
   sales development, comparison of competitive claims, development of technical
   understanding and the hammering out of
   agreements and terms (Rice 1982).
10) Probably, the most important factor that is
   often disregarded is the reversal of roles
   that takes place at a trade show. Rather
   than the salesman visiting a prospect's
   office (where there is the probability of
   interruption by phone calls and other job
   responsibilities), the prospect visits the
   salesman's exhibit. Now, the prospect is
   away from his office and away from his
   regular pressures. The prospect has come
   to the show because he wants to see what's
   new. He is expecting and wanting to talk
   to salespeople; he wants to talk, to see,
   to touch and to try the products.

What are the Disadvantages of
Participating in a Trade Show?

Of course, the trade show may not provide each
and every product the exposure it needs. In
fact, there are some disadvantages to participating in trade shows which must be considered.
1) Product comparisons with competitors could
   do more harm than good.
2) Producing a display, staffing it and
   getting the display to show can be both
   cost and time prohibitive.
3) The show may be poorly attended.
4) Statistics produced by the show management
   to attract exhibitors may be in error.
5) Geographical limitations may exist for the
   product and/or the show.
There are other reasons why a trade show may not
be the best marketing alternative for a small
business. However, those reasons are entirely
dependent on the product, the marketer, and the
show. Extreme caution could be observed before
engaging one's effort into exhibiting at a trade
show. The best advice is to find out as much as
possible about participating in a trade show
before committing.

Is Exhibiting in a Trade Show
Worth the Cost?

It appears from the growth in both the number
and size of trade shows that the price is
economically feasible. In a study conducted
earlier, a majority of qualified buyers stopping
at a trade show booth to get information said
they had not been called on by a salesperson
from that exhibitor.

Astoundingly, of the buyers who stopped at a
booth to ask a question or pick-up informational

literature, 83 percent were not on the regular call list of a salesperson. In other words, many attendees who are attracted to an exhibit during a trade show can be classified as a new prospect (Rice 1982). Thus, a minority business with a potentially smaller sales force may be on a more equal footing when competing with more established and larger businesses.

The trade shows continue to out-perform personal sales calls as a prospecting medium, at least according to the trade show industry. The Trade Show Bureau (TSB) in a recent study found that the average cost-per-contact at trade shows in 1985 was $106.80. According to McGraw-Hill Publications Company's Laboratory of Advertising Performance, the average cost-per-sales call in 1985 was $229.70 (Business Marketing Feb. 1987).

How Many Prospects Will Stop at the Booth of a Small, Minority Manufacturer With all the Larger Companies Present?

When taking a space at a trade show for the three or more days of exhibiting, it is a place of business -- a place to meet and converse with customers and prospects. Similar to any other place of business, the number of attendees to visit an exhibit (potential customers) can be increased if they are encouraged to come specifically to see an exhibit, rather than waiting on incidental passers by.

Of course, one of the first things to do is simply let people know that your company will be at the show. The show management often prepares promotional material, like posters for windows, stickers for correspondence, public relations guidebooks which list all exhibitors, insignias for advertisements, admission tickets to the show for special customers and other ideas (Konikow 1982).

Many exhibitors offer special prices on merchandise bought at the show. Special prices are especially effective when the products are not expensive and do not require a large commitment (Konikow 1982).

Developing a pre-show strategy aimed at getting the best potential prospects to visit the exhibit at showtime is imperative. An exhibitor must be discriminating with time before and during the show. Quality prospects are more important than the quantity of prospects. To identify the qualified prospects, all pre-show literature and promotions should be directed toward them.

Prospect Qualification

It is possible to use the pre-show promotion phase to accomplish some prospect-qualification. Pre-show promotions should be given well in advance of the show so that there is time for a mailing, a reply, and a fulfillment to be completed before show time. Then, it is possible to qualify prospects before they visit the exhibition (Hanlon 1982).

Other exhibitors make a mailing to solicit a response in which the respondent qualifies himself as a prospect. The use of an incentive in the form of a premium offer to secure the prospect's cooperation in supplying the qualification information is one technique. In return for the information, exhibitors often send a redeemable coupon for the premium offer that is presented to the exhibitor at the show (Hanlon 1982).

Beyond trying to attract the quality prospect, the quantity of qualified prospects also is important. There is no need to participate in a trade show unless a certain number of attendees with buying power are present. Estimates of attendance supplied by the show's management is sometimes inflated, but until a better system is found, their statistics must suffice.

Another alternative is to use product-interest data developed from audience surveys. Not everyone from a particular job function or business category is necessarily interested in seeing an exhibitor's products. That percentage of the audience that is interested in seeing a particular exhibitor's products indicates the most realistic measure of his total prospects (Exhibit Surveys 1986).

Finally, if all else fails, Exhibit Surveys of Middletown, New Jersey, suggests using its "16 percent rule." This guideline states that on the average, 16 percent of the audience will be interested in seeing an exhibitor's products. If the expected overall attendance is 50,000, then the exhibitor can expect the interest of 8,000 prospects.

Potential Audience

Rarely can a minority businessperson reach, or even attract, all of the prospects in attendance at a show. The "potential audience" is the number of total prospects that a businessperson has a good chance of reaching at his exhibit. In all of its show surveys, Exhibit Surveys, Inc. determines the audience interest factor (AIF) -- the percentage of the audience who tend to visit many exhibits. The AIF averages 45 percent. This means that a small business owner has a good chance of reaching 45 percent of his total show prospects. Depending on the type of show, the AIF will vary. Shows having a vertical industry representation of the audience will usually have a high AIF. Vertical industry representation means the products exhibited are from the same or similar industrial classifications, while horizontal representation would have products from several industrial classifications. Here are averages that Exhibit Surveys uses based on whether the primary industry segments of the exhibitors and audience are vertical or horizontal.

An audience survey can determine the actual AIF for each show. To calculate the potential audience for an exhibitor, simply multiply the estimate of his total number of prospects by the most appropriate audience interest factor.

TABLE 1

Primary Industry Representation	Audience Interest Factor	
Exhibitors	Audience	Percent
Vertical	Vertical	57
Vertical	Horizontal	48
Horizontal	Horizontal	39
Horizontal	Vertical	35
Current All Show Average		45

In Which Trade Shows Should a Small, Minority Business Exhibit in Order to Attract the Largest Potential Audience?

A rational decision whether to participate in a particular trade show must be based on a definition of the exhibitor's motives, on an assessment of the strengths and weaknesses of that show, and on the abilities of the exhibitor financially. All to often past observations have indicated that this rational approach to trade show participation has been seldom applied (Alles 1973).

An exhibitor can start by looking in "Exhibit Schedule" published by Successful Meetings magazine in Philadelphia, Pennsylvania. The Trade Show Convention Guide from Budd Publications in New York is another source. Robert Elster has compiled a directory which has 1,150 entries. Entitled Trade Shows and Professional Exhibits Directory, 1st ed., the directory is arranged by subject with descriptions of trade shows, consumer shows, associations, conventions and similar events. Entries include details such as space rates, audience type, and special features. The Annual International Directory of Meetings and Conventions includes lists of facilities throughout the United States and show management companies, both should prove helpful in searching for information about sites and contacts.

Once finding a show that looks right for the company's product offering, write the show management for informational literature supplied to prospective exhibitors. Remember, this literature is a sales pitch, but it should give a good background about the nature of the audience, exhibitors and attendees.

If a list of exhibitors at previous shows is available from the show management or old promotional materials, then a good indication of the appropriateness for individual exhibitors can be determined. Examine the list to see what products were exhibited by which companies (Konikow 1982).

Now That I've Decided to Participate in a Trade Show, What are my Objectives?

Once getting involved in a trade show, the exhibitor should decide which objective is the primary reason for participating in the show and strive to realize that objective. This main objective will be the basis for creating guidelines, making decisions, determining investment and evaluating performance (Konikow 1982).

The exhibitor should keep in mind that trade shows attract many of their audience from the area surrounding the show location. Rightly, a geographical marketing objective becomes an important consideration. If at all possible, the small, minority businessperson should select a show where his product will gain the most from an intense sales effort. The exhibitor should then select the companies and particular individuals in those companies who will be a primary target.

One last consideration is appropriate. Participating in a trade show just because the competition will be present is not good rationale for participation. When the motive for participation is not centered around personal marketing objectives, there probably is no need to show up (Konikow 1982).

How Does an Exhibitor Prepare for Participation in his First Trade Show?

The exhibitor should begin planning the display as early as possible. No preparation should be left for last-minute scurrying. Before planning for the display, the exhibitor should make contact with the show management to review all requirements for participation and the support services to be offered. Often, space for some shows must be reserved one year in advance. The earlier reservations are made, the more choices available to the exhibitor regarding locations with high visibility. Likewise, the exhibitor should avoid areas near a traffic bottleneck, a dead end, or next to competitors (Exposystems 1984).

Next, the exhibitor should determine how much he can afford to invest in the show. An exhibitor's largest expenditure will probably be the booth, followed by the exhibit space rental (Exposystems 1984). Over the past decade, exhibit construction and space costs have taken less of the trade show exhibitor's dollar, but show services and transportation costs are claiming a much larger portion. The Trade Show Bureau supplied data which comparatively analyzed the 1983-84 period with 1972-1974. In their report, the current breakdown of the exhibitor's cost to participate are:

Exhibitor rental space 21%
Exhibit construction 21%
Show services 21%
Transportation 13%
Refurbishing exhibits 12%
Special personnel 5%
Specialty advertising 2%
Miscellaneous costs 5%

This data is based on 131 exhibits in 41 shows studied in 1986 (Business Marketing Feb. 1987).

Designing the Display

Since such a large investment goes into the display booth, the exhibitor should determine how the display will be used at the show and after the show. Similarly, the exhibitor must determine how the display is to be transported and where it will be stored. If the exhibitor realizes what uses he expects of the display, then the determination of the investment is made much easier.

Booth Space

The most common unit of space is a 10-foot by 10-foot booth. Some shows have smaller units. Price differential between booth spaces are determined by floor location. If space is available and the exhibitor can afford it, he can purchase as many booths as he likes. The best bet is to purchase only what you need.

Staffing the Booth

For the small manufacturer, hiring additional personnel to man the booth can be cost prohibitive. But, the exhibitor should realize that the key to successful results at the show is to support an eye-catching display with an effective sales approach.

Follow-up and Evaluation

Follow up all trade show inquiries as soon as possible after the show. Quickly contacting a qualified prospect indicates the small, minority businessperson is highly interested in that attendee's business. The slower competition will miss the opportunity.

The exhibitor should have a supply of business cards and lead forms available for the duration of the show. The lead form is a record of the prospect's name, address, phone number and primary interest in the product. Professional surveys and direct inquires of attendees can give immediate feedback for reference (Exposystems 1984).

In addition, the trade show sponsor may provide a list of registered visitors. Find out if the sponsor will provide such a list to all exhibitors. From such a list an exhibitor may be able to produce additional potential customers.

After the show, the minority businessperson should look at the results to determine if his or her objective(s) were met. Perceiving at the outset what role the trade show is to play in the marketing mix will help the evaluation process. At each show there is a lot of money and time invested, so special attention should be paid to planning, execution and thorough evaluation. The obvious elements to evaluate are: the number of inquiries, the number of sales, market competition, product comparisons and sales, and presentation effectiveness.

Summary and Conclusions

For minority businesses with budget limitations,

selecting the proper means to market a product is essential to success. Whether other critical marketing decisions have been made or not, an initial and effective means of promoting a new product can be exhibiting in a trade show. Obviously, for industrial goods a trade show may be more effective than for consumer goods, but the variety of shows available allows for participation regardless of the product's class.

Trade shows offer some advantages other forms of promotion may not:
1. It permits demonstrating the product firsthand to a potentially large audience in a short time.
2. The cost is relatively inexpensive on a cost-per-contact basis.
3. It utilizes one of the most effective methods of creating demand - personal selling.
4. With one concerted effort, a small minority business may accomplish the equivalent of other forms of promotion in less time and perhaps with less money.
5. It can allow small, minority businesses to compete head-to-head with larger and established companies.

Consequently, participating in the right trade show can have a positive effect on a small, minority business unlike other forms of promotion.

References

Alles, Alfred (1973), Exhibitions: Universal Marketing Tools, New York: John Wiley and Sons.

Alpern, Lynne and Ester Blumenfeld (1987), "No Business Like Show Business," Business Atlanta, (April), 86.

"Data Give Trade Show Specifics" (1987), Business Marketing, (February), 46.

Exposytems (1984), Stalking the Elusive Client: Your Guide to Trade Show Success, Tampa, Florida: Maler Haley International Company.

Hanlon, Albert (1982), "Exhibiting at Trade Shows," Inform-A-Gram, 26, Aurora, Ohio: National Association of Exposition Managers, (April), 5.

Konikow, Robert B. (1982), "Exhibiting at Trade Shows," Inform-A-Gram, 26, Aurora, Ohio: National Association of Exposition Managers, (March), 1.

Marketing With Exhibits for Success and Profit, (1986), Middletown, New Jersey: Exhibit Surveys, Inc.

Rice, Charles W. Jr. (1982), "97/39 or How a Trade Show Saves You Money," Inform-A-Gram, 30, Aurora, Ohio: National Association of Exposition Managers, (May), 1.

"Trade Show Prospecting Shows Cost Advantages," (1987), Business Marketing, (February), 46.

CHAIN STORE MERCHANDISING POLICIES FOR ETHNIC HAIR CARE PRODUCTS IN A MAJOR URBAN MARKET[1]

Thaddeus H. Spratlen, University of Washington
Ronald Robinson, Howard University

Abstract

Merchandise policies are compared for hair care products in two drugstore and two supermarket chains in Washington, D.C. Based on an area sample of stores, responses of store managers are reported along with data on shelf exposure in evaluating the performance of ethnic and non-ethnic product categories. The results provide a basis for interpreting the managerial implications of current merchandising policies for marketing Black hair care products.

Introduction

Hair care products are of particular importance to Black business enterprise and minority marketing in the cosmetics industry. They represent one of the rare instances in which Black firms have a substantial market share -- an estimated 50% of manufacturers' sales. (Drug & Cosmetic Industry 1986, p. 34) Blacks may purchase as much as one-third or more of category sales. Because of the extensive variety of product items in ethnic hair care, they serve as important generators of store traffic for retailers in the drug, variety and supermarket businesses in the central city. Indeed, sales of such products are of sufficient importance to warrant a separate section designation in many chain stores which serve a predominantly Black consumer market. High levels of promotional spending further indicate that competition for consumer recognition and loyalty is quite keen. Yet very little attention has been directed towards in-store merchandising policies for ethnic hair care products.

This initial effort is aimed at exploring the potential and importance of research on various aspects of merchandise management in the category of ethnic cosmetics marketing. Our focus is on merchandising with respect to the Black consumer segment.

In this paper we analyze several aspects of retail merchandising of ethnic hair care products. Our main purposes are to describe the relative importance of ethnic products in the overall hair care product category and to identify key policy issues at the retail level which face marketers of ethnic hair care products. Particular attention is given to the managerial implications of current merchandising policies for marketing Black hair care products.

---

[1]Research for this paper was completed while the first-named author was on sabbatical leave at the School of Business Administration, Howard University. Special thanks are due dean Milton Wilson for the support provided during the 1986-87 academic year.

Methodology

An area sample of selected chain stores was conducted in Washington, D.C. during the summer of 1987. Cooperation was obtained from two major supermarket chains and two major drugstore chains. Because of resource limitations, our study was limited to the city rather than the metropolitan area. Further, only drugstores and supermarkets were included. Their inventory management and in-store merchandising practices made it possible to compare brands and space allocation. Small retail distributors of cosmetics, convenience stores and beauty or styling salons were omitted because they could not be analyzed in comparable terms (e.g., linear feet of shelf space or number of brand facings, etc.).

The sampling frame was designed initially from the Zip Code listing of all chain drugstores and supermarkets in the city which were operated by the cooperating firms. Random systematic sampling procedures were used in selecting store units.

All Zip Code areas in which all cooperating chains had stores were initially included in the study. Areas or stores were eliminated under the following conditions. Areas were eliminated when only one of the cooperating firms had stores there, (e.g., Safeway in 20032 and 20037 as well as Peoples Drugs in 20036). Special purpose Zip Code areas were also omitted (such as those assigned for major universities).

A total of 17 Zip Code areas were sampled in the study -- eight in the Northwest, five in the Northeast, and two each in the Southwest and Southeast. In terms of stores a 20% sample of drugstores and a 25% sample of supermarkets were obtained for the study. The sample consisted of 20 supermarkets and 15 drugstores. Because of closures and the unavailability of store personnel, data were obtained for 19 supermarkets and 12 drugstores. Two of the drugstores were located in the downtown area. The remaining 10 drugstores and all of the supermarkets were located in inner city and outlying neighborhoods.

As additional background information it should be noted that the population of Washington, D.C. is over 70% Black or African-American. Its relatively small size in land area (63 square miles) and high population density (10,121 per square mile) make it quite suitable for the area sampling approach used in the study.

Two types of information were collected in the study. Space allocations in linear feet and display arrangements for hair care were recorded for each store. Store managers were asked several questions regarding merchandising policies. We were especially interested in finding out who makes decisions about the products to be carried and the space allocation for hair care products as well as the relative importance of various performance results in evaluating hair care products.

Findings

Survey results are reported for three major aspects of merchandising policies: space allocation and display of merchandise; decisionmaking for product lines carried and space allocation; and performance evaluation for the product category. Only descriptive measures are presented in this paper.

Space Allocation and Merchandise Display

Comparisons of space allocation for ethnic hair care products are presented in Tables 1 and 2. Note that over three-quarters of the stores have more than 10 linear feet of ethnic hair care products on display. At the upper level of shelf exposure, five of the 31 stores have over 90 feet of shelf space devoted to this product category.

TABLE 1
Ethnic Hair Care Space Allocation
(in linear feet)

Shelf Space (ft)	No. Stores	Per Cent
10 or less	7	22.6%
11 - 20	1	3.2
21 - 30	3	9.7
31 - 40	2	6.5
41 - 50	4	12.9
51 - 60	3	9.7
61 - 70	4	12.9
71 - 80	1	3.2
81 - 90	5	16.1
Total	31	100.0%

TABLE 2
Ethnic Hair Care Space Allocation
As Per Cent of All Hair Care Space Allocation

Per Cent (Category)	No. Stores	Per Cent
10 or less	7	28.0%
11 - 20	6	24.0
21 - 30	5	20.0
31 - 40	3	12.0
41 - 50	1	4.0
51 - 60	3	12.0
Not Reported	6	-
Total	31	100.0%

For 12 stores ethnic hair care products comprise over one fifth of the total space devoted to hair care products. In three of the 25 stores for which information was reported, over half of the space is devoted to ethnic hair care products.

Nearly three-fourths of the reporting stores maintained separate sections of ethnic hair care products. Most of the stores with combined displays were supermarkets. As an aside, it should be noted that in two instances, store managers reported that the ethnic hair care section was kept quite small and in a separate area in order to reduce losses from pilferage.

Merchandise Policies and Decisionmaking

In 15 of 21 reporting stores the district or regional manager had primary responsibility in deciding the merchandise lines to be carried. A similar pattern existed for determining space allocation as well. The jobber or wholesaler had this responsibility in five stores. The store manager rarely made either of these decisions.

Performance Evaluation of the Product Category

At the time the study was being designed we were unaware of the extent to which merchandise decisions were made by individuals other than the store manager. Hence, we asked them to indicate the relative importance of several performance criteria used in evaluating product categories. The results are shown in Table 3. The ratings were based on a scale of 1 (Unimportant) to 5 (Important). The pattern of evaluations was similar for both drugstores and supermarkets. However, sales volume and turnover criteria were slightly more important in drug stores than in supermarkets.

TABLE 3
Importance Ratings of Product Performance for Ethnic Hair Care Products

Criteria	Mean	S.D.
Sales Volume	4.24	1.26
Turnover	4.04	1.15
Promotional Support	3.05	1.35
Mark Up	2.48	1.25
Dealer Incentives	2.26	1.24

Apparently comparisons within the broad or overall product category are not made on a regular and systematic basis in many stores. Data on within-category comparisons were not known or reported in 13 of 31 participating stores. But in 11 of 18 comparisons that were reported, ethnic hair care products had better sales performance results than hair care products as a whole.

Managerial Implications

The kind of research initiated in this study points to the lack of knowledge about merchandising policies and practices at the store level. For example, it is clear that it is at the regional and district level that major decisions are made regarding merchandise lines as well as space allocation. Indeed, as reported by Snyder (1985, p. 108), many chain retailers have switched from direct buying to reliance on "master distributors," who serve as buying intermediaries for HBA product items. What is not known (and is unlikely to be determined) from research at the store level is what influences are at work to shape district and regional decisions. Much the same could be said about the role of jobbers and wholesalers in the area of hair care merchandising. Further, questions arise as to what their relationships are with store and higher level management in drugstore and supermarket chains. it is also clear what seems to determine when jobbers and wholesalers are assigned key decisionmaking responsibilities and when the responsibilities are retained at the district and regional level of the firm.

Our results provide some information on the criteria used in evaluating product performance. But is this consistent with the judgment of district/corporate level decisionmakers? Answering this question will involve research beyond the store level.

Thus key policy issues facing marketers of ethnic hair care products include the following:

**Identifying decisionmakers at the district and regional level in each firm.

**Determining how to reach and influence the decisionmakers.

**Establishing the relative importance of push vs. pull methods in merchandising ethnic hair care products.

**Defining and using variations in product performance evaluations as an integral part of marketing strategies for ethnic hair care products.

More extensive and larger scale research of the kind initiated in this study will help to inform policies and strategies needed to market ethnic cosmetics in the years that lie ahead.

In-store research provides a useful starting point for describing and understanding merchandising policies that apply in the marketing of ethnic hair care products. It can supplement information form trade sources as well as consumer-based research. However, benchmark standards of comparison are needed in order to apply the results to store operating decisions and policies of ethnic hair care product marketers.

Conclusions

Store-level research on merchandising policies and practices can contribute to our understanding of key issues and policies regarding ethnic hair care product marketing at the retail level. However, it is clear that research must be extended to the district and regional level in order to identify key source of decisionmaking responsibility. The role of jobbers and wholesalers must also be examined beyond the store level.

Our results have provided some descriptive measures and relationships of store-level merchandising. But the measures and the relationships must be examined in much greater depth in order to be useful in marketing and merchandising ethnic hair care products. Nevertheless, the tentative observations presented initiate analysis and thinking regarding shelf exposure and decisionmaking for merchandising ethnic hair care products at the retail level.

References

Carson, Hamilton C. (1986) "Cosmetic & Fragrance--Review and Forecast," Household and Personal Products Industry (HAPPI) 23, No. 12 (December), pp. 40-42, 46, 48, 50, 52, 102.

Snyder, Glenn (1985) "Supers Step Up Ethnic HBA Efforts," Progressive Grocer (March), pp. 107-120.

Spratlen, Thaddeus H. and Pravat K. Choudhury (1987) "Political/Ethnic Issues in Marketing Cosmetics to Black Consumers," 1987 Conference Proceedings, American Marketing Association. Chicago, IL: the Association. Manuscript, p. 4.

Weil, Arthur W. (1985) "'Special' Needs Spur Growth of Ethnic Market," Product Marketing (September), Vol. 14, p. 11.

Drug and Cosmetic Industry (1986) "Hair Care Report: Fragmentation Beckons," (November), pp. 33-34, 36, 102.

Marketing News (1985) "Minority-Marketing Growth Boosts Black Trade Journal," (March 29), p. 15.

THE MARKETING OF THE HISTORICALLY BLACK COLLEGE

Sundar W. Fleming, North Carolina Central University

Abstract

In spite of limited financial resources and other environmental factors, historically black colleges have made substantial contributions to modern society. Now, many rapidly changing factors are adversely affecting black colleges and their enrollments. Only those colleges that effectively market themeselves will experience dynamic growth and vitality. This paper will delineate marketing strategies which will help black institutions evolve within a changing academic community.

During the 1990's the marketing of most colleges will be vitally necessary as i) the traditional college age population is projected to decline and ii) federal financial resources are becoming more scarce. Although the marketing of historically black collegs (HBC's) is no different than the marketing of other comparable sized institutions, the marketing of HBC's is more critical. This is the case since many HBC's have low levels of public awareness outside the black community, and as a result, it is difficult for them to receive positive local, regional and national media coverage as compared to majority institutions. Also better use of marketing mix variables by HBC's are necessary because they have high proportions of low income students, small endowments, but most importantly, HBC's no longer have monopolies on the matriculation of local black students. Virtually, all institutions are drawing on the pool of potential black students. And as competition for black students intensifies, it breeds better use of marketing mix variables. Simply put, well managed marketing mixes help all institutions and particularly HBC's attract minority and white students.

To add credence to the above argument, Garibaldi has delineated the following future negative factors that will affect the stability of most colleges:

- Scarcity of financial resources
- Substantial declines in enrollment of 18 to 24 year olds
- Intense competition for more able students
- More dropouts and stopouts among first-time enrolling students
- Consequences of court ordered desegregation for many public institutions
- Increased cost of a college education
- Fewer and smaller educational grants and loans for students.[1]

Certainly, these negative factors represent a challenge to all institutions which only well focused management and marketing skills can alleviate.

Obviously, the mission statement of an institution helps to set its image; hence, the mission statement serves as the springboard of recruitment and other marketing strategies. This paper will develop a framework for HBC's to better market their missions, images and products.

Although this paper will assume that HBC's are alike, it is extremely important to highlight that there is much diversity in (the over 110) HBC's. Historically black colleges differ in size, the amounts and types of financial support systems, age and tradition, and leadership motivations. This paper will address HBC's and their potential marketing strategies in a homogeneous fashion; this will be done considering that most HBC's do have similar mission statements as an outgrowth of their formations to provide higher education for blacks (after the Civil War).

The historically black colleges must market the quality of their products in order to improve their images within the greater educational community. HBC's, as other institutions of higher learning, have goals of information dissemination, research development, and community service, and products of developing critical thinkers or educated individuals.

Black colleges continue to have outstanding teachers and graduates alike and must market such. As Vernon Jordan has noted, black colleges have granted undergraduate degrees to 75 percent of all black Ph.D.'s, 75 percent of all black army officers, 80 percent of all black federal judges and 85 percent of all black doctors. In addition, black leaders such as Thurgood Marshall, Martin Luther King, Jr., Andrew Young, Ernest Morial, and Richard Arrington are all graduates of historically black colleges.

HBC's must market the fact that for many black students the best alternative for gaining

---

[1] Antoine Garibaldi, "Black Colleges: An Overview," Black Colleges and Universities Challenges for the Future (New York: Praeger Publishers, 1984), p. 7.

knowledge is the historically black institution. This is usually true because in comparison with majority colleges black institutions have more experience at training black scholars; and hence, they should better understand and serve the academic needs of black students. According to a study by the Southern Education Foundation, black institutions must market that the "Black students' academic performances are higher at institutions with college life usually the traditional black college." As stated by Black Issues in Higher Education, black students on white campuses complain of frequent racial discrimination and report little or no integration into general campus life.[2] With all of the above true, the question to be answered is how does the black college effectively market its academic programs and successes in order to maintain and increase enrollments?

Survey Results

One hundred fifty community leaders and alumni of historically black colleges were mailed survey instruments to seek their opinions of the historical black college and its recruitment environment. At this juncture, 59 of the selected participants (39%) have responded to the survey instrument. The following are major findings of the study on which marketing strategies are based:

a)   Local leaders and alumni, within a 50 mile radius, are much more likely to be familiar with the goals and activities of a local black college (as compared to leaders and alumni outside of a 50 mile radius);

b)   Many leaders and alumni of HBC's (47%, 28 of 59) feel that black students would rather attend a HBC as opposed to a majority institution;

c)   Percentage of leaders identifying the following factors as being extremely important for the student selection of a college—

   -degree leading to a good job (92%, 54 of 59)
   -academic programs of the institution (83%, 49 of 59)
   -costs of college (90%, 53 of 59)
   -family opinions of college (68%, 40 of 59)
   -high school leaders' opinions of college (56%, 33 of 59)
   -perceived appearance of campus (59%, 35 of 59)

---

[2] _____, "Black Students' Academic Performance, Satisfaction with College Higher at Black Institutions," Black Issues in Higher Education (Cox, Matthews and Associates, June 1, 1986, Vol. 3, No. 6), p. 1.

d)   Most leaders (54%) suggested HBC's need to play a much stronger role in their local and regional communities. In other words, HBC's must become better aware of their publics and more visible in their communities.

Even though, this study was performed on community leaders and black college alumni, it seems reasonable to suggest that potential and current students need to be surveyed if the black college is to have an accurate picture of its market (and particularly the recruitment) environment. HBC's should investigate and uncover the perceived images held by potential students and each college should intensively question currently enrolled students with respect to the following:

a)   What is your hometown and how far is it from campus?

b)   What is the economic level of your family and what are the key elements of your financial support system?

c)   When and from whom (or what media) did you first learn of the college?

d)   Have other family members attended or will attend the college?

e)   What was your primary motivation for attending the college?

f)   Did you strongly consider attending other colleges and if so, please name?

Obviously, such student data will solidify the above uncovered alumni and community leader information; hence, black colleges are, herein, strongly encouraged to seek annually pertinent data from their publics with special attention given to potential and present students.

Marketing Recommendations

To begin, it is again, recommended that HBC's seek vital primary and secondary data of its key publics (alumni, trustees, present students, recruiters, faculty and staff, donors, and competitors). Networks in the community such as churches, fraternities and sororities, alunmni chapters and sister institutions function as critical informational support systems.

On campus, the career placement center serves as a reservoir of essential marketing information since the career placement center collects data on job recruiters and it maintains data bases on job opportunities, job performances and accomplishments of graduates. Other valuable on campus collectors of potential marketing data are the offices of admissions, alumni affairs, and student affairs; these offices must have current and accurate demographic data on both past and present students.

Marketing research is necessary to uncover "who we are and why" and "who we serve and how well." Also, marketing research helps to develop a framework for improving the design and communications of the product. The product of the black institution (education) should be designed to satisfy the needs and motivations of its customers (students).

Once there is a degree of understanding of the college's missions, plans and its marketplace, the institution must establish a strategic marketing plan, which is a component of the overall institutional strategic plan. Such a strategic marketing plan allows the marketing roles of the college to be defined; it defines potential students to be attracted and recruited; and it helps to set key marketing budgets and equally important, it serves as a framework for the evaluation of marketing efforts. The magnitude of the strategic marketing plan indicates that it must have executive direction and management at the vice-presidential level. All major components of the campus must function within the guidelines of the strategic marketing plan.

As the study indicates, local alumni tend to be familiar with the external activites of the college. As a start, the black college should contact local, prominent alumni to help with the college's image building and developmental processes. Taking the conclusion that local alumni have high awareness of campus activities a step further, it signals a strong need for HBC's to initiate regional and national contacts of alumni and to implement regional and nationwide alumni follow-up surveys. Of course, these surveys should include systematic media presentations on regional and national levels. In this regard to alert alumni of the surveys and the potential value of the data to the institution, it is, herein, suggested that the college advertise the data collection campaign within cost effective media.

To further augment the collection of alumni data, HBC's can request that each identified alumnus provide the names and addresses of at least two unidentified alumni. This will necessitate that all known alumni be provided with an updated listing of identified alumni. Such an alumni data base system should be computerized and updated at least annually.

Really, the black college (as a whole) has not fully exploited its alumni base. If properly utilized, alumni can serve as major springboards for student recruitment efforts (especially recruitment efforts outside of the local environment), national fund-raising campaigns, and even the recruitment of noted faculty and administrators. The alumni of the black college must be actively encouraged to play major roles within the overall marketing efforts of the institution.

Continuing, considering the key college selection, student factors identified within the study, a definite student recruitment plan must be developed for each black college. To be effective, the recruitment plan must be generated from the strategic marketing plan of the college. As a first cut, the recruitment plan should be directed at having significant impacts on in-state and regional high schools. Such efforts will require campus recruiters and admissions officers to make and maintain key contacts within the regional school districts.

HBC's should define primary and secondary markets for high school students. Major recruitment and image-building efforts on the part of alumni, faculty, and current students should be targeted initially to primary markets (and key high schools) and after time as recruitment has evolved more focus should be given to secondary markets. This does not mean that national recruitment is ignored; what it does mean is that major communications are first oriented towards the primary and secondary markets of the institution (especially early within the student recruitment campaign). In other words, marketing efforts are focused upon those geographical areas and high schools which are likely to produce more dramatic results within the recruitment campaign. Also, once recruitment efforts have succeeded in certain regions and high schools, new geographical areas can be targeted.

As mentioned in the Wall Street Journal, it must be noted that colleges should "frequently back up their on-campus recruiting with efforts aimed at improving high school instruction and curricula; raising test scores for college admission; guiding students to the right college-preparatory courses; and giving them and their parents information about financial aid."[3]

Most HBC's should consider implementing some if not all of the following recruitment tactics:

a) Convene a group of current students to provide valuable insights to the recruitment plan and staff;

b) Survey current students to identify other potential students (special efforts should be made towards those current students who have younger brothers and sisters);

c) Initiate a parent contact program in which parents of current students contact the parents of potential students;

---

[3]Michael McCarthy, "Colleges Press Drives to Inspire and Enroll the Minority Student," Wall Street Journal (June 2, 1987), p. 1.

d) Survey students who were accepted, but did not enroll, in order to uncover why they did not enroll and from this group, who may yet enroll;

e) Develop a system in which potential students who visit, call or write to the campus are identified and formally written by recruitment counselors;

f) Utilize national high school student listings (such as from the Educational Testing Service) to uncover potential students and begin direct mail approaches toward identified students;

g) Initiate alumni recruitment training programs in order to educate and encourage prominent alumni to actively recruit potential students;

h) Offer after school and weekend instruction to selective high school juniors and seniors to enhance the knowledge base of potential students, and to encourage them to attend college;

i) Begin to consider retirees (and other nontraditional students) of the local community as markets for special interest courses;

j) Finally, encourage local former students who did not graduate to return to school (local media coverage will obviously help in this regard).

It must be, herein, stated that the recruitment of new students runs simultaneously with the retention of present students. In essence, the decline in enrollments of many HBC's can be explained by low rates of student retention. Key marketing strategies which must be effectively implemented are those which will positively affect the retention of current students. Specific retention tactics include:

a) Intensify efforts to ensure that current students seek advisement from properly assigned advisors; make constant contact with advisees--scheduling counseling sessions with current students;

b) Require students to immediately repeat courses in which they receive failing grades;

c) Have periodic academic meetings with students to stress the academic environment of the college experience (meetings can be chaired by the appropriate academic deans);

d) Provide tutorial laboratories in areas such as grammar, mathematics and reading;

e) Impose strict class attendance policies to encourage in-class participation of student;

f) Finally, encourage all students to strictly observe and abide by course prerequisites.

To augment student recruitment and retention, HBC's must pay careful attention to their overall communications goals and plans. This means that the black institution must channel positive campus related stories throughout the mass media. HBC's definitely need positive communications to help with their image building campaigns. Such campaigns must be promoted both regionally and nationally.

As the study indicates, many alumni feel that black students would rather attend a HBC as opposed to a majority institution and most alumni also suggest that HBC's need to play stronger roles in their communities. Both of these suggestions can be effectuated within a well planned media campaign.

Specific low cost promotional tactics include the following:

a) Significant student and faculty accomplishments and college development efforts should be reported to appropriate newspapers; also, major campus-related efforts should be developed into feature stories;

b) Campus sponsored events should be promoted in public service media (i.e., television, radio, and the local print media);

c) Important campus sponsored events should be used to attract a broad range of publics (i.e., legislators, community leaders, high school students, and business executives); high visibility events should be designed to develop positive images of the college;

d) Faculty and other key campus personnel should be encouraged strongly to give counseling, speeches and prsentations within the community;

e) Campus direct mail brochures and other promotional materials should be standardized with respect to the college's logo, slogan, etc.;

f) Finally, great use should be made of newsletters to alumni and community leaders.

All of the above mentioned suggestions are low cost marketing strategies (or tactics) which help to better the survival rate of HBC's and other smaller colleges. This set of recommendations is not meant to be all inclusive, but it is meant to serve as a springboard for the black college and its designing of marketing programs which will assist the college's positive evolution.

Summary

As many institutions of higher learning have recently experienced declining student enrollments (and this trend will continue over the next several years), the future oriented college will survive and even prosper based on early detection of falling enrollments and retention losses and early formulation of effective, counteracting marketing strategies.

A key factor for enrollment declines of colleges is the rapidly changing environment and the resulting slow altering of the marketing mix variables in response to the changes. First, black colleges must not only compete for prospective students with other historically black colleges but also, they must now compete in the same market place as traditionally white institutions. This fundamental factor coupled with a now much lower governmental financial support system necessitates better focused fiscal managment and better designed and implemented strategic marketing plans.

As mentioned herein, special and more targeted attention must be given to all publics of the historically black college (i.e., alumni, current students, faculty, trustees, administrators, community leaders, job recruiter and donors). Even though marketing strategies have high initial costs, the ultimate accrued benefits of effective marketing programs clearly outweigh their costs. And in conclusion, the futures of many HBC's are indeed bleak unless such strategic marketing plans are effectuated now.

References

_____ (1986), "Black Students' Academic Performance, Satisfaction with College Higher at Black Institutions," Black Issues in Higher Education, (June 1), Vol. 3, No. 6, Cox, Matthews and Associates, p. 1.

Garibaldi, Antoine (1984), "Black Colleges: An Overview," Black Colleges and Universities Challenges for the Future, New York: Praeger Publishers, p. 7.

McCarthy, Michael (1987), "Colleges Press Drives to Inspire and Enroll the Minority Student," Wall Street Journal, (June 2), p. 1.

INDEX OF AUTHORS

Awadzi, Winston 126

Baxter, Richard 112
Berl, Robert L. 28
Bolden, Vicki L. 126

Calcich, Stephen 37
Choudhury, Pravat K. 41
Cooke, Ernest F. 87, 112
Cooper, William 144
Cunningham, M. Grant 147

Dunn, Sarah 144

Edmonds, Linda 33
Ellis, Richard 130

Fleming, Sundar W. 155

Greene, Walter E. 117

Hankel, Karen Dale 37
Harris, Allen C. 51
Hilger, Marye Tharp 65
Ho, Helene 64
Hoover, Robert J. 65
Hsu, Margaretha M. 83

James, E. Lincoln 51
Johnson, Rose L. 13

Kiel, Mark 144
Kim, Yong-Ju 64
Kosenko, Rustan 74

Lazer, William 3
Lee, Monle 87, 112
Liebman, Mary Margaret 57
Linhardt, Wayne C. 18

Meadow, H. Lee 8
Mihalik, Brian J. 147
Miles, Benton 144

Okrah, Alexander M. 133
O'Leary, Joseph T. 46

Panigrahi, Bhagaban 103
Peyton, Reginald 28

Qualls, William J. 97

Rahtz, Don R. 74
Richmond, Tyronza R. 133
Robinson, Ronald 152
Rogers, Hudson P. 28
Rucker, Margaret 64
Ryan, William T. 121

Sachdev, Harash 13
Sackmary, Benjamin 69
Saegert, Joel 65
Samli, A. Coskun 1, 33, 78
Shapiro, Stanley J. 92
Shaw, Eric H. 3
Sirgy, M. Joseph 78
Slurzberg, Lee 23
Smith, Allen E. 3
Snuggs, Thelma L. 97
Spratlen, Thaddeus H. 41, 139, 152
Stuart, Jon C. 103

Tamilia, Robert D. 92

Uysal, Muzzafer 46

Wilkins, Henry T. 83
Williams, Jerome D. 107
Wilson, E. Marie 69

Printed by Printforce, the Netherlands